Guidance Techniques
for
Elementary Teachers

Guidance Techniques
for
Elementary Teachers

RALPH GARRY
Boston University

CHARLES E. MERRILL PUBLISHING COMPANY,
COLUMBUS, OHIO
A Bell & Howell Company

Photographs courtesy of Steven Trefonides, Boston

LIBRARY OF CONGRESS CATALOG CARD NUMBER: 63-12589

5 6 7 8 9 10 11 12 13 14 15-76 75 74 73 72 71 70 69 68 67

PRINTED IN THE UNITED STATES OF AMERICA

To Henry Bonner McDaniel
Stanford University

Preface

The American school is quietly undergoing change, particularly the elementary school. One of its universals has been the self-contained classroom. But a second has been the steady diversification of the teacher's role. As our jobs and occupations have become more and more specialized as a result of technological change, society has looked to the teacher to be more intelligent and more capable. Today the teaching machine, programmed learning, team teaching, instructional television, team learning, language laboratories, and other innovations are steadily changing the teacher's role. As greater amounts of professionally prepared instructional materials and the means of delivering them through new teaching aids become available, the teacher becomes more an organizer and analyzer. Her work may well become more diagnostic — analysis of individual talent, progress and error, and selection of appropriate learning and remedial practice. The teacher's role will also entail greater responsibility for systematically providing for healthy personal and social development of children.

Guidance Techniques for Elementary Teachers is devoted to helping the elementary school teacher develop the skills that will make her most effective in the modern classroom. Recognizing that the classroom teacher is at the heart of efforts to introduce guidance programs in the elementary school, the book emphasizes the principles and techniques that will enable her to assume this responsibility.

The focus of *Guidance Techniques for Elementary Teachers* is on basic psychological, sociological, and physical health principles and their applications for the teacher. Techniques, such as sociograms, sociodramas, the Social Distance Scale, Guess Who, record keeping, measurements of physical health and growth, case histories, and intelligence tests, are introduced, described in step-by-step detail, and evaluated in terms of their intrinsic validity and *their usefulness for the elementary teacher*. While some of the techniques have been used primarily in clinical treatment, with appropriate training they can be fully as useful to the teacher in analyzing growth patterns and planning programs for children in the classroom.

The book provides a comprehensive view of the child's world through treatment of family relationships, health and physical development, personal development, social development, and the school and community context. Part One presents basic information on obtaining, transmitting, and interpreting information. Parts Two-Five follow the same pattern: the first chapter in each of these parts discusses the kinds of information needed in a particular area of the child's world and provides descriptions of the techniques for obtaining this information; the second chapter contains developmental and normative data against which the information can be compared. The final chapter in these parts suggests ways of using the information to foster desirable personal and social development of children. Part Six, which examines the child as a group member of the class, the school, and the community, considers how these groups influence him and suggests ways in which environmental situations can be handled to encourage achievement and adjustment.

Acknowledgments

This book is the work of many people, for although the words are mine, the content reflects the work of many psychologists, guidance specialists, and teachers. I am indebted to the many elementary teachers who shared their problems, their experiences, and their wisdom. In reading this book, many will discover incidents that they have reported to me. In all instances, identifying data has been deleted or changed to protect the identity of the child. Miss Muriel Gamble deserves special recognition for her work in introducing guidance practices into her classroom and for her detailed accounts of such efforts. Finally, there are the children whose problems and achievements reflect the ills and strengths of our society. I hope that this book contributes to their well-being.

RALPH GARRY

Little Cranberry Island,
Maine

Table of Contents

Guidance Techniques
for
Elementary Teachers

Part One

OVERVIEW

Chapter 1

INTRODUCTION

DEVELOPMENT OF GUIDANCE PROGRAMS

In the last four decades there has been a steady growth of guidance programs in the secondary schools of the United States. The major emphasis in these programs has been on vocational and educational guidance. Several factors prompted this particular emphasis in preference to programs intending to foster personal-social development. Vocational-educational guidance was an observable need of adolescent youth, a need which was emphasized during the depression, when jobs were scarce and again during the postwar years when the veterans returned to civilian life. This need was particularly acute in cities, where the major developments in guidance programs occurred. Useful tools in the form of specialized tests of vocational and academic aptitude and interest developed rapidly, and eventually vocational-educational guidance was adaptable to group procedures. During the same period of time, very few developments in guidance occurred at the elementary school level. To be sure, many communities had some form of child guidance clinics established to aid maladjusted children, but guidance programs designed as part of an organized plan to foster the personal-social growth of all children were conspicuously lacking.

Historically, the primary purpose of the elementary school has been the development of skills in reading, language, and numbers—skills needed to manipulate and deal with the environment, especially the man-made part of language, numbers, tools, machines, customs, and the like. However, it has become increasingly clear that not only are skills in the proverbial three "r's" needed but also that man must be able to live with himself and with other men. More than technical skill is required to hold jobs, maintain marriages, and avoid conflict between social groups. Understanding and accepting oneself, being able to join with others in common activity, knowing and accepting the rules and procedures of society, having realistic goals which are within one's capability and harmonious with the social order are as important as technical skills. These facts have been painfully apparent for a long time, but a sudden awareness of man's capacity for destroying himself with his technological inventiveness, if he is not equally inventive in solving his social and political problems, has given dramatic urgency to the problem and its solution. In our industrialized, urban society with its shifting structure, the school has become increasingly responsible for providing for these aspects of child development.

The educational goals which have been set for the public school have expanded to include "self-realization" and "effective human relations." These goals have been reflected in an expanding guidance program, first at the secondary and now at the elementary school level. To be effective, such a guidance program must function as an integral part of the school program, not as an adjunct appended to an existing educational program. The operational objectives of the educational program are described in its curriculum—broadly, the sum total of what the child experiences in school; narrowly, the selection of tasks to be performed and the organization of material and method of presentation for learning. Within any curriculum, the tasks to be mastered have to be organized into an arrangement which permits some systematic attack. This almost invariably places the emphasis on subject matter and skill rather than on developmental activity but does not preclude the latter. Yet it is in relationship to certain aspects of developmental activity that guidance exists as an essential aspect of the educational program. The ways in which the lives of children are managed during the process of learning affects not only their progress in mastering the tasks confronting them but also the concept they develop of themselves. Daily experiences affect their feelings of adequacy, their fears and desires, their aspirations and hopes, their sense of self-worth, their perception and relations with other children and adults. Not only is their intellectual development being shaped but their personal and social development as well. These latter elements are the concern of the guidance program, an organized plan for promoting optimal development of children in the personal-social aspects of their lives. An organized plan implies specific objectives to be achieved in the area of mental health, personal adjustment, and social relationships; a division of duties between the available personnel—teachers, guidance specialists, and administrators—for promoting development in these areas and for identifying and treating those children experiencing adjustment difficulties; and a planning and provision of experience in some sequential fashion in order to attain the desired objectives.

The particular form and content of guidance programs at the elementary school level is nebulous and in the process of evolving. Two prime questions have to be answered, the first as to what the content of the program should be, and the second what the relationship between guidance specialists and elementary school teachers should be.

DIFFERENCES BETWEEN GUIDANCE IN THE SECONDARY AND ELEMENTARY SCHOOLS

It would be unfortunate if the secondary school guidance program were chosen as a model, as has been suggested, and emphasis given to providing vocational guidance, occupational information, and counseling. Though the secondary school programs may be ready-made and experienced personnel available, certain fundamental differences between the needs of children and those of adolescents cannot be overlooked because of the implications these differences have for program.

The secondary school guidance program is intended to compensate for the departmentalized instructional program which focuses on subjects more than on children. The guidance program is designed to integrate the several aspects of the high school life of an adolescent. In addition, its purpose is to aid the high school student in meeting and solving the characteristic adolescent problems—choosing a career, finding a job, adjusting to physical maturation, making adequate heterosexual adjustment, and developing a philosophy of life. The age, vocabulary, and conceptual development of the adolescent make verbal procedures, both group and individual, practical and effective. It is possible to depend on verbal procedures in providing information, aiding in understanding, and finding solutions to problems of adolescents.

Contrast this situation with that of the elementary school. The children are much less mature, they have had limited experiences, their vocabulary is limited, and their conceptual development is incomplete. All of these factors restrict the effectiveness of verbal procedures with children between the ages of five and twelve. The contrast between *showing* a child what or how to do something and *telling* him what or how to do something is so great that any program dependent upon the verbal procedures common to high school counseling programs can have only limited success.

THE IMPORTANCE OF THE TEACHER IN THE ELEMENTARY SCHOOL

Still another major difference must be considered: in the elementary school the child spends nearly the entire school day with a single teacher. She, along with the parents and peers, is or can be a major influence on the behavior and adjustment of the child. Working the entire day with the child, as an individual and as a member of a group, the teacher will, in the main, accomplish more good or do more harm than will a counselor having limited periodic contact with the child. Demonstrating this point is the following event which occurred in a first grade classroom one winter day after lunch.

> The children filed in, pulled off their boots and coats, and took their seats. The teacher stood silently at the front of the room making no sound while the last words and laughs were exchanged. Moments passed while the teacher stood silent, hands clasped, waiting for the ultimate hush to come. Then with the crispness of a drill master, she barked, "Richard, were you alone in the room with Virginia at noontime?"
> "No," replied Richard.
> "Seymour, were you alone in the room with Virginia at noontime?"
> "No."
> "Jimmy, were you alone in the room with Virginia at noontime?"
> "No."
> "No one was in the room with you, Virginia, while I was out at noontime, was there?"
> Virginia, almost hidden by the desk before her, shook her head.
> "And what did you do, Virginia? Shall I tell the class?"

Again no sound, just a headshake.

"Then you'd better tell the class, Virginia."

No sound from Virginia.

"Well, I'll tell you what she did, class. She went up to my desk and took the box of gold stars and threw them all over the floor. And then she took a gold star and put it on her number paper and put it on top of the pile! And she didn't have a hundred on it either!"

"Was that a very nice thing to do, class?"

"No," the class echoed.

"What do you say, Virginia?"

"I'm sorry," squeaked Virginia.

A few minutes later, the teacher had a group of children surrounding her for a reading lesson. Ruler in hand, she punctuated the reading with sharp raps demanding attention, scolded whisperers, and scowled at shufflers. Hearing a noise across the room, she shouted, "Harold McBee, get back in your seat or I'll have you on the wastebasket! Yesterday was your birthday, not today." True to her warning, moments later she had Harold sitting on the wastebasket, her durance vile, for not being quiet.

This scene, though real, is an extreme illustration of an unhealthy classroom atmosphere and shows the need for an organizational plan for elementary guidance programs which allow for the significant role that individual teachers in the elementary school play in their full days with children. Any increase in the guidance skills of the teacher, in her understanding of child behavior, and in her ability to provide a nurtural environment for children, will work to the benefit of all or nearly all the children in the classroom. This is one of the most important considerations in planning the organization of guidance programs in elementary schools. This is not to say that there are not special skills and tasks which teachers do not have or cannot do, skills and tasks requiring a specialist. It does mean that the specialist, in large part, will work through the teacher and not as a separate department.

GUIDANCE SKILLS NEEDED BY THE ELEMENTARY SCHOOL TEACHER

One of the main purposes of this book is to provide information about techniques that teachers can use in carrying out their part in an elementary guidance program. It is especially important that teachers become skilled in the guidance area because there are and will continue to be many schools that do not have specialized assistance. Whatever provision is made for the development of a guidance program will depend upon teacher-skill and teacher-initiative.

Guidance programs at the elementary level call for skills that are suitable to the particular developmental levels of five to fourteen year old children and objectives consistent with the developmental tasks of these age levels. Vocational aptitude testing, occupational information, and educational guidance, so important to the secondary school, appear most unrealistic as components of elementary guidance programs. Instead the procedures needed are those which assist the transition from home to school with its more impersonal and expanding social demands; the development of capacity to relate emotionally to others; the encouragement of social participation and acceptance; the provision for success, self-esteem, and respect from peers and adults; and the prevention of emotionally blocking and crippling events. To achieve this, information adequate to individual appraisal is needed in order to identify individual needs, including difficulties of adjustment requiring specialized treatment.

Starting with the premise that the elementary school teacher is the key figure in developing a guidance program at this level, the important considerations become:

How does the teacher view children?
What does she understand of what she sees?
What is she able to do about it?
What is she willing to do?

This book should aid the teacher to see children more accurately, understand more of what she sees, provide suggestions for manipulating the environments and assisting the children, and stimulate and satisfy her motives as a result of more effective actions.

Ordinarily one would begin with a description and discussion of the principles of guidance and from this groundwork develop the technical applications which relate to them. A different approach is to be found here, starting with the premise that in theory, at least, most teachers subscribe to such principles, but that understanding of them evolves from attempts to make them operational through the kind of practices they follow in working with children. Invariably, the teacher is faced with a decision about what to do with, or for, a certain child or group of children. This book contains information which will enable teachers to work more effectively in promoting the personal-social development of children, not as amateur psychologists or psychiatrists but as professional educators. Success in such efforts should lead to greater understanding of human behavior. The risk in such a course is readily apparent—the blind application of recipes and formulas without reference to guiding principles. Yet principles and philosophies are as much the children as the parents of practice.

Psychologically, we are born blind. We learn to see. We learn to *make* sense out of the physical world and the psychological world as well. The latter is more difficult because the clues are less tangible. Just as words have different meanings depending upon the context, so behavior can have different meaning. As we can see from the following example, incomplete and misinterpreted information thwart attempted understanding of behavior.

> A second grade teacher, walking from desk to desk giving assistance and correcting errors during an arithmetic lesson, came to the desk of a girl who usually had most of her problems worked correctly. But not this day. Few were right. As she corrected the problems, Miss Seymour jokingly said, "Well, I tripped you up today, didn't I, Martha?"
>
> Martha began crying. The teacher comforted her, assured her she would do better tomorrow, and went on to the next child. But she didn't dismiss the event as a momentary upset as she might have several months earlier, before undertaking study in guidance. She paid closer attention to what Martha had to say and how she acted. She overheard several conversations between Martha and a classmate, Cathy. Martha was upset because her father had been called back into the army. She couldn't conceive of just what the army was or why her father had to go there, but she knew war meant possible death. And maybe it really wasn't the army; she vaguely knew that sometimes fathers left their homes and families and got divorces and didn't come back. Observing the support and understanding that Martha received from Cathy, Miss Seymour realized the value of the close friendship between the two girls. Because she had looked more closely at the occurrence, the teacher also realized the steps that should be taken and found opportunity to help Martha understand and accept what was happening.

In other situations, teachers can observe accurately enough without knowing the meaning of their observations—for example, the teacher who knew Johnny had to urinate frequently was aware of a history of diabetes in the family but did not see any connection which suggested a possible underlying physical cause for Johnny's frequent trips. Understanding what one sees implies an acceptance of the proposition that behavior is caused and that it may be explained, especially if one is willing to look behind the scenes for clues.

To say that behavior is caused is to imply that it is meaningful and purposeful, rather than accidental and blind; that today's events and experiences will influence tomorrow's behavior and today's behavior can be understood if we look to the past for causes. It is much more difficult to accept this proposition than to state it. First of all, there are so many myths and superstitions prevalent about human behavior: "chip off the old block," "redheads are temperamental," "every family has its black sheep," "distrust a shifty-eyed person." Second, we adults are often more interested in controlling behavior than we are in directing and guiding behavior. It is much more simple to order a child to put an object down than it is to show him how it works and how to handle it. This is not a suggestion that every act of a child be analyzed as to its origin; nevertheless, in the press of events, especially during a day with thirty or so children in a classroom, demands are such that a teacher will repeatedly respond to an aggravating child with attempts to control his behavior rather than reflect on its meaning and causes. To do the latter takes conscientious effort, sometimes more than we are willing to give.

Understanding behavior and doing something about it, if something can be done, are closely associated for the teacher. Generally speaking, if she is interested in understanding human behavior it is because she wishes to be more effective in her work with children. Increased understanding of behavior should be paralleled with increased skill in manipulating the environment, physical, social, and psychological, in order to permit and promote behavioral changes in children. Skill in situational manipulation is especially important to the elementary teacher because of the limitation inherent in the use of verbal procedures with young children.

THE ELEMENTARY TEACHER'S ROLE

This brings this book to a starting point. Most teachers believe they have enough to do. Full-fledged guidance programs, replete with cumulative record-keeping, tests, anecdotes, parent conferences, etc., will appear as more chores conceived by administrators to laden already overworked teachers. Teachers will do more if the doing fulfills their own motives, gives them more satisfaction, increases their pride in accomplishment, and enhances their sense of professional performance. Incorporated in this text are a variety of procedures which teachers can use and which, once used, should aid them to see children more clearly and with greater understanding. The techniques that teachers use should not only facilitate their work but under administrative direction produce information essential to a well-developed guidance program. This includes an appreciation of the limits of teacher-skill and the value of specialized services and community resources in solving some of the difficult problems with which all teachers are confronted.

It has been argued with some justification that guidance and "good teaching" are identical in the elementary school, particularly if the teacher plays the crucial role. It is true enough that the teacher is the focal point through which the entire school organization and program is presented to the pupils. But a guidance program can no more be left to chance arrangement and organization than a curriculum can. Guidance is a procedure for arranging personnel, materials, and methods to foster and promote optimum personal-social development of children, just as curricula are arrangements providing for the intellectual and scholastic development of children. In actual operation, all aspects of the educational program merge in effect; however, each phase serves its specific function, and guidance is no exception.

The phrase "good teaching" implies a simple, unitary concept instead of the complex of functions which it is. When a group of twenty-five elementary teachers were asked to identify the various roles they saw themselves engaged in with their class, they listed over fifty separate roles. The roles named by more than three teachers were (in rank order):

Clerk	Police-	Coach	Furniture-	Traffic Officer
Advisor	woman	Disciplin-	mover	Typist
Nurse	Janitress	arian	Motion-	Organizer
Teacher	Mother	Interpreter	picture opr.	Supervisor
Banker-	Friend	Judge	Counselor	Confidant
Cashier	Referee	Dictator	Milkman	Maid

Even though one must concede that the various titles are not used with precise meaning by the group of teachers, the list, nevertheless, implies a diversity of functions being filled by the teacher. Two observations are germane: first, definition and delimitation of the role of the elementary teacher are needed; second, training and organization of teaching personnel are necessary with respect to the functions assigned teachers.

It is one thesis of this book that the function of the teacher with respect to the personal-social development of children is an educational function and can be distinguished from that of the specialist whose work is re-education or therapy. The distinction will be elaborated later in the text, but in the main the teacher's function consists of systematically providing opportunity for personality and social growth and development in accordance with recognized needs of children and society. Although the specialist may assist the teacher in her educational function, he also has a separate sphere of action concerned with therapy or re-education. His work focuses on persistent personality or character structure and behavior patterns which have to be altered before healthy growth and development can proceed.

THE ELEMENTARY SCHOOL GUIDANCE SPECIALIST

In view of the purpose of this book it is proper that emphasis be given to the teacher's role in elementary school guidance. However, there are guidance services to be provided by other school personnel. Although the position of the elementary school guidance specialist is still in the process of being defined, the functions to be performed by him are contained in the following list of duties:

General services

1. Being responsible for the gathering, organizing, and keeping of significant pupil data.
2. Being responsible for organization and administration of testing programs.
3. Developing of procedures for identification of pupils having special needs.
4. Cooperating with school administrator in planning and execution of school program as far as personal-social development of children is concerned.
5. Cooperating with community agencies in cooperative case-work.

Services related to teaching staff

1. Helping teachers carry out procedures for collecting, interpreting, and using behavioral data.
2. Planning and execution of in-service training program with respect to child guidance, for example, case conferences.
3. Assisting staff in working with parents, for example, reporting, parent conferences, etc.

4. Helping teachers work with individual children with adjustment problems.
5. Helping teachers understand and accept all children.
6. Being aware of and providing for mental health needs of teaching staff.

Services related to children with adjustment problems

1. Gathering and interpreting data about the maladjusted child through observation, tests, interview.
2. Aiding teachers to understand and deal effectively with children with learning or adjustment problems.
3. Coordinating efforts of school staff in carrying out individual treatment program for child.
4. Aiding principal in work with parents in carrying out satisfactory plan.
5. Cooperating with local groupwork and casework agencies concerned with individual child.
6. Working directly with child as needed.

Other services

1. Assisting parents in recognizing, understanding, and taking appropriate action for helping child.
2. Coordinating services of personnel and community agencies to provide optimum program for promoting educational, social, emotional, physical, and moral development of boys and girls.
3. Promoting harmonious school-community relations through parent-child-teacher contacts.
4. Working with community agencies in program for improvement of community conditions and solution to pressing community problems.

From this list of duties, it can be seen that effectively organized and harmoniously operating working relationships are needed between the guidance specialist, the principal, and the teacher, if a guidance program is to be effective. In addition to guidance specialists, others of the following personnel may participate in the guidance program:

1. Attendance officer
2. Visiting teacher
3. Speech therapist
4. Reading specialist
5. School nurse
6. Physician

7. Dentist
8. Psychologist
9. School social worker
10. Psychiatrist

The diversity of communities and the novelty of elementary guidance programs make it difficult to apply set criteria or find uniform organizational arrangements for evaluating or describing guidance programs at this level. Organizational patterns are likely to vary widely from community to community. In one, the specialist primarily responsible for the program may be a school social worker; in the second a school psychologist; and a guidance specialist in the third. Nevertheless, one can identify the services to be performed, the available staff, and the informational base from which a program operates.

THE ELEMENTARY SCHOOL GUIDANCE PROGRAM

Elementary school guidance services are designed to aid the child's personal and social development from the time of his entrance into school until he moves to the secondary school. Information regarding the physical, mental, social, and emotional development of children is needed from time of admission to the elementary school until departure. Such information should be kept current and available to personnel having need to use it. A brief check list of information and procedures is presented for purposes of a quick review of the guidance program.

Individual Inventory Services. Which of the following procedures are systematically used for obtaining information about child and family?

1. Personal data blanks or questionnaires
2. Physical examinations
3. Interviews with child or family
4. Teacher observations
5. Anecdotal reports
6. Teacher ratings
7. Autobiographies
8. Samples of creative work
9. Projective techniques
10. Interest inventories
11. Pupil diaries
12. Records of leisure and hobby activities
13. Personality inventories

14. Standardized tests
15. Previous school records
16. Home visits
17. Case studies
18. Case conferences
19. Sociometric data

What types of information are contained in the cumulative record?

1. Identifying data—child name, sex, birthplace
2. Identifying data—parent residence, occupations, etc.
3. Family background data
4. Detailed physical and health history
5. Test data—IQ, aptitudes
6. Test data—achievement
7. School records, achievement
8. Attendance record
9. Pupil interest, hobbies
10. Pupil adjustment, emotional
11. Pupil leisure and club activities
12. Pupil social adjustment

Given personnel and information, the guidance worker must be concerned with the use being made of the information and the guidance program being developed. A program can only function on an ad hoc basis if no attempt is made to assimilate the accumulated data. Not only must the necessary data be available on each child, but some compilation and summary is needed if an effective program is to be operated. Information about the community, its socio-economic and occupational structure, its ethnic composition, and its social problems is needed. Knowledge of the types of difficulties and adjustment problems being experienced by children is important, not only in school but after school. If malnutrition as a result of economic difficulties is prevalent, different solutions are needed than if the origin is not economic but instead due to faulty dietary habits. Schools serving child populations in high delinquency areas, or groups in which a high frequency of broken homes occur, or districts in which a high proportion of both parents are working have to anticipate the kinds of needs and difficulties emerging because of the community structure. Suburban communities in which youngsters are widely dispersed and dependent upon transportation by parents are likely to present needs different than densely populated urban areas lacking recreational facilities. All these illustrations point to the need for demographic analysis of the information available about a given community and its school population if intelligent provision is to be made for group needs.

Within this framework, a variety of uses should occur with respect to the information available in order to meet the developmental needs of children.

Providing for personal-social development of all children
1. Preschool orientation program.
2. Elastic system of original school admission.
3. Individual personality appraisal of kindergarten children.
4. Every-pupil program of measurement and evaluation to keep constant check on potential and achievement.
5. Availability of adequate, scientifically prepared cumulative record.
6. Use by school personnel of cumulative record.
7. Teacher review of cumulative record at beginning of the school year for individual program planning.
8. Recording of significant observations through anecdotal records.
9. Provision for individual differences in children through adaptation of techniques, methods, and materials within the classroom.

Identifying and providing for children with special needs
1. Screening of children for sight, hearing, and other physical handicaps or difficulties.
2. Individualized and small group remedial reading instruction.
3. Provision of specialized assistance for children with special needs; speech therapy, sight-saving instruction, speech-reading instruction for hard of hearing, special classes for mentally retarded, transportation for physically handicapped.
4. Identification and provision for children with special talents, e.g., art, music, science, etc.

Identifying children with adjustment difficulties
1. Staff alertness to screening, and appropriate referral of children with adjustment problems.
2. Recommendation of medical, psychological, and psychiatric clinic services for children needing them.
3. Cooperation with agencies working with children.

Working with parents
1. Providing parents with information about school program and regulations.
2. Providing parents with knowledge of guidance services and program.
3. Effective reporting procedures to parents on child progress which includes information on physical, emotional, and social growth as well as academic.
4. Provision for parent-teacher conferences on a regular basis.

The preceding listing provides the teacher or principal a useful gauge for reviewing the guidance services available in her school and a valuable preliminary to the reading of this text.

ORGANIZATION OF THE BOOK

Although this book is divided into six parts, the same organizational pattern is found in each part. First, a chapter on the kinds of information needed in that particular area and a description of techniques for obtaining the information; second, a chapter containing developmental and normative data against which the information may be compared; and finally, a chapter suggesting ways of using the information to foster the personal and social development of children. This same pattern is reflected in the next three chapters with the difference being that these next chapters are more general and attempt to provide basic information on obtaining, transmitting, and interpreting information. The final section of Part One is a case history, an attempt to present a reasonably complete picture of a child as seen by a teacher. Case histories vary in form, content, and analysis according to the intent and training of the person preparing the report and the techniques used in gathering the information. Case histories prepared by teachers contain much more observational and anecdotal information than clinical information. They tend to be more concerned with behavior and especially school achievement than with emotional and motivational aspects of personality. The analyses are less technical and not to the depth of the clinical report. Nevertheless, they can be operationally sound and fully as useful in analyzing growth patterns and planning programs for individual children.

It would be just as sensible to place the case history last, as the culmination of the information gathering. The reason in presenting it here is to show a child described as well as pedantic words can describe him. Here is the whole, to which the pieces we will study belong. Perhaps the pieces will appear more sensible because of this order. The succeeding five parts of the text concern themselves with the child's relationships with his family, his health, his personal and social development, and finally with the school. Each part ends with several selected references chosen for their usefulness to the classroom teacher.

Chapter 2

OBTAINING INFORMATION

THE DANGER OF SNAP JUDGMENTS

In each day of her life with a particular class, a teacher is involved in making judgments and interpretations of the behavior of the children. Phrases such as "willful disobedience," "attention-seeking," "insecure," "trustworthy," "aggressive," "shy" reflect description, interpretation, or judgment of children's behavior. "Not working up to his ability," "not trying as hard as he should," "poor word recognition," "slow learner," "pleasing personality," and "bright child" reflect the impressions and judgments of the teacher, or her attempts to analyze or explain a child's behavior. It is inevitable and essential that teachers should arrive at judgments or conclusions regarding the behavior of individual children. Attempts to guide the development of children towards socially desirable goals require constant evaluation of progress and problems encountered. The very nature of teaching necessitates making many judgments regarding human behavior. Unfortunately, such judgments are too often faulty due to insufficient information, inaccurate information, or inability to interpret the information. The following illustrations of such judgments and interpretations have been taken from the observational case studies of children made by teachers.

Report	*Comment*
Jimmy comes from a semi-well-to-do home. The mother is a socialite so she doesn't spend too much time with Jim. Most of his time is spent with his nurse. Jim is an only child so he has been given everything . . .	Does it follow that socialites don't spend time with their children, or just this particular mother? Note the cause-effect relationship implied regarding indulgence of only-child as explaining observed behavior.

Report	*Comment*
. . . Jim doesn't get along with the other boys his age. He says they bore him. . . . Jimmy's superior intelligence may be partly inherited because his mother and father are very brilliant. He speaks French and German, plays the piano very well. . . . He was able to distinguish tunes before he was four months old and he knew colors at three months. . . . He never received much affection, so he became very cold emotionally. He looks for sympathy but never receives it.	A broad generalization. In what situations doesn't Jim get along? Jimmy may be very bright, and he may have developed color preferences by three months but much more is indicated in this description. How accurate? Again a broad generalization about amount of affection and its relation to present emotional responsiveness.

✿   ✿   ✿

Rob is in the eighth grade, is 14½ years old, nearly six feet tall, and thirty pounds overweight. Father, born in the old country, is a shop supervisor. Mother died when Rob was 6.

Rob attended both parochial and public elementary schools. The record shows he has been a discipline problem as far back as the fourth grade. His fourth grade teacher states he was "excitable, fearful, uncontrolled, and a day dreamer who didn't adjust too well to his companions in school or on the playground. He is restless in school and mischievous if he thinks he will not be discovered. Is polite to the point of exaggeration and extremely courteous. Has a habit of running

Considerable factual information presented in condensed form, but with little apparent relationship between the separate facts.

up to little girls, throwing his arms about their necks and kissing them. Takes piano lessons and practices every day."

Most of the time he is neat appearing. His attendance is good, has passing grades until this year. Average intelligence.

Reports received from teachers state:

English: Behaves well in class, enjoys oral reading, work untidy and unfinished; delights in giving out books—has egocentric attitude.

Latin: Nothing but a nuisance. Failing.

Mathematics: Unsatisfactory work. Restless. Always looks for an excuse to leave class. Feel he needs help, perhaps a psychiatrist.

Physical Education: Will not participate on some days, just creates a disturbance. Smaller boys annoy him, getting him upset and defensive.

Conclusions: Rob's lack of stability and stick-to-it-iveness is a carry over from primary school days, probably due to his need of love.

The separate reports represent a compilation of discrete bits of information primarily concerned with class performance and interspersed with suggestions of behavior which may indicate serious problems. Yet none of the reports provides sufficient information to permit a judgment.

The Importance of Separating Fact from Interpretation

It is readily apparent in the preceding observations that many judgments and interpretations are implicitly made, interpretations which stem from the teacher's perception of the behavior and her evaluation of its meaning. It is easier to see the inaccuracies and misconceptions made by others as we read their reports of child behavior, overlooking the extent to which all perceptions are distorted. Unless carefully trained and consciously concerned, human observation is fraught with error, first from oversights and inaccuracies in actual observation, second, from distortions of perception. You are probably more conscious of the automobiles on the highway which are identical with the one you own than you are of others, although the latter may be more numerous. You probably are aware of nearly every sportscar which you see, but are unaware of an even greater number of Fords or Chevrolets. The explanations of this selectivity are quite reasonable, but, however reasonable, the result is inaccuracy in observation. More serious is the fact that our own motives and attitudes often cause us to misconstrue what we observe. As we watch an event we more than passively observe, we actively attempt to make sense out of what we see. Two short anecdotes readily illustrate this tendency:

> There is no companionship between Billy and his parents as they are not home enough to develop such a feeling. I believe Billy's companionship with the handyman is a way of substituting for the missing parental love. Billy feels inferior to his classmates because he is so thin and small compared with the average child in the class. He keeps to himself to avoid being ridiculed or teased by the children in the class, and to side-step embarrassment.

Listing the facts observed in the preceding, one learns:

1. No companionship between Billy and parents.
2. Parents frequently out of the home.
3. Billy has a companionship with handyman.
4. Billy is thin and small.
5. Billy keeps to himself when with his class.

But for nearly every fact an interpretation or explanation was offered telling from the observer's viewpoint that such behavior meant:

1. Companionship with handyman is a substitute for missing parental love.
2. Being thin and small makes Billy feel inferior.
3. His keeping to himself stems from a desire to avoid ridicule.

And the second anecdote:

> Philip thrives on attention. The more attention he gets, the more he demands. Because he was the first child, he got unlimited attention for the first few years and after his sister was born he still got unlimited attention because of his speech difficulty. When he was able to talk, the attention gradually began to shift to his younger sister with the result that Philip began inventing his own attention-getting mechanisms.

The entire report is more an attempt to explain why Philip seeks attention than an observation of behavior, even though incorporating several contradictory explanations:

1. First children get unlimited attention which is
2. taken away with the birth of the second child, but
3. not in this case, for he continued to get attention because of speech difficulty; but since correction
4. has had to resort to other devices.

It is this overwillingness to interpret and explain behavior that is a danger resulting from naive application of a little psychological knowledge. Too often we mix a little psychology and a lot of our own prejudice in such interpretations. If nothing else, experience in working with children with adjustment difficulties teaches one to reserve judgment and not be deceived by the too obvious.

Anyone working with children, whether clinician, group worker, or educator, is constantly making decisions as to appropriate actions to be taken with children. These decisions and actions follow from the perception and interpretation of a given situation and its historical antecedents. The value of a written, factual record is that it permits us to review and re-analyze the situation at times when our judgment or interpretation proved faulty. If we have recorded only our interpretations and omitted the facts, we are subsequently forced to proceed by trial-and-error rather than through re-analysis and understanding. It is important, then, that we separate fact from interpretation.

FACTS, NOT VALUE JUDGMENTS, ARE NEEDED

We must distinguish between the behavior we observe and whether we approve or disapprove of it. For instance, in the following excerpt from a case study:

> Tommy Bird is a friendly red-haired boy who has just reached his thirteenth birthday. He is in the eighth grade. The Birds live in a pleasant bungalow in a *good* residential section of this city. Mr. Bird is a transportation supervisor and provides a *good* standard of living and a few luxuries for his family. Mr. Bird is a *very* intelligent man with an *excellent* disposition. He is devoted to his children, but at the same time firm, and they obey him promptly and pleasantly. Mrs. Bird is an *exceptionally* fine woman . . .

Judging from the frequent use of such adjectives as good, excellent, exceptionally, very, we are provided not only with certain information but also impressed by the fact that the observer personally *approved* of what he saw, that according to *his* set of values the parents were admirable people.

Not only should we separate our interpretation of the behavior from the events we observe and record, but also we should eliminate any intrusion of our private value system by which we respond by liking or disliking, approving or rejecting. Anecdotes and observational records in which we fail to accomplish this are comparatively useless as the following sequence of anecdotes taken from a cumulative record shows:

ANECDOTAL REPORTS: RICHARD G————.

Kindergarten

Physical Characteristics

Short—neat and clean—has a very distinct voice. General health good. Has a good sense of rhythm and can skip. Posture is good but doesn't sit still for any length of time. Doesn't have much self control.

Social Adjustment

Has had a hard time working in a group. Very immature, self-centered and has no respect for others. Slow about obeying and has not learned to conform to classroom regulations. Powers of concentration poor, flits from one thing to another.

Intellectual Development

Uses very good English—asks sensible questions—has the ability to understand and follow group directions but his power of concentration is short unless intensely interested in what he is doing. Has a clear understanding of what takes place in his everyday world. Quick to see likenesses and differences. Has ability to do first grade work but probably will find it hard to settle down to routine.

Miss V————, Kindergarten teacher

Of all the reports on this child, the one by the kindergarten teacher presents the clearest picture. It is mainly factual, even though most of the description is general. A few specific illustrations would be useful.

Grade One

Physical Characteristics

Short, stocky, rugged. Has had tonsils removed. Nervous and easily excited.

Intellectual Development

Good progress which could be improved by better conduct. A wealth of background material that he is over-anxious to relate. Fine ability which at present is hampered by poor personality adjustment.

Social adjustment

A poor group member, with little respect for the rights of others. Still self-centered but less boisterous in expressing himself. Good, natural, even disposition but lacks

This teacher adds little information. Her anecdotes show frequent use of adjectives good, poor, fine, etc., which are not meaningful unless one is acquainted with her scale of values. She speaks of poor adjustment but even disposition which needs further explanation.

control of his emotions and personal desires. Boundless energy and enthusiasm.

    Miss W———, Grade One

Grade Two

Richard has quieted down somewhat but it is a great effort for him to be natural. His work is good in spite of his behavior. He is a very disturbing influence on the room and is most difficult to manage.

    Miss X———, Grade Two

No attempt is made in these grades to group facts into physical, intellectual, and social.

Grade Three

Richard has been a definite problem in every way. He has the ability to do excellent work but because of his exceptionally poor work habits, he has not done the work of which he is capable.

He is emotionally immature—demanding attention and showing off. He needs constant urging to finish any work and is not receptive to praise or censure.

    Miss Y———, Grade Three

Failure to provide specific information regarding behavior leaves the reader confused and groping with what appears to be an increasingly severe problem.

The term immature appears repeatedly in the ancedotes. Is this to imply that the behavior patterns have not changed since the kindergarten, or does each teacher mean something different?

Grade Four

Richard is a definite behavior problem. It has been impossible to allow him any playground privileges at recess or noon this year because he needs constant alert supervision at every moment. This has been the consistent report of all his teachers thus far. Highly nervous and easily disturbed by classroom activities, he finds it difficult to concentrate for the period of time necessary for completion of any assignment. Praise or punishment have no lasting effect.

Although immature in personality traits and motor adjustments, Richard has a brilliant mind which is active when interested.

He has a neat, well-dressed appearance and is always courteous. He doesn't resent

Praise or punishment (such as?) have no lasting effect, yet he is courteous, doesn't resent criticism and wonders about group adjustment.

criticism and wonders why he cannot conform to group routine.

Miss Z——————, Grade Four

Note: Richard was so difficult that the principal felt it necessary to transfer him to the other fourth grade in the school.	The principal felt it necessary? . . . or did Miss Z feel it necessary?

Grade Four

Here is our sixty-four dollar problem. Bright child-lazy child, quick child-irresponsible child, small child who is at your heels at all times demanding attention. Lovable child to me—some find him not so lovable. Terrifically irritating at times. Talks like a little old man.	The most literary of the anecdotes, reflecting as much the difference in the two fourth grade teachers as it does about the child.

What will become of him when he has grown up? I wish him the best of everything, but I wonder.

Certainly these anecdotes, reported in full, reveal how much can be written and how little said. Each of the teachers has her own picture of the child, to be sure, but the reports paint a blurred and fuzzy image of him. Yet if there is any single skill needed by a teacher in the area of guidance, it is the skill to observe accurately and report clearly.

When children are referred to psychologists or psychiatrists for assistance, these specialists depend upon a series of contrived devises and techniques such as tests, play therapy, case histories, etc., to obtain the information needed for diagnosis. They use these varied procedures not only to obtain a complete range of information, but also because they seldom have first-hand access to the life of the child. Seldom can they observe the child for long periods in his natural environment. This the teacher can do. Properly developed, observational skill is a powerful tool, and a tool which is almost exclusively the teacher's, for she has daily contact with the work and play life of the child, as well as direct access to the neighborhood and home of the child.

TECHNIQUES FOR
GATHERING NECESSARY INFORMATION

The teacher's problem is to obtain sufficient accurate information to permit her to make sound deductions about the behavior she observes in her class. There are many procedures for gathering information, ranging from simple to complex, from those that teachers can readily use in practice to those that require skilled clinical training. The particular technique to be used depends upon the information needed by the teacher in order to successfully carry out her duties as a teacher. The first task of the teacher is to decide what she wishes to know about all the children in the classroom—the minimum amount of knowledge she needs about every child—then subsequently, what more she wishes to know about particular children. The gathering of data about children is not an end in itself. The school exists for the education of children, not for the accumulation of records. Cumulative records which remain in the principal's office unused by teachers may be a source of satisfaction to the principal but are scarcely a labor of love for his faculty. The starting point in gathering information about children is to determine what facts must be had about all, and then the further facts needed by the teachers in order to perform their work as effectively as possible.

The knowledge we gather about a child can be subdivided into three categories:

1. Knowledge about the child as a person.
2. Knowledge about the child's world.
3. Knowledge about the child's relationships.

Although the following list is not exhaustive, it covers the major categories of information desired in each area, with the minimum essential information starred (*). Adjacent to each section is a listing of techniques for obtaining information which are adapted to or especially useful in a particular area. These techniques range from simple to complex. Some are restricted to a given area, others are useful in all. Most important among the latter are observation, interviews, questionnaires, check lists, and case histories. In the first chapter of each part in the book, the techniques will be described as they apply to a given area of development.

Knowing the child as a person	*Technique*
Identifying data*	
Name	
Address—telephone	Questionnaire
Birthdate—age	Interview
Sex	
Parent or guardian	
Parent address—tel.	

Physical Health
    Height°
    Weight°
    Vision°
    Hearing°   Physical examination
    Physical examination (general or detailed)   Medical report
    Dental examination   Observation
    Vaccination record
    Energy level
    Motor development and coordination
    Health history of previous illnesses, injuries
    Nutrition of child

Intellectual
    IQ°   Standardized test
    Reading readiness   Teacher report
    Special aptitudes
    Achievement°

Emotional
    Attitude toward self-acceptance°
    Attitude toward self-esteem
    Attitude toward self-guilt   Case history
    Fears   Rating scales
    Worries   Problem check lists
    Problems of adjustment°   Creative work
    Symptomatic behavior
    Motives, goals, level of aspiration

Knowledge of the child's world

In-School
    Attitude toward school°   Observation
    Attitude toward learning°   Questionnaire
    Participation in activities   Check lists
    Interests°

Out-of-School

    Family background
        Adults in home
        Children in home
        Parental occupation
        Socio-economic status
        Cultural status
            Attitude toward music   Case history
            education, art, leisure, etc. Interview

    General home life

    Religious influences

Hobbies

Interests

Reading interest, activity

Sports

Leisure activities

Social activities

Knowledge of child's relationships

Family
    Parent attitudes toward child*
        Accepting, rejecting, over-prot.,
        indulgent, ambitious, etc.
    Nature of discipline
    Child attitude toward parents
        Hostile, submissive, affectionate,
        indifferent, aggressive, etc.
    Child relationship with siblings
    Child attitude toward other adults,
        teacher

Peer group
    Status with classmates*
        with agemates*
    Friendships
    Neighborhood associates
    Clubs, team activities

Case history
Interview
Questionnaire
Observation
Projective techniques
Sociograms
Social distance scales
Guess-who
Personality inventories
Autobiography

Chapter 3

COMMUNICATION OF INFORMATION

THE CUMULATIVE RECORD SYSTEM

In the days of the one-room school, attended by all grades and taught by a teacher long resident in the community, the teacher was her own cumulative record system. She was well-acquainted with the community and the families in it. The number of children she worked with was comparatively small; she taught them not for a year but for as long as they attended school. Her store of information on each child was limited only by her memory; her use of the information was limited only by her wisdom and her interest. The birth of the city changed most of this, for instead of all grades in one room, only one grade existed per room, and instead of all subjects taught by one teacher, specialized teaching developed. Add to these changes the developing knowledge of the dynamics of human behavior and the teacher discovered she could no longer depend exclusively on her memory, her interest, or her wisdom. She needed to know what had occurred in the grades preceding hers; she needed to seek help on occasion from specialists in analyzing the behavior of certain children. So the cumulative record was created to systematically store significant information about a child's growth and development over a period of time.

The difficulty with cumulative records is that they become attics, crammed with nonessential as well as potentially useful material. The key to cumulative records lies in the phrase to "systematically store significant information." Although any author can list a range of information which *should* be stored in cumulative records, its significance depends on whether or not it can and will be used by school personnel.

To be sure, the several parts of the text stress the significance of certain information as it relates to child development, and most discussions of cumulative records adopt a similar viewpoint. If the cumulative record is seen as a device for storing information for use, then significant information is that which will be used. The effectiveness of the cumulative record system depends upon the interest and the training of a given faculty. A school staff that is establishing a record-keeping system should ask: How useful is the information and what information will be used? not, What information would we like to have? The latter question produces the attic of useless data, an educational wasteland of precious energy. The school staff which has a cumulative record system should ask: How useful is the information we have been gathering? Inevitably, they will discover that the data is over-balanced, e.g., there will be much information on academic performance, disciplinary problems, and health, but little of value on personality or social development. Roughly a third of the information will be useless, being opinion without fact. Very likely half of the remainder will seldom, if ever, have been used, and therefore is of little significance. The starting point for a cumulative record system, by these criteria, does not lie in the purchase of file cabinets and the design of record systems, but in the training of the staff.

A review of anecdotal reports shows that teachers consistently neglect certain aspects of development and report on others. Violations of rules and regulations, health problems, tardiness and absences are more likely to be consistently reported, but information on personal adjustment and social development will be most consistently neglected. One survey of 167 elementary school teachers of an urban school system which prides itself on being a "better" school system showed that 46 teachers reported data on social growth as being least useful and 59 the data from test records as being least useful. Items such as "uses creative abilities" and "uses self analysis as a means to improvement" were thought difficult to interpret, but seemingly essential items in the social growth category were "is dependable," "is emotionally mature," and "follows directions." Most useful information in the cumulative record was the record of grades. It was apparent from further analysis, that the teachers found the check list of short phrases difficult to interpret. Given descriptive information in anecdotal form which was more complete and objective, the teachers preferred such information to the customary check list.

All of the limitations in record systems cannot be attributed to staff limitations, for investigation of record-keeping systems will frequently show that the block is a mechanical difficulty, e.g., the records are kept in the principal's office for his exclusive use, or they are kept at such a distance from the teacher that access is difficult enough to discourage use.

The Functions of Cumulative Records

In general, cumulative records can serve three functions of the school—pupil accounting, teaching efficiency, and pupil guidance. The activities relative to each of these areas which are served by cumulative records are listed below:

Pupil accounting	*Teaching efficiency*	*Pupil guidance*
Identification of pupils, residence, etc. Maintaining attendance records. Maintaining fiscal records relevant to daily attendance.	Familarizes teacher with class. Provides record of previous school performance. Grouping of pupils. Identification of individual strengths and weaknesses for special work. Preparing report cards. Improving accuracy of estimated performance of pupil.	Provides leads regarding causes of behavioral difficulties. Conferences with parents and pupils. Background for case studies. Aid in courses and career studies. Information about home background. Provides clues to pupil interests and motivation.

Any and all of the activities listed are valid functions of the school, and a cumulative record is indispensable to many of them. Irrespective of how much or how little information is to be gathered, certain basic concepts should be adhered to in the design of the record:

1. Organization by time sequence. The cumulative record is an attempt to provide a record of a child's growth and development and the sequence of events affecting it. The record should be continuous and indicative of relationships between phases.

2. Continuity of form and content. The data being gathered and the format of same should show continuity from grade to grade and school to school.

3. Balance of information. The range and frequency of information obtained should provide a rounded picture of the child. A record of grades, achievement test data, or disciplinary problems is scarcely a full picture of a child's development in school.

4. Comparability of measures. A procedure for scaling test scores and other measures should be adopted so that scores are comparable.

5. Design for use. The design of the records should be such that efficiency in storage of information does not take precedence over efficiency in use of information, e.g., the space provided on most folder type records for recording personality data, anecdotes, avocational activities, etc., is so limited as to discourage recording and review.

Content of Cumulative Records. Segel[1] studied the cumulative records of 177 school systems and recorded the frequency in which specific kinds of information were recorded. Listed in rank order, these are:

1. Scholarship
2. School progress
3. Attendance
4. Entrance and withdrawal
5. Home conditions and family history
6. Intelligence tests
7. Social and character ratings
8. Health
9. Space for notations
10. Achievement tests
11. Extracurricular activities
12. Vocational and educational plans
13. Residence record
14. College or occupation entered

---

[1] D. Segel, *Nature and Use of Cumulative Record*. U.S. Office of Educ. Bull. #3, Washington, D.C.: U.S. Govt. Printing Office, 1938.

15. Special abilities
16. Photograph
17. Out-of-school employment

Several of these items are clearly more important to secondary schools than to elementary schools (#12, 14, 17). No single item was included in the cumulative records of more than 80 per cent of the schools reporting, and the most noticeable characteristic was the lack of uniformity in the records. For instance, most of the records called for some judgment by the teacher on social and character traits. The number varied from three to eight in most records with those most frequently mentioned being accuracy, conduct, cooperation, courtesy, dependability, effort, honesty, industry, initiative, leadership, obedience, personal appearance, punctuality, reliability, and self-control. Unfortunately, the traits to be rated are seldom described, with the result that a high degree of overlap occurs among ratings of several traits, i.e., dependability, effort, industry, obedience, and reliability are different names for the same behavior as far as teachers' ratings are concerned.

The information essential to the elementary school which a cumulative record should contain is the following:

1. Identification and Progress Items
   name and address
   date of birth and place
   sex
   date entered school system
   grade entered
   date left school system
   date re-entered school system

2. Scholarship Items
   age at entrance first grade
   present grade
   teacher's name
   number of days attended
   number of days tardy
   scholarship ratings

3. Educational and Aptitude Test Items (if any)
   year, grade, and chronological age of student
   names of tests and forms used
   dates of administration
   raw scores

percentile score (including local percentiles if available)
MA, CA, IQ, percentile of intelligence tests

4. Health Items
dates of school health and dental examinations
record of diseases incurred
physical defects
dates parents informed of any unusual condition,
    recommended action, action taken by parents
results of treatment

5. Home Conditions and Family History
names of father, mother, (or guardian)
residence (if any different from child)
brothers and sisters, number older and younger
education of parents
marital status of parents
language spoken in home (if not English)

6. Leisure Activities
intellectual activities
social activities
athletic or physical activities
cultural activities
hobbies

7. Social and Character Items
(If ratings are to be used the trait should be clearly described
and the steps on the scale identified, e.g., example taken
from American Council on Education Cumulative Record for
Grades 1-3.)

Cooperation (Ability to participate jointly in activities with
others)
Generally cooperative—enters freely and helpfully into group
activities.
Selectively cooperative—takes part where he obtains satisfaction from activity but does not participate in other situations.
Independent—prefers to do things by himself, so is not likely
to enter group situation on own initiative.
Passive—does not realize value of cooperation or does not care
enough to make effort to bring it about.
Antagonistic—is definitely resistant to group activities.

(If anecdotes are to be used provision should be made for objectivity of reporting and screening of items for importance
prior to being made a permanent part of record.)

In reviewing the foregoing items, those listed under identification, scholarship, tests, health, plus address of parent or guardian, constitute a minimum essential record for school purposes. The remaining items are as important, perhaps more, to an understanding of the child and his progress in school, but their inclusion should depend on the use that school personnel will make of them. Figures 1, 2, and 3 show three different formats for recording and keeping such information.

PROBLEMS IN THE MECHANICS OF RECORDING
AND USING INFORMATION

The common predictable items like grades and test scores do not present the mechanical problems that irregular data such as anecdotes offer. Most cumulative records, whether printed on the sides of a manila folder, on a card, or on questionnaires which get stapled into a manila folder, make adequate provision for space for a grade in each subject for each quarter that the child is in school. The testing program is sufficiently stable that space can be provided for each test score. The mechanics of handling anecdotes is more difficult because they vary in length and time of occurrence. A simple solution to this problem can be obtained through the following procedures. Standard 8½ x 11 inch pages are run through the mimeograph machine in order to have three horizontal lines drawn on the page which divide the page into quarters (see Figure 4). Each teacher is given a supply of these pages for recording her anecdotes. Different color paper can be used, if desired, to distinguish health anecdotes from disciplinary actions, etc. In almost all instances a single anecdote can be written on a quarter of the page, using front and back. If more space is needed, as it might be in an interview with a parent, as many quarter pages can be used as desired. (The quarter page size is suggested because experience shows this is usually sufficient space; however, the pages can be run to provide thirds or halves of pages should more room be desired for general recording provided the size is kept uniform.)

During the course of the school year the teacher will record her anecdotes, one per quarter page (see Figure 5). Each anecdote will have a caption or title placed on the bottom line which will identify the date of the anecdote, the subject, and the person writing it (last name or initials). At any time during the school year, but certainly by the end of the year, the teacher will review the anecdotes and

PHOTOS (Dated)

| LAST NAME | FIRST | MIDDLE | NICKNAME | RELIGION | DATE AND PLACE OF BIRTH | M F SEX | W C Y COLOR |

ADDRESS AND TELEPHONE

PREVIOUS SCHOOL RECORD: Names and Types of Schools Attended, Achievement in Subjects and Activities, School Difficulties Encountered, Summary of Test Results.

PHOTOS (Dated)

Names and Type of School Attended

Home Room Teacher

Age as of Sept. 1

School Year and Grade

SCHOOL ACHIEVEMENT

These Columns Are for Analyses of Development in the Subjects Indicated. A Check in One of the First Five Columns and Across from the Subject Will Indicate the Degree of Achievement in That Pupil. Development Will be Indicated by Entering the Letters O (Outstanding), A (Above Usual), U (Usual), B (Below Usual), S (Seriously Below Usual) Across from the Subject.

ACHIEVEMENT: Outstanding | Above Usual | Usual | Below Usual | Seriously Below | Use of Language * | Interest and Effort | Work Habits | Achievement Considering Personal Handicaps and Advantages

LANGUAGE ARTS
- Reading
- Spelling
- Handwriting
- Communication — Oral
- Written

SOCIAL STUDIES
- History
- Geography

Science

Arithmetic

Arts and Crafts

Music

Health Education and Physical Education

* In this column the general use of language in discussion and writing in any subject will be considered.

Figure 1

38

NAME OF TEST	Month	Score	Grade Level	%ile	Norm Used	NAME OF TEST	Month	Score	Grade Level	%ile	Norm Used	NAME OF TEST	Month	Score	Grade Level	%ile	Norm Used
TEST RECORD																	
SCHOOL APTITUDE [Use M. A. and I. Q. if Preferred]																	
READING																	
ACHIEVEMENT AND OTHER TESTS																	

INTERPRETATION OF SCHOOL ACHIEVEMENT In Relation to the Test Record and Other Pertinent Information Contained in this Record.

ATTENDANCE [Reasons if Irregular]

SIGNIFICANT INTERESTS, OPPORTUNITIES AND EXPERIENCES [Activities and Accomplishments in School and Out That Give Evidence Regarding Interests and Powers]

FINANCIAL AID [Type and Amount]

HEALTH AND PHYSICAL CHARACTERISTICS [Vigor or Lassitude, Assets, Handicaps or Limitations. If School Has a Separate Health Records Indicate Contagious Diseases, Immunizations, etc.]

American Council on Education
Washington, D. C.

WT._____ HT._____   WT._____ HT._____   WT._____ HT._____

DESCRIPTION OF FAMILY

	Type of Occupation	Educating Degree and Kind	Country of Birth		

FATHER

MOTHER

STEP PARENT OR GUARDIAN

SIBLINGS | Sex | | | Birth Date | |

NOTE OTHER SIGNIFICANT ITEMS: Health, Duration of Either Parent, Citizenship, Change in Type of Occupation of Parents, Language Spoken, Type of Community, Opportunity for Privacy and Play, or Other Factors Such as "Broken Home". Indicate Dates of Significant Changes.

Notes

DESCRIPTION OF BEHAVIOR [Made Only by Those Who Have Had Sufficient Opportunity to Observe the Child] For the Major Headings of Responsibility, Sociability and Cooperation Check Under the Grade Level the Definition That Best Describes the Behavior of the Pupil. For Each of the Habit Categories Follow the Directions Given Below. Answer the Questions by Writing Yes or No. None of the Descriptions Should Be Interpreted as Ratings.

Grade Level

RESPONSIBILITY

- Responsible: Recognizes Opportunities to Assume Responsibility and Carries Through to the Best of His Ability Whatever Is Undertaken.
- Conscientious: Applies Himself with Conscientious Effort to What Is Assigned to Him.
- Generally Dependable: Usually Carries Through Undertakings, Self-Assumed or Assigned by Others, Requiring Only Occasional Reminder or Compulsion.
- Relatively Dependable: Shows High Persistence in Undertakings in Which He Has Particular Interest But Is Not Likely to Carry Through Other Assignments.
- Undeveloped: Needs Much Prodding and Supervision Even in Undertakings of Moderate Duration or Difficulty

SOCIABILITY

- Secure: Appears to Feel Secure in His Social Relationships and is Accepted by the Group of Which He Is a Part.
- Uncertain: Appears to Have Some Anxiety About His Social Relationship Although He is Accepted by the Group of Which He Is a Part.
- Neutral: Shows the Desire to Have an Established Place in the Group, but is, In General, Treated with Indifference.
- Withdrawn: Withdraws From Others to an Extent that Prevents His Being a Fully Accepted Member of His Group.
- Not Accepted: Has Characteristics of Person or Behavior that Prevent His Being an Accepted Member of His Group.

COOPERATION

- Generally Cooperative: Enters Freely and Helpfully Into Group Activities.
- Selectively Cooperative: Takes Part Where He Obtains Satisfaction from Certain Group Activities but Does Not Participate in Other Group Situations.
- Independent: Prefers to Do Things by Himself so is Not Likely to Enter Into Group Situations on His Own Initiative.
- Unawakened or Passive: Does Not Yet Realize the Value of Cooperation or Does Not Care Enough to Make an Effort to Bring It About.
- Antagonistic: Is Definitely Resistant to Participation in Group Activities.

Influence

- To What Degree Has He Influence in a Group? Use D (Dominating), S (Strongly Influencing), C (Consulted), V (Varying), F (Follower) or Others Explained in Notes.

GENERAL HABITS

- [Indicate by H (High) U (Usual), or L (Low) the Maturity in Development, in Relation to Age, Reached in Each of the Following Habits:]
- Promptness: Habitual Meeting of Opportunities and Obligations on Time.
- Courtesy: Good Manners and Thoughtfulness of Others.
- Respect for Rights of Others: Willingness to Share Fairly in Privileges, Activities and Properties.
- Respect for Property: This is Shown if He Recognizes Others' Rights in Property. Does Not Take What is Not His Own or Wilfully Injure It.

WORK HABITS

- Span of Attention: Length of Time for Which He Can Concentrate on an Undertaking.
- Working Tempo: Rate at Which He Works.
- Efficiency in Use of Time: Extent to which He Has Learned to Start Quickly, Organize and Carry Through a Task.
- Industry: Conscientious Application to His Work.
- Persistence: Extent to Which He Continues to Work on a Task in Spite of Difficulties.

Figure 1—Continued

40

EMOTIONAL STABILITY	Is He Markedly Apathetic?		
	Is He Markedly Excitable?		
	Is He Markedly Sensitive?		
	Is He Markedly Stable?		
	Has He Marked Feelings of Inferiority?		
	Has He Marked Feelings of Superiority?		
	To What Stimuli Does He Show Marked Response?		
	What Influences or Conditions Disturb Him?		

ADDITIONAL COMMENTS CONCERNING THE PUPIL'S BEHAVIOR AND DEVELOPMENT

(Describe Typical Behavior and Significant Variations From it. Explain Particularly About Emotional Responses.)

END OF YEAR SUMMARY WITH SUGGESTIONS FOR THE FUTURE

[Include Recommendations for Summer Reading, Study and Other Experiences.]

Were The Recommendations Followed?

FOLLOW-UP.—Next School Attended, with Dates.

Cumulative Record Cards for Grades 4, 5 and 6

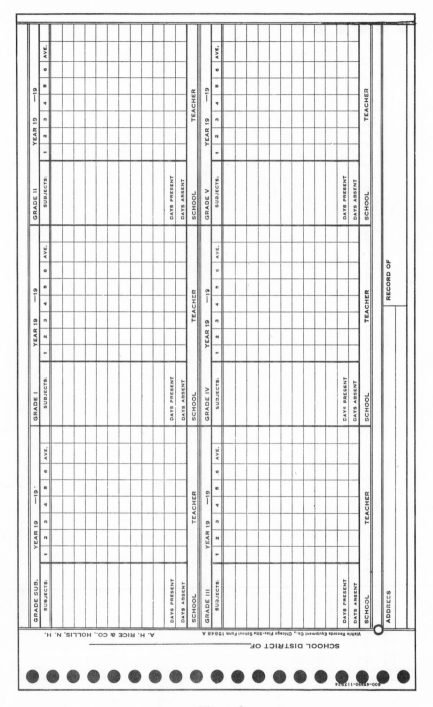

Figure 2

42

RECORD OF _____ ADDRESS _____

Visible Records Equipment Co., Chicago Flex-Site School Form 15848 B

DATE OF BIRTH _____ PLACE OF BIRTH _____

NAME OF PARENT OR GUARDIAN _____

OCCUPATION _____

ENTERED FROM _____

TRANSFERRED TO _____

SUB.	I	II	III	IV	V	VI	VII	VIII	PHYSICAL DISABILITIES.
HEALTH									
CONDUCT									VACCINATED?
EFFORT									

STANDARD TESTS — NAME OF TESTS

	DATE	AGE	GRADE	STAND. SCORE	CLASS MED.	PUPIL SCORE

GRADE VI — SUBJECTS:

	YEAR 19 —19									
	1	2	3	4	5	6	AVE.			
DAYS PRESENT										
DAYS ABSENT										

SCHOOL _____ TEACHER _____

PROMOTED TO H. S., DATE _____

GRADE VII — SUBJECTS:

	YEAR 19 —19						
	1	2	3	4	5	6	AVE.
DAYS PRESENT							
DAYS ABSENT							

SCHOOL _____ TEACHER _____

GRADE VIII — SUBJECTS:

	YEAR 19 —19						
	1	2	3	4	5	6	AVE.
DAYS PRESENT							
DAYS ABSENT							

SCHOOL _____ TEACHER _____

43

ELEMENTARY SCHOOL
PUPIL CUMULATIVE RECORD

HINGHAM PUBLIC SCHOOLS
HINGHAM, MASS.

LAST NAME	FIRST	MIDDLE

FATHER

MOTHER

GUARDIAN

	BIRTHPLACE	OCCUPATION

FATHER

MOTHER

PUPIL

	YEAR	MONTH	DAY	HOW VERIFIED

PUPIL'S BIRTH DATE

LANGUAGE SPOKEN AT HOME

PUPIL LIVES WITH - 1. 2.

ADDRESSES	TELEPHONES

PHYSICAL

DATE		WEARS GLASSES		VISION			HEARING		THROAT	DEF. SPEECH	TEETH	REMARKS
YEAR ENDING	HEIGHT	YES	NO	R	L	B	RIGHT	LEFT				
		WEIGHT	GENERAL HEALTH			X-RAY	VACCI-NATION		CONTAGIOUS DISEASES		TOXIN ANTI-TOXIN	

Figure 3

44

DATE	GRADE	ADDITIONAL PHYSICAL DATA	DATE	GRADE	HOBBIES	DATE	GRADE	INTERESTS

DATE	GRADE	SCHOOL ACTIVITIES	DATE	GRADE	OUT OF SCHOOL ACTIVITIES

SCHOOL PROGRESS RECORD

YEAR	GRADE	SCHOOL AND ROOM	DAYS PRES.	DAYS ABS.	TIMES TARDY	TIMES DIS.	READ.	ARITH.	SPEL.	SOC. STUDIES	ORAL	WRIT	SCIENCE	PENMAN SHIP	ART	MUSIC	TEACHERS SIGNATURE

(COMP. spans ORAL and WRIT)

DATE

SPECIAL PROGRAMS SUGGESTED BY NURSE OR PHYS. ED. DEPT., AND ANECDOTAL RECORD

DATE

DATE LEFT   REASON

DATE ENTERED

	LAST NAME	FIRST	MIDDLE
M			
F			

AGE - GRADE DISTRIBUTION														
BLUE	5	6	7	8	9	10	11	12	13	14	R.A.	IMP.
RED	KD	1	2	3	4	5	6					

NEW SCHOOL

PREVIOUS SCHOOL

Figure 3—Continued

PERSONALITY TRAITS

	GRADE	GRADE	GRADE	GRADE	GRADE	GRADE	GRADE	GRADE
PERSONAL APPEARANCE	1 2 3 4 5	1 2 3 4 5	1 2 3 4 5	1 2 3 4 5	1 2 3 4 5	1 2 3 4 5	1 2 3 4 5	1 2 3 4 5
COURTESY	1 2 3 4 5	1 2 3 4 5	1 2 3 4 5	1 2 3 4 5	1 2 3 4 5	1 2 3 4 5	1 2 3 4 5	1 2 3 4 5
TRUSTWORTHINESS	1 2 3 4 5	1 2 3 4 5	1 2 3 4 5	1 2 3 4 5	1 2 3 4 5	1 2 3 4 5	1 2 3 4 5	1 2 3 4 5
CONSTRUCTIVE LEADERSHIP	1 2 3 4 5	1 2 3 4 5	1 2 3 4 5	1 2 3 4 5	1 2 3 4 5	1 2 3 4 5	1 2 3 4 5	1 2 3 4 5
WORK HABITS	1 2 3 4 5	1 2 3 4 5	1 2 3 4 5	1 2 3 4 5	1 2 3 4 5	1 2 3 4 5	1 2 3 4 5	1 2 3 4 5
CO-OPERATION	1 2 3 4 5	1 2 3 4 5	1 2 3 4 5	1 2 3 4 5	1 2 3 4 5	1 2 3 4 5	1 2 3 4 5	1 2 3 4 5
SELF-CONFIDENCE	1 2 3 4 5	1 2 3 4 5	1 2 3 4 5	1 2 3 4 5	1 2 3 4 5	1 2 3 4 5	1 2 3 4 5	1 2 3 4 5
EMOTIONAL STABILITY	1 2 3 4 5	1 2 3 4 5	1 2 3 4 5	1 2 3 4 5	1 2 3 4 5	1 2 3 4 5	1 2 3 4 5	1 2 3 4 5

1=EXCELLENT   2=ABOVE AVERAGE   3=AVERAGE   4=BELOW AVERAGE   5=POOR

ANECDOTAL RECORDS

(Fold Two)

47

DATE	GRADE	NAME OF ACHIEVEMENT TEST	FORM	SCORE	C.A.	CLASS NORM	%ILE	AGE EQ.	GR. EQ.

MENTAL ABILITY

DATE	GRADE	NAME OF TEST	FORM	SCORE	C.A.	M.A.	IQ.

DIAGNOSTIC TESTS

DATE	GRADE	NAME OF TEST					

APTITUDE TESTS

DATE	GRADE		FORM	SCORE			

REMINGTON RAND INC.-13 806-BP X37 # 1 & 2 T

(Fold One)

Figure 3—Continued

(Fold Three)

ADVISERS COMMENTS

ACADEMIC NOTATIONS AND ANECDOTALS

DATE	GRADE																	

CONFERENCES WITH PARENTS

DATE	GRADE																

49

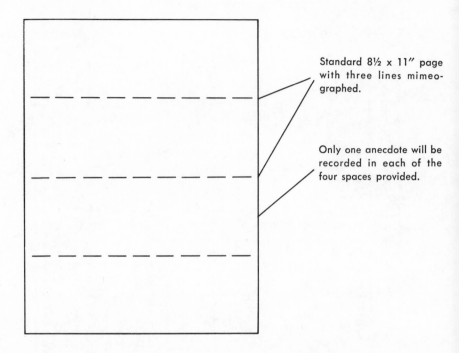

Figure 4.   First step in preparing form for anecdotal reports.

destroy those which, in her judgment, have no permanent value. Those to be kept will be cut apart along the lines and pasted on the inside of the cumulative record or on a stiff backing which will be kept in the record. The pasted anecdotes will overlap each other so that only the bottom line—the line with the caption on it—is visible (see Figure 6). Such an arrangement permits approximately 25 anecdotes to be pasted to a single backing with the title of each showing. The anecdotes will be arranged in chronological order with the earliest pasted at the bottom of the backing, and proceeding chronologically with the most recent one closest to the top. The pasting operation can be speeded by providing a backing which is "pre-glued" by having three vertical stripes of glue applied by the printer, and needing only moistening. With the anecdotes arranged in this order, any single anecdote is easily accessible by date or title because each is visible. Furthermore, all anecdotes on a single topic, e.g., all disciplinary actions, can be immediately reviewed.

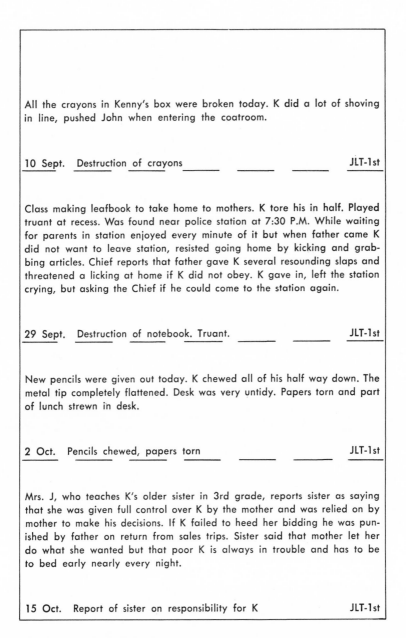

All the crayons in Kenny's box were broken today. K did a lot of shoving in line, pushed John when entering the coatroom.

10 Sept.   Destruction of crayons   JLT-1st

Class making leafbook to take home to mothers. K tore his in half. Played truant at recess. Was found near police station at 7:30 P.M. While waiting for parents in station enjoyed every minute of it but when father came K did not want to leave station, resisted going home by kicking and grabbing articles. Chief reports that father gave K several resounding slaps and threatened a licking at home if K did not obey. K gave in, left the station crying, but asking the Chief if he could come to the station again.

29 Sept.   Destruction of notebook. Truant.   JLT-1st

New pencils were given out today. K chewed all of his half way down. The metal tip completely flattened. Desk was very untidy. Papers torn and part of lunch strewn in desk.

2 Oct.   Pencils chewed, papers torn   JLT-1st

Mrs. J, who teaches K's older sister in 3rd grade, reports sister as saying that she was given full control over K by the mother and was relied on by mother to make his decisions. If K failed to heed her bidding he was punished by father on return from sales trips. Sister said that mother let her do what she wanted but that poor K is always in trouble and has to be to bed early nearly every night.

15 Oct.   Report of sister on responsibility for K   JLT-1st

Figure 5.   Anecdotes prior to cutting and attaching to backing as illustrated in Figure 6.

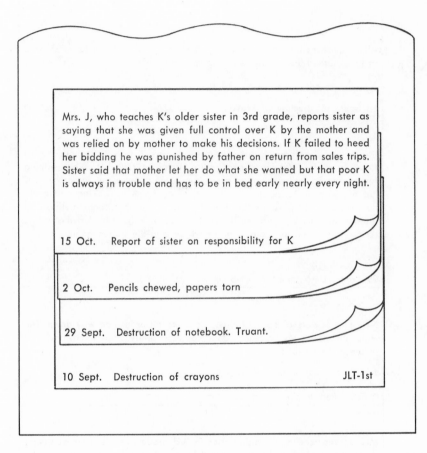

Figure 6. Anecdotes reports as inserted in cumulative record.

Assimilating the information contained in cumulative records is a most difficult task for teachers. Ideally, each teacher should sit down with the cumulative records of her class prior to the beginning of the school year and review their contents, not only to familiarize herself with the individuals but, more important, to plan her instructional programs to provide for the individual differences observed in the group. To do so necessitates not only that she review considerable data about a given child, but also that she organize them into some comprehensible form. To make her work even more difficult, she has to view each piece of information in two frames of reference—the individual child and the group. She has to see its pertinence to the development of the child and also relate it to the range and levels of ability of the group, for she selects her materials and organizes her teaching as much in relation to the group as to the individual.

Limitations of Class Record Sheets. A common form of recording data is the class record sheet on which the names of the class are recorded alphabetically and information on a variety of items—age, mental age, intelligence quotient, achievement test scores, etc.—is recorded. The class record sheet not only tends to blur the information about an individual, but it is confusing with regard to the class, for the scores or data in any single column on the page are in random order. Should she arrange the class by mental age instead of alphabetically, the teacher will have children of similar mental ability adjacent to each other on the page, but they are still mixed to some degree when she looks at any other column, e.g., achievement test score. What she needs is a device which permits her to rearrange scores at her convenience without losing sight of the individual or the group. Quite obviously IBM cards and a tabulator could be used to mechanically rearrange and tabulate any set of data on a page in any predetermined order. But IBM equipment is not yet standard equipment in schools.

Pupil Data Card. A cruder, but nevertheless serviceable, device is presented in Figure 7 showing the front and back of a 4 x 6 inch card which overcomes the difficulties previously discussed. Around the margin of the card are a series of boxes in which data can be recorded —Date of Card, Health, Age, Height, Weight, Vision, Hearing, Absences, and Conduct—across the top; IQ, MA, Misc., Choice status on sociogram on the right side; and Achievement Test Scores along the bottom. Associated with each box is a + and − symbol (in two

12/62	Ov	Un	Ov	Un	+	–	+	–	+	–	+	–	+	–	TEST &
Year	Age 8	Ht 52	Wt 50	Vision	Hear ok	Absnt	Condt								DATE

Name ROGER R.   Grade **3**   IQ 1961   +   BiNeT 122   –

F Occup Asst. MGR. JONES Co.   **M Occup** SECRETARY   MA 9.8   + / –

Sibs (B-G-Age) PAUL – 6   + / –

Residence 27 WINTER ST.   **Socio-Econ** UPPER–MIDDLE   **Chosen** Rjtd + / –

Grades	Read	Arith	Spell	SocSt	Sci	Or-Comm-Writ	Art	Music
Super'r								
Avg					X			
Infer	X	X	X			X		

Achvmnt Test   Date   Form

RdCmp	RdVoc	TotRd	ArCmp	ArRsn	TotAr				Total
	1.8								1.8
+ –	+ –	+	+ –	+ –	+ –	+ –	+ –	+ –	+

(Detail) Interests, Talents, Ambition	Needs (Describe)	Adj Diffic	
Art		Self-Estm	
Music		Indpndnce	
Sports—Team		Soc Accp	
Sports—Indiv	Afraid to join boys'	Fears	
Models	games.	Anxieties	
Collects	Cries easily, gives	Shyness	
Crafts	up quickly.	Perfctnst	
PhysSci	Meticulous about	Aggr—Self	
NatSci	work.	—Othr	
Entertnm		—Obj	
Literature		MotorCoor	
	Prefers girls'		
	activities to boys'		

Date	Test	Age	Score	%	GE	Date	Test	Age	Score	%	GE
1961	DURRELL READ	7.6			22						

Figure 7. Pupil Data Card.

54

instances OVer and UNder). The procedure followed is to record a given bit of data in a box and block out the + square if the student is in the top quarter of the class in that item, or block out the − square if the student is in the bottom quarter of the class. The exceptions to this are vision, hearing, absence, and conduct, where the blocking out of a minus square indicates presence of a problem. In the center of the card are identifying information and grades in various subjects classified as superior, average, and inferior. These last items do not have blocks on the margins, inasmuch as the achievement test data is used in lieu of grades, but where test data is absent grades could be marked on the margin.

It is apparent that important data for a given child is immediately available. For instance, in the illustration shown, it is apparent that the boy described (Roger, see Chapter 5 for further description) is 8 years old, average in height and weight, no hearing and vision problems, IQ of 122, under-chosen by his classmates, and retarded on achievement test scores. What is not immediately apparent is that a group of cards can be simultaneously inspected by riffling them, much as one does with cards while shuffling or spreading them for counting. This procedure makes the blocks at the margin of the card visible with the result that one can immediately detect children of superior or inferior standing in any of the characteristics shown. Moreover, the cards can be arranged from highest to lowest for any trait, then rearranged in different fashion for a second characteristic. One can divide the cards into smaller groups (as one might sort pupils into groups for instructional purposes) and then by inspection of each card, determine the specific level of achievement present in that group. Obviously, the cards would have to be riffled from top, side, or bottom depending upon items being inspected. The cut diagonal corner at the upper right corner makes any card which is upside down in the pack immediately detectable.

The cards may be turned over and information relative to hobbies and interests checked on the left with supplementary comments written, and adjustment problems noted on the right half of the card. Additional space is available at the bottom for recording further test data, e.g., earlier achievement test scores. Some teachers prefer to leave the backs blank for whatever notations they may wish to enter. The card illustrated shows how it would look with such information about Roger added.

The card is purposely kept small so that the set for a class can be carried in pocket or purse and easily manipulated. It is not intended to be a substitute for a permanent record card or a cumulative record. Rather, it is seen as a device which would make it possible for teachers to record in manageable form early in the year as much information as they could use. Further the cards would make possible more adequate planning for the instructional program at the point when the teacher knows the least about the class. As the school year passes and the teacher's knowledge of individual pupils and class as a whole increases, she would have less and less recourse to the set of cards. Special problems arising would undoubtedly result in reference to the cumulative record for detailed information.

Limitations and Precautions in Using Cumulative Records

Cumulative records, like weather reports, have to be viewed with some reservation and used with certain precaution, for they are far from infallible. Nevertheless, both permit improvement in prediction of performance and by so doing serve many useful purposes. Curiously enough we take error in weather reports for granted, but find it difficult to use cumulative records with the same healthy skepticism. By being aware of possible limitations and using certain precautions, we can reduce the errors.

Errors in reporting
1. Negative events tend to be more frequently reported than positive.
2. Unusual incidents are reported more often than common, hence the data presented is not typical behavior of the child.
3. Data included in cumulative records is heavily weighed with respect to scholastic achievement. Information in other areas is often quite sparse.
4. The events reported in anecdotal form may be taken out of context and reported in isolation.
5. The reports of untrained observers are less factual and more interpretative, often revealing more about the observer than the child.

Errors in interpretation
1. Failing to see trends in data and over-looking the fact that growth is a long-term process and change is seldom rapid.
2. Assuming that the past permits perfect prediction of the present, i.e., "you can't change human nature." Teaching is predicated on the knowledge that human nature is changeable and that

introducing new influences and new situations permits differences in rate and direction of development.

3. Selective perception of facts in the record. There is a tendency toward over-emphasis of facts which coincide with one's preconceptions and convictions and neglect of those which contradict one's prejudices.

4. Over-generalizing from insufficient information. IQ scores are repeatedly used as a basis for over-generalizing, e.g., assuming that bright children will automatically do well in everything. Items regarding race, religion, social background may be used as damagingly.

5. Failing to recognize that some of the data in the file is subjective interpretation, not fact.

It is not unusual to hear teachers express the thought that they prefer not to look at the cumulative records because they feel it causes them to form prejudgments about the child which can be unfair. They prefer to let the child have the chance to start with a clean slate. This attitude is healthy, for our actions and attitudes as teachers should never operate to discourage children from doing their best, and certainly during the more malleable years of personality development we should adopt attitudes which encourage children's optimal growth. Yet this attitude is one of expecting miracles to occur when, in fact, children tend to persist in patterns of behavior. The value of the cumulative record lies in the clues it can give as to possible causes in the background, and to the positive information which makes better individual and class program planning possible.

Ethical Concerns with Cumulative Records. Many schools have their "special" or "confidential" file in the principal's office containing information which it would be indiscreet to record in the cumulative record. The indiscretion rests not in the facts involved but in the fact that apparently one or more members of the staff may be unable to treat such information in confidence. The precaution is wise for it is the responsibility of school personnel to safeguard the confidence of information regarding the private lives of children and their families.

Any interview with parents ends with the teacher possessing information about the child and his family which ranges from public to private knowledge. Intimate details of family relationships and experiences may be related by the parent which, if public, could be extremely harmful to both child and family. In this situation, the teacher or principal frequently has a difficult choice to make in deciding just which information she will record or communicate to other members of the school staff. When an item is recorded in the cumulative record or recounted to a member of the staff, it is being introduced into channels of communication. A question is immediately raised as to the ethical responsibilities of the teacher regarding the communication of information. Does her loyalty lie with the school department, i.e., the state, or does it lie with the parent or child, i.e., the individual? Other professions and occupations face similar questions, but their question of loyalty is more clearly defined than that of the teacher. A member of the intelligence section of the armed forces or the Federal Bureau of Investigation is obliged to communicate information irrespective of its effect upon the individual. His responsibilities and loyalties are unequivocally identified with the government. The medical, legal, and ministerial professions and, to a large degree, the social work profession are unequivocably identified with the individual, in that information given a member of these professions by an individual is privileged, e.g., the lawyer cannot be compelled under oath in court to reveal information given by his client. The status of information in possession of members of several of the professions, psychologist and teacher, for examples, has not been established by court decision; hence attitudes of teachers with respect to information is discretionary in that it is dependent upon professional and personal ethics. The suggestions which follow must be interpreted as advisory.

A distinction has to be made between the public information of the school and the private information of the individual. For the accomplishment of its purpose the school needs and maintains certain information about the child as listed:

1. *Vital Statistics*
   Birthdate and place
   Parents' names
   Residence
   Children in family
2. *Personal Data*
   Health record
   Scholastic aptitude test data
3. *School Record*
   Attendance
   Grades
   Achievement test data
   Promotion record
   Anecdotal information

Disciplinary problems and disposition
Special interests and activities
Classroom and school department
Termination
Transfer
Graduation
Withdrawal

The information accumulated under the foregoing headings relates exclusively to the identification of the individual child and his performance in school. The point at which the school concerns itself with personality factors affecting scholastic performance and assumes responsibility for facilitating healthy personal and social adjustment is the point at which the school enters the private world of the child and assumes obligation to respect the privacy of the child and his family. In essence this means that school personnel have to guarantee the confidential nature of such information and all will treat it in similar fashion. In medicine and social work the guarantee is achieved by permitting only members of the profession bound by the same code of ethics to have access to the information. Such a procedure would only be partially effective in education because of the variable training required for entry into the profession and the presence of large numbers of teachers who are only partially trained.

The second feature which affects the situation is the previously described discretionary nature of the teacher's position with respect to the information. The responsibility for guaranteeing the privacy and confidential nature of information rests with each individual teacher. This means that she will not record in a cumulative record or relate orally any data which will not be held in confidence by the recipient. In schools in which the administrator expects all information to be recorded, the teacher is placed in a position of conflicting loyalties—responsibility to maintain a confidence and responsibility to the institution which employs her. Her only resolution of this situation is to advise the parent that she cannot insure the confidence. Lest this point appear belabored, one has only to recall events which occur in many lives—children are born illegitimately, parents live out of wedlock, men are convicted of criminal action, alcoholism or drug addiction occurs, and a host of other events take place which can be harmful to children if they become public knowledge.

If information is to be taken in confidence, it must be respected. If it cannot be, then such information should be avoided or else it should be made clear that its confidential nature cannot be guaranteed.

General Criteria

As a result of the discussion presented in this chapter, certain general criteria can be established regarding the contents of the cumulative record:

1. Items relevant to the legal responsibility of the school should be recorded.
2. Only those items which the school staff is trained and willing to use should be recorded.
3. Only those items which have permanent value should be recorded in the cumulative record form.
4. Only those items which provide recognition, distinguish one individual from others, and offer diagnostic or prognostic utility should be incorporated in the cumulative record.
5. The cumulative record should be organized for continuity of data and facility of use.
6. Items of confidential nature should not be recorded in the cumulative record unless it will be respected by all members of the staff.

Chapter 4

DYNAMICS OF
HUMAN BEHAVIOR

Man has been engaged for centuries in two great searches for discovery—one, the explanation of the physical world, and the other, the explanation of himself. Both searches have been forwarded by penetrating insights and conjectures in science and in literature, just as they have been stalled by rational explanations, which, in time, were proved rational but erroneous. Until the advent of the scientific method, a systematic mapping of observation, measurement, and experiment which anchors explanations in verifiable fact, the difficulty in verification lay not in determining whether or not there was some truth in a given explanation, but how much truth. Especially in explaining behavior, where we tend to overgeneralize from limited observation and to overextend hypothetical concepts (for example libido and instincts), the task of determining the limits within which any hypothetical explanation functioned, and without which it wasn't applicable, has been extremely difficult.

In spite of improvements in mapping, many doubtful accounts of human behavior hang on with surprising tenacity. Many people consider delinquency or any form of maladjustment the result of an inborn perversity which characterizes human beings. The notion that man is inherently evil has been nurtured through centuries in some religious thought. In earlier parts of this century, human behavior was widely attributed to instincts—hereditary, unlearned patterns of behavior. Courage, mother love, athletic prowess, and a thousand other human attributes were viewed as "instinctive."

Systematic observation has shown that in major degree most of the so-called "instincts" are learned. All mothers do not love their children blindly and automatically. Some mothers literally hate their children, resenting having to care for and feed them. Whatever the reasons—illegitimacy, physical deformity, or assorted others—it became clear that all mothers do not love their offspring, i.e., mother-love is not instinctive.

Organic explanations were advanced to account for human behavior, suggesting that normal behavior resulted from the optimal functioning of physiological organs, glands, central nervous system, etc., and that abnormal behavior was the result of injury or disease affecting particular organs. This account was not too far advanced from the medieval notion of an evil spirit taking possession of the body, in part or whole. In the latter instance, the evil spirit was to be exorcised by magic; in the former, by medication, diet, surgery, or other weapons in the medical armory.

Reflexes, modifiable and unmodifiable, were seen as a possible psychological explanation. One possessed some reflex responses and acquired others through learning. Through conditioning, these responses combined into hierarchies of complex behavior patterns that accounted for all man's varied activities. At the opposite end of the spectrum was the explanation that man's actions were derived from his will, not from the blind accretion of conditioned reflexes.

Each explanation possessed within it a given remedy: punishment, medication, reasoning, manipulation of stimuli, etc. As exploration of human behavior continued, and as remedial action based on erroneous explanation failed; as the scientific method was applied to individual and group behavior, and as consideration of behavior was extended to man as a species rather than restricted to man in a given tribe, nation, or race, principles accounting for specific aspects of human behavior emerged. Contained within all the explanations is the concept that human behavior is caused, and that to understand the behavior one must look to the causes. Too often, many of the actions of adults towards children are the result of an assumption that the behavior of the child is capricious and impulsive, random and inconsistent, needing essentially to be controlled by adults. However suitable a given control may be for given occasions and however inept adults may be at ascertaining the causal factors, an understanding of behavior and the attempt to modify behavior necessitates a search for causes.

An episode occurring during an observation of three pre-school children gives meaning to the foregoing conclusion.

ANALYSIS OF A BEHAVIOR SEQUENCE

Conditions of the Observation

This situation involved three children—Randy (our subject), Arlene, and Ann. The girls were observed in the home of Randy and Ann's grandparents. Arlene, a visitor and friend whom Ann had not seen since the previous summer, had come with Ann to her grandparents' house to play. The ages of the three children were as follows: Randy, four years; Arlene, four and a half; Ann, Randy's cousin, five and a half. Prior to the observation the three children had been playing outdoors; at Ann's insistence they had come indoors to watch television. This observation is an example of childhood frustration. The observer was the only adult present during the observation. For the most part the pre-frustration period was marked by much mutual laughter and friendly play conversation involving all three girls. (See Figure 1.)

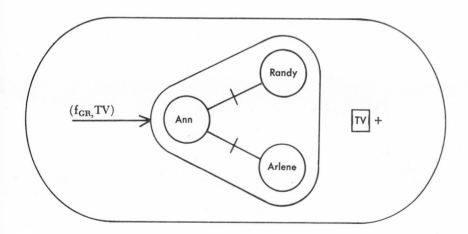

Figure 1. Diagram of group situation at beginning of observation. (The group has come indoors at Ann's insistence to watch television. Arlene is Ann's friend, Randy, her cousin, but Arlene and Randy are barely acquainted. The group is actively engaged in watching television. Arrows indicate "forces" in operation in the field (f_{GR},TV), either individual or group.)

The Behavior

Ann reaches into a playpen (empty) and pulls out a baby blanket. She offers an end to Arlene who takes it and says, "Oh, thanks, now we can be warm." Randy, who had until this time been watching television, turns to the two girls and sits watching them. Giggling and talking back and forth, Ann and Arlene proceed to wrap themselves with the blanket. (1) Randy walks to the two girls, who by this time have climbed upon two bridges of chairs directly in front of the television set. Randy grabs Ann's end of the blanket and starts pulling. She says to Ann, "It's my baby's blanket." Ann answers, "Oh no, oh no, it's my blanket and we're playing with it—you can't." Still pulling at the blanket Randy sobs, "I want it—big dope." (A1) At this point, Ann begins to hit and push Randy. Randy standing her ground under the volley of blows, hits back somewhat feebly. (See Figure 2.)

(2) After about twenty seconds, Randy walks back to her chair and turning toward (3) Ann and Arlene says, "You're stupids, I hate you stupids." All three children watched the television program quietly for a minute. During this time, Randy, without a trace of a smile climbs about on her chair. (4) These

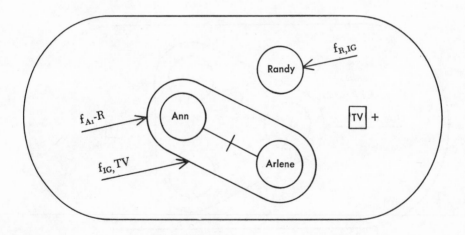

Figure 2. Diagram of situation after rejection of Randy. (Ann's wrapping blanket around herself and Arlene excluding Randy, f_{A_1}-R, creates a barrier preventing Randy from being a part of the in-group, which presumably still maintains a mild interest in the television, f_{IG},TV. Randy's motive is to rejoin the group, $f_{R,IG}$.)

movements were impressive to the observer because of their bored aimless quality. (A2) Ann looks sternly at Randy then wraps the blanket more firmly about their heads. Ann drapes it about her head in a squaw-fashion; Arlene follows suit with her half. (5) Randy, still in her chair at the other end of the room, stands up and straddles the arm, shouting, "Giddyap." Randy stops, looks toward Ann and Arlene and says, "I have a pony, giddyap." In a loud and belligerent voice Ann counters, (A3) "Who cares." Randy climbs from her chair and approaches Arlene and Ann. Arlene and Ann, giggling and kicking, wrap their arms more firmly about the blanket. (6) Randy takes a position between the two girls and the television set and announces, "I'm going to turn the radio off." (7) Next, she turns to Ann and says, "I hate you, you're stupid." (8) Randy leaves the room and enters the adjoining room in which a group of adults are seated. She stands watching them from a distance and then

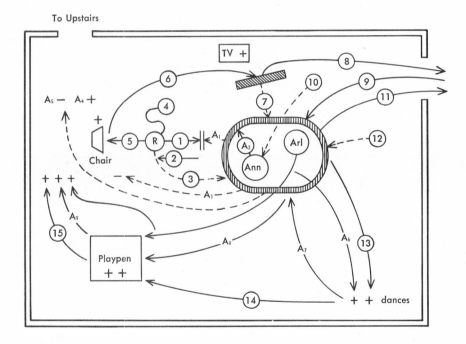

Figure 3. Schematic Diagram of actions of Randy in attempting to attain goal illustrated in Figure 2. (Direct movements are indicated by solid lines, verbal action by dotted lines, temporary goals by +.)

runs back into the sun-parlor where Arlene and Ann are now watching television from the floor. They are seated on the baby blanket. (A4) In a mild voice, Ann suggests, "Let's go upstairs, Randy?" Without hesitation, Randy, all smiles, answers, "Yes." Ann snaps, "Oh no." (A5)

(9) Randy approaches Ann, grabs her corner of the blanket and starts tugging. Ann says, "You leave it alone. It's my blanket." Randy continues tugging. Ann threatens her in a loud voice, "I'll pinch your face." Randy answers, "Oh no, I'll pinch your face." Ann clenches her fists and screams in a loud voice, "Oh no, oh no you don't." Randy lets go of the blanket and stands pouting before the two girls. (11) Once more she leaves the room. In about twenty seconds, she returns and (12) approaching Arlene says, "You go home, kid, you're stupid." Randy then seats herself on the floor before the television set. The three children watch the program quietly for almost a minute.

(13) Getting to her feet, Randy announces, "I'm going to dance." This she did by jumping up and down and waving her arms in time to the music. "Me, too," says Ann, (A6) as she leaves the blanket for the first time during the observation. Arlene moves to a nearby chair to escape being kicked by the "dancers." During the dances the blanket gets kicked under the playpen to remain for the duration of the observation.

Turning to Ann, Randy says, "I'm dancing." Ann looks at Arlene and (A7) then turns to Randy saying, "Who cares." Ann then returns to her seat next to Arlene. Randy continues to "dance" until the music stops. Going to a nearby foot-rest, Randy with much effort pushes it into position in front of the play-pen. Ann starts to laugh and (A8) climbs into the play-pen with Randy. Arlene standing off to one side shakes the railing. Randy suggests to Ann, "Let's jump." Ann laughingly agrees. The two girls continue their laughing and jumping until interrupted by an adult. Ann turns (A9) to Randy and Arlene, "Let's play upstairs." All three run out of the room. (15)

INTERPRETATION

At least two main hypotheses can be ventured in explanation of the behavior observed: (1) Randy feels displaced by Arlene in her friendship with Ann and strives to re-establish it, or (2) Randy wants to be a part of the group activity. For the first hypothesis, Randy's goal, the condition which satisfies her motive, is shown in Figure 4A. The second hypothesis is illustrated in Figure 4B.

In all situations we are confronted with goal directed *behavior* from which we can infer the motives or drives which produced it.

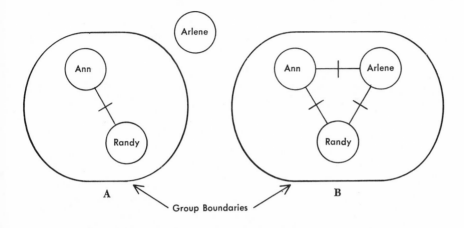

Figure 4. Diagram of two possible goals of Randy
in behavior described.

Our conjectures about motivation can be validated only by checking them against the events which terminate the activity by satisfying the operant drive. In many instances the end state which terminates the activity has to be interpreted symbolically, e.g., owning a foreign car may satisfy one person's desire for prestige, and another's desire for economy; hence it is usually desirable to observe behavior in a number of situations in order to test which hypothesis is most valid. In Randy's case we can test each of the two hypotheses, and any others which one might formulate, against the behavior and the drive-reducing terminal state.

Randy is apparently satisfied (generally inactive) at the beginning (Figure 1), but Ann's wrapping of the blanket around herself and Arlene disrupts the equilibrium by excluding Randy from the group. In the face of this rejection and the interposed barrier, Randy no longer watches TV but makes a direct attack on the barrier. Failing in the direct attack because of Ann's assault, she retreats, now pulled by two conflicting forces: wanting to be in the group but also wanting to avoid harm. She resorts to verbal aggression. Her restless movements suggest increased tension, a by-product of the frustrating conditions. She suggests a substitute activity, playing pony, which Ann rejects with a terse "who cares." Ann's movements with the blanket during this period accentuate the attractiveness of the goal. Randy counterattacks by threatening to block the satisfaction Ann and Arlene are having with the TV, follows up with more verbal aggression, then finally withdraws to the other room—possibly to seek adult help, possibly to give the impression of going for help, possibly to escape the frustration. She returns immediately and, all smiles, accepts Ann's suggestion to play upstairs, but is immediately thwarted again as Ann first offers the bait, then casts it aside. Again Randy makes a direct attack, but fails, once more leaving the room. For the first time in the entire series of actions, Randy attempts to divide Ann and Arlene, with "Go home, kid, you're stupid." Up to this point all of Randy's actions have been aimed at restoring conditions to the pre-blanket phase, when all three were mutually enjoying a group activity.

Randy attempts another substitute activity and is temporarily successful until Ann rejects the dancing. Randy immediately tries again to create a substitute activity which is completely successful because both Ann and Arlene are attracted to it, and the group activity subsequently resumes with Ann's suggestion that they play upstairs.

Briefly, the theme of the episode is that Randy, repeatedly rejected by Ann, attempts to relieve her frustration and satisfy her desire to be one of the group by a variety of actions. She finally succeeds by creating a substitute goal which ends the rejection and reinstates her as a member of the group. In a way, the situation can be characterized as "bringing the mountain to Mohammed." Judging from the termination condition, Randy's motives are illustrated by Figure 4B.

The preceding discussion is a thematic analysis of a child's behavior in a single situation. This approach to behavior analysis can be applied to interpretations of actions over a long period of time, as in a case history, or to diagnostic evaluations of creative and projective materials such as art work, stories, play, etc. By comparison, a more static evaluation can be made by tabulating the frequency of given kinds of behavior, as shown below, for Randy:

Direct attack on barrier	— 2
Verbal attack	— 2
Substitute goals	— 3
Withdrawal	— 2
Counterattack	— 2
threatens turn TV off	
Arlene, go home	

Both approaches are useful in analysis of case material; the latter is often used for listing a person's assets and liabilities, strengths and weaknesses, for classifying symptoms, and for appraising the severity of problems. However, effective solutions depend in greater degree on understanding why a person is doing what he is doing. Systematic and successful use of either technique requires extensive training in psychology.

At this point, many readers will be tempted to dismiss the analysis as much ado over nothing, contending that the behavior described is perfectly normal. Unfortunately, classifying or naming does little to explain its meaning or how it came to be, and worse, the word "normal" has so many possible meanings and is used so loosely within these meanings that it is almost useless as a classification. Normal can be synonymous with typical, in the sense that negative behavior is typical of age 2½ to 3, or, somewhat differently, normal may mean characteristic for a given person. Often, the term normal implies frequency. For instance, fear of the dark may be normal for seven-year-olds because 30 per cent are fearful (note that in this usage the behavior may be frequent but not typical, inasmuch as only a minority show it). Sometimes the word normal implies desirable behavior, but in this context, its meaning obviously depends upon whose standards of desirability are being used. Often the word normal infers that the behavior is socially or morally approved, i.e., it may have legal, cultural, or religious sanction. Inherent in these different usages are many conflicts. For instance, stealing, which may be normal behavior for a nine-year-old in the sense that many children at this age commit minor theft, is abnormal behavior when judged by ethical considerations or legal prohibitions.

A longer discourse would provide more explicit definitions of the word normal as used by statisticians, psychiatrists, psychologists, lawyers, etc., without adding very much to the conclusion offered here—that because of its innumerable connotations, the word normal is of little value in explanations of behavior. As used by teachers it often implies that they do not have to be concerned about the behavior or take action to change it.

Randy's actions in response to her needs and to the developing situation provide us with a miniature model for analysis which has certain particular advantages. As Randy grows older her actions will be increasingly covert and symbolic. We learn to hide or cover our reactions and to express them indirectly as we grow older and more experienced. Younger children are more immediately responsive to the pressures and tensions which they experience. The openness of their actions makes more direct interpretation possible.

The Role of Learning

In reviewing Randy's actions, behavior which at first glance appeared almost accidental takes on much greater significance. She showed herself to be an inventive person, taking varied actions in an attempt to surmount the barrier of the blanket. She attacked the blanket directly. Failing in this she resorted to verbal aggression threatening attack. Three times she established substitute activities, once with partial success and finally with complete success. This did not exhaust her resourcefulness because before she attained the desired solution, she attempted two counterattacks and two withdrawals.

We observe a child systematically varying her actions in an attempt to attain her goal, and in the process learning varying modes of adjusting to a frustrating situation. Had she succeeded initially in knocking down the blanket and forcing Ann to let her join the group, she would probably repeat this behavior on subsequent occasions. As a matter of fact, she may have learned to avoid direct attack against a stronger opponent, but reserve it for situations involving smaller or younger children. Her verbal attacks may have released some tension without bringing her closer to her goal. She did not call for adult assistance, even though she left the room. Her winning strategem was the introduction of a substitute activity which attracted the others. Randy will probably try this again on subsequent similar occasions because she has learned it produces success—learned because it leads to satisfying ends and hence is reinforced. In time, if this is the most effective technique she can devise for such situations, it will probably become habitual, just as aggressive actions can become habitual against weaker persons (unless restrained or punished by adults). These consistent modes of behavior combine to become functional parts of one's personality.

Learning is crucial to the development of personality, and central to our attempts to understand and interpret behavior. Were there no learning process, one's actions in a given situation would depend solely upon the impulses in effect and the pressures or forces at work in the situation. Behavior and actions would be primitive, wasteful, and inefficient. Learning makes it possible to acquire standardized ways of responding to known situations, approaches to be used in novel situations, and knowledge and skill that can be brought to bear in any situation. Because of learning, our interpretation of any person's actions depends not only on the immediate situation but equally on motives and behavior patterns acquired as a result of previous experience. We are aware of the origin of some of our actions, for some learning occurs in conscious and insightful activity. But we are unaware of the origin of a large portion of our behavior, some because it occurred at a time or in a way of which we were not conscious, and some because it is the product of experiences long-forgotten, e.g., many extreme fears recognized as irrational go back to childhood experiences now consciously forgotten. Much learning occurs almost blindly, some by trial or error, some by conditioning, but it is nonetheless permanent, however unconscious it may be. Randy is in the process of learning procedures for meeting frustration and for reconciling her desires with those of others in a social situation. Years from now, when, instead of insisting that others submit to her suggestions, or withdrawing, saying that she really doesn't feel like doing anything anyway, Randy says: "Oh, let's see if there isn't something that everybody wants to do," she will have little or no recollection of the learning experience just described which helped mold this reaction as her habitual response.

This illustration of the learning process is vastly oversimplified, because so many diversified experiences combine to shape the motives, attitudes, habit patterns, skill, knowledge, etc., which comprise a given personality. But the influence of each event, varying in degree, is nonetheless important in the total result. As limited as scientific knowledge may be, the processes are neither mystical nor mysterious.

Effects of Frustration

Randy's actions are interesting for another reason. They are typical of an individual's reaction to frustration, that is, an external event or act of another person which blocks the satisfaction of an aroused motive or drive. In the situation observed, Randy desires to be included as a member of the group watching television. When Ann wraps the blanket around herself and Arlene, she excludes Randy and blocks the continued satisfaction of Randy's desires. Frustration usually produces two immediate effects, the first is a strengthening of the drive, the second is the production of aggression. The strengthened drive is noticeable in increased activity and tension, and increased striving to find a means of attaining the goal—in Randy's case to restore the status quo of which she has been deprived. The aggression is noted in attempts to displace the barrier or attack the instigator. Randy shows increased tension—aimless crawling about on the chair, increased striving for readmission to the goal area by claiming the blanket is hers and by attempting to establish substitute goals.

In the face of continued frustration, and particularly the greater the degree of it, actions tend to disintegrate or the person attempts to escape the situation. Regressive behavior can ensue (actions characterizing an earlier age level). Randy could begin to whine or cry or beg in a more infantile manner, or climb into the play-pen and act more babyish. She could withdraw, physically or psychologically, in fact she does leave momentarily, but the reasons for this action are not clear. Still another less adaptive approach is the adoption of a defense mechanism as a means of releasing the tension and aggression and obtaining partial satisfaction. But before discussing defense mechanisms, one must take a closer look at motivation.

MOTIVATION AND BEHAVIOR

ACQUIRED MOTIVES

In discussing Randy's behavior, several terms have been used repeatedly: motive and drive, behavior, goal, and need reduction. Drive and goal have been functionally related in that drives are described in terms of goals. The relationship between these aspects of motivation may be shown as follows:

Drive $\longrightarrow$ Behavior $\longrightarrow$ Goal $\longrightarrow$ Drive Reduction

Drive gives rise to activity directed toward the attainment of a goal which satisfies the drive and results in its reduction. The drive reduction reinforces the behavior which was instrumental in attaining the goal so that on a subsequent reoccurrence of the drive that behavior is likely to be repeated. The drive generates activity which continues until the attainment of a goal restores equilibrium or provides satisfaction. Drives may be thought of as tension systems, somewhat like clocksprings, which produce activity until a balance is restored, i.e., the spring is unwound. Some explanation is needed first, however, of what winds the spring, that is, what creates the tension systems; and second, which systems are affected. On a physiological level, the tension systems can be traced to chemical and physical changes in the tissues of the body which trigger glandular responses and produce reactions sensed as hunger, thirst, etc. Without attempting to consider any one of these mechanisms in detail, it has been verified that tissue needs give rise to the various physiological drives which in turn prompt the activity necessary to insure survival.

This is too simple an account to explain the complexity of man's manifold activity, for he does much more than look for food when hungry, fluid when thirsty, and the shade when overheated. Indeed, some men will continue to eat when stuffed, others will drink fluids which blind or cripple them, and still others drive military equipment in boiling desert sun shooting at one another. The explanation falls short because man's motives and behavior are vastly complicated by learning. In the mere satisfaction of his hunger he learns to get hungry on a time schedule, learns to prefer or abhor specific foods, and learns a complete repertory of skills for obtaining food. Consider meat. Some like it raw, others cooked; some prefer it fresh, others spoiled. Some will not eat it at all because of social custom, others not on a given day. Some forms are eaten for the first meal of the day only, others are specific to other meals. Some hunt it, others raise it, others work for money to buy it. All these examples demonstrate the effect of learning on the simple satisfaction of hunger.

Learning, however, not only conditions the method of satisfying physiological drives, but more important, it accounts for the more significant personal and social drives which man acquires, and which govern the greater part of his history. Experimental and clinical evidence show that man acquires drives which may be classed as personal and social motivation. He learns to fear objects, situations, and conditions which are harmful; he strives for goals which he has learned to desire. He faces conflict when his desires are antagonistic as, for example, when a student wants to study because he desires to graduate from college, but at the same time wants to play ping-pong with his friends in the dormitory. Or a child may want to read a book after his bedtime yet be afraid of punishment from his parent if he is caught with his light on. In simple form (including the original scheme), these acquired drives may be diagrammed:

Many of our basic social motives arise through simple conditioning. Conditions surrounding the satisfaction of physical needs—such as being held, being in some other person's presence, being talked to, hearing footsteps approaching, the kind of food offered, etc., etc., acquire a positive valence because they are associated with the satisfaction of the physical drive. They soon become goals in their own right—children seeking to be picked up or played with. Although the psychological and social processes by which we acquire motives are not fully explored and understood, the nurturant process, however pleasant, indifferent, or brutal, produces in human beings an interlocking series of personal and social motives, behavioral patterns for expressing them, and specific objects or conditions capable of satisfying them. All of them are elaborated and refined by the experiences of living.

This complexity makes it impossible to establish a definitive list of motives. Any descriptive term for a drive or motive stands not for some thing or for some given condition but for a complex behavioral pattern. Yet the concept is useful in understanding behavior. In addition to the physiological drives of hunger, thirst, sex, pain avoidance, and temperature balance, each person acquires personal drives for esteem and recognition, achievement or mastery, and affection, plus social motives for acceptance, belonging, conformity, and approval. The distinction between the two categories is not sharp, the personal motives being less dependent upon participation in, and approval of, groups. In actual experience, we are seldom striving to satisfy a single motive at a time—meals involve not only physiological needs, but social; becoming a teacher can satisfy a desire for mastery, recognition, social acceptance, and physical security. Nevertheless, an understanding of the dynamics of behavior and the relationships of learning to behavior makes it possible to make some sense out of children's behavior and through our understanding to take directed rather than blind steps in child guidance.

From the beginning, the teacher faces children possessed of motives acquired through previous experience. Essentially her task is twofold: to direct the established motives to socially desirable objects and to manage her relationship with the child in such a way as to create subsequent motives which are personally and socially beneficial. Children enter school with an acquired motive for social approval. All teachers utilize this motive, with greater or lesser effectiveness, to educational ends. The teacher may insist that the child be quiet, docile, and submissive if he is to receive her approval; or she may stimulate him to be curious, eager, and enthusiastic (if she doesn't fear noise and the consequent criticism of the teacher in the adjoining room). She may manage her classroom so that the children view each other as competitive threats and enemies; she may encourage cooperative group activities which encourage friendship and the evolution of a group-oriented social approval. Surely the teacher who appoints a different child each week to be the row monitor and to report to her all minor infractions of _teacher-established_ regulations is setting child against child in a system of mutual spying and tattling which can only create interpersonal antagonism. The fact that so many children develop a deep-seated antipathy towards school and learning, wanting to get out of school at the earliest opportunity, can only be attributed to the experiences which teachers and the school provide the children. It is quite true that many parents have little regard for schooling and encourage a similar attitude in their children. It is also true that the children's actual experiences in the school confirm this attitude rather than creating an attitude that school is a place where one finds personal satisfaction. The effects upon attitudes and motivation are probably more significant than the factual information and skills acquired.

Frustration and Barrier Behavior

In the process of acquiring motives, one also learns to seek certain objects or conditions because of their capacity to satisfy the motive. Here, one has to distinguish between an object and the goal it symbolizes to a person. Recognition is a common motive. One person may satisfy this drive by going over Niagara Falls in a barrel, another by the applause he receives for theatrical performance, another by patient laboratory research work, another by the doting smiles of his mother. Many conditions and objects are capable of satisfying particular motives or combinations of motives, and the particular ones adopted by a person are a result of learning with all its social, ethical, and other ramifications. Inevitably, one encounters barriers which block one's access to the chosen or imposed goal, whether long or short range. We saw Randy blocked in her desire to participate with the other two girls. We see students prevented from completing college by lack of ability, resources, or other limitations. If this were the only difficulty, solutions would be comparatively easy to find. One could assist the individual to attain his goals some other way, or help to find substitute goals equally satisfying to the aroused motives. Several complications forbid this desirable solution. The attainment of most goals involves other people, people who have their own desires and drives which demand satisfaction, and drives which may be conflicting or disrupting. These people exist within a social milieu which places exaggerated emphasis on some behavior.

We, for instance, stress competitive and aggressive behavior where the Indian may stress cooperative or submissive behavior. The social milieu sanctions some responses and forbids others, e.g., be aggressive against persons of equal or greater strength but not against the weaker. Further, one's motives are not static but shift and change in terms of the events which occur during the attempts to satisfy them. Finally, one's motives are not a harmonious, mutually integrated, set of forces, but, instead, include many conflicting drives. The interplay of these various elements condition the kind of motives, frustrations, and response patterns which develop.

It is important to consider several aspects of the barrier which impedes progress towards a chosen goal. The simplest of these is the locus of the barrier: it is perceived as either blocking the path to the goal, or blocking the individual from activity. Figure 5 illustrates the two conditions. In the first diagram (A), the goal is blocked but the individual has freedom of locomotion—he can strive to get around or over the barrier, leave the field, or change goal-objects. A range of actions is available, both adaptive and non-adaptive. In the second diagram (B), the barrier is blocking the individual, rather than the goal, and the individual is denied locomotion. The simplest illustration of the latter situation would be a dominant-protective mother whose insistence on managing all aspects of her child's life represents a total barrier which prevents his acting independently on his own behalf.

A second aspect of barriers is that they can be internal as well as external, imagined as well as actual. For example, a child may have difficulty with reading because of vision, with basketball because of motor coordination, or with arithmetic because of limited aptitude. These barriers are actual but internal rather than external. Another child, as a result of difficulties in learning, may, in spite of a high measured aptitude, come to perceive himself as incapable, particularly in arithmetic. Considerate teachers may reduce his feelings of inadequacy so that he can work at his potential, but, faced with an achievement test—which is not a teacher-who-is-kind-to-you-in-spite-of-your-inadequacy but "AN OBJECTIVE EVALUATION," all his concerns are aroused and in his effort to do well he works doubly slowly and as a result performs below his capacity. The barriers in this instance are self-imposed, imagined, yet nonetheless real in their effects.

Finally, the barrier, figuratively speaking, may be a state of anxiety arising from conflicting motives, or conflicting actions possible with respect to the goal. In almost any situation we face choices between

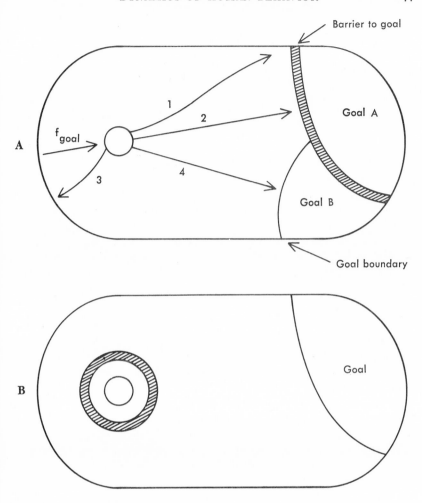

Figure 5. Illustration of barrier situations. In A the individual is prevented from attaining Goal A, which is strongly desired, by the presence of a barrier. He has freedom of action to (1) strive to discover possible routes past barrier, (2) make direct assault on barrier or even on self in the form of self-blame, (3) withdraw from the situation, actually or through fantasy, or (4) seek to attain substitute goals which permit partial satisfaction. In situation B, the individual is immobilized by the barrier and has no choice but to overcome or submit. Overcoming the barrier permits striving for goals and continued development. Submission blocks the continued development and differentiation, physically, psychologically, and socially, essential to attainment of maturity.

equally attractive goals. A junior high school boy may want to date
a girl, or walk home with a girl after school, and at the same time
desire to maintain his status with his gang of friends who feel that
going with girls is undesirable. Every time a person shops for food
for the family, or plans to buy an automobile or other object, he must
choose between apparently equally desirable objects. This conflicting pull between objects of equal attractiveness is illustrated in Figure
6A in which two objects endowed with positive valence by virtue of
personal desire exert equal force, leaving the individual torn between
the two choices. Oftentimes, the choice is resolved by the easier
accessibility of one object (Figure 6B), i.e., the person may be
closer to it, as the choice between two automobiles may be resolved
by buying the less expensive (more accessible) car. Most approach-
approach conflicts are solved rather easily, or at least with satisfaction, inasmuch as either choice satisfies. But tension can occur when
one or both of the alternatives includes a concealed negative valence
which creates partial avoidance behavior. In the situation described
of the boy uncertain about the choice between girl and gang, his
difficulty may be heightened by having to face the jeers and catcalls
of his friends if he dates the girl. The difficulty in choosing between
two jobs is often increased because positive and negative elements
counterbalance and there is limited information about the disadvantages of each.

Approach-avoidance situations are common occurrences in the
physical and psychological environment of children. A boy may want
to play football but fear the physical punishment involved; a young
child may want to play in the ocean but be frightened by the waves;
a youngster may not want to do the chores assigned him but want

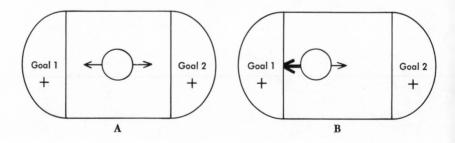

Figure 6. Schematic diagrams of approach–approach conflicts. **A.**
Equal attraction. **B.** Equal attraction but greater accessibility to Goal 1
increases force in that direction.

the allowance he receives. Teachers and parents are continually using rewards and bribes to induce children to perform tasks which have no intrinsic positive valence for them. Parents impose the threat of disapproval or of rejection in order to obtain desired behavior on the part of the child. In some instances, both the positive and negative valences are inherent in the event (Figure 7A), but more often the object has a given intrinsic valence which is altered by actions of persons in power (Figure 7B). The boy desiring to play football illustrates the former; a child wanting to read a book after bedtime, the latter. Many times a child will run the risk involved in approaching or avoiding, where the penalty or praise is externally imposed. He may conveniently forget to do the chores, hoping that it won't affect his allowance; he may read the book in bed by flashlight, hoping he won't get caught and if caught will receive no more than a reprimand.

Greater difficulty is experienced where the conflict is internalized. For instance, a child's desire to be an autonomous, independent individual may run counter to his parents' ambitions and desires. To fulfill his own individuality carries with it the fear that he may disappoint and hence lose the love of his parents. If he follows his own desires, his fear is increased. He can avoid this by conceding to his parents' desires. While this eases his fears, it increases his frustration, with a resulting vacillation between fear and desire. Fears and guilt feelings interact with motives in such a fashion, oftentimes to the great distress of the individual. For example, a child may be curious about his own sexual characteristics or those of the opposite sex and be pushed to explore and discover the differences. Counterbalancing this desire is a feeling that such actions are likely to result in dire

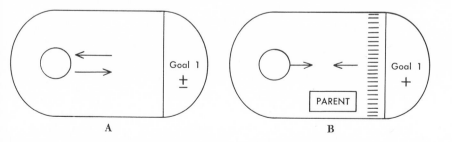

Figure 7. Schematic diagrams of approach-avoidance conflict. **A.** The goal possesses equal positive and negative valences, but in **B.**, the positive valence of goal is counterbalanced with negative force invoked by parent.

events, so strenuously have the taboos regarding sex been inculcated. Exploration, if it occurs, will be secretive and guilt-ridden. The emotional relationships with parents involve many such conflicts. The parent is the source of love, and the source of punishment. The expressions of love for the parent are constrained by sexual taboos which have the ultimate purpose of directing the love to its consummation outside of the family.

A third variation in conflict arises between two avoidance drives (Figure 8) directed toward escaping unpleasant or painful outcomes. A child may not want to do his school work but not want to stay after school to finish it. An adolescent may be fearful of going out to find work for himself and establish his own livelihood, yet want to avoid having to live with critical parents. Usually the solution comes through an attempt to escape the conflict. The child may pretend to be ill and avoid going to school; the adolescent may join the army to avoid both unpleasant circumstances. But events may serve to present his escape and force his staying in the field. The parents of the first child may insist on his going to school, or the teacher may come to the home to inquire about his absence and encourage the parents to return the child to school. The boy may not be permitted to join the army because his parents refuse permission. Being forced to remain "in the field" will result in an increase in tension, in vacillation, in exaggerated outbursts of aggression, increased dependency, of escape through fantasy.

Many conflict situations occur which are of minor importance and even though not resolved can be dismissed, but the more significant the motives which are involved, the more central to the basic satisfac-

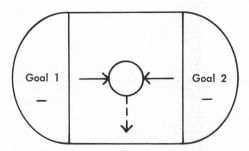

Figure 8.   Schematic diagram of avoidance–avoidance conflict with resolution through attempt to escape field.

tion and development of the individual, the greater the difficulties which ensue. When the conflicts either are or appear to be insoluble, a continual dilemma is faced, which, if it cannot be resolved, must be avoided. One by-product of conflict situations is anxiety, a general emotional response characterized by a forbidding apprehension of impending threat of danger or disaster. The emotional tension associated with anxiety makes discrimination between alternate courses of action more difficult with the result that the individual finds himself encountering an even greater range of difficulties because he is unable to make comparatively minor choices. The state of conflict becomes generalized to a wider range of problems. Anxiety differs from fear in that the latter is generally conceived as being specific, objective, and met by an avoidance response. In fear, one is afraid of something which can be identified and avoided. In anxiety, one is afraid, feels threatened and helpless, without being able to ascertain the origin. The highly dependent child may basically resent the dominant parent who forces his submission. An expression of the feeling could threaten the loss of his prime source of protection and affection. His feelings of anger and resentment will create anxiety, for to express them runs the risk of disaster.

The occurrence of anxiety and associated emotional tension creates a drive state which necessitates satisfaction in its own right, by taking action which permits elimination of the anxiety, usually the adoption of a defensive device permitting an avoidance of situations giving rise to anxiety. For instance, the dependent child may unconsciously strive always to be a very good child who completely pleases his parent, solely to avoid the anxiety.

Some writers, Freud, Horney, and Sullivan among others, attribute a broader source and functioning to anxiety. Horney[1] describes anxiety as a feeling of helplessness in the face of a harsh or hostile environment. The child sees himself as unable to cope with the hostile world and forced to depend upon the adults. Attempts to make free use of his resources and develop his own individuality risk the loss of the adults upon whom he depends; to express his anger at the restrictive treatment he is forced to accept is equally dangerous. Rather than express himself as he is, he adopts a pose, an assumed role, as a strategem, which is, in effect, an alienation of himself. In the interests of safety, he subordinates his own desires, thoughts, and potentials to a defense system which permits him to avoid the basic anxiety he feels. As long as the defense system remains intact and is not threatened, the person can reconcile the conflicts, but anxiety is

---

[1] K. Horney, *New Ways in Psychoanalysis.* New York: Norton, 1939.

created when the defense system faces attack, for if it were to break down, the original conflict would have to be faced. The feigned role not only permits an escape from the original conflict but becomes a self-perpetuating device which avoids situations that would undermine it. The greater the difference between the assumed self and the real self, the greater the anxiety.

Considerable experimental and clinical evidence verifies the functioning of anxiety in human behavior, even though the complete ramifications of its development and operation are not entirely understood. Certainly the basic approach and avoidance diagrams represent too simple an explanation of anxiety to account for its fullest manifestations. On the other hand, the extent and degree to which the child perceives the total environment is uncertain, and the effort to establish anxiety on a global basis may exaggerate its importance.

DYNAMICS OF ADJUSTMENT

We have seen how an individual, with given physical equipment and basic physiological needs, is confronted with the need of learning behavioral procedures which provide him with the satisfaction of his drives in a manner suitable to the society. He is faced with strong conformist pressures exerted immediately by members of his family but fundamentally by the society with its particular social, cultural, and technological synthesis. He is taught to value certain goals, he acquires given motives, and he learns appropriate and approved patterns of action for joining the two. He develops consistent patterns of thought, feeling, and action which constitute a personality, a more or less effective product of efforts to synthesize the physical, psychological, and social realms of experience. Inevitably, he experiences frustration and conflict because of inconsistencies or discrepancies—between his goals and society, between his talents and his goals, between his motives and his opportunities; conflicts between what he would and should do, his fears and his wishes. In a society such as ours, with its mixture of value systems and ethnic groups and complicated by the impact and approval of change of social structure, the occurrence of conflict is much greater than in a stable, homogeneous social system. The incongruities in a society which equally values humility and victory, aggression and piety, individuality and togetherness, acquisitiveness and generosity, and as many more dualities, provide a fertile field for conflict, frustration, and anxiety.

In the face of these experiences, procedures have to be discovered for providing satisfaction of drive and release from tension and anxiety. Figure 9 lists three aspects of adjustment in the face of

ACTION PATTERN	DYNAMISMS FOR REDUCING TENSIONS	LEVELS OF ADJUSTMENT
Offset (attempts to reduce the importance of the goal or replace with equally attractive goals)	Substitution Sublimation Compensation Rationalization Reaction Formation	*Integrative* Striving for solution where possible, ceasing where impossible. Establishing substitute goal. Sublimate drive in socially approved pursuits.
Attack (aggressive action directed towards goal, barriers, or substitutes for barrier)	Displacement Projection	*Defensive Compromise* Defense mechanisms which provide partial satisfaction or release from tension in non-injurious channels, e.g., attention-getting, negativism, compensation, displacement, identification, fantasy.
Submit (immobilization or fixated behavior in face of persistent failure)	Identification Introjection Isolation	
Avoid (withdrawal or escape from frustration)	Regression Fantasy Phobia Repression	*Disintegrative* Delinquency, destructiveness, assault, suicide, phobias, psychosomatic illness, apathy, regression, delusions, psychosis.

Figure 9. Types and levels of adjustment to frustration and conflict situations.

frustration—the action patterns, the defense mechanisms for reducing tension, and levels of adjustment. In the face of frustration one can release tension and express aggression by (1) minimizing the value of the goal; (2) attacking the barrier, the person or representative who set up the barrier; or (3) attacking a substitute for either, e.g., a smaller, weaker, or helpless person, object, or group; (4) accepting the situation as immutable and submitting to it, or (5) attempting to escape from the frustration through withdrawal.

Such actions may be carried out literally through overt, direct actions or they may be executed symbolically through various defense mechanisms. Just as all individuals have innate physiological needs to maintain their physical well-being by providing adequate satisfactions for hunger, thirst, sex, fatigue, so they strive to satisfy their personal and social needs: feeling adequate under all situations and conditions and feeling socially secure and approved. The physiological needs remain active until equilibrium is restored; the psychological needs impel us to restore psychological balance and equilibrium and to protect the integrity of the individual in the face of frustration or conflict. When direct solution is impossible, or seemingly so, compromise solutions are adopted in order to avoid the catastrophe of permanent failure. We make excuses rather than acknowledge inadequacy; we blame others rather than admit failure; we daydream of imagined accomplishments in lieu of defeats; we lose appetites, or have headaches, or difficulty in sleeping in the face of unresolved conflicts. Lacking primary satisfaction, we accept the best secondary compromise.

A varied series of techniques classified as defense mechanisms are used in attaining compromise solutions and releasing tension. They are listed in the second column of Figure 9. As arranged, they are associated with the action patterns most characteristic. The associations established are not complete. For instance, projection can be and often is used not only as a form of attack but also of offsetting the importance of the goal. Fantasy provides not only a means of escape but may be associated with aggressive or submissive action patterns.

Nevertheless, the listing indicates the main objectives being accomplished. Another characteristic of the list is that those towards the top of the list tend to be the healthier actions—healthier in the sense that they meet with greater social approval. The devices of pathology are a functional part of any social system. In our social system, we encourage compensatory and aggressive defense mechanisms. We look askance at the use of fantasy or trance states as defense mechanisms, yet in some cultures these mechanisms are approved. No connotation is intended, however, to suggest that defense mechanisms are undesirable of themselves, any more than one would say the automobile is responsible for the death toll in highway accidents or that it is a cause of juvenile delinquency. The death toll is the result of the way in which man uses the automobile. Defense mechanisms are *unconscious devices* used for reducing psychological tensions. Like automobiles, they are the servant of any master. The same dynamics which serve to defend the individual from tension and conflict can also serve the attainment of individual maturity and integrity. Fantasy can be the instrument of creative imagination, identification the instrument of worthy aspiration. Each dynamism can be and is used to serve many ends, as can be seen in the following illustrations.

Defense Mechanisms

Substitution: replacing an unrealistic or disapproved goal with an attainable or socially approved one.

Aspiring to be a bookkeeper instead of an accountant.

Sublimation: channeling socially unacceptable impulses into socially approved actions.

Release of aggressive impulses by boxing, or writing stories of violence.

Compensation: overemphasizing a trait, ability, or characteristic to avoid inadequacy in another area.

The dull child trying to act alert, or the bully.

Rationalization: shifting the blame from self to other cause; diminishing the desirability of a goal; finding socially acceptable explanations for actions.

"Oh, yes, I've seen her ring. It's a lovely *little* diamond."
"I don't care if I am fat as long as I feel good."

Reaction-formation: acting in the opposite way from what one unconsciously feels or has previously acted.

The dominant-rejectant mother who overprotects her child. The child who objects to being kissed because he's no longer a baby.

Displacement: releasing unacceptable aggressive impulses or actions in less dangerous avenues.

Having been berated by employer but afraid to respond in kind, the father overly criticizes wife or child for a minor mistake.

Projection: attributing to others the wish or fault to be avoided in oneself.

"What difference does it make, everybody cheats on income tax."
"She's always picking on me" (the child who is constantly annoying the teacher).

Identification: taking satisfaction from the accomplishments of other persons in the absence of one's own achievement.

The mother of the real or pseudo-prodigy.

The perennial "old-grad."

"My father's the biggest . . ."

Introjection: adopting the external demands as one's own wishes.

"I wouldn't think of leaving food on my plate" (the person who is overweight).

Isolation: unconsciously separating one's feelings from the events with which they were associated.

A listless, disinterested attitude towards events.

Regression: giving up in the face of frustration and retreating to behavior characteristic of an earlier (more satisfying) age.

Disruption of toilet habits in a young child after the birth of another baby.

Phobia: recurrent, persistent, irrational fear of object or situation. (Often associated with repression and displacement.)

Excessive fear of pets or water, etc.

Fantasy: deriving satisfaction from imagined occurrences in lieu of actual.

An orphan who relates long and varied tales of his father's marvelous deeds and his many, many possessions.

Repression: the inhibition of dangerous impulses or conflicts; forgetting unpleasant occurrences or unwanted memories.

Forgetting a dental appointment.

LEVELS OF ADJUSTMENT

The action patterns taken to overcome difficulties, relieve frustration, and resolve conflicts can be viewed as ranging from constructive to destructive. At the constructive end are those which reflect and contribute to an integrated personality able to strike a satisfactory balance between internal and external needs and demands. The exact components of the balance are not fixed, but, in the main, include two sets of relationships: the one with self, and the other with society. The first includes an acceptance of self, of one's motives, defenses, strengths and weaknesses, and an evaluation of one's self that provides for sufficient self-esteem to avoid being overcome by guilt, so that gratification of one's physical and emotional needs is possible without infringement on the equal rights of others. One not only has to accept the reality of one's self, but the reality of the world as such in order to withstand hurt and disappointment, to be able to learn from experience and develop sufficient flexibility to change as needed, and to be able to maintain a degree of autonomy in the face of social and cultural demands. On the side of social relationships, one should be able to function adequately in group situations—vocational, recreational, familial—with spontaneity and appropriate emotionality. In short, it means harnessing one's talents to an appropriate satisfaction of personal and social needs, and viewing the results with perspective. All individuals resort to defense mechanisms from time to time to ease tensions, but the more they become a predominant mode of response adopted to maintain some degree of need satisfaction and release from frustration, the more they represent a compromise solution accepted in lieu of complete defeat. The inability to establish any kind of compromise leads inevitably to destruction of self or society, literally or symbolically. Apathy, regression, psychosomatic illnesses, psychosis, and suicide are forms of disintegration of the self. Delinquency, assault, and destruction are forms of attack on the society. Either course leads to disaster.

Teachers must understand the behavior they observe in children in order to function more effectively in guiding children to maturity, and to gauge the import of behavior in relation to level of adjustment. Teachers see children who are timid and children who are aggressive. They encounter children with physical and emotional handicaps. They observe emotional outbursts, learning difficulties, social adjustment problems, speech defects, and other signs of disturbance. Teachers have to decide whether or not to take specific action and, if so, what course to follow. The problem is less one of identifying problem behavior than it is of determining the seriousness of the difficulty and the most suitable method of approach.

We are more conscious of problems that children present to us, or to their classmates, than to problems which they may be experiencing in themselves. The most obvious illustration is that of an aggressive or attention-demanding child compared with a timid or withdrawn child. We cannot escape the one, but we can easily overlook the other. This follows from the fact that teachers too are goal-centered. They have their motives, their purposes to be accomplished, and they are conscious of events which prevent their progress with individuals or classes. Inattentiveness, restlessness, talking without permission, wasting time are items of children's behavior which come first to our attention because they obstruct us. We need a focus which permits us to see a child as he sees himself and as he is seen by his classmates, to give him and us clues to the problems he is experiencing within himself, regardless of their expression—aggressive belligerency, timid withdrawal, or passive daydreaming. As we

try to view children from this perspective, we have to decide whether
it is necessary or desirable to step in, or whether to trust to the
remedies or opportunities available in the natural course of events.

Each handicap, whether physical or emotional, carries with it some
degree of isolation from the environment. With physically handicapped children, the physical defect makes some aspect of the world
unavailable. The blind child is cut off from visual stimuli, the cardiac
from active games. In addition, he develops an attitude towards the
handicap which may amplify the isolation. Mental defectives experience a degree of isolation because of their inability to comprehend
parts of the environment or to experience it in the ways others do.
Emotional disturbances provide their degree of isolation. The shy
child experiences emotional barriers which restrict his commerce and
communication with other children. Even the aggressive child, who
at first thought might appear excessively intrusive into environment,
experiences his particular degree of isolation from the rejection and
counteraggression he stimulates in others. A crude measure of severity of difficulty can be obtained by appraising the degree of isolation
from the environment and its duration in time.

A distinction must be made between the social significance of a
problem and its psychological significance. Truancy, delinquency,
injury to others, and arson are serious when gauged by their social
impact. Feeding problems, temper tantrums, companionship problems, bullying, lying, fearfulness, and suspicion are of limited social
significance. Yet in psychological terms, the latter can be as fully
or more significant than the former, for they can signify problems of
major duration or scope.

Teachers have access in part or whole to the three major arenas
of the child's activity—the family, the school, and the recreational.
Within each of these settings they have the opportunity to acquaint
themselves with the function of the child in several primary aspects
of his personality:

> *Physical:* food habit—poor or excessive appetite, food preferences
> and aversions; toilet habits—control, excessive modesty or
> curiosity, concerns; locomotor—physical energy and coordina-
> tion.
>
> *Emotional:* control—inhibition, spontaneity; affectional relation-
> ships; frustration tolerance, control and directing of aggression
>
> *Intellectual:* learning progress; adaptability, curiosity.
>
> *Imaginative:* creativity, resourcefulness, initiative.
>
> *Social:* degree of participation—self-esteem vs. group centered,

isolation, intimacy, status and role; attitudes—suspicious, negative, cooperative, etc.

Authority: degree of autonomy, independence; submissiveness vs. rebelliousness; feelings of guilt or shame.

There is no ready yardstick for measuring severity of any problem. The necessary clinical judgment and discrimination develop gradually through repeated experience, and the process is similar to that by which any discrimination is learned. Large differences are more easily discerned; repeated trials and corrections increase the capacity for finer discriminations. The teacher does not need the refined discriminations and analysis which characterize clinical diagnosis. She can, however, make broad distinctions among: those conditions which are best ignored, those where specialized treatment is essential, and those in the intermediate range which require her best efforts. Essentially, the teacher's task is not to diagnose adjustment problems, but to detect them and refer those which obviously need specialized assistance. Two rules of thumb can be offered as guidance in the process of discrimination. In reviewing the major areas of a child's life and the particular aspects listed earlier, the greater the degree of isolation from the environment, that is, the more numerous the areas in which he experiences difficulty, the greater the severity and the need for specialized treatment. Second, the greater the child's resistance to whatever program the teacher follows, the greater the need for special assistance.

Some explanation is desirable on these points. Usually the teacher notices a disturbance in which a child repeats the same or similar behavior constantly, suggesting an underlying tension and inability to modify his behavior in the light of experience. In other instances, a series of different disturbances, ostensibly unrelated, are observed. For instance, a child may be experiencing learning difficulties in the classroom, may not participate in the play activities with his companions, and may evidence lack of care from the home. The greater the range of involvement, and the longer the duration (a reason for cumulative records), the more serious the difficulty. Systematic staff conferences for discussion of cases can be most beneficial, not only in developing greater comprehension of the dynamics of behavior and insight into the seriousness of problems, but also in providing perspective on appropriate courses of actions. Many teachers' meetings, often a dull series of announcements better disseminated by written bulletins, could serve as stimulating sessions of professional growth, were they devoted to specific analysis and suggestions for action regarding individual cases of child adjustment.

The second rule of thumb suggested concerns the child's continued resistance to change. In situations where the teacher has planned a program in the hope that it will provide desired opportunities for change, and where, in spite of her efforts, the child's behavior pattern persists, outside assistance is needed. It may still be that the problem is situational; that it may exist in the relationship between teacher and child and be no problem to the child in any other area. Many children are well-adjusted in their family relationship, in the group relationships, and, in general, in school, but encounter specific difficulties with particular teachers. This does not necessarily reflect upon the teacher, for few, if any, human beings are capable of ministering to all children; and teachers are no exception to this limitation, however reluctant we may be to acknowledge it. Whatever the cause, both can benefit by help from specialized sources.

THE ROLE OF THE TEACHER IN TREATMENT

Because the resources available in the community for treating adjustment problems are limited, and because the school has easy access to nearly all children, there is a strong temptation to delegate to the school full responsibility for the treatment of these problems. It is true that in many instances the school is the only social force in contact with or available to the child and that if any remedial action is taken it will be taken by the school staff or not taken at all. Nevertheless, the school's effort should not be confused with psychotherapy nor should it become a basis for expecting the school to function in such capacity. The teacher's educational role, whether restricted to scholastic development or extended to include personal and social development, is necessarily a managerial and directorial function which runs counter to the role of the therapist. A clarification of function should help to define limits of action for the teacher.

Figure 10 diagrams the differing aspects of the roles played by teacher and therapist. The essential distinction hinges on the contrast between education and re-education. In a general sense, education consists of the systematic provision of opportunities for growth based on the assumption that the individual will avail himself of them, consciously or unconsciously, for the fulfillment of self. When educators speak of self-realization as a prime goal of education, I believe they mean it in this sense. Not only does the teacher provide the opportunities, but she also simultaneously works to remove barriers impeding progress, in short, to set the individual free for healthy development. Re-education is used in a contrasting sense, implying

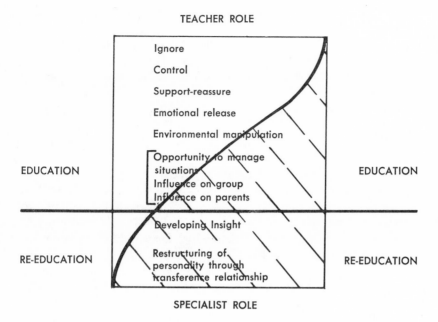

Figure 10. Diagram of complementary and contrasting roles of teacher and therapist.

that an existing condition must be restructured before the individual is free to avail himself of the opportunities at hand.

This is similar to the difference between suburban development and urban renewal. In a sense, a planning board with its zoning laws is similar to an educational program in that it directs the growth of a community along lines presumably best suited to its ultimate development. An urban renewal program is akin to therapy in that existing structures must be removed or altered to make way for a better organization and development consistent with changed conditions. It is much more difficult to accomplish the latter, for not only must a plan for potential development exist, but the habit patterns of existing usage must be broken, and the emotional attitudes and traditional patterns of the community must be penetrated and redirected before such a program is possible. Some citizens combine to push an urban renewal program, others resort to the courts and various legal tactics to impede or prevent such change. Small wonder that urban renewal requires such strenuous effort and frequently fails. By contrast, suburban development proceeds more easily, often erratically, in that the communities fail to make the best usage of their resources, although embroiling themselves in less conflict.

The functions of the teacher and the therapist parallel the two aspects of the illustration just given. The teacher with her resources, her "zoning laws," and her plan of development (the total curriculum) provides for development more or less suitable to individual capacities and needs. The specialist, be he guidance worker, psychologist, or psychiatrist (and especially the last named—inasmuch as many of the functions of the guidance worker and the psychologist fall into the educational sphere of operations), works at personality renewal —to coin a phrase. His work involves using his talent and skill to penetrate the existing habits of behavior and emotional defense, to restructure interpersonal and intrapersonal relationships in order to free the growth forces of the individual for healthier development.

Five main tactics used by teachers are identified in Figure 10: ignore, control, support, provide emotional release, and manipulate environment. While it is true that all behavior is meaningful, it should not be inferred that all behavior is significant or that all behavior should be acted upon. One hazard of exploring the meaning of behavior, especially in the novice stage, is the tendency to overinterpret behavior. There is an inherent satisfaction in naming and classifying events, for the ability to apply a concept implies one's mastery of it. One derives a feeling of control or authority from being able to designate a parent as a "dominant-rejectant" type, or seeing a child expressing "sibling rivalry," and labeling a thumb-sucker or pipe-smoker as an "oral-incorporative" type. Minor incidents are easily magnified into major types. Much behavior that is observed should be ignored as far as any need to act upon it is concerned, mainly because much behavior is self-correcting. By this is meant that the individual frequently recognizes for himself the effect and meaning of his actions and is able to make corrections; also, the normal interplay of environmental forces with personal needs provides opportunities for needed development and change.

Where behavior is persistently maladaptive, the teacher may act to control the expression of the behavior. The youngster who has repeated temper tantrums, the youngster who is repeatedly hitting or poking other children, the youngster who consistently avoids participation in class activities, can be directly controlled by the teacher. She can suppress the temper tantrums by refusing to tolerate them; she can insist that the aggressive child keep his hands and feet to himself; she may demand participation in class activity. The teacher should recognize that when she controls the expressions of behavior, she is essentially suppressing only the behavior, and rarely affecting the needs or the drives which gave rise to it. For the protection of the child or his classmates, such actions may suffice. The probability is great, however, that the behavior will find expression in other areas or at other times when the teacher or another adult is not present to regulate its expression.

Support or reassurance is the first level of treatment provided by teachers. By a variety of devices, the teacher reassures the child that he has the capacity to meet the seductions, the obstacles, and the challenges presented in life and supports his ego as it comes to grips with the tasks it faces. Buhler[2] presents an excellent example:

> Wilma, tall and handsome, at twelve was taller than all the girls and boys in the seventh grade. She became quiet, withdrawn, unwilling to enter games. The organization of social dancing precipitated a crisis. Wilma developed physical symptoms—sore foot, sore throat, headaches, absences from school—which medical examination showed to have no physical basis. Her teacher visited the family, noted many expressions of the family to Wilma such as "It's no disgrace to be tall . . . a large girl has to be careful of her behavior . . . can't cavort like a puppy . . . must be dignified . . . stripes and frills not becoming . . . shouldn't wear jeans . . . etc."
>
> Fortunately for Wilma, the teacher had been tall as a child and could recall her embarrassment. Not only was she able to interpret the situation to the parents, introduce square dancing in lieu of social dancing, make arrangements with the home economics teacher to have Wilma model in a fashion show—"all models are tall because they wear clothes so well," all of which constitute manipulations of the environment, but more important she could talk to Wilma about her childhood, sharing stories and embarrassments at particular experiences, and by so doing provide Wilma with the support needed to face the difficulties and possibly as well, a model with whom to identify.

The provision of support doesn't anticipate any fundamental change, but it helps the individual find assurance in his own resources for coping with the tasks or difficulties he faces. This support is the most significant treatment that the teacher can render children as they muster their resources in seeking to balance the impulses they experience with the external demands and restrictions they meet.

Remedial teachers base their work essentially on such support;

---

[2]C. Buhler, *Childhood Problems and the Teacher*. New York: Holt, Rinehart and Winston, Inc., 1952, pp. 181-183. Material used with permission.

they replace the forbidding standards of school grades and age norms with tasks appropriate to the child's capacity and thus increase his confidence in his own ability to succeed. Three phases occur where support is essential:

1. Maintaining the child's confidence in his capacity to succeed while meeting the sequence of tasks inherent in maturing.
2. Aiding well-adjusted children in periods of crisis: serious defeats, family deaths, etc.
3. Providing reassurance in cases of chronic difficulty where little change or improvement can be hoped for: physically and mentally handicapped children.

The second important treatment technique used by sensitive teachers and therapists alike is the provision of opportunity for emotional release. The expression of feelings, guilt and shame, is a time-honored procedure which recognizes that "telling is good for the soul" because it releases tension, and the externalizing of feelings makes their management easier and their replacement by positive feelings possible. An important distinction must be made between the provision for emotional release by the teacher and that by the therapist. The terms management of and replacement of feelings implies the presence of sufficient controls to manage the impulses and feelings expressed and the existence of positive feelings in sufficient depth. Seriously maladjusted children have often been so abused that the hatred or the fear with which they struggle would be overwhelming if released and would sweep aside whatever precarious control they have maintained. The task of working with such feelings is the province of the psychiatrist. The best the teacher can do is to manage her classroom so as to reduce the exposure to frustration and siphon off some of the feeling indirectly, rather than open the floodgates of feeling. The vast majority of children have or are in the process of developing reasonably adequate controls and achieving an understanding of their feelings and socially acceptable means of expressing them. The opportunity to express the feelings, whether in group discussions or private conversation, reduces tension, contributes to acceptance and understanding, and permits development and integration of controls.

Environmental manipulation is the teacher's main stock in trade. To begin with, she creates an environment through her selection of program and management of its details. Her procedures may introduce large or small measures of frustration, they may possess inherent built-in controls and opportunities for draining tensions, or they may create mutual interpersonal support or conflict. No matter how suitable and well-arranged her selection of material and arrangement of program, necessity for alteration will occur. At this point, the teacher's capacity to effectively manipulate the environmental conditions in order to create situations which induce desired behavior or block destructive behavior is important. The historic sitting of a child in a corner, or banishing him from a room, or changing his seat closer to the watchful eye of the teacher, are ancient illustrations. Signal interference whereby one catches the child's eye and by minor gesture prevents an action, or by moving into proximity to a child to exert a restraining influence without overt word or act, are more subtle forms of environmental pressures. The skilled arrangement of groups, so composed that the interplay of personality contributes to essential development is a still more sophisticated approach. Shifting assignments, introducing and assigning roles in games, providing opportunity for enrollment in club groups, exerting influence on parents in order to bring an alteration in the home environment, are all further examples of means through which the teacher literally creates situations which provide avenues for development.

The curving line through the face of Figure 10 suggests that in small part teachers aid in the development of insight and personality formation through identification, just as psychiatrists may utilize educational techniques in a clinical setting. The procedures are not mutually exclusive, and, as shown in the illustration of Wilma, can occur simultaneously. Nevertheless, for the teacher the development of insight and the use of identification occurs incidentally rather than systematically. The systematic application of techniques for the purpose of development of insight or the use of the transference relationship to provide for personality restructuring requires the skilled training of the clinician, and hence these techniques are grouped under the major designation of re-education.

At the risk of oversimplification, the clinical treatment of adjustment problems depends upon the talking out or the living out of the problem. In the first situation, the therapist uses words or play with children, either individually or in groups, as a means of helping a child give up his defenses, understand himself and the people with whom he lives, and, through increased understanding and acceptance, develop his capacity to cope with objective reality. In the latter situation, the therapist utilizes the emotional feeling of the patient toward the therapist to promote change. The tendency of patients to displace the affectionate or hostile reactions associated with their parents on to the therapist, the transference relationship, serves as the vehicle whereby infantile feelings are experienced and released, precipitating a process of emotional development which permits the attainment of more mature emotional relationships. Both procedures depend for their success upon a close relationship between patient and therapist; in the former, words are ostensibly the medium for change, in the latter, the transference relationship.

The limited capacity of children to express their feelings verbally has led to the development of procedures which permit children to act out the difficulties and feelings as they experience them. Play therapy is frequently used where the child is exposed to a range of toys and games with which he is permitted to play in whatever fashion appeals to him. The toys he chooses, the arrangements of the objects, the use he makes of them, the method of approach, the points at which he blocks or disrupts in play, the statements he expresses while playing, not only reveal the source and the nature of the disturbance but provide the therapist with a way of gaining access to the emotional life of the child.

Paralleling the treatment of the child, particularly with younger children, a parent may be simultaneously engaged in treatment sessions with clinical personnel, in order to restructure the parent-child relationship.

The following chapters will contain illustrations to show, in different spheres of development, the operation in an educational setting of the general techniques outlined above. The distinction between education and re-education has been suggested to demarcate the limits of the teacher's role. Essentially, her efforts are to reassure, to dispel fears and build confidence, to increase self-understanding and to help develop new methods for meeting thwarting events. This cannot be done unless the teacher, in her basic relationship with child and class, is skilled in her primary function of providing a well-balanced program which permits achievement and avoids the emotional tensions arising from failure, scolding, and threats. Well planned and executed programs avoid the fears and anxieties, the frustrations and inadequacies, which amplify adjustment difficulties. But even with the assurance of a skillfully designed program, children will exhibit difficulties in adjustment arising from a variety of other sources. In these instances the teacher has to attack causes rather than symptoms through the devices available to her, knowing all the while the limits of her skill and role. Not to know the limits of one's capacity and responsibility creates two disastrous effects: the feeling of being responsible for the well-being and successful adjustment of all children, with the inevitable guilt and self-chastisement which follows the inevitable failures; and second, the blind self-seduction of seeing oneself the justified manager of the lives of children.

TEACHER CASE STUDY

To give meaning to what has been discussed and to invest it with the reality of acual events, the following case history reports the efforts of a teacher in working with a child, describing her successes and failures, and, most of all, showing the patience and care needed to create an environment in which change can occur.

Case studies vary in form and content with the training and orientation of the practitioner preparing the report and the means used to obtain information. Thus, case studies prepared by a social worker, a clinical psychologist, and a psychiatrist will differ. Further, the kind and depth of analysis employed will differ, the social worker stressing environmental factors, the psychologist psychometric data, and the psychiatrist interpersonal dynamics. A teacher's approach to a case study—and by implication to a child experiencing adjustment difficulties—must of necessity be different. Her basic training and primary commitment is to teaching and learning, not to clinical diagnosis and training. Any procedures which she uses must be suited to her knowledge of the dynamics of behavior and to the kinds of contact she has with children.

The following case history describes a teacher's work with a child in the course of her day-to-day duties. In effect it is more of an operational case study than a clinical case study, for the teacher, after planning her course of action, concentrated her efforts on assisting the child to find more satisfying means of fulfilling her needs.

The teacher's actions were predicated on four assumptions:

1. Symptomatic behavior results from frustration of emotional needs.
2. Satisfaction of emotional needs will yield increased learning, reduced aggression, greater social acceptance, and improved adjustment.
3. Certain common needs can be postulated for all children: (1) Physical (economic), (2) love and affection, (3) social acceptance and approval, (4) self-esteem, (5) achievement, and (6) freedom from fear and intense guilt.
4. Unfulfilled needs can be identified from behavioral manifestations and actions taken in a school setting to satisfy them.

CASE STUDY

Problem behavior

Illegible, erratic penmanship and general untidiness of clothes, papers, desk, and floor were the first clues to the disturbed personality of Gail. Closer observation showed frequent symptoms of frustration. If a child was in her way, she pushed him roughly aside; if she were reprimanded, she would become either belligerent and noisy, or sullen, discouraged, and bitter. She frequently insisted that nobody would play with her and that her only friends were "dumb kids." Some times when she couldn't complete her work, she sobbed noisily, her face flushed, her eyes and mouth twitched, and she complained of headaches or stomach pains; at other times she would ignore the work and stare into space with a tense, angry look on her face. Gail had her pleasant moods too, but even on these occasions her behavior indicated tension—motions jerky, laughter excessive, anxious about being included in group.

Thus initial contacts indicated aggression resulting from frustration and psychosomatic symptoms.

Identifying data

(Source: cumulative record) Gail, short, slightly overweight, neatly dressed and fairly attractive was 9 years 9 months of age on entering grade five. Cumulative record shows a wide discrepancy between superior Stanford-Binet IQ of 126 and academic achievement. Attendance record has been extremely poor (see below) yet health record indicates no physical impairment or recent serious illness.

Gail is the third of four children—two older sisters 16 and 15 attending high school, and younger brother just entered kindergarten. Father, a college graduate, employed as a school custodian; mother a trained nurse, age 49. Family resides in rented six-room apartment in a suburban duplex.

Background information

(Sources: cumulative record, interviews with school nurse, previous teacher, and mother). Information discloses problem to be serious and long-standing.

Mother reported Gail was a "wanted child." Born five years after second daughter, she was petted and adored by the entire family, was especially attached to mother, sleeping with her, dressed by her, and highly dependent on her. Kindergarten report describes Gail as attractive, uninhibited, friendly, bright.

When her brother was born, Gail, age 5½, was bewildered and lonely and cried considerably while the mother was in the hospital. First grade teacher reports superior achievement, but occasional temper tantrums, thumb-sucking, and appearing depressed. Second grade teacher reports excellent work, that Gail had many friends, but was "temperamental." Mother states that Gail adored this teacher. During March and April Gail was absent with pneumonia and scarlet fever and mother thinks subsequent emotional problems may have ensued from extremely high temperatures during this period of illness.

During the third grade, the mother worked the 3-11 P.M. shift in a hospital, seeing Gail only at breakfast and for a few minutes after school. Gail frequently begged to stay home from school to talk to mother. Gail was cared for by older sisters, was rebellious, occasionally spanked because she resented being put to bed at same hour as baby brother. Teacher reports that Gail was disobedient, antagonistic, frequently expressed hatred for teacher, classmates, and family. School achievement began to drop. Teacher, aware of IQ. and previous achievement, frequently scolded Gail about her school work. By February Gail's behavior became critical: she was not doing her school work, her behavior appeared regressive, reports describe her as drooling, crawling about schoolroom on hands and knees. School health department advised that the child be removed from school and placed in hospital for diagnostic study.

Mother preferred to handle the problem herself, giving up her job, putting Gail to bed for several weeks under care of pediatrician, buying a summer home, and reorganizing family life to make Gail feel "secure and loved." She reports that she neglected her housework to play with Gail and her brother, read to them frequently. Father would hold Gail every night until she fell asleep. The loss of mother's income, expense of summer home, and medical expenses forced the older girls to give up music lessons and have fewer clothes and luxuries. Oldest sister cooperative, but Jean resented limitations resulting from her "crazy sister."

Gail returned to school in September, much improved after summer in the country. Her fourth grade teacher was interested in Gail but traditional in classroom discipline. Her reports indicate that Gail was high-strung and nervous but making fairly good progress in school work. (No achievement test data available.) Mother reports that Gail both loved and feared her teacher. In February the child again had to be removed from school because of extreme nervousness and lack of bowel and bladder control. Hospitalized two weeks for medical and phychiatric study. No physical or mental disorder found; weekly visits to psychiatrist arranged. Mother reports that visits were discontinued after a few weeks because the psychiatrist was not seriously alarmed about Gail.

Again after a summer in the country, Gail returned to school well tanned and ten pounds heavier to begin the fifth grade.

Projective techniques

In order to identify Gail's primary needs with some objectivity, several protective techniques suitable for use in the classroom were administered. Gail's scores or responses are indicated.

THE WISHING WELL

Need for	Score	Norm
self-respect and sharing	14	6
love and affection	12	6
belonging	10	5
achievement	8	8
security	4	2
freedom from fear	2	5
freedom from guilt	4	8

High scores indicated need for attention, companionship, participation and cooperation with others, and affection.

The class was asked to write their three wishes, with an explanation given so that just material goods were not asked for, but rather wishes which would make their lives more peaceful and happy. Gail's wishes were:

THREE WISHES

1. I wish I was an only child.
2. I wish I had more smart friends.
3. I wish I knew if my mission in life was to take care of poor children without any brains.

Gail's first two wishes indicate her wish for a greater share of her parental affection and possibly less conflict or competition from siblings, and a need for status and belonging with her intellectual equals. (Her only friend at this point was a dull, meek girl of limited ability.) The implication of the third wish is more obscure, possibly suggestive of need for ego satisfaction or a situation of unquestioned superiority.

SOCIAL DISTANCE SCALE

Gail chosen as	by boys	by girls	total
best friend	0	2	2
friend	3	4	7
okay	3	5	8
not cared for	11	2	13
disliked	0	3	3
	17	16	33

Two-thirds of the boys and one-third of the girls ignored or rejected her. Three-quarters of the children in this class received higher scores. Her evident need for group status, belonging, and companionship are reflected in the response of her peers on this scale.

A modified form of the *Who's Who* produced the following characterizations of Gail by her classmates:

DESIRABLE TRAITS		UNDESIRABLE TRAITS	
Stays calm	1	Unhappy	4
Unselfish	2	Lazy	2
Well poised	2	Poor leader	4
Friendly	1		
Good in clubs	3		
Modest	1		
Protects the weak	3		

The total response was similar to the Social Distance Scale in that the positive and negative elements were about equal, with no clear consensus seen. Only one-third of the class recorded a higher number of positive ratings yet paradoxically only one-tenth had more negative traits marked.

SOCIOMETRIC STATUS

Seating

Gail received
1 first choice
2 third choices
1 rejection

Gail chose
Louise (mutual)
Janet
Patricia

Gail rejected
Suzanne

Gail chosen by
Louise (mutual)
Helen
Alice

Gail rejected by
Suzanne (mutual)
Patty

Geography committee

Received
1 first choice
4 third choices
1 rejection

Chose
Janet
Dorothy (mutual)
Beth

Rejected
Louise

Chosen by
Louise
Diane
Dorothy (mutual)
Elaine
Suzanne

Rejected by
Beth

Gail and Louise, a rather colorless, timid child whom Gail dominates and treats with occasional disdain, are neighbors who play together and fight together more frequently. Interestingly enough she rejected Louise, presumably her best friend, on the committee work sociogram, choosing instead three superior students and consistently successful school achievers. On both sociograms, Gail chose Janet, a highly chosen, friendly, sympathetic girl who, apparently sensing Gail's problems, has unobtrusively tried to be friendly and helpful. Nevertheless, neither of these choices was reciprocated by Janet.

Although Gail is not an isolate, the sociograms suggest a need for belonging in a group of children who would understand, accept, and encourage her, and whose acceptance would reinforce her sense of self esteem.

Analysis

Gail's general behavior pattern of aggression and psychosomatic symptoms of illness indicated unmet emotional needs. Data from all sources indicated a long-standing problem, probably precipitated by the birth of the younger brother. Although information regarding early childhood is meager, the favorable reports at kindergarten and first grade level indicated the problem apparently dated from this period of time and is at the behavioral level. Data suggested unmet needs primarily in relation to affection, self-esteem, and social acceptance, and to a lesser degree of achievement. The loss of the equivalent of one year's time from the last two school years had produced a shift from superior achievement status to retarded educational achievement and definite lacks in certain skills. She could be expected to recover by virtue of high intelligence if this ability could be released and brought to bear.

Because the problem was apparently the outgrowth of circumstances and family relationships which failed her during early childhood, the teacher could have dismissed the problem as the responsibility of the parents and not of the classroom teacher. Moreover, since the emotional problems were of serious proportions, as evidenced by regressive behavior and complaints which necessitated long periods of exclusion from school, they could justifiably be referred to clinical psychologist or psychiatrist. The fact that the family had not ignored its responsibility, but had initiated a program to ease home tensions and foster improved mental health for Gail, with the additional knowledge that the psychiatric examination had found no evidence of serious physical or mental disorder, lent positive indication that satisfaction of the child's needs was not impossible or improbable. Since Gail's actions made it difficult to progress satisfactorily towards reasonable educational goals and her irrational behavior made progress difficult for her classmates, sensitivity to the child's needs and a programmed attempt to meet them was not only desirable, but a responsibility of the teacher. Improved classroom relationships could alleviate many of the frustrations which blocked Gail's progress.

Having concluded that the basic needs to be satisfied were affection, self-esteem, social acceptance, and achievement, the teacher undertook a course of action designed to (1) minimize frustration in these areas, (2) meet specific situations as they occurred in light of the analysis, and (3) keep detailed observational reports for purpose of further analysis, clarification, and subsequent evaluation of progress. The anecdotal reports which follow are selected from extensive notes recorded by the teacher during both the information-seeking and the program-execution phases. The analysis of the information and the action taken are indicated.

1. When asked why her arithmetic was not completed, G answered belligerently: "I can't do my work because the children keep looking at me and laughing. They're making fun of me and make me nervous." The children reported that they could not help smiling because G was kicking the chair of the girl in front of her, grumbling, humming, and making facial grimaces that attracted their attention.

Asked G if she would like to sit up front near me, where she would not be so nervous. She became almost hysterical as she sobbed: "No, I want to sit up at the back of the room where I won't bother anybody. Everybody is mean to me." Gathering her materials she rushed to the last seat, placed her head on the desk and cried. She made no attempt to complete her work, but when the arithmetic period was over returned quietly to her seat.

Analysis: With her need for achievement blocked by her inability to perform the arithmetic and pressed by what she felt to be rejection by her classmates, G withdraws.

Action: On the basis of the sociogram, seated G with a group of four girls (all either chosen by her or choosing her) simultaneously taking advantage of the shift of class seating to place the group near front of the room where her moments of tension would be more apparent to teacher and her disturbing behavior less likely to draw attention and displeasure of classmates.

Second, appointed G as monitor of attendance book which was kept in Principal's office and which could be sent for as needed. This permitted teacher to meet moments of high tension by sending G to office, giving her a chance to relax, become friendly with Principal and secretary, receive an encouraging word from teacher on return, without

fear of other children feeling she was getting undue attention.

2. Gail's composition work was above average but her choice of
topics unusual. Her paper was often dirty and written so wildly
it was difficult to read. One example: Once there was a pretty
little boy and his mother loved him the best in the whole world,
but he got pimples on his face and he wasn't pretty any more.
Then the mother was ashamed of this poor ugly little boy and
couldn't stand to even look at him and she didn't love him any
more. Then the nine-year-old sister took him to a great doctor
and the boy was cured. Everybody kissed the girl and said she
was a great heroine and the family lived happily ever after.

> *Analysis:* Need for affection and approval by family evident
> in the theme of the story as well as a favorable outcome
> to the story. If the story is viewed as directly reflecting her
> life and feelings, the "great deed" may suggest some guilt
> about her feelings of rejection and jealousy towards her
> brother and an attempt to compensate for them.
>
> *Action:* Asked G if the story was original or had she read
> it. When G said she had made it up, Teacher replied:
> "You seem to have a talent for telling stories; perhaps
> you'll be a writer when you grow up. Why don't you keep
> a notebook of stories about these children and their family?
> Perhaps I can help you, and if they are good enough we'll
> have them typed and make an attractive cover for them."
> Also asked her to make a new copy in best penmanship
> for display on bulletin board.
>
> Discussion of this and subsequent stories provided a natural
> springboard for discussing G's personal problems. Both
> discussion and her writing offered possibility for release
> for tension. Her satisfaction with the procedure also per-
> mitted an indirect attack on encouraging neat work with-
> out appearance of nagging and the reinforcement of the
> idea, without sermonizing, that mothers love children
> equally.

3. Low scores on achievement and diagnostic arithmetic tests
indicated that G did not know her multiplication and division
number facts so that she was put in the third division where
she would get needed drill and extra help. She resented being
placed with the "slow children" and was sullen and disinterested
during the drill period. When easy division examples were
assigned to her group, she completed only one example and
watched the first division as they did more difficult work at the
blackboard. When teacher suggested that G had better finish
her work if she wanted a good mark, she remarked: "I get a

headache when I do baby work. I wish I could go home; I feel sick." Her face was flushed and she blinked her eyes as she talked.

Analysis: Need for achievement and status by being part of superior group.

Action: G was allowed to remain in the first division for instruction periods but was encouraged to join the third division when number concepts were being developed or special drill periods were going on. When she chose to attempt the written work of the first division she was given the privilege of asking Janet or another child to point out her error when she got "stuck." If the difficulty was too great she was to move to a division receiving oral instruction, in order to avoid a building-up of tension and frustration. To maintain her own self-esteem, she had to complete two first division problems before she went home for the day or take them home for completion. This was to make her realize that work was essential to maintain a place in the first division.

Over a period of time several actions were initiated with the aid of her family and classmates:

a. Family bought an abacus for younger brother and G was encouraged to teach boy his number facts.

b. Family purchased and played games with G involving arithmetic. G was encouraged to bring these to school and play with other children at lunch, and on occasion to play them with the third division in order to "help teacher."

c. Father made G a "hundred board" as part of an English project which G explained to class, teaching herself more about number concepts than she taught the class.

d. Parents used board to help child with number concepts, kept graphs of progress. G used board to help Louise.

4. In an attempt to bolster G's ego and to provide frequent opportunities to talk with the child, teacher asked G if she would like to be her personal secretary, with duties of taking attendance, polishing desk once a day, and keeping books and papers straight. G's eyes brightened momentarily, but then she replied: "No thanks, you're always saying that my desk and floor are a mess, so you don't really think I do a good job. You're only giving me charity and I hate charity."

Analysis: Merit has to be earned if children are to accept it as a true gauge of worth. An unearned reward failed to build G's self-esteem; at the same time her own integrity was such that she rejected the offer.

Action: Since this particular job had previously been offered to only a favored few, the teacher decided to rotate the position, which had the advantage of providing all children an opportunity, including G as her turn occurred, without its appearing a special privilege.

5. G was upset and nervous as she confided to the teacher and several girls that she was afraid to go to a Campfire meeting after school because the leader did not like her and had threatened to put her out of the group if she did not behave. She explained she had to pay her dues if she wanted to go to camp in July. Teacher suggested that another child could pay G's dues. Janet said: "Come along with me—I know Mrs. L. doesn't like you but I'll try to keep you out of trouble."

G was absent the next day. Janet reported that the Campfire leader "really did pick on Gail" and that G got "awfully fresh" and was told to go home. Instead of leaving immediately, she upset the meeting by screaming: "I hate you and I don't want to belong to your old club. My mother will take me to our own camp."

Called G's mother and learned that G had returned from the meeting in such a disturbed state that she was unable to eat her supper, and had cried herself to sleep. Because she had a headache and was upset, mother had kept her home in bed for the day. Mother suggested she wanted to talk with teacher about her "problem child."

Analysis: G's need for belonging and acceptance makes her want to be in the group, but feeling rejected by the woman in charge she invites retaliation by her challenge. G attempted to save face by rejecting the group in return.

Action: Encouraged G and Janet to talk about incident without interruption as they "aired their gripes." Without indicating approval or disapproval, asked why Mrs. L. was leader; did she get a good salary? No, she didn't get paid, worked hard, and was nice to the girls who behaved. The two girls bragged about their naughtiness, agreed they hadn't cooperated, and finally decided they were mad because the rest of the girls were older and excluded them from their projects. Mrs. L. had suggested that a junior group should be started but at least six girls were needed to form a group.

Contact with Mrs. L., classroom talks by Janet and G, complete with uniforms, resulted in a new group being established, with the further provision G could demonstrate her contriteness for her behavior by improved action. Contact with Mrs. L. provided teacher opportunity to explain G's needs and suggest action for providing for them.

6. During an unusually high-spirited day, G prevailed upon her group to elect her chairman for a social-studies project. Two days later, G resigned as chairman and the group told her they didn't even want her in the group. At this point G was biting her lip to keep from crying. Fortunately, Janet, with rare insight, sensed the situation, and putting her arm around the frustrated child said: "We need you in our group. We're doing a play and you're the best reader in the room."

Later in the day G explained: "My sister Jean is a stinker, and the whole thing was her fault. I asked her to help me plan the work sheet so everyone in the group would have a part in the project and she told me to stop trying to act so grown-up, that I was only a baby and to stop bothering her because she had her own homework." When asked why she didn't call on her oldest sister, G said: "Jean's the smartest and has wonderful ideas but she hates me and I hate her too." Then she added: "I dreamed last night that Jean had a catastrophe and I was the heroine."

> *Analysis:* Again frustration of affectional, acceptance, and achievement needs, but yet certain gains are indicated. G is beginning to fight for status by persuading her peers to elect her, she is acting out the problems directly rather than withdrawing or developing psychosomatic symptoms.
>
> *Action:* Allowed G to describe her hostile feelings, which allowed her confusion to come to the surface without fear of censure, giving teacher a chance to share confidence and demonstrate concern. Because of evident need for identification with Jean, a plan for constructive cooperation was laid, the first phase a secret between G and the teacher. G was to offer to do the dishes for Jean for a month in return for help with homework (the secret lay in the fact G would earn a Campfire merit for doing the dishes). Second, the teacher talked with Jean (with G's consent) who responded favorably, and a needed lift was given to the girls' relationships.

7. G seemed to revert to her old apathy after the geography group episode. In one instance where G made no attempt to write answers to history questions, teacher, feeling that G was being stubborn and that patience and understanding were not producing results, stood over her insisting on her writing the answers. Although this took only five minutes, G's face became flushed, her mouth and nose twitched, and she trembled notice-

ably. Teacher called nurse who took G home. She did not return to school for a week.

Analysis: Disappointed by the child's reversion to earlier symptoms after notable progress, the teacher attempted to force the situation, only to end convinced that her "strong-arm" method was a mistake with a child whose emotional needs took precedence over her school achievement needs.

Action: Rather than risk a repetition of the two previous years when G had stayed out of school for several months, teacher worked out a plan with the mother whereby G would remain home for a day or two when fatigue, tension, or pending emotional distress indicated. The mother agreed that it might satisfy G to be her mother's "only-child" while the other children were away at school, and agreed to cancel other plans on such occasions to care for and spend time with the child. The plan seemed to work for G never took advantage of the arrangement, was anxious to return to school, and better able to cope with her problems. The mother's needs were satisfied by the implication that only she could meet the situation when a stalemate was reached; she was not made to feel that she was to blame for the problems.

8. During a dodge-ball game in the school yard, G threw the ball so wildly that the girls groaned and their opponents, the boys, shouted with delight. Startled and dismayed, G left the circle and ran to the corner of the yard, refusing to re-enter the game. Returning to the building, the teacher casually took the girl's hand, and as they walked along G said: "I should think you'd hate me for being such a pest. No wonder the kids don't like me."

Analysis: G's desire for approval and status led to a panic reaction in the face of an abrupt and unexpected failure. Nevertheless, she was able to take the teacher's hand and while walking with her admit that her behavior had been unwise.

Action: Teacher reassured G that she liked her whatever the performance had been, went on to relate an event at a childhood birthday party when she had left her own party to hide under a bed because her feelings were hurt and had refused to come out, spoiling the party for everyone. G laughed at the idea of the "teacher under the bed" but saw the point of the story, agreed not to tell the other children, but to remember it next time she was tempted to be a poor sport.

9. G's birthday: Following customary class procedure G wore a gold paper crown and was queen for a day. She conducted opening exercises, gave an excellent safety talk, heard the class sing *Happy Birthday,* and was allowed to do all errands. The principal, recognizing the crown, wished her a happy birthday and gave her a book of plays. G was relaxed, happy, and unusually pretty all day. Her school work, especially her penmanship, was greatly improved. At the end of the day she thanked the class and teacher for helping her to have "the most wonderful birthday in my whole life."

> *Analysis:* The children seemed to sense the special importance of the day to G and responded accordingly. For once, all needs appeared to be met.

10. G was much more confident and relaxed after the birthday episode, asked if one of the plays could be presented to show Principal she appreciated the gift. Although there was the usual argument, whispering, and giggling that attends such productions, the play was presented with G as heroine, a popular boy as hero, and supporting cast of ten. Interestingly enough, the play concerned a princess who had to be taught humility before she could find true contentment and happiness. The play was a success, the Principal congratulated the children, and G received commendation for both her coaching and acting. She was radiantly happy. Mother reported that although the child was excited she slept unusually well that night.

Summary

Although Gail had to step down from the role of princess to accept some of the hum-drum of school routine, with the inevitable reoccurrence of some of the old behavior, nevertheless, for the first time in four years she completed a full year with only a minimum of absences, her symptoms of psychosomatic illness had disappeared, her aggressiveness was under temporary control, and on her report card, all subjects showed honor grades except penmanship, sewing and art. Although her emotional needs had not been fully met, and little information was available on whether changes had occurred in the family relationships which gave rise to the problem, G was better equipped to meet frustration. Certainly her family had given serious and intelligent cooperation to a program which had been primarily executed in a school setting where the needs for esteem, acceptance, achievement, and to some degree affection, could be met.

REFERENCES FOR PART ONE

Carmichael, Leonard. *Manual of Child Psychology*. New York: John Wiley & Sons, Inc., 1946.

Gessell, Arnold. *The Child From Five to Ten*. New York: Harper & Row, Publishers, 1946.

Henry, N. B. (Ed.) *Mental Health in Modern Education 44th Yearbook, NSSE, Part II*. Chicago: University of Chicago Press, 1955.

Hountras, Peter T. *Mental Hygiene: A Text of Readings*. Columbus, Ohio: Charles E. Merrill Books, Inc., 1961.

Miller, Frank W. *Guidance Principles and Services*. Columbus, Ohio: Charles E. Merrill Books, Inc., 1961.

Redl, F., and Wattenberg, W. W. *Mental Hygiene in Teaching*. New York: Harcourt, Brace, & World, Inc., 1951.

Shaffer, L. F. and Shoben, E. J. *Psychology of Adjustment*. Boston: Houghton Mifflin Company, 1957.

Traxler, A. E. *Techniques of Guidance*. New York: Harper & Row, Publishers, 1957.

Willey, Roy De Verl. *Guidance in Elementary Education*. New York: Harper & Row, Publishers, 1960.

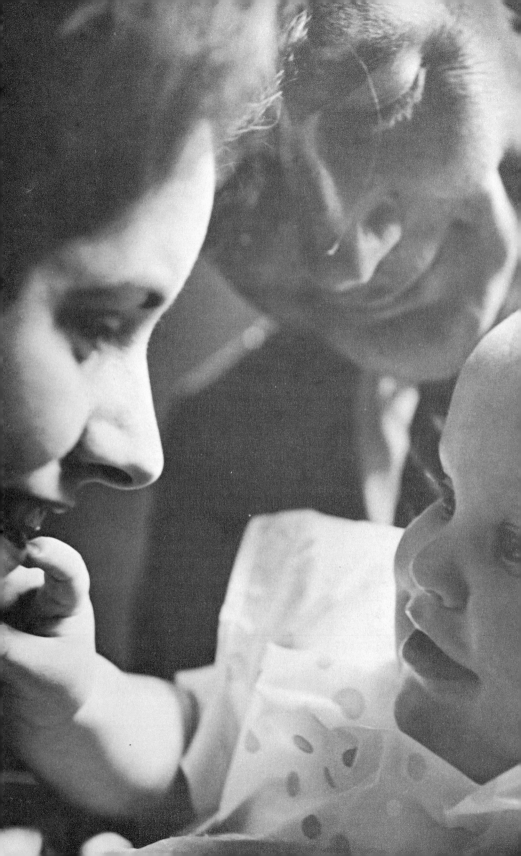

Part Two

FAMILY
RELATIONSHIPS

Chapter 5

OBTAINING INFORMATION ABOUT FAMILY RELATIONSHIPS

If children were raised by robots, we could describe the differences in their personalities and concentrate on seeking an understanding of these differences through study of the child. Fortunately for children, at least for most of them, the responsibility for child-care rests with parents, not robots. And parents vary considerably in the way they act in their role of parent. These variances provide the matrix in which children's personalities develop. Any given parent behaves toward a child in ways which are generally consistent from situation to situation (he may even be consistently inconsistent), yet this behavior distinguishes him from other parents. This consistent pattern of treatment provides the learning situations for the child from which his social and emotional habits form and ultimately expand into an adult personality and character.

We could ignore these differences in the home and work exclusively with the child as he is; in fact, with most children this is precisely what occurs. We present children with opportunities, demands, experiences, trusting they will be sufficiently adaptable to meet and take advantage of them for the benefit of their development. In part, this approach is possible because we choose to ignore many aspects of attitude and adjustment—trusting to time and event; in part, it is possible because most children, as a result of adequate parental relationships, have the capacity to devote their energies to growth and development. Yet even in the narrow range of demands involved in academic achievement, we encounter children experiencing difficulty in fulfilling their potential, and when we look at the broader spectrum of behavior involved in personality development and social adjustment, we find many children who appear half-crippled. It is with these children in particular that we must look to differences in parental actions if the school is to successfully fulfill its functions as a medium for promoting child growth.

THE SCHOOL'S ROLE

The emphasis here is on parent actions, not on parent personality or feelings or traits, and further, on patterns of action, not single, isolated episodes. The teacher's concern is with the child and his progress in development, and indirectly with the parent as it affects this progress. Parent behavior consists of words, gestures, facial expressions, and physical actions to which the child responds in terms of learned meanings. We are concerned with the relationship between these actions and the responses the child has developed to them. This has a twofold purpose, the first, one of focus and the second, one of limits. Our focus is on the child and how he came to be as he is, not on the parent personalities as such, or "goodness" of the home as judged by any set of moral standards. Knowledge of parent-child relationships, which contributes to such understanding of children, is relevant to the school's purpose. Yet, there are limits which the school personnel should set for themselves. The school as an institution has found itself delegated an ever increasing number of responsibilities—lunch programs, banking, juvenile delinquency prevention —without inquiry as to whether such duties are within its purpose. The mission of the school with respect to parents is not to remodel the home life of the child, nor to mediate family relationships, but to obtain that information which assists the school in fulfilling its primary task of education.

CONFLICTS BETWEEN
THE HOME AND THE SCHOOL

Much discussion can be heard of the beauties of home and school cooperation, but little of fundamental conflicts between the two which block the achievement of this happy millenium. Certain of these are relevant to an inquiry into the approach to the home for purposes of obtaining information; certain are more pertinent to the discussion of working with parents presented in Chapter 7, but consideration and appreciation of the conflicts latent in the difference between the roles of home and school should contribute to more harmonious relations.

The home is a refuge and a guide for the child, a place where he can relax and not feel guilty about his shortcomings because he knows he is accepted and loved as he is. Not that parents do not criticize and make demands on children, merely that most parents do not attach a price tag to their love; protection is a function of the home. Parents protect, defend, find excuses for their children, and in doing so, they help children gain a feeling that they are worth something, and, gaining that, acquire a capacity to face the evaluation of strangers whose judgment is not tempered with affection.

The school is the place of law and order, in the sense that the law is impersonal and detached, applying to all alike in the social world of regulations and demands which have to be faced. The school represents a world of objective evaluation. The teacher represents society and its impartial demands for compliance. To the teacher, then, the protectiveness of parents is a nuisance, for it often stands in the way of what she sees is needed in the development of the child. It irritates her that parents apparently avoid seeing the child as he is (by the teacher's scale of values) and make excuses for the child. Yet, a successful approach to parents demands an appreciation of the basis of the parents' subjectivity.

Incorporated in this subjectivity is the recognition that the child is a reflection of the parent and that "objective evaluation" of the performance of the child is automatically an evaluation of the parent. This realization penetrates the parents' personal feelings. Any approach which suggests to the parent that his assistance or help is needed, that he may have ideas or solutions to given situations, is less likely to stimulate anger at impending criticism and protectiveness for the child than an approach which says: your child is difficult, or your child is a failure.

A further complication occurs which is less a conflict between home and school than a complication of social relationships. In growing up, each of us acquires a picture of the status system in our society and our position in it. We are aware of persons in the community—the "Important People"—to whom we should be deferential, the persons with whom we can be familiar, and those whom we disregard. One cannot help feeling timorous in approach to families of higher social status, for it implies in part that one is "stepping out of one's position." Increasing this difficulty is the fact that in many communities, one finds many teachers who were born and raised in that community, often having taught nowhere else. Such teachers cannot help feeling uncertain, for the social relationships of the community often run counter to the professional relationship. Many of the adults cannot help seeing the teacher as "the Jones girl," or "little Susie Casey," rather than as a professionally trained teacher. Furthermore, all the adults were once children, once attended school, and in those years developed attitudes towards and about teachers. Entering a school building, however new, with its desks and drawings, written alphabets around the wall, maps and books, all the paraphernalia so familiar and so reminiscent, recaptures not only the memory, but the mood of childhood, and we approach the teacher, however young or old she may be, in part the child of yore as well as the adult of today. Not all of us remember school as a place of joy; many of our memories are tinged with anger and resentment. Stop and think for a moment of your grade-school teachers and you find yourself thinking of those who were cruel as well as those who were stimulating. It is not strange, then, that these mingled feelings of teacher and parent introduce many subtle currents into their meeting in a parent-teacher conference or home visits.

Still another difficulty to be faced by teachers is that their training in education does not include any work in adult education. They are trained to work with children, not adults. Interviewing and counseling techniques are rarely included in their training programs, yet these are the essential tools needed in working with parents—interviewing as a means of obtaining information, counseling as a means of giving and interpreting information, and of modifying attitudes. To obtain skill in interviewing and counseling requires extensive training which is beyond the scope of this book. However, a number of suggestions can be presented which will enable a teacher to operate more skillfully in her contacts with parents.

POINTS OF CONTACT

The most frequent point of contact between teacher and parent is an indirect one—the child. His behavior in school reflects influences of the home; his attitudes at home reflect the school. Into each situation the child carries the satisfactions and disappointments he is encountering in the other. However, the image presented is blurred and indistinct, and only direct contact sharpens it. It should be mentioned, in passing, that the blurred image parents receive is partially due to the fact that children have an indistinct memory of the events of the school day. A few moments at the end of the day or a half hour at the end of the week to raise the question with the class: Now what have we done or learned today; or what have we accomplished this week?, prompts recollection and evaluation and reinforces the retention of learning and a sense of accomplishment, as well as offering unexpected dividends in communication to parents about the school program.

Direct contacts between teachers and parents occur at school functions such as Parent-Teacher Association meetings, open house, National Education Week, through parent-teacher conferences arising out of reporting procedures, and during occasional visits by the teacher to the home or the parent to the school. Where schools use questionnaires to obtain information about the child, this represents another point of contact. School functions seldom provide the privacy needed for discussion of child progress and often fail to provide opportunity for even minimal social contact. Too many Parent-Teacher Association meetings find the teachers huddled together in a row of seats, a segregated minority out of contact with the remainder of the group, painfully doing their duty. More imaginative arrangements provide panel discussions involving parents and teachers, home-room discussion groups, demonstrations by teachers of various aspects of the school program, discussion groups on child development, all of which permit teachers and parents to take on form and shape in each other's perceptions. These social functions should serve the vital need for the acquaintance essential to opening avenues of interchange between parents and teachers so that the occasion which demands deeper understanding is not blocked.

The significant points of contact are the parent-teacher conferences initiated for discussion of the child's progress in school and his evolving needs, irrespective of whether these conferences occur in the school or home setting. Essentially, the purpose of such a meeting is to get and give information, in a phrase—to conduct an interview.

Three questions arise regarding such interviews: where to have them, when to have them, and how to conduct them.

There are advantages and disadvantages which can be listed for the conference held at either school or home:

CONFERENCE AT SCHOOL

Advantages	*Disadvantages*
Time saved because no travel needed.	Inconvenient or difficult for some parents to come to school.
No transportation expense.	Easier for parents to pretend.
Teacher derives "security" from being on her own "home grounds."	No observation of circumstances of home possible.
Privacy assured.	Atmosphere makes for greater restraint and more formality.
Setting makes direction and control of interview easier.	Parent can avoid conference by canceling or failing to keep appointment.
Arranged to suit convenience of teacher.	

HOME VISIT

Advantages	*Disadvantages*
Parent interviewed and observed in "natural habitat."	Greater time consumption.
Opportunity for observation of organization and functioning of home.	Frequent interruptions.
Opportunity for observation of parent-child relationship.	Teacher may feel like and appear to be an intruder.
Arranged to suit convenience of parent.	
Contributes to greater rapport with child.	

Most of the items listed are self-explanatory, but a few words of explanation are in order. Conferences at the school take much less of the teacher's time and yet can be as productive as home visits, in most instances, if the teacher is skilled in interviewing. Unfortunately, most teachers know very little about interviewing. For the majority of children, however, the school conference is sufficiently rewarding. It has the further advantage to the teacher, if she feels at all unsure of herself, of providing the reassurance that comes from being on one's own territory.

THE HOME VISIT

The most important advantage to the home visit is the chance it provides to observe the welfare and organizational level of the home and derive some sense of the kinds and amount of stimulation a child living in that environment receives. Second, it permits the teacher to watch the child-parent relationship in operation. It is not unusual during a home visit that the occasion arises for the parent to limit or control the child's behavior. His approach to such natural situations can be quite revealing. Another advantage that accrues from a home visit, at least with children in elementary school, is greater rapport. The teacher's visit symbolizes to the child that he is important to the teacher and that she is concerned about him.

The time chosen for a meeting of parent and teacher is a discretionary matter for which certain general guide lines can be established. Certainly, as a minimum, a conference is in order whenever a child manifests problems or difficulties which are not relieved by the actions of school personnel. This scheme has two major disadvantages: first, it is an action based on desperation in which the school is in effect saying that it has exhausted its repertory and is appealing for help, and second, it places the parent in a position in which he is likely to act defensively. In spite of these disadvantages, this minimal approach need not fail, provided the school has previously established satisfactory relations with parents at other points and times of contact.

Certainly, the inability of the child to achieve in keeping with his capacity, or his inability to establish adequate personal and social relationships, suggests the need for contact with the home, as the following observations by a teacher show:

> I started to take a personal interest in Lynn (a cute, jet-black-haired, five foot, hundred pound girl of 13 years in the fifth grade) when I gave the children a questionnaire to answer at the beginning of the year. All the children except Lynn found it easy to understand and answer. But for Lynn, it was difficult to read. Observing Lynn, I noticed that she was very quiet and didn't enter the activities of the other children. During free play she sits quietly by herself, at lunch she eats alone. Her only chum appears to be an older girl whom she meets when school is out. In team sports, Lynn shows a marked hesitancy to participate, and is usually last chosen. A check of her cumulative record, in addition to showing marked reading retardation, reveals consistently good health. When I urge her to join she seems eager, yet a little afraid. When she does participate in the activity she has good coordination and handles the ball with skill. She is a fast runner and quick on her feet. One day in class. when the children were discussing parents, Lynn said that she didn't have a father and that she only lived with her mother. I

recalled the records listed a stepfather. When I found a time to ask Lynn about her stepfather, she replied that he was not her father, and that her father had died when she was a little girl. She is not neat about her clothes and doesn't care about her appearance, having told me, "Why should I care what I look like, nobody looks at me anyway."

Concerned about her isolation and her shyness, I thought it advisable to visit her home. I found Lynn's family lived on the top story of a dirty and unkempt four-story cold-water apartment house in a poor neighborhood. The mother works part time to supplement the income the stepfather receives as a candy-machine operator. The family consists of the mother and Lynn, the stepfather and his three children, two girls, 8 and 5, and a baby boy of two years. Ann, 8, attends the same school but doesn't accompany Lynn to school, saying, "You have to stick by your friends and not your sister." Lynn retains the name of her father.

The visit was very revealing. In the course of it, the mother told me that Lynn's father hadn't worked much when he was alive and consequently spent much time with the girl. She always spoke about her father and wanted to know about him. This so angered the stepfather on one occasion, that he said Lynn's father was not to be mentioned in the house again. The mother related that work and care of the house and children left her little time for Lynn, who wouldn't spend any time with the stepfather as did the other three children. She described an occasion on which Lynn became very upset because her stepfather brought lollypops home to the children but none for Lynn, telling her that she was too old for lollypops.

When the stepfather came home, I inquired if he knew how Lynn was doing in school. He said that he signed her report cards but that he did not have time to see if she did her work, that the only time he saw her was at dinner and when they went to church. He added, "You know my children take up a lot of my time." The mother interjected that Lynn was his child also and this started an argument which ended with the stepfather accusing Lynn of always starting a fight with her brothers and sisters.

Lynn criticizes the stepfather for giving the other children more food than she gets, is very antagonistic towards Ann, but expresses affection for the five-year-old sister, taking her to and from school, making things in school for her. The mother reports that she has caught Lynn hitting the children many times, even the baby brother. On one occasion she ripped a dress that an aunt had given Ann for Easter.

Certainly, the home visit in this instance reveals basic problems in Lynn's development, and sufficiently to justify special assistance if available. Lacking such assistance, and recognizing the fact that the family situation may not be amenable to change, the teacher, nevertheless, can act much more wisely in attempting to provide Lynn with the opportunity for developing healthy relationships with the younger children with whom she attends class.

It is better to have had the first conference with a parent before problems develop, because it establishes the contact and rapport with parents necessary for exploration of greater difficulties. Two procedures commonly used for establishing and maintaining contact with parents are meetings scheduled at the time of the child's entry or transfer to the school, and second, at one of the report periods during the year. Many schools use a parent conference as a basis for beginning the cumulative record. The least time-consuming procedure for children entering the first grade is to schedule a pre-school round-up during late spring, to which prospective first-graders and parents are invited—the children to spend a part of the day in school getting acclimated, the parents for a short interview with a school official to obtain basic family data for the cumulative record. A more effective arrangement is that of providing released time for teachers during the first weeks of school for parent conferences. By releasing children from school at noon time on two afternoons per week during the first two weeks of school and scheduling interviews with parents at twenty-minute intervals, the entire group can be accommodated.

A similar arrangement can be extended through all grades. A preferable arrangement in the higher grades is to wait until approximately mid-year and use a parent-conference scheduled on a similar arrangement as a basis for reporting child progress in lieu of the report card for that period. There are a number of advantages easily seen in such arrangements: the freer exchange of information, better maintained cumulative records, a more matter-of-fact approach to problems of child development, and avoidance of any feeling of being singled out on the part of the parent or child. Parents view the conference, not as a sign that the child is in trouble, but as a chance to share views of the child's progress. When the only contact between teacher and parent occurs over problems, the parent develops an attitude that no news is good news and that a visit from the teacher means trouble.

The following guide for home visits was devised to assist teachers in the initial stages of conferring with and interviewing parents. By discussing the main items listed and then continuing with a consideration of some of the important elements of interviewing, procedures for obtaining information from parents can be clarified. The guide serves a conference at school as well as a home visit.

GUIDE FOR HOME VISITS

Purpose:
1. To obtain information to increase effectiveness in teaching: skills—socialization—self-realization
2. To impart information about child development and progress

Preparation:
1. Appointment or casual call
2. Review available information regarding child
3. Consider kinds of information you need

Openings:
1. Immediate event, e.g., illness
2. Specific purpose of interview—get acquainted, particular problem, etc.
3. Specific interest or accomplishment of child

Your opening should establish rapport, relieve anxiety, give direction to the ensuing conversation.

Information-getting:

Questions:
1. How do you feel Bill is doing in school?
2. What plans do you and your husband have for Bill?
3. How do you arrange for Bill's friends?
4. What gives you the most pleasure about your child?
5. What gives you the most worry?
6. Is there anything you would like the school to do for you, or Bill?
7. OPTIONAL—health, diet
   worst faults or habits
   best qualities
   attitudes about school
   et cetera

Observe:
1. Physical setting—welfare level, variety of experience, organization
2. Activity level of home—active, alert, tense, quick—slow, procrastinate, easy going.
3. Discord in the home (conflict—harmony) in general—conflict, quarrels, complaining—tolerant, friendly

4. Sociability of family (expansive–reclusive)–active socially, mixers, seeking new contacts–passive contacts, recluse
5. Acceptance of child: devotion-rejection
6. Protectiveness re: child–acceleration, pushy–babying, protecting
7. Dominance of child–order, suggestion, submit, autocratic, democratic, laissez faire

Information-giving:

1. Child performance relative to ability
2. Child performance relative to group
3. Special needs of child
4. School and class program: goals and procedures

Closing:

1. Have you any suggestions in particular that you would care to make regarding Bill's program at school?
2. Express appreciation of time and thought given by parent
3. Invitation to visit

Responsibility of Teacher:

1. Recording–will the record-keeping protect confidential information?
2. Discussing–teacher is professionally responsible to maintain and protect confidential information
3. Use–welfare of child

THE PARENT CONFERENCE

An interview with a parent differs from a conversation in that it has a purpose or an objective. In the main, the teacher's objectives will serve one of three purposes of the school: to further the youngster's progress in developing the skills to be acquired from the school's educational program, his social development and adjustment, or his personality development and adjustment—in short the major objectives of the curriculum and guidance program. The interview will be devoted to getting the information needed to help the teacher achieve these objectives and also, to provide the parent with information on the pupil's progress in school.

Three steps are needed in preparing for the interview: first, to make an appointment with the parent by letter, note or telephone; second, to organize present knowledge about the child; and third, to identify the questions needing answers. The child should know that the meeting has been scheduled. It is most important that the teacher take the time to review what she knows about the child, both from her own direct experience and that contained in the cumulative record. In the day-to-day task of teaching thirty children, the facts one knows about one child are inevitably intermixed with all the events of all the days with all the children. One has to consciously stop and review and organize information about a particular child in order to develop a meaningful, well-integrated picture. The importance of this step cannot be over-emphasized. The study of parent reactions to conferences with teachers shows that their satisfaction and approval of the conference varies directly with what they learn about their child's progress. When the teacher's information is vague and uncertain, parents tend to be irritated or view the session as wasted time. The third step of formulating the questions which need answering also depends upon a thorough review of what is known.

The opening of the meeting should establish a friendly relationship based on mutual interest and identify the purpose of the meeting. It is important to be at ease and cordial, and the time honored procedure of being complimentary about the child helps establish a friendly contact. Praise, to be effective, has to be real. A glibly offered compliment is recognized for what it is. A better approach is to describe or discuss a specific interest or accomplishment of the child, preferably one not connected with the school. Many children exist for teachers only as pupils, not as children with personal interests and accomplishments. To be able to discuss specific activities of the child that are not connected with school shows that the child exists as a person for you, not merely as a pupil.

Two short excerpts from a case study concerning a third-grade boy, Roger (mentioned previously in Chapter 3, pages 53 to 55), retarded a year in reading in spite of his superior intelligence, concerned with orderliness, and quite detached from his class, can be offered as illustrations:

> While Roger was getting ready to go home, we talked about the home and who lived there. I found there was Nana who kept house and took care of Grandfather who is quite old, the two boys, Roger and his brother, Hal, and Mother and Father. The parents both work, leaving before the children go to school, and returning home in time for dinner at night. Nana, it seems, not mother, makes all the decisions.

Teacher: Roger, I'd like to come up to your house and meet your family. Do you think I could go home with you some afternoon?

Roger: Well, I don't know.

T: Would you like me to visit you?

R: Yes I would, but my mother won't be home.

T: I could come some evening.

R: I would be in bed. I go to bed at seven o'clock

T: Is Saturday afternoon possible?

R: Well, we clean house and Nana has to cook on Saturday. My mother goes to parties in the afternoon.

T: Would mother be willing to stay home one afternoon so I could come and call?

R: Well, I don't know.

T: Will you see if you can fix it up for me?

R: Well, my father has to have his nap. We children have to play outdoors, and not make too much noise.

T: You talk it over with Nana and Mother and see if you can arrange it.

R: I'll see what I can arrange.

Unknowingly, the teacher had done more than acquaint Roger with her plans to visit. She had given him a task which he considered near the limit of his capacity, for he was being asked to disrupt what he saw as well-ordered routines, firmly established to satisfy adult needs. The teacher recognized that it didn't sound promising. She might have chosen to end the discussion with Roger differently, retaining the initiative by saying she would telephone, but she preferred the method she had adopted because it made the child a participant and contributed to his feeling important.

Two weeks elapsed before the teacher received a call from the mother arranging to visit the school on a Monday afternoon, the last day of her vacation. When she came into the room, the mother was all the same color, gray. She took off her coat and she was still all gray, no relief from it, even in a pin. Her voice was colorless, her smile, sad. Part of the interview follows:

T: Hello, Mrs. R. It is so nice of you to give up a part of your afternoon to visit me.

M: Well, it is the only afternoon that I can come, you see I work, and this is the last day of my vacation.

T: I do appreciate your coming, and now I have

some good things to tell you. (Cumulative records had revealed, although he had superior intelligence, his academic achievement had lagged. He had repeated the first grade, and by the third grade still revealed a deficit of one year in achievement. The teacher assumed that the family, of comfortable, upper-middle status, was disappointed and sensitive about Roger's progress.)

M: Not really, I've never heard any before.

T: I'm glad I'm the bearer of good news. (The mother relaxed a bit and a slight flush came to her cheeks.)

M: This is the first year Roger has really liked school.

T: That makes me happy, for I have had a feeling as the days go on he seems to enjoy himself more.

M: Yes, he wants to read and write at home and that is new. I just haven't time to help him and I don't know how either.

T: If you want to help him, I will be glad to show you how, as best I can.

M: I'll do what I can. (Teacher got a book and showed mother how to begin. It lasted about two weeks, the teacher subsequently learned.)

The teacher correctly surmised the parent's feelings. Her opening anticipated and circumvented them. Within a short time, the two were discussing the boy's progress as collaborators. The teacher was in position to discuss more basic questions affecting the boy.

The opening phase of an interview is of critical importance. When the meeting has been requested by parent or pupil, the initial direction is usually provided by them. When the teacher has called the conference, or when it has been scheduled as part of the school program, the initiative rests with the teacher. Consider possible reactions to the topics and questions to be raised. Try to anticipate points of sensitivity or defensiveness. Scan the cumulative record for information which will provide clues to existing attitudes. Such consideration permits one to avoid areas of hypersensitivity or to approach them in such a manner or at a time when a responsive attitude is ensured. A premature introduction of a topic invites a negative response which is likely to continue for the duration of the interview and preclude its success.

In situations where some hostility on the part of the parents can be anticipated, teachers can utilize an illness of the child to good advantage to establish initial contact. Whatever reasons a parent may have for feeling hostile toward school authorities, it is difficult to exercise such feelings in the face of a friendly and concerned inquiry about the well being of the child.

In the guide for home visits, the section under information-getting lists several questions that can be asked and several points that can be used for observation. In the main, it is better to choose your questions to suit the occasion, to let the parents talk, following their sequences, expressing a desire to learn about the many interesting things that happened as a child was growing, using occasional questions to help clarify or open new areas of information—the parent's hopes and concerns, techniques used in managing the child, personal relationships in the family, the family way of life, the impact of specific events of birth, death, job loss, and illness. As one gains more experiences with interviewing, specific questions of the type presented in the guide will be unnecessary. In getting started, such questions can help because they eliminate the uncertainty arising from wondering what one should say or ask. More important, the questions are open-ended in that they encourage an extended answer rather than a yes or no reply.

The questions listed are chosen for specific purposes. "How do you feel Bill is doing in school?" is an exploratory question intended to identify parent attitudes toward the school and the child's achievement. Often, the parents will turn the question around and ask you to tell them, opening the discussion, but when they are concerned or angered by events they have an inducement to express it. The question on plans taps the parent's ambitions for the child, if any, and permits the teacher to gauge the possibility of their fulfillment in relation to her knowledge of the youngster.

If parents are to fulfill their role, they must see childhood friendship and group activities as important. The third question, regarding how parents arrange for such activities, inquires into the value parents attach to such activities. The questions treating the items which please and worry the parents attempt to tap the affectional relationships existing between parents and child. To show the value of such questions, the answers of the parents of three first grade boys to two of these questions during a home visit by the teacher reflect specific differences. (Q4 is the answer to the question concerning pleasure; Q5 concerning worry.) As brief as the answers are, they reflect sharp differences in the feelings and concerns of the parents.

The first time Michael came to school (two weeks after school started) his mother brought him into the room and kissed him goodbye. Michael said goodbye, walked over to me and said, "Are you going to show me how to read and write now?"

Responses of mother to questions during home visit

Q4?   Every night before I go to work, my husband and I sit on this couch and listen to Michael in the next room playing by himself. All his toys and desk are in there. What fun he has on the old couch. I'd like to get a new one but my husband says Michael would miss the old one. What an imagination the boy has. He puts a rope around the pillow and it is a horse. He takes the part of the horse, galloping and all the other noises of a horse. Then he's the sheriff, talking and acting like one; then a cowboy; first one character and then another.

Q5?   I worry about him when he's outside playing, but he's too big to keep in the yard. There is so much traffic in the neighborhood, Michael isn't allowed out after supper.

✿   ✿   ✿

Ronald, too, had been late to enter school. His mother had him by the hand and dragged him into the room. He stood near her and would not take off his hat or coat. For weeks he wouldn't take his hat or coat off until after recess.

Responses of mother to questions

Q4?   Because he is so good to his sister.

Q5?   Doesn't keep his clothes clean. I don't let him wear his good clothes to school because he won't come in after school to change. I'm so busy looking after my mother, that I can't go out after him.

✿   ✿   ✿

According to the cumulative record, Donald spent most of his time in kindergarten fighting. While being corrected, he'd sulk or run off. Sometimes, rather than go to school, he'd run off, although at school, he seemed generally happy.

Stepmother's and father's responses to questions

Q4?   (Stepmother)   Because he thinks so much of me. I have had him for only a year. He tries to help me with the work. When I light a cigarette, he always gets me an ash tray. I was at the doctor's when you called before. I was in the hospital this time.   (Father)   Donald sure does everything he can for my wife. His own mother had him but did not take care of him or really want him. He is really happy here.

Q5?   (Stepmother)   Because he is beginning to stutter when you speak to him. He is copying the girl downstairs.

He's taking a nap now. (Father) Yes, the stuttering is a
bad habit he's got to stop. (Calling to the boy) Come on
out, son. (Donald entered and walked over to his stepmother with a smile.)

At any point in the series of questions, the interviewer should feel
free to follow up worthwhile leads that develop and not feel compelled to undeviatingly ask a planned series of questions. Teachers
are so accustomed to asking questions during recitation in school
that this style of questioning creeps into an interview, and, instead
of open-ended questions, the teacher finds herself asking questions
which encourage short answers or yes-and-no replies. Particularly
during the first interviews, the teacher should monitor herself and
ask herself what portion of the time she used in talking. If it exceeds
half, she is dominating the conversation.

It was pointed out earlier that an advantage gained from home
visits is the opportunity for observation. Many facets of the home
will present themselves for observation; several have been selected
here for primary attention and deserve elaboration.

1. *Physical setting.* The amount and kind of stimulation a child
   receives in his home and neighborhood is a significant factor in
   his development. The physical setting should be viewed in these
   terms, not in terms of economic well-being. A home may be
   sumptuously carpeted with oriental rugs and decorated with
   expensive works of art, yet be as sterile for a child as an impoverished tenement flat. Is the home adult-centered, and the
   child handled expediently, ignored, neglected or unstimulated,
   or is the home child-centered, wherein he receives attention,
   stimulation, suggestion, and organized action? Homes will vary
   in degree between the two extremes presented here, and in each
   of the subsequent items, yet the contrasting points provide the
   poles for scaling judgment.
2. *Activity level—how active is the family.* Many youngsters find
   themselves functioning within a tightly drawn schedule of
   meals, lessons, recreational activities, etc. Others have few demands to meet and are engaged in few activities.
3. *Discord in home.* Does the home impress you as harmonious,
   organized, pleasant to live in, or confused, discordant, and unpleasant? What are the routines of the household? Are they
   rigidly or erratically adhered to? The difficulties of many youngsters arise from their being unorganized and confused, rather
   than maladjusted. The patterns of family life and the emotional

tenor of the family are so inconsistent that they fail to develop a feeling that life has a certain stability and continuity. Without extraordinary effort, the school can serve a constructive role through the degree of organization that it can introduce into children's lives.

4. *Sociability of family*. Is the family isolated, detached from social activity, characterized by an emphasis on privacy and individuality, or is it sociable, friendly, hospitable, with an emphasis on cooperation and group activity?

5. *Acceptance-rejection of child*. Is the attitude and behavior expressed toward the child approving, encouraging, affectionate, or critical, punitive, or blaming?

6. *Protectiveness of home*. Is the child over-babied or overtrained, by having things done for him that he is able to do himself, e.g., eating, feeding, or is his development pushed by excessive teaching, training, lessons, etc., and treatment as if he were older? The alternate to these two forms would be where the parents make no effort to accelerate the child's growth, encourage him to develop at his own pace in activities appropriate to his age level.

7. *Dominance of child*. What degree of freedom does the child have? Is it so complete that he is free to do and choose as he desires with little or no restriction, perhaps even to be able to order adults, or is he restrained within strict bounds and arbitrary control, having to seek adult permission in all situations?[1]

The interview can be closed quite directly when the time arrives. If the interviews are occurring on a set schedule as they might be at the school, the closing can often be anticipated in the opening remarks by a statement such as this, "As you can see, I'm meeting with each of the parents to discuss their child's progress," which serves not only to establish the purpose of the interview, but to inform that the interview is one of a series. If, by the end of the time allotted, it is evident that further discussion is needed, arrange a second interview by a statement to the effect, "We need time to discuss this more fully," or "I would like to continue our discussion but I don't want to keep Mrs. X (the next person) waiting. Could we set another time for a meeting?" When the meeting is not one of a series, a direct closing statement can be interjected, "I'm pleased to have had this

---

[1]For further information on observation of variables of parent behavior, see H. Champney, "The Variables of Parent Behavior," *J. Abn. Soc. Psychol.*, 1941, 36, 525-542, and H. Champney, "The Measurement of Parent Behavior," *Child Development*, 1941, 12, 131-166.

chance to discuss Jim's progress," or "Is there anything else we should discuss?" An indirect closing is to ask the parent if there is anything he would like to have the school do for the child, or if he has any suggestions to make regarding the child's progress. Such a statement signals that the teacher has completed his reasons for the interview, but it has the added advantage of informing the parent and maintaining the atmosphere that parent and teacher share the responsibility for the child's progress, and that the school exists in part to aid parents in accomplishing their goals for their children. More often than not, the parent will make no particular suggestion, leaving the interview obviously at an end, with the moment at hand for expressions of appreciation and farewell.

Before getting into more detailed discussion of techniques of interviewing, it is necessary to repeat that the teacher has the responsibility of respecting and protecting confidential information received during the course of any interview.

TECHNIQUES OF INTERVIEWING

If you have ever stood knee-deep in the ocean surf, you have an impression of the dynamics of an interview. There are times when the ocean is almost still, the waves moving into the shore with barely a crest showing the movement of time; when the tide is running, the force of the water as it pushes into the beach, or the undercurrent as the ebbing water cuts the sand from underfoot, is keenly felt; and when a strong wind adds its force to the tide, the impact of the water as it hammers the shore is overpowering. Interviews range from the comparatively static and calm public opinion poll to the intense, at times overpowering, clinical interview. Calm or intense, interviews are as dynamic as the ocean, with a constant interplay occurring between and within the participants as their attitudes, perceptions, and feelings affect the course of the interview and determine its outcome.

An interview is not just a series of questions and given answers, but a personal interaction between two persons in which their motives and perceptions influence the sequence of responses. We take for granted that a parent will talk to a teacher when she calls. More than courtesy brings a parent from his home to the school, and this, more-than-courtesy, involves the motives possessed by the parent. These may be thought of as existing at two levels: those deeper and more central motives inherent in the parent-child relationship, and the peripheral motives pertaining to the interview request itself. Ignoring the more complex pattern of motives involved in the parent-child relationship for the moment and turning to the secondary but nonetheless important motives inherent in the interview itself, one finds the parent ready to enter into communication with the teacher because it represents a means to an end he considers desirable, a means to bring about some change or action he desires, or to maintain a situation he approves. The parent sees the teacher as a person exercising an important influence in the child's life, a person whose good will he wishes to maintain in order that his child may receive maximum benefits. The second aspect of motivation inherent in the interview is the intrinsic satisfaction derived from the interview itself, and also from the personal relationship which evolves with the teacher. The term personal relationship is not intended to connote anything on the nature of friendship or like, but rather the satisfaction derived from discussing topics of interest with a person who is receptive and understanding. Without the initial impetus which brings the parent to the conference, and the satisfaction with the parent-teacher relationship as it develops, such conferences would be impossible.

BARRIERS TO COMMUNICATION

The teacher's first task as an interviewer is to convey the impression that he has a genuine interest in the parent and an acceptance of him as a person; second, that he is a person to whom the parent may express facts and feelings without fear of being offending or of being condemned; and third, that he is not attempting to coerce the parent. Often, the images we hold of ourselves tempt us to say too easily that we fulfill these requirements. A brief consideration of some of the barriers inherent in the teacher's position which prevent him from appearing in the foregoing role, points up the difficulties. The teacher is a person in authority, representing an official government agency, who has control of the child. A parent will be cautious that neither his words or actions lead to harm to the child. For instance, a parent may be most reluctant to acknowledge that his spouse is receiving psychiatric care, or for another example, that a child was born out of wedlock, for fear that the teacher would condemn or blame the child for these events. Such fears have a basis in reality. For example, enough teachers have made enough children resent being intelligent by their criticisms, e.g., (to a homogeneous group of superior students) "I certainly expected more from this class; after all, you are supposed to be smart."

Another less formidable barrier is sometimes the youth and, often, the inexperience of the teacher. A parent may be uncertain of the maturity of a young teacher and hesitate to relate experiences, or he may question, with some basis in fact, whether or not the teacher's life has provided a broad enough range of experience to permit him to understand the parent's experiences. Not a few teachers live rather restricted lives, both before and after becoming teachers. Third, as a result of espousing idealistic standards, teachers are tempted to judge unfavorably lives of parents and children which depart from not only the ideal, but from conventional norms. For example, a fifth grade teacher was surprised in going through a series of themes written on the topic, "My Father," to read the favorable, obviously sincere report of one boy about the satisfactions he obtained from the many recreational activities which he shared with his father. She was surprised because the boy's father was an ex-convict. The teacher had made the a priori judgment that he couldn't be a "good man." As a matter of fact, when she received the papers, she had looked first for this boy's — suggestive perhaps of unusual curiosity? Later contact with the father and greater knowledge of the home showed that whatever the social transgressions that had resulted in his imprisonment, he was more than adequate as a father. These are a few of the barriers which exist in the parent-teacher interview. Still more may be introduced unknowingly by the teacher.

Bias in Communication

Although the interview is a fluid event and consequently plagued by inaccuracy as far as consistency of measurement is concerned, nevertheless, trained interviewers can and should obtain comparable results from an interview. Training and experience are required to minimize or overcome bias which the interviewer himself introduces, bias which may be quite subtle. Bias can be introduced by facial expressions, by manner or gesture, and by the phrasing of questions. It may exist, not because of any overt action by the teacher, but merely because of her appearance or status. Consider this question: Don't you think parents are too lenient with children nowadays? It reveals the point of view of the person asking the question and provides a clue as to the expected or approved answer. The respondent senses the bias and gauges his answer accordingly. Minor characteristics or expressions reveal attitudes as much as words. Pursed lips, a frown, or a shake of the head can reveal the interviewer's reaction as much as a spoken opinion. Parents from working class families may be restrained by social-economic differences, considering, and rightly so, that the teacher supports the middle-class points of view and doesn't speak the language or understand a working-man's viewpoint.

Another position in which teachers trap themselves is prejudging the parents on the basis of the child's behavior instead of waiting with open mind for the interview with the parent. Such prejudgments reveal themselves in questions or comments which the teacher puts to the parents, e.g., "I don't know where I got the idea that Billy was your youngest (pampered) child." Finally, it is not unusual to find a parent criticizing the school or previous teachers, or describing some difficulty or conflict in which they find themselves involved. In the face of criticism, the teacher feels compelled to defend the school; in the face of a problem, he is tempted to give advice and propose possible solutions. Both violate the basic requirement of a successful interview: the first, because it places the teacher in a position of conflict with the parent, and the second, because it implies that the teacher believes the parent is unable to arrive at his own solutions and is dependent upon superior advice. The teacher's ego-involvement in his work and that of the school leads him to step out of a neutral role in the face of criticism or to attempt to explain to the parent "the facts" of the situation. Explanations of fact start with the assumption that man's behavior is entirely rational. Our actions seldom follow simple logic. We are seldom aware of all our reasons. Our emotional responses are as significant as our intellectual in determining behavior, and to complicate matters, the meaning of behavior is as often symbolic as direct. The approach needed is not a rational explanation of fact but a question as to what it is that makes the person feel as he does.

The physical setting functions to assist or impede an interview. Arising to walk toward the classroom door to greet the parent establishes a more receptive mood than remaining seated or standing at the desk. A handshake closes the initial gap between persons more than merely asking the person to be seated. Asking the parent if he has a moment or two to view some of the work of the children in the class and walking around the room explaining some of it provides a shared activity as a warm-up to the interview. Seating the parent across the desk, rather than beside the desk, interposes a barrier between parent and teacher which may go unnoticed but which is not unaffecting. There may be occasions when such a seating has its merits with a parent who dominates the interview or crowds the teacher with demands, but in this instance, it is a recognized protective device. Some persons need such protection; for instance, the executive who always remained standing while insisting his subordinate be seated because this was the only way he could offset his feelings of inferiority derived from his five-foot stature, or another manager who kept his swivel chair elevated to maximum height while seating his visitors or subordinates in lower chairs.

It should be apparent to your visitor that you think the interview important. Desks stacked with papers, or books, or other paraphernalia of teaching, suggest the interview is an event to be crowded into the busy day. To continue working at a task for a few moments while asking the parent to wait suggests there are other activities more important. Obviously, there are moments in which the task at hand has to be brought to a point where it can be set aside, but to engage in busy work to impress one's visitor is foolishness. The child's cumulative record is better kept in a drawer, where it can be referred to if events require. The folder on the desk arouses curiosity and occasionally a feeling of resentment at supposed secret information. Note-taking is inadvisable, for the presence of pencil and paper and the recording of comments inhibit the response of the speaker. One's memory is sufficiently accurate to retain the essence and most details of an interview. What one writes during an interview and what one ignores provide hints to the respondent which can lead to biasing. The act of writing distracts the interviewer's attention from the flow of events in the interview and leads to missed cues which often are important.

Gestures can be used to facilitate the interview. The interviewer can manage his body position to help establish and maintain a conductive atmosphere. Sitting back in the chair, relaxing, helps the parent feel at ease; leaning forward toward the parent suggests greater interest or support at a time when he may find it difficult to express himself. Pushing the chair back from the desk creates greater space, reducing intensity. These and other movements are possible, and are suggested, not by way of creating a list of automatic gestures intended to stereotype communication as once was done in elocution lessons, but to emphasize the dynamic nature of the interview and the interplay of all facets of the situation. The interviewer, on the judgment growing out of experience, has to gauge which action is appropriate to the particular situation. A parent, rather than deriving a sense of support when the teacher leans forward, may feel crowded and inhibited; hence, one's actions and words have to be based on one's perception at the moment.

It was pointed out earlier that an interview has an objective or purpose. Seldom will that purpose merely be getting acquainted. Parent-teacher meetings and open-houses can satisfy that need. Usually, there will be particular information that is needed by the teacher in order to better execute her task of teaching, or there will be a problem needing the mutual efforts of parent and teacher for solution. This purpose dictates the course of action of the teacher and the roles of the participants. The teacher's role is to manage her actions to overcome the existing barriers in order that maximum communication occurs and to direct the interview by attitude and question to the achievement of the objectives established. To this end, the teacher encourages and discourages, by gesture, expression, question, and comment—replies that are appropriate and those that are incomplete or irrelevant. The teacher may indicate by a pause that she is waiting to hear more, or by direct question or comment such as: We seem to have wandered off the topic; or by direct question: Could you enlarge on that? She may reflect the feelings expressed in the words which is, in a way, feedback to accelerate or continue the flow of thought. A frown can indicate a question of dissatisfaction with the response.

These procedures are dependent on the fact that a social interaction such as an interview is supported by certain established norms of behavior to which the participants are expected to conform. One is expected to behave courteously, to respond to questions, to speak truthfully, and to defer to persons in positions of authority. In a sense, these are some of the ground rules operating in any social interaction which facilitate it. Yet, like any set of rules for any game, they are effective only as long as one desires to engage in the game. Not to imply that an interview is a game, but to draw a parallel that these norms of behavior are dependent upon the parent's being motivated toward somewhat similar goals as the teacher. Thus, he must be deriving intrinsic satisfaction from the interview itself, that is, from the interpersonal relationship that develops with the teacher, and second, he must feel that the purposes of the interview are consistent with his deeper or primary motives.

To this point, the discussion has concentrated on the external aspects of the interview as they affect the rapport and understanding or lack of it developed during the interaction between parent and teacher; only hinting at the internal frame of reference of each of the participants which are as significant to the outcome of the interview as are the management techniques utilized by the teacher for steering the progress of the interview.

We can return now to the interview with Roger's mother recorded earlier and analyze the situation for both sets of components. The teacher initiated the conference because she felt Roger needed help. As she first met the boy at the beginning of the year, she knew he lived with mother, father, younger brother, mother's father, and housekeeper. Both parents worked, providing a comfortable living. From the cumulative record, she learned he had superior intelligence, yet was retarded a year in reading achievement in spite of having repeated first grade. Anecdotes related his fearfulness at new tasks, his preference for girls as playmates rather than boys, and his reluctance to play group games. She watched him creep into the classroom the first morning, immaculately groomed, gulp when greeted, drop his lunch box, and embarrassedly take his seat.

As Miss Johnson, the teacher, took pains to speak to him frequently during ensuing days and ask him to do little things such as getting a pencil for her or taking a paper to her desk, she saw him respond like a faithful puppy pleased at being able to do anything asked. She watched him dally over his work so he could stay after school to finish it. Asked if his mother wouldn't worry, the boy had responded that he had made arrangements so he could stay. As she learned more about his achievement level and placed him with a smaller group of like ability, she saw him begin to gain confidence as he found he could keep up with the other children. As he gained confidence, slowly, he continued to remain after school for extra activity. He struggled with his reading, and it wasn't until the teacher introduced the unit on Indians that she saw a spark of enthusiasm which she steered into some recreational reading in books she selected at his reading level. Yet with these gains, the patterns of behavior reported by preceding teachers continued.

By now, Miss Johnson felt herself sufficiently well acquainted that she could benefit from a conference with the mother, both from the additional insight she could obtain with further information and from the influence she might be able to exert with respect to Roger's progress. She asked the boy if she might arrange a visit with the mother.

Consider the demands placed on the mother by this request as they are diagrammed in Figure 1. Two sets of factors exist, pulling in opposite directions, one facilitating an acceptance of the request, the other impeding.

Miss Johnson has no way of knowing the specific factors existing in the situation. The delay in response suggests possible hesitation and mixed feelings about the request. She assumes that the difficulty

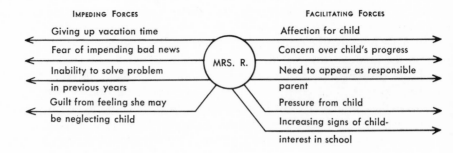

| IMPEDING FORCES | | FACILITATING FORCES |

Figure 1. Conflicting forces affecting response to request for conference in case of Roger.

Roger has experienced in learning is threatening or disappointing. She knows from the child's appearance that he is well-cared for; hence, she assumes some regard is shown for the child, but she also suspects that the home is strongly adult-centered. Her position as Roger's teacher provides her with the right to information pertinent, even if personal, to her professional function with the child. The mother's acceptance of the interview and her visit to the school has a tentative quality in which she reserves the right to reserve information or withdraw, depending upon the course of events. The outcomes of the conference clearly depend upon the degree to which the developing relations between the mother and Miss Johnson affect and overcome the existing barriers, and satisfy Mrs. R's basic motives which have not yet been identified.

Miss Johnson's appreciation of the mother's "giving up part of (her) afternoon" elicits the response that she not only is giving up her afternoon but part of her vacation. The teacher's reply is not to inform the mother, directly or by implication, that she should be willing to give up some time for the child, but to the effect that it will be worthwhile, especially when she hears the "good news." Within a few moments, the diagram of external forces in play has shifted to that appearing in Figure 2.

If anything, the giving up of vacation time, instead of being an impeding force, may have been converted to an asset. It and the fear of impending bad news have been countered; to some extent her concern about the child's progress has been eased, and the pressure to satisfy the child's desire for the mother to visit no longer exists, for the mother can safely say to the child that she has visited the teacher, even if she chooses to leave immediately. Another force has been

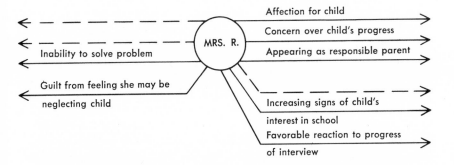

Figure 2. Structure of forces after opening of interview with mother of Roger.

introduced in its stead—the beginnings of rapport with the teacher. Within the course of a few more comments, this is to be strengthened, and the possibility of a solution to the problem introduced. Miss Johnson has established the impression of warmth and sincere interest and of having the ability to accept and use constructively whatever information she receives. The rate at which the teacher is given access to information and the depth of the feelings to be revealed, depend not only upon her skill in interviewing, but even more upon the personality of the parent and her perception of the teacher.

Earlier, it was pointed out that interviews range from the public opinion poll to the clinical interview, because the public opinion poll is seen as impersonal and detached, lacking in any relationship between interviewer and respondent. A question as to what one's income is, or does one favor fluoridation, is likely to receive either a distorted answer or a rejection, because the question is viewed as improper in the circumstances. In a clinical interview, much more intimate topics are discussed matter-of-factly because the respondent sees such discussion as within the context of the interview or therapeutic conference and within the scope of the relationship developed between therapist and client. The therapist is perceived as a person aligned with the client in assisting the latter in obtaining a solution to difficulties confronting him. The public opinion pollster has no personal relationship, no continuity of contact; in fact, he may be viewed as a possible thief or government agent in disguise.

The teacher finds herself in an intermediate position. She is partially aligned in common purpose with the parent in working for the welfare of the child, but at the same time she has responsibilities to a social institution which prevents her being accorded the same relationship and confidence that a therapist receives.

In this discussion, the roles of teachers and therapists are viewed in the abstract. Some therapists with some clients find themselves facing similar difficulties. Certainly, a prison psychiatrist has similar problems. In addition, it has been shown that the teacher is in a position of power with respect to the child; parents may fear this power. Many parents will refuse to call the attention of school administrators to unhealthy, sometimes, cruel, behavior by teachers for fear of recrimination against the child. The progress of the relationship between Miss Johnson and Mrs. R. depends in part upon the nature of the parent-teacher relationship as well as on the personality and attitudinal factors involved.

The interior of the circle representing Mrs. R. has been blank in the discussion of the play of forces affecting the interview. But as the teacher comes to know the mother, she discovers as one would expect, a highly complicated personality, partially observable, mostly hidden, even to Mrs. R. She discovers a woman deprived of her mother role by a dominant housekeeper, an autocratic father who continues to treat her as a minor child (see Chapter 7 for further case history information), and a dependent husband unable to establish his own authority. She works partially in support of the family, partially to escape the home. She identifies with Roger, seeing him as being like her in his wishes and fears. She has adopted a pattern of submission and withdrawal as a reconciliation to the conflicting pulls. Although she wants to be the mother, she cannot fully be the mother, and, to maintain her self-esteem, she turns to other avenues. We see a complex of motives—escape from painful situations and dependence—conflicting with her needs for self-esteem and nurturing of her children.

At the same time, she has developed a set of attitudes resulting from her experience, identifications, and education. She stresses cleanliness and order, believes that children should be submissive and non-demanding, thinks it undesirable for sons to play with children of another religious faith. These are only part of the entire complex of personality characteristics, attitudes, and habit patterns which will affect her perceptions of Miss Johnson and the subsequent course of their relationship. Miss Johnson as well possesses personality traits and attitudes which enter into the interplay taking place during the interview. She may resent a mother, who "blessed with children," fails to provide as a mother should; instead, preferring to work and "neglecting" the children. Or, she may sympathize with Mrs. R. and her having to work, recalling her own mother who had to work to support a family. Instead of being sympathetic to Roger, she may dislike boys in general, or boys who aren't ruggedly masculine, and these attitudes reveal themselves, affecting the progress of the relationship.

The interview, then, develops as a dynamic relationship, depending basically upon the motivation and attitudes of the participants. These factors determine what the participants bring to the session, what they seek, and how they will perceive and respond to each other. In addition, the relationship depends upon external pressures and social norms. Such pressures and norms can determine whether or not the interview is likely to happen and if it happens what is needed to continue it. The course of progress that develops can be steered by the teacher, who, cognizant of her own role and possessing skill and experience in interviewing, can direct the interview toward achievable goals. Rapport may be established and a sound relationship developed as in the first diagram in Figure 3; or contact may be established but then disrupted by conflict of interest or antagonism (Figure 3B). In some cases, the teacher's own lack of insight and training will hinder contact; however, in other cases,

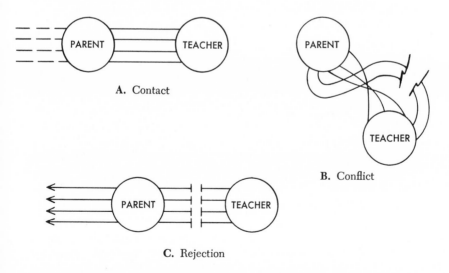

Figure 3.   Possible outcomes of interview contacts between
parent and teacher.

the parents' attitudes may be such that even the experienced and sensitive teacher will be unable to develop a satisfactory relationship.

SUMMARY

Given an understanding of the dynamics of the interview, certain specific suggestions can be made by way of summary.

1. *Prepare for the interview*—by reviewing cumulative record, organizing what you know about child and family, determining the objectives of the interview, making appointment, providing time and privacy for the interview, avoiding previous judgment and personal prejudice on your part. Adopt an attitude of being of service to parent and child by asking yourself how you can be of help to them.

2. *Conduct the interview.* Be at ease, allow time for parent to get acquainted, begin with pleasant topics, then introduce the subject of the interview starting at a point of real interest to the parent. Let him talk; *listen;* help him supplement his statements by asking him to enlarge or tell you more on a given topic. Introduce questions which are not likely to obtain refusal or cause antagonism before moving onto points where tension will be great. Focus on what parents do instead of what they think they are doing.

    Don't assume the role of the teacher of the parent. Give him equal status. Ask direct, non-ambiguous, non-technical, preferably open-ended questions early in the interview, specific later in the interview. Avoid questions which imply the answer. Be sensitive to the feelings and concerns lying behind the parents' statements and help them to voice these feelings. Distinguish between giving a suggestion and giving advice. The latter position implies the advice-giver is competent, the recipient incompetent.

3. *Direct the interview.* Tactfully keep on the subject of the interview, pacing the interview to keep within time limits and within the readiness of the parent to deal with the questions. Close the interview when the objectives have been obtained or a stalemate is reached. The interval between the ostensible end of discussion and actual departure can often reveal important information. Tension has relaxed, and the parent may express opinions or attitudes which he had previously been reluctant to voice. Often, the interviewer can obtain an answer to a question just prior to actual departure which would have been rejected earlier in the interview.

Chapter 6

PATTERNS OF
PARENT RELATIONSHIPS

Evaluating and interpreting the information derived from home visits and parent interviews, is one of the most difficult tasks that can be undertaken. The complexity of the relationships involved in the different aspects of parent behavior, coupled with the limitations in scientific and clinical knowledge, hamper interpretation and introduce a large probability of error. Any interpretation made with respect to the effects of parental treatment of children should be tentative. It should be based on the reaction of the child to the treatment rather than the reverse of assuming that a given behavior pattern automatically produces certain personality patterns in the child. The fact that different children respond differently to the same treatment necessitates caution in interpreting the interaction of parents and children. One child will respond aggressively to an autocratic parent, another submissively. While certain generalizations may be drawn, they are helpful as guides, not dictums.

In looking for a framework within which analysis and interpretation of parent behavior is possible, the lack is immediately seen. We have many large scale studies of groups of children which provide normative data of growth and development, but few such studies of families and particularly the patterns of behavior in children associated with given modes of parent behavior. Consideration must be given to three influences operating in relation to parents and their treatment of children: (1) cultural and social influences; (2) age trends in children; and (3) parent action patterns. In any single parent-child relationship, we are primarily concerned with the dynamics of the particular pattern of the parents, but the effects of the society, as well as factors of the child's development, should not be overlooked.

The sociological studies of social classes show that variations in value systems and action patterns occur at the different social strata, and that these differences have their effect on children's behavior. Several designations have been assigned to the different classes: upper class, middle class, and lower class, or white collar and blue collar. The occupational and income groups included in "middle class" and "white collar" are not identical, but for general purposes they are seen comprised of managerial, professional and semiprofessional, technical, sales, and clerical. The "lower class" or "blue collar" class is composed of semi-skilled and unskilled workers. Given residential areas and the schools therein can usually be designated as predominately populated by members of a given social class. Many exceptions, where schools served a mixture of the various status groups, occur, and there are few schools that are entirely composed of children from a given social class. But the predominance of a given group is typical, particularly in the elementary school where the smaller size of the school tends to restrict its student population to a smaller geographic area.

The findings with regard to child-care show that social classes differ in discipline, attitudes and values, and parent relationships. Middle class parents are more likely to reason, to praise, to demonstrate affection to their children, to impose fewer restrictions and be less severe in punishment. Lower class mothers will use more physical punishment, deprivation of privileges, ridicule, be more restrictive and more severe in punishment. Children in middle class families are permitted to express more aggression towards their parents, are encouraged to develop self-reliance and initiative. The children are more likely to be achievement conscious, as far as school-work is concerned, and to use verbal aggression. Children from lower class families find their expressions of aggression against parents discouraged and punished, modesty as far as physical exposure stressed, and thrift emphasized as desirable. They find more disagreement between their parents and certainly are exposed to different attitudes with respect to political, economic, and social issues. Their aggression is more likely to be physical than verbal in form. Even within ethnic groups, differences occur which reflect the social status of the family. Nevertheless, differences also occur between ethnic groups, e.g., religious attitudes, which need more systematic study as far as their effects on children are concerned.

AGE TRENDS OF CHILDREN

The child is not a passive recipient of the culture and his parents' ministration, but an active respondent who contributes in his own right to the chain of events which shape his personality. The more we study children, the more aware we become of the dynamic potential which children possess for interacting with the influences which bear on their lives. The longitudinal studies of children bring to light behavior of children towards their parents which is characteristic of given ages.

Very briefly, for these phases will be discussed more fully later, the six-year-old shows his dependence on his parents through his efforts to get close to them, to have their approval of his undertakings, and to obtain their praise. Simultaneously, he reveals the early stages of what should become increasing independence by his resistance to punishment and increased negativism to direct commands from parents.

The seven-year-old expands on these differences increasing his identification with his family through efforts at imitating and copying them, speaking with pride of accomplishments of his parents, seeking their praise, at the same time showing increased resistance by challenging their authority by doing a job his way rather than theirs and by not hearing them when they call.

The conflict between these two courses reaches something of a peak at eight when they fluctuate between excessive independence or open resistance, particularly towards the mother. The child's relationships with his father appear smoother and less intense than with his mother whom he strives hard to please, knowing the while that he is turning away from his childhood dependence to newer spheres of authority and standards of behavior.

The nine-year-old has achieved greater detachment from his parents; in part the result of increased participation and acceptance in a group of his peers, in part because of his own developing personal standards of behavior. He shows this in increased critical evaluation of events in his own right, reflecting his own standards and evaluating his own behavior. He still is sensitive to parental criticism and seeks closer relationship with his father in activity rather than affection. A growing loyalty to his friends is evident.

During the tenth year, the child reaches a balance, culminating the developments of the early school years and anticipating the coming adolescent years. He has less conflict with his parents, greater independence, is more impersonal and detached, being able to accept the use and need of rules and regulations and referees.

The balanced ten-year-old gives way to an ambivalent eleven-year-old who, though he desires the support of his parents, is more objective about them as persons, sensing their limitations. His increasing identification with group values, self-assertiveness, restiveness, and variations in mood, symbolize the prelude of adolescence.

PARENT ACTION PATTERNS

The actions of parents have to be viewed in the context of the society and the segment to which they belong and in relation to sequence of events characteristic of children's development. As we gather data from interviews and observations of parents, they seemingly defy classification, so many are the aspects of behavior in which they can differ. Even when a classification system is adopted, parents do not neatly fall into one or another of the categories. A parent may fluctuate in his behavior, now rejecting, now affectionate; he may change in time, treating each successive child differently, restricting the older, indulging the younger; he may treat children of opposite sex in differing manners. Parents together present various combinations. A mother may become increasingly protective of her children as a by-product of the father's rejection. In opposite vein, the identification of a child with a given parent may stimulate hostile or resentful feelings in the other parent. But in spite of all these limitations, it is helpful to explore the relationship between some aspects of parent treatment and child behavior.

Two of the more important aspects of parent behavior are considered simultaneously in the following pages: Acceptance-Rejection and Dominance-Submission.

Parents can be classified into one of the four categories resulting from a combination of the degree of affection and the degree of dominance exhibited: dominating behavior that is either accepting or rejecting of the child, and submissive behavior that is either accepting or rejecting.

A comparison of the characteristic behavior of children found in association with a given pattern of parent actions, helps in the identification of possible causative factors and of apparent needs with respect to change. The adult pattern is listed in one column, the associated child pattern in juxtaposition. It should be clear that rarely will a child exhibit all of the symptoms listed, and that the less clearly defined the parent behavior is, the more variable will be the symptoms of the child compared to those listed.

DOMINANT-ACCEPTANT PARENTS

Another term for this parent might be the loving autocrat, the parent who always knows what is best for his child, caring for him with affection and love, though not always unselfishly. The dominance takes two noticeable forms: in one, the relationship is characterized by high demand for superior performance by the child; in the other, the child is smothered in love, scarcely able to escape the arms of his devoted parent. The children of high-demand parents work effectively in class as long as the task is well-defined but falter in situations requiring initiative and self-direction. The hurdles they are expected to jump are so high and inflexible that fear of failure is constantly threatening. Adequate performance, normally satisfying to a person, is insufficient for them, for it doesn't attain the high standard they have come to expect. A grade of "B" can signal failure for it is less than the goal that has been established for them. Knowing the expectations of the adult in authority at least gives them the assurance of knowing they are on the right path. Suggestions that these children decide on their own goals are threatening and increase their anxieties; such suggestions increase the possibility of their not fulfilling adult expectations and standards. These youngsters, like all other children, recognize that as long as an adult-established grading system exists, it will ultimately have to be reckoned with; however, unlike many children, they lack the assurance of their own or a peer-centered scale of values as a counterbalance.

A few excerpts from a home visit by Jane's fourth-grade teacher illustrate this type of relationship and the consequent behavior of the child:

> The mother had invited me to tea ... Jane was the hostess ... had very nice manners, but very little to say ... everything

Dominant-Acceptant Parents

Behavior of Parents to Child

1. Overcautious and Overdevoted Parents.
   A. Encourage extreme dependence
   B. Supervise Social Contacts
      1. Don't allow child to play games or sports with others
      2. Bring and fetch child to and from school
      3. Choose child's amusements and companions
   C. Overdress and over-care for child
   D. Make child's decisions
   E. Try to meet all child's needs

2. Overambitious Parents
   A. Expect too much
      1. Demand more than child is capable of
      2. Expect superiority
   B. Develop child to full capacity
      1. Stifle inefficient tendencies
      2. Encourage abilities

Child's Reactions to Parents

1. Overcautious and Overdevoted Parents
   A. Dependence on parents— strong attachment
   B. Poor social relations— shyness
   C. Neurotic fears
   D. Immaturity
   E. No initiative—submissive
   F. Egocentric—selfish
   G. Sense of inferiority
      or
   H. Extreme independence
   I. Antagonism to parents
   J. Desire to escape

2. Overambitious Parents
   A. Works to capacity, tries hard, works zealously and well
   B. Ambitious
   C. Develops false values
   D. Fear of failure—anxiety
   E. Inhibited initiative— submissive
   F. Feeling of inferiority

in the girl's room was in perfect order. The mother assured me the room always looked like that.

I asked the mother how she felt about Jane's work. She replied that Jane was a terrible worrier but that she was capable of doing her arithmetic, and if necessary the mother would help her. I (teacher) explained I hadn't noticed any difficulty.

As to future plans, the mother said, "We hope she'll do well . . . I want her to go to college."

Asked what gave her the most pleasure and what worried her the most, the mother replied, "Jane is the neatest child, haven't you noticed? Never leaves things around . . . doesn't want any commotion. In fact, she usually gives in to her younger sister . . . I like to have her stay near the house so I know where she is. Jane is fussy eater . . . When she has good days in school,

she wants to be a fourth grade teacher like you, but when she
has work to finish, she wants to be like you, but teach the third
grade because things are easier ... I've wanted Jane to be a
Brownie, so I became a Brownie leader. If I'm at the meeting,
I know she'll go every week."

In school, Jane was very uncertain about her school work, repeatedly asking if she had to do assigned work, coming to the teacher
after each problem or two to see if it was correct, being very pleased
to find it was. She always asked permission to do many things which
the children knew to be their privilege, such as moving their desk
to a better location if they could not see the blackboard. If Jane took
school papers home which showed errors, her mother would often
call, asking for books or work to help Jane at home.

The second behavior pattern occuring in the dominant-acceptant
category is the child encased in parent affection, whose behavior is
most easily designated as "immature." At the risk of using a term too
often misused through failure to distinguish between physical, emotional, and social maturity, these children, though physically mature,
act more infantile, both emotionally and socially, than their con-
temporaries. Harold, as seen by a student observer, exhibits many of
the symptoms of children in this category:

> I could see no particular physical weakness to account for
> Harold's mother describing him as "sickly" and her insistence on
> daily vitamin pills. Although he was not muscular or athletic look-
> ing, he was better than average height and weight, tending to be
> somewhat fat, and short-winded when he ran.
> I asked Harold if he wanted to go to the park down the street
> and watch the baseball game the boys were playing. His mother
> came on to the porch and said that he could go if I watched
> him very carefully. When the boys saw us coming they asked
> me to referee. I agreed if Harold could get into the game. Harold,
> however, said, "My mommie told me never to play with these
> boys." I assured him that it would be all right with his mother
> as long as I was there. Whenever he came to bat someone
> would always shout, "The sissy is up, he's a sure out." ... When
> his shoestring came untied he asked me to tie it for him, telling
> me that his mother always tied it for him. ... Later, he told
> me his mother had fixed it so that he had friends by inviting
> three boys to the house for a party, telling them she wanted
> them to play with Harold because they were the best boys in
> the neighborhood, and that if they continued to play with Harold,
> she would give them parties.
> At supper the mother seated Harold next to her, kept repeat-

ing what a wonderful boy her precious little darling was because he ate everything his mommy gave him. At the end of the meal, she hugged him and gave him a kiss. . . . When bedtime came, the mother got up to take Harold to bed. In reply to the older brother's disapproval she said, "I wouldn't feel good to think that I didn't help him get ready for bed!" reminding the older brother that she used to do the same for him. During a telephone conversation which Harold overheard, his mother mentioned that someone had died. Harold ran up to his mother saying he hoped she would never die. The mother reassured him that she wouldn't, but Harold stayed next to his mother clutching her hand, and unwilling to let go of her.

The attention these parents give their children is such that it denies the children the kind and amount of experience needed for normal social-emotional development. The kindergarten and first grade teachers see the excessively dependent child during the first days of school. The transition from home to school, with its full-fledged entrance into the outside world, if a difficult step for many children who demonstrate this during their first few days. It is a major step for parents as well to give up their child to the school. The dependent child persists in his unhappiness and the parent encourages and supports him by insisting on bringing the child to school, coming to meet him, and sometimes asking to remain in the room "to help the child get used to it." It is true that the task is more difficult for these children because of their lack of opportunity to venture and explore outside of the home during their pre-school years.

Occasionally a child, either with the support of brothers, sisters, and one of the parents, or basically more vigorous, develops sufficient ego strength to break through the envelopment, but not unscathed, for the very strength of the drive needed to escape finds continuing expression in extreme independence and antagonism toward authority.

DOMINANT-REJECTANT PARENTS

This classification includes those parents who openly reject the child, coupling the rejection with open aggression against the child, usually in the form of punishment, and those parents who reject the child but disguise the rejection in a protective veneer which allows them to masquerade as dutiful parents. Several anecdotes describing Rod illustrate the first of the situations:

Rod is a well developed child of nearly eight years in the third grade, average in height and weight. He tries to look neat in school but seemingly gets little help from home for his stockings usually have holes in the heels, the buttons are all off his clothes and he's held together with safety pins, which bothers him greatly. I sewed some buttons on his shirt and he cuddled up and said to me, "I wish you were my mother, you love me, dontcha?"

Rod was born while his "daddy" was overseas in military services. When the father returned, he separated from the mother for two years, disowned the boy, and accused another man of being Rod's father.

Last year, I noticed Rod on the playground, always in a fight, disliked by the children for his aggressive acts, "never to blame" for what happened. He was restless, would never play at anything very long, would almost always be in a fight before recess ended, often being beaten up by bigger boys.

Rod reports making his own bed and lunch every day. He cringes everytime anyone is near him. I enrolled him in the Boy's Club, but he soon lost his admittance card because of too many fights.

Whenever he is corrected in school, Rod is always "in the right" and will argue incessantly for his position. He hates it in school as it is all noisy. During reading, he comes to my desk, sits beside me, cuddling up closely, looking at the book. He has little persistence, but after school, when all is quiet, he does his arithmetic and does it well, and finishes any other work that is incomplete.

During Christmas preparation, he told me he had asked Santa Claus for a new toothbrush. I asked him why he hadn't asked for toys. He replied, "My mother won't let me have any." He has me save his papers, telling me that mother throws them away.

Every morning, when I get off the bus at 7:45, Rod meets me and comes in and dusts and talks. He hates to have 8:15 come, when the other children come in. I've been allowing him to do his arithmetic lesson before school and he seems to concentrate better on his work.

At Valentine's Day, he was delighted to fix the room. He received ten valentines. I made sure that all children received some. Rod was thrilled. He took the valentines home, but his mother destroyed them.

Bedlam broke loose today in school. Rod was loud, boisterous, repeatedly interrupting, sometimes swearing under his breath. He hit different children, tripped some, broke a balloon a small child had. He was in trouble with the janitor, the patrol boys, everyone. The principal shook Rod up. Next noon Rod was in another fight.

I visited the home, to listen to the mother blame all her faults on the child, saying that Rod was to blame for all the trouble around the house, saying "I can't stand the damned brat." Discussing his work in school, the mother doubted that he was getting any good marks by himself, saying that he probably cheated to get them.

The dynamics in this parent-child relationship are clear. The mother rejects the child because she sees his presence as the cause of the conflict in the home. Rod becomes the scapegoat for her guilt feelings, for she is unable to acknowledge her direct responsibility for his birth, and he becomes the target for the hostility of her husband who sees the boy as a constant reminder of his wife's infidelity. Deprived of the affection of his parents, Rod lives a precarious emotional existence, finding scant substitution in the kindness of his teacher.

DOMINANT—REJECTANT PARENTS

Behavior of Parents to Child

1. Rejective
   A. Neglect
   B. Lack of affection
   C. Lack of attention
   D. Corporal punishment
2. Overprotective—
   Prevention of the child's doing anything to reveal the unsoundness of parental rationalization.
   A. Refusal of independent behavior
   B. Child not allowed to "grow up"
   C. Parental control of the purse strings
   D. Overcritical and overambitious
   E. Insistence on adherence to social customs and group standards
   F. Insistence on moral taboos
   G. Indifference to effect such insistence has on child's emotional and mental adjustment to life

Child's Reactions to Parents

1. Aggressive sexual behavior
2. Stealing
3. Lying
4. Shy, retiring, socially inadequate
5. Lack of emotional response
6. Lack of effort—and concentration
7. Attention-getting
8. Truancy from school and home
9. Radicalism

incurring the open aggression of his classmates and the sanctioned aggression of the adult punishments when he expresses his aggression resulting from his emotional deprivation.

Somewhat less apparent to the observer is the behavior of the parent whose rejection is disguised in a protective cloak, by means of which the parent creates excuses for criticizing or punishing the child permitting the expression of the rejection in socially approved behavior, i.e., the punishment of a "bad" child.

Sidney is nine, the second of seven children of a deliveryman, average in height, frail of build, disliking school (parochial) intensely, enthusiastic about sports, particularly baseball.

Each brother nearest him in age does well in school; Sidney receives poor grades, although he does appear to try and complete his nightly assignments with fair regularity. When his nightly lessons are finished, he joins his brothers in reciting to his mother, usually waiting until his brothers are finished, before approaching the mother. Failure to answer results in scolding. Sidney then becomes upset and nervous and unable to finish. Often called stupid, Sidney explains his poor grades by "I'm stupid." The father attended college for three years but was unable to complete because of finances, vows that all his children will go to college. The mother, who failed to complete high school, and has little knowledge of academic life and difficulties beyond junior high school, shares the view and is convinced that her children will do as she wishes, even if they must be forced.

Sidney has difficulty in pronunciation of certain sounds. His mother has been sitting him in the living room, in view of his brothers, and insisting on his speaking correctly and clearly. On a particular occasion, the boy was being drilled in the pronunciation of "S" which he pronounced incorrectly, forcing air from the back of his mouth on either side of his tongue:

(M-mother, F-father, B-brother, S-Sidney)

M: Now you sit here, Sidney, and pay attention to your father and me. Never mind the others.

F: Sit up straight and pay attention.

M: Now say the word SPECIAL.

S: (slowly) SPECIAL (said faultily)

M: No, that isn't right! Watch my mouth, say it like I do. S-S-S-P-E-C-I-A-L!

S: (slowly) SPECIAL (Sidney pronounces initial S correctly, but mispronounces the middle C.)

F: Pretty good, Sidney. Now say it all the same way.

S: SPECIAL (The pronunciation is incorrect.)

M: No, no, no! Can't you see the way I do it? Do like you're whistling through your teeth. (Mother makes S sound.)

S: (Imitates her correctly)

M: Now say SPECIAL the same way.

S: (hesitates a few seconds)

F: Say it! What are you waiting for?

S: SPECIAL (mispronounced)

M: What's the matter with you? Can't you even say a thing like that? It's simple. What's the matter with you? (Shaking the child's arm)

B: Gee, he can't even say s-s-s-s-s- right!

F: You be quiet. He can say it! He can say anything you can say. He's just stubborn.

M: You'll have people laughing at you, if you don't talk right. Now say the word SAINT.

S: (again hesitating) SAINT (faultily)

M: Oh go to bed, you dope! You'll say it right if I have to make you! Go to bed!

S: (leaves room, visibly upset and near tears)

Sidney finds himself subjected to the taunts of his brothers and playmates who will jeer at him saying: "Hey, Sidney, say S-S-S-TINK!" His response is to withdraw and isolate himself. He is continually admonished in school for his poor diction regarding assigned spelling words, so much so that when the teacher reprimands him, it becomes the class fun period with the children taking delight in his embarrassed efforts.

One occasion when Sidney mispronounced (although he spelled the word correctly) soldier, the teacher repeatedly attempted to get him to say the word correctly. Each failure brought forth greater mirth from his classmates. Finally, the teacher reprimanded the class saying: "Now children, that isn't nice. Sidney can't help it if he isn't as smart as you. That's the way God made him."

Sidney went home, hoping he would find peace, to tell his mother that the reason he had difficulty was because he wasn't as smart as the other pupils, thereby hoping to escape the adult demands. An ensuing visit to the school by the mother, resulted in the suggestion that Sidney be transferred to the public schools. The suggestion was acted on favorably.

Sidney's parents adopt a near hostile attitude toward the boy, creating situations which are managed to a conclusion of guaranteed failure, which justifies parent criticism of the child for his "wilful stubbornness." Parents attempt to motivate him by "shaming him into it," scoldings, threats, and punishment. His escape is to avoid and retreat from the painful situations, to avoid speaking, to condemn himself.

Phil's reaction pattern to rejection is hyperactivity and destructiveness. Phil differs from Sidney in that he is an only child in his first year of school. Observational reports indicate the parent-child relationship:

> (Child seated at dinner table with parents; observer in adjacent room.) Phil beat his spoon on table in a persistent staccato, exclaiming he didn't want hamburger for supper. Mother replied he must eat his hamburger as it was good for him. Phil replies: "I will not eat it. I will not eat it," continuing to beat the spoon on table. Mother eventually relents, warms some macaroni.

✿   ✿   ✿

> Phil playing with blocks on living room floor, father seated in arm-chair reading evening newspaper, mother in kitchen washing dishes. Phil built tower of blocks, systematically destroying them with rain of marbles. Then he turned to playing toy automobiles. Picked up one and threw it at observer (no apparent reason), who caught it and hid it behind back. Phil commenced to scream for toy. Refused, he began to jump up and down until given toy, when he ran into other room, returning a moment later without it, striking me on arm and saying, "I don't like you; you're mean to me; everyone's mean to me."

✿   ✿   ✿

> While both parents were watching television, Phil left his seat, began to rummage for toys in box, making considerable noise. Father yelled at him, "Cut out all that racket you little brat or I'll break every bone in your body." The boy continued to make noise. The father got up from his chair and hit the child. Phil jumped up and down screaming he hated his father, continuing until his mother promised him a nickel to be a "good boy."

✿   ✿   ✿

> Phil's mother presented him a model airplane as a gift. He picked it up, looked at it, threw it on the floor saying, "I don't like airplanes; why didn't you buy me a boat instead?" The mother told him to be a good boy and play with the airplane and she'd buy him a boat next time.

✿   ✿   ✿

> The boy was sitting on the front steps, not playing with neighboring youngsters. Mother came down stairs, instructed child

to go and play immediately. Boy refused, the mother insisted. Boy turned and ran upstairs. Mother turned to observer and said, "I just can't understand that boy. He's getting to be more like his father every day."

   ❁   ❁   ❁

Phil and another boy of the same age playing hide-and-seek outside. Game continues for ten minutes until on one turn Phil is unable to find other boy. At first he continues to search, but not finding his playmate, he commenced leaping up and down shouting first, "Where are you, where are you," and then, "If you don't come out I won't play." Eventually, the other boy revealed himself, whereupon Phil ran up to him, striking him on the abdomen.

   ❁   ❁   ❁

In school, Phil is described as moody, sulky, disagreeable, often absent from school for refusal to attend.

All three boys, Rod, Sidney, and Phil, described in this section show the symptoms of rejection. Rod and Phil reveal their aggressive response to the parental dominance and rejection in hostile and destructive acts. Sidney is too dominated to overtly aggress. Performance of the three boys in school is erratic, fluctuating between effort and restlessness. As yet, the aggression has been more directly released rather than symbolically in theft or lying, appearing characteristically as a rebelliousness against persons in authority and direct destructiveness.

Sidney's parents clearly impose impossible standards of performance and utilize his failure to succeed as justification for punishing and restricting him, thus providing a vehicle for their rejection. With Phil the parental relationship is less consistent, for he receives some attention, occasional bribes, occasional ignoring, interspersed with rejection. However, he is not prevented from recognizing the parents' feelings in their true light.

In Rod's family, the causes and the dynamics of the relationship were quite apparent, but the reasons underlying the rejection of the other two boys are obscure and would require intensive study for understanding. Many causes exist to create the grounds for rejection: unplanned children the parents did not want; homes broken by death, desertion, or divorce; poverty, worry, and parental demoralization; personality maladjustment of parents; difficulties of adjustment evolving out of family mobility, loss of employment; and other causes.

Submissive-Rejectant Parents

Neglect is the term that most aptly describes the manner in which this group of parents treat their children. They are not openly cruel or hurtful to the children—they merely do not take adequate care of them. The children may be completely neglected or they may have some of their wishes excessively gratified by gifts of money, toys or other pleasures, but their needs for affection, protection, and adult direction are ignored. The submissiveness appears as a lack of control, a giving into the wishes of the child, a lack of proper supervision and discipline. The parent may protest that he is unable to "do anything with the child," or the neglect may be rationalized by excessive participation in community organizations and groups to the extent that the parents are so busily engaged in social activity and enterprises devoted to the "good of the community," that they "just don't have any time at home" because "there is so much to be done."

The symptoms portrayed by neglected children present a confusing array ranging from food fussiness to cruelty and delinquency. In one sense, the children are confused, for their parents do not particularly appear at fault; they are seemingly interested parents, they are not unkind to the children, with the result that the child has no apparent source of rejection and no target for release of his feelings. Having the opportunity to do as he desires, the child develops some independence, may see himself as luckier than other children who "have to mind their parents," may develop adequate relationships with other children. Oftentimes, other children, and particularly a gang, represent his sole source of identification and personal attachment. The values of the group are his source of values, their goals his goals. He lacks the counterbalance of values absorbed from identification with adults, making him particularly susceptible to group pressures. The so-called "socialized delinquent" evolves in this group. Lacking adult directions, he absorbs the standards and goals of the group in which he finds membership, and, if the group identifies with delinquent values, this child acquires these as a natural product of development.

> Eddie is a second-grader already showing the developing symptoms resulting from the neglect of his parents. Born late to a couple with three other children—one in high school, two in college—by the time he entered the first grade Eddie has been given little of his parents' time. The father is a successful merchant, the mother involved in many organizations within the community. The family enjoys a comfortable living, owning their own, well-equipped and beautifully furnished home. Rarely is

anyone available to attend to the child. During the afternoon, his mother is out, leaving the housework to a part-time maid. The father is often absent on week-ends because of business demands. Two televisions preoccupy the family time in the evenings, one in the dining room for use during meals, the other in the living room. Eddie seldom views a program of his choice, because the parents watch one set, and the older sister the other. He goes to bed whenever he desires.

Although Eddie has many toys, they are quickly broken, partially because the members of the family push them from place to place, sometimes destroying them, referring to them as junk, other times because Eddie loses them or leaves them in the driveway. Eddie speaks with a lisp, stutters on occasion, more frequently at home than anywhere else.

At school, Eddie is very friendly with boys and very hostile towards girls, perhaps because of his older sisters' open hostility for him. He enjoys the company of older boys, and is accepted by them in their games. He shares his toys with them, receives frequent calls from them and invitations. With younger children, Eddie is often ringleader and usually leads the group into some mischief.

Eddie is a curious and capable pupil in school but he gives up easily when he makes a mistake. Emotional and easily em-

SUBMISSIVE—REJECTANT PARENTS

Behavior of Parents to Child	*Child's Reaction to Parents*
1. Cannot control child	1. Gets attention by misbehaving
2. Give in to child just to get matter settled	2. Moderate degree of independence
3. Use lax, inconsistent discipline	3. Makes desperate attempts at getting affection
4. Neglect child—movements unsupervised	4. Defies authority
5. Do not provide advantages	5. Fussy about food
6. Do not make an effort to improve child's condition	6. Expresses himself well verbally
7. Indifferent toward child; ignore him	7. Gets along well with age mates
8. Fail to provide him with money or toys	8. Likely to try to misrepresent the facts
	9. Mistreats animals
Extreme symptoms	10. Destructive
9. Desert child	11. May become juvenile delinquent
10. Put child into an institution	
11. Join social organizations; spend no time at home	

barrassed, he is prone to whine and cry. On other occasions, he shows off excessively.

The variable behavior of neglected children is quite evident in Eddie.

From society's viewpoint, it is fortunate that he lives in an area that has a healthy social orientation, for the values Eddie is exposed to support socially-approved behavior. His parents take excellent care of his physical and material needs. His health is excellent; he is well-clothed and fed and amply supplied with material objects. On the emotional side, his experience is one of neglect and indifference, and the first stages of the varied symptoms of the neglected child are noticeable.

SUBMISSIVE-ACCEPTANT PARENTS

Indulgence is characteristic of parents in this category. The child's needs and wants are satisfied, and anyone else's needs are secondary.

SUBMISSIVE—ACCEPTANT PARENTS

Behavior of Parents to Child	*Child's Reactions to Parents*
1. Unable to deny the demands and requests of child even though they are unreasonable	1. May show signs of nervousness, insomnia, nail biting, enuresis, precocity in sexual development
2. May side with child, defend him against attack from other authority	2. Selfish and wants things for himself. Dislikes sharing with others
3. See few faults, if any, in child and magnify his virtues	3. Failure to grow up emotionally and remains infantile in behavior reactions
4. Will make any kind of financial sacrifice for the child	4. Makes excessive demands for what he wants, is tyrannical in forcing compliance to his wishes from parents and others
5. Coddle the child during illness and curb his independence when faced with danger	5. Difficulty in giving up aggressions; has not learned self-control
	6. Uses temper tantrums, crying, whining, or plaguing in a childish way to enforce his demands. Tends to push and take things forcefully
	7. Difficulty adjusting to routine; at school he has difficulty adjusting to the school situations

Adults, to these children, exist expressly for the purpose of satisfying their desires. Games are to be played by their rules, activities regulated by their wishes. The indulgence experienced by these children differs from the overprotective, dominant mother who inhibits the child's growth in smothering affection, because he is free to expand his demands over his parents, not forced to submit to their attentions. As a result, he develops little notion of shared satisfaction or little tolerance for frustration. Faced with the demands of adults other than his parents, e.g., teachers, and expected to accord other children their rights, the indulged child's response is an immediate expectation of concession by the others, and, failing to receive that, aggressive assault to attain his ends. His aggressive responses, instead of being channeled into socially acceptable avenues as a result of learning to accept demands, are directly expressed and rationalized on the grounds that the other person didn't "play fair," by insisting on equal rights and failing to give in. Hence, if the children of Dominant-Rejectant Parents reveal their aggression in rebellion against authority, these children of Submissive-Acceptant Parents have unchecked aggression.

Two sets of excerpts of observational studies of a boy and girl serve as illustrations:

Anne is ten, the youngest of three daughters of foreign born parents, who were educated in this country, the mother through high school, the father through college.

Anne's mother came in from town with some things she had brought for the two older girls. Anne, seeing none for herself, stamped her feet, and made the mother promise to take her into town the next day and buy something . . . Anne asked if she could go to camp during the next summer with other girls in her class; the mother refused because Anne was too young and something might happen to her.

Anne asked her older sister to take her to the Rodeo and was accepted if she promised to be a good girl. Twice that week Anne slapped her mother and refused to go to the store for groceries unless the mother gave her money to buy candy. Anne went to the Rodeo on Friday.

Anne took piano lessons, did quite well for a while, but after the fascination wore off, she refused to practice, so the teacher suggested she give it up for a while. Now she plays the piano when her parents or sisters are talking on the telephone.

Anne usually spends Saturday morning watching TV and having her meals served to her. One evening, the family was watching TV, when Anne entered and immediately switched stations. She began to stamp her feet when the mother asked her to change it back, and cry when her sister tried to change it. The mother told Anne she wouldn't get the new dress she'd been promised if she didn't change it. Anne replied that she didn't care. A few days later she showed me her new dress.

The mother or one of the older sisters always gives Anne her bath and reads her a story before bed.

        ✿   ✿   ✿

Jimmy, a healthy, handsome, blond-haired, brown-eyed, only child of well-to-do parents, is quite attached to his parents. Saturday and Sunday is usually spent doing whatever Jimmy suggests. One Saturday, when the mother said that she had to visit a sick friend, Jimmy sulked until the mother promised to stay with him. He expects to see his parents whenever he returns from school or being out and becomes angry and worried if they are not there. He accompanies them on all trips, because the father believes he won't be properly cared for by anyone else. One night when his parents had gone out, Jimmy awakened at 11:00 PM and, learning the time, arose to telephone them that they had promised to be home by 10:30. He insisted on waiting up until they returned.

Jimmy expects his father to drive him to school every morning, although it is only a five minute walk. After playing with his toys, he leaves them lying around, but gets quite angry if he can't find one he wants after his mother has picked them up. He expects her to bring him a toy everytime she goes to the store, and is angry if she doesn't. When Jimmy has outbursts of anger, the father is likely to get excited and scold Jimmy, threatening various actions. But Jimmy says that he knows his father is always scolding, but won't do anything.

Jimmy has two close friends with whom he plays, being accepted as the leader. He exercises his authority, telling them what to do, what to play with, how to play. When he thinks the games aren't being played correctly, he criticizes, scolding his companions, issuing orders and commands to change. He uses his imagination effectively to introduce ideas to make games more exciting.

The two children described in the preceding anecdotes are accustomed to being indulged, and they accept the services of others as their natural birthright. They find it difficult to share with others and to function in a group where their leadership is not accepted. If they are blessed with talent, they can succeed in this role in child groups, but lacking it or persisting in infantile actions as a result of parental indulgence, they find themselves barely tolerated. In the face of frustration, they respond with temper tantrums. If their indulgence is associated with material well-being, these children may often manipulate the group by management of toys, money, equipment, etc.

DEMOCRATIC PARENTS

The mechanisms of democracy are often confused with the principles or values inherent in democratic relationships. It is not uncommon to find a miniature judge and jury system installed in the upper elementary grades for disposing of violations of classroom rules and regulations, as if the form of democracy implies the existence of the substance, and the latter is to be derived from the former.

A formal machinery for sharing power may be essential to democracy as a political arrangement, but it is not essential to primary or face-to-face groups. The relationships existing within a group of adults or children may be democratic without the election of officers, the voting on decisions, or holding a family council. Essentially, it depends on the kind of relationship existing between the members of the group—is there regard for individuals, is there cooperative effort toward mutual goals, is there room for individual development. In such a climate, individuals, child or adult, can be true to their own individuality without feeling threatened by another's difference, can restrain themselves so that others may receive equivalent satisfaction, and can work effectively toward both individual and common goals.

The behavior patterns may be, in part, imposed, in the sense that the responsible adult, whether parent or teacher, forbids certain behavior, and rewards others, recognizing that so-called "democratic behavior" is as much a learned behavior pattern as temper tantrums are learned techniques for achieving one's goals. The word pattern is significant because isolated demands for democratic behavior in a context which is basically opposed fails to produce the needed integrated pattern of perception, feeling, and action desired. Thus the teacher who responds with an exasperated grimace to the questions of certain children who acquire concepts slowly, unequivocally contradicts any verbal exhortation to the contrary. The importance of the total context can be illustrated in a few anecdotes taken from home observations of two children, a boy and a girl.

> The mother showed me about the home—she was particularly proud of her husband's art work (avocational), told me that Dave had liked to draw when younger but of late had turned

more to science. The father had been working with him, had gotten some chemicals for experiments but insisted that Dave not work on them alone because of danger involved.

Both parents agreed their biggest recent concern had been Dave's school work. When younger, he had gotten all A's but lately C's and D's and, according to the teacher, showed little interest. The father restricted the boy's activities, eliminated TV and movies until he catches up. They thought themselves partially at fault for taking his excellent performance for granted.

When report card time came again, Dave showed his card to his father with a smile, for it was much improved. The father told Dave that now he'd learned the consequences of not doing his work, he could have his freedom back. Subsequently, the mother showed me a pamphlet of a set of encyclopedias they were planning to buy for the boy's birthday.

The boy enjoys basketball and baseball, has fair skill, participates in them after school every day, weather permitting. After supper he'll work with his father on an experiment, if he doesn't have homework. The mother related that one afternoon when she wasn't feeling well, Dave told her to go to bed, and that he'd play with the younger brother until his daddy got home. She accepted the suggestion, and the boys played together all afternoon.

Lately, Dave has been talking about becoming an atomic scientist. They encourage him in his interest, hope he may choose such a goal, but think a decision premature. The boy is generally affectionate towards adults who are related to him, but more recently the mother has noticed that he wants to shake hands with a few of his father's business associates.

*   *   *

Both Herb and Ev try to be fair in all dealings concerning their two daughters—their love for both girls is genuine and deep. Debbie, the younger, has regular hours, bed at eight, rise early, school at nine. This disciplinary action, however, does not hinder expressions of love as such; taking extra time to cater to such whims and holding her on her lap or brushing through Debbie's hair and tucking her in bed. Debbie is given jobs to perform and receives a weekly allowance. She knows what her parents expect of her and tries to please them. When she is told by her mother that it is bedtime she gets ready immediately and without complaint. If for some reason Ev isn't at home to tuck her in, Debbie doesn't complain. Both parents try, by example, to set an atmosphere of friendliness, cooperation, and love. Ev herself felt out of place as a child, not wanted and awkward, and she doesn't want her daughters to feel this way. She lets her daughters know how proud she is of them and how much they mean to her. If Debbie is away from home for a visit, she will often bring each member of the family a small gift. Debbie often goes places with her parents to various events, but Ginnie, the older sister, now enrolled in college, oftentimes prefers staying at home to going out with her parents. The parents have encouraged the girls to enjoy foods of different lands, to appreciate all types of music, and to sing and dance.

The foregoing excerpts, taken from more complete case studies, give the flavor of the parent-child relationships existing in these two

DEMOCRATIC PARENTS

Behavior of Parents to Child

1. Acceptance of child
   A. Unconditional love
   B. Respect for dignity and independence of child
   C. Faith in child
   D. Normal expectancy of ability
2. Role
   A. Leader not dictator
   B. Honest, fair in dealings
   C. Reasonably shockproof
   D. No sibling preference
   E. Understand child's basic needs
   F. Sense of humor
3. Interests
   A. Opportunity to play, to create
   B. Appreciation of child's interests
   C. Sharing, planning together
   D. Responsibilities
4. Discipline
   A. Reasonable limits are set and observed
   B. Consideration for everyone in family
   C. Firm but kind
   D. Proper emphasis on cleanliness, routines, manners, but *not too extreme*
   E. Consistency

Child's Reactions to Parents

1. Self evaluation
   A. Feels adequate, secure, confident
   B. Can face disappointment
   C. Self-esteem
   D. Realistic
   E. Reasonable control over emotions
2. With peers
   A. Friendly, dependable
   B. Accepted, respected
   C. Good sport
   D. Fair
   E. Does not "bear grudge"
   F. Plays well with others
3. At school
   A. Has confidence in adults
   B. Reacts comfortably
   C. Kind, helpful
   D. Works up to capacity
   E. Concentrates well, does not worry
   F. Interested
   G. Cooperative
   H. Accepts responsibilities
4. Toward society
   A. Respects people's property
   B. Appreciative of rights of others

families, and breathe life into the more abstract descriptions listed in the table.

Democratic parents can cover a fairly wide range of behavior. Some parents who may clearly be labeled "democratic" are neutral, even cold, in their affectional relationships with their children, practicing democracy more as a set of principles to which they intelligently adhere. Others, somewhat less consistent, perhaps, in showing varying degrees of dominance on different occasions, nevertheless are more affectionate.

Chapter 7

WORKING WITH PARENTS

The task of educating forty million children is sufficiently demanding of all the resources of teachers that to add eighty million parents would be completely overwhelming. To suggest working with the parents of children is to suggest a task of such scope that one immediately understands some of the reluctance of teachers when home visits and parent conferences are suggested. Teachers implicitly recognize not only the difficulty of the task but their limitations as well, for their training and experience in teaching do not include training in the fundamentals of parenthood.

ACCEPTING LIMITATIONS

Although to work with parents is, in large degree, to educate parents, this does not imply that parent education is a teacher responsibility. Parent education has been and will continue to be for some time largely self-education, and the teacher's role in this process will be that of suggesting directions to speed its course. In working with parents, any teacher faces definite limitations which should be openly recognized.

The first mentioned was that of inadequacy of training and experience. It has been facetiously remarked that once a person becomes a parent he is automatically disqualified from giving advice on problems of parent-child relationships. Certainly, a person can maintain a blithe assurance on the simplicity of being a parent if he has never had children, but the longer one is a parent the less is his naive assurance about the simplicity of the task. With or without actual experience, the teacher's own training focuses mainly on the intellectual and academic and not the emotional and personality development. Even when she is interested and concerned about healthy personality development, she recognizes that persistent non-adaptive behavior by the child requires complete diagnosis demanding specialized training. The teacher's function in instances where she recognizes that physical and psychological factors introduce problems beyond her skill is to identify the existence of a problem and suggest sources of help. Were our communities sufficiently equipped to meet the problems of personal adjustment, her task might end there, but, unfortunately, the needed help is more often than not unavailable, so that the teacher is forced to face the problems presented by children day after day without assistance, groping for a solution or at least some degree of relief as well as she can.

Even where help is available, the teacher still has the educational task at hand. Access to the family is often restricted by the fact that in a greater number of families both parents are working. The mother is no longer easily available for meeting with school personnel. Not only is she not available, but her work demands with her absence from the home means that community agencies, particularly the school, are expected to assume the responsibility for duties which she cannot fulfill.

The effect on the teacher is to make her job more generalized, in that she finds herself required to carry an expanding range of functions at a time when most vocations are becoming progressively more specialized.

In the suburbs, the dispersion of families over wider geographic areas makes both teacher and parent dependent upon private transportation in order to make contact. The parent is no longer within walking range of the school.

Assuming that the physical obstacles presented by changes in the working and living patterns of families can be overcome, the teacher must recognize that she cannot expect to redesign the child's personality or his relationships with his parents. By knowing them as they exist, she can undoubtedly work within this framework with some progress, but in many instances unless some redesign occurs, the teacher's hands are tied. Two examples, both presenting specific limitations illustrate this. The first offers more opportunity to the teacher for successfully fulfilling her functions:

Adele is almost nine, a tall, blonde girl in good health but for her repeated hacking cough. Recent and thorough medical examinations and tests reveal no physical basis or allergy to account for the cough. The girl's muscular coordination is excellent. She has a keen interest in school and is an excellent student able to adjust herself to all conditions. She is apt to undervalue herself: often when an activity or task is suggested she responds with interest coupled with self-derogation, e.g., her response to a suggestion that she weave potholders for Christmas (a task easily within her capacity) was, "I should like to, but I know I can't do it." Adele expresses a deep attachment to her mother; speaks non-committally of her father; and her attitude towards her younger sister is that she "gets in my way all the time" and is "something to be endured."

The family resides in a medium-sized "ranch-type" home in a suburb. The father is a successful chemist who devotes his leisure time to improving the home.

The home visit was quite revealing. After a general exchange of information and a few pleasantries I [teacher] inquired about Adele's cough. At first, the mother was reluctant to discuss the cough, saying her daughter would outgrow it in time, but after talking about other topics for a few minutes, the mother suddenly began to talk freely about the irritation. She said that Adele had developed a hacking cough when she was an infant—the doctor called her a croupy baby.

The mother felt a keen responsibility for her daughter because her husband, absent in military service, did not have a chance to see his daughter until she was a year old. She disliked having anyone handle their child and said that when anyone came to call she snatched Adele up and rushed to put her in her crib because she was so afraid that friends would bring in germs. Living with her mother-in-law at the time, she treated her the same way, insisting that she wash her hands every time before touching the child. She relaxed after her husband's first visit, and did not have this apprehension at all at the time the second daughter was born.

There was a decided difference in the father's treatment of the two girls. He is amused when the younger child talks out of turn and takes pride in her being a "real tomboy," but he will not permit Adele to talk back and repeatedly admonishes her to be ladylike. It is also evident that he is apt to remind her of her faults and rarely encourage her. The mother related that when Adele brought home her first report card for the year (4 A's and 2 B's) the father reprimanded her for not having all A's.

The teacher had visited Adele's home to inquire about the girl's persistent cough and had learned that as far as the best medical authorities were concerned the causes were not physiological. The mother expressed her relief at this knowledge but was reluctant to infer the possibility of psychological origin, insisting that Adele would "outgrow" it. By the end of the interview, the teacher had a different perspective on her task. Accepting the negative medical findings, she could see possible relationships between the cough, the family history, and the prevailing attitudes and actions of the parents toward their children. The mother's anxiety regarding the cough was undoubtedly communicated to the child but with what meaning is unknown, e.g., did it imply to the child that she was physically inadequate or that the mother resented having the responsibility for caring for her without the help of the father. The exact meaning of the mother's anxiety about the child remains unknown. The mother's attention during this period was pleasing in some respects but thwarting in others, for it blocked much normal infant behavior such as tasting and feeling different objects. The father's return took away some of the mother's attention and imposed an added set of demands. The birth of the younger sister created a double set of standards for the children, giving special privileges to the younger child.

With the knowledge derived from the home visit, the teacher sees Adele's needs for increased self-esteem and an opportunity to talk about some of the feelings which she restrains beneath her ladylike demeanor. It is not enough that she continue her excellent academic performance, but that she derive a sense of accomplishment and personal adequacy from it. These experiences the teacher can provide, knowing them to be a counterbalance to the family, and yet not fearing that the results will be harmful. She sees the much greater amount that could be accomplished if the parents could obtain insight into the existing interpersonal relationships in the family, yet she cannot bring it about; she is not certain that her own guesses are accurate; she met a reluctance by the mother to look at possible psychological causation; and while she may further suggest it as a possibility, she has to accept the limitations created.

Tim, too, has a respiratory ailment, asthma, which he has had since early childhood, but unlike Adele, he is failing in school and is rejected by his playmates, who call him "Monkey," partly because of his nervous mannerisms and wide-eyed stare. Tim is ten. He lives in a single-family dwelling with parents, older sister (14) and younger brother (7). The father is frequently away from home at his work—selling.

The parents are repeatedly being called to the school because of Tim's failing marks. He was retained in the third grade (because the teacher "had it in for kids from their neighborhood," was the parent's explanation), spent most of the time "daydreaming" until the mother offered him five dollars if he'd improve. However, he was promoted on trial, and he received the five dollars. The next year the parents transferred Tim to a parochial school because "they give such a good foundation." Four successive Mondays in October Tim was absent from school because of an asthma attack incurred Sunday night. The doctor didn't question the authenticity of the asthmatic attack, but thought the timing of them unusual.

Interviews with the parents reveal that the parents (at least in recent years as the schoolwork has deteriorated) have fluctuated between permissiveness and harshness in their treatment of Tim. The parents have rationalized the boy's behavior, first blaming the teacher, then the asthma, but now, in a new school and with asthma being treated, and Tim's behavior becoming worse, the parents have been pressed to the point of whipping the boy. The mother describes herself as highly nervous, alternately begging, bribing, and pleading with Tim, until she finally loses all control and whips him. She recounts the previous evening when she had instructed Tim to "do your homework like a good boy . . . all right, just 15 minutes of TV, then do your homework . . . Tim, it's an hour since you said you'd do your homework . . . Tim, stop scuffling with your brother and work . . . all right then don't do it and go to school tomorrow and not know it, it's time to go to bed now . . . go to sleep, I don't care if you haven't done your homework . . . go to sleep, it's ten o'clock . . . all right, get up, and I'll help you . . . stop making noises and pay attention . . . Tim, you're not trying." Finally, it ended by whipping him and sending him to bed. During several conversations the mother usually referred to the younger brother as "her little sweetheart" and the older sister as "my big girl, and my big helper," but her references to Tim were to the effect that he was "the one who causes all the trouble." She said that when the father is away she lets Tim sleep with her because he seems to sleep better, it's company for her, and she thinks he may be allergic to his bed. She notes that because the father is away so much of the time she does everything to try to make things pleasant for him, but evidently Tim, with the help of his brother and sister, will have the father so upset in a few hours as to be shouting. She expresses fear of the father incurring a nervous breakdown because he gets so depressed over the week-ends.

During an interview at the home with the father, Tim was continually interrupting with requests seemingly aimed at aggravating the father, such as "Hey, Dad, can I drive the car," "Can I have five dollars, huh," "How do they make cars, Dad?" Then he started running around the father, holding on to his pants, shouting he'd tie the father up. Irritated, the father told Tim to "be a good fellow and do your homework." Tim grinned and retorted, "You can't make me, I'll beat you up." "For Pete's sake, Timmy, be a good fellow." The aggravation continued to build up until finally the father stepped toward Timmy threateningly, which caused the boy to run yelling into the house. The father expressed fear that the mother will have a nervous breakdown because she has been getting more and more nervous.

Tim's functioning is impaired in all areas—health, school work, peer and family relationships. The asthmatic attacks are now closely associated with periods of stress and serve as a device not only for escape from a situation but also for perpetuating the special attention he obtains from his mother, being permitted to share the parents' bed in the absence of the father. Solace is not the only satisfaction derived from these occasions, for the mother suggests it prevents her being lonesome while the father is away at his work.

Whatever its origin, the asthma is now a mechanism in a complex set of relationships within the family, involving the psychosexual development of the boy. It is significant that Tim is the leader in the "uprising" against the father on the week-ends, that he feels capable of challenging the father, yet at the same time it appears he may also be provoking the father into punishing him. It is apparent that there is little the teacher can do. The interplay of events is so intricate and the linkage between causes and effects so subtle, that it is difficult for the teacher to specify her best moves with the boy. It is possible that gains in the academic sphere will be hard-won and require infinite patience.

In accepting the limitations imposed by her training, her function as a teacher, and the difficulties in obtaining adequate access to the child's home life, the teacher finds herself recognizing and accepting limitations which the parents present. Some of the more obvious limitations are those imposed by the lack of education, both parents having to work, isolation resulting from migrations in pursuit of work, and families broken by death or divorce.

Equally significant are limitations which ensue from emotional and psychological disturbances. We acquire our school achievements by means of cognitive processes during which we are aware of much that is occurring, but our patterns of emotional reactions are built up by affective processes which we only barely perceive.

Much of the way in which parents treat their children is a function of the treatment they received as children, of the relationships existing between themselves and the members of their families, and of their personalities. Their feelings are deeply ingrained from long exposure during childhood and are not easily altered by the accretions of knowledge which the school adds. They forget much of what they have learned.

BASIC CONFLICTS

In Chapter 5, in the discussion of obtaining information about the home life of the children, attention was called to several points of conflicts likely between parents and teachers—the protectiveness of parents for their children, and the effects of community social relationships on teacher-parent contacts.

There is yet another aspect of home and school which is predisposing to conflict. The mission of the school is to assist the child to attain mastery over the environment. The skills he is expected to acquire during his years in school are those which permit him to cope with the natural (physical) and artifactual (man-made) parts of the environment. The task of parents, in large degree, is to aid the child in attaining mastery of himself, so that he can function effectively psychologically and socially. The two functions are not completely separate, nor do they of necessity conflict, but they are largely separate and often clash in practice. Most parents relegate the entire academic teaching function to the school.

Most teachers seldom take an active hand in shaping the emotional development of the child (not that they do not affect it). The teacher soon knows it when the parents fail to perform adequately, and the results affect the capacity of the child to achieve. The parent finds his job made difficult by the teacher's failure to program effectively for the child. Children who find themselves failing because of being unable to fulfill arbitrary and impossible standards of performance imposed in the schools have difficulty in developing as adequate persons. Events such as these in either sphere, real or imagined, can easily produce a clash between home and school.

Dicky Arsenal is a case in point. A twelve-year-old, fifth-grade boy (once retained), excessively fat, and hence unable to participate effectively in sports or games, Dicky was failing in school.

Although his measured intelligence was average, his grades, fair in the primary grades, had been consistently poor the last two years, and his achievement tests showed him a year or more below grade level. Anecdotal reports made by the teacher say:

(Oct. 29) Report cards given out today. Dicky got failure in reading, spelling, arithmetic, passing in others. Reading placement is 3.4; he is using a third grade reader as a supplementary reader.

(Nov. 3) Room ready for mothers visit tomorrow. Children have planned reading from Weekly Reader, show of arithmetic work, and discussion of early explorers. Chairs are wide enough to permit mothers to sit with child. Dicky says his mother is coming because she wants to see me about something anyway.

(Nov. 4) Mothers came to visit at two o'clock. Dicky's mother sat with him and whispered words to him during reading, and helped with arithmetic. Dicky didn't volunteer during discussion.

Girls prepared the tea, came back and invited mothers into next room. As I rose to join them, Mrs. Arsenal approached and said: "Hey, I want to have a word with you." Asked if she wished to talk now or after the other mothers departed, she retorted: "I don't care where or when, what I want to know is why you said my kid is dumb. He's a smart kid, smarter than most. Why I never saw such a report card. He used to get A's and B's."

Since it was a matter of personal nature, I said that I'd prefer to talk at another time with her in private.

"Time and place be damned," was her answer. She'd got down here when she was sick and it was hard for her to come and she didn't care who heard her. It was time somebody found out why teachers gave good grades to just their favorites. She continued in the same vein, her eyes snapping fire and her mood fighting mad, telling me how teachers simply pulled their grades out of the clear blue sky, had personal favorites, were mean and unfair, and bore grudges against children.

This continued for nearly ten minutes until Mrs. J., the other fifth grade teacher rescued me by coming to the door and asking us not to forget the tea which was waiting.

Calling attention to essential differences in the purposes of the family and the school makes it easier to recognize them for what they are, accept their differences, and prevent their being hidden sources of conflict perpetuating barriers to communication. Although the specific objectives of family and school may differ, their final purpose, as far as children are concerned, is to help them attain maturity as competent, personally adjusted, ethical human beings.

A final source of difficulty is created by differences in attitudes and values. Teachers support middle-class values encouraging hard work, efficient use of time, desire for education, respect for property, personal restraint, and sexual inhibition. The children in their classes, however, come from a wide range of homes, espousing as diversified a set of attitudes and moral values as hats in an Easter parade.

Like it or not, it is the home which defines the child's status, interprets his experiences to him, and establishes his basic attitudes, not only by what is spoken in the home but more by what occurs in the home. The blocking of highways around a Midwestern city to prevent transportation of milk during a price war will be approved by one set of parents praising the farmers for taking action to break the monopoly of the big dairy associations but will be disapproved by another set of parents who decry the farmers who prevent children in the city from getting their milk or needlessly interfering in business. Whatever the teacher's viewpoint, she can't agree with both, anymore than she can agree with many activities of parents which run counter to her set of moral values and personal prejudices.

> Mrs. Clark and her two children live in a housing project which has well-kept trees and lawns, old but well-kept gardens. The hallway leading to the apartment was clean and the walls were free of smudges and marks. Mrs. Clark greeted me pleasantly. She was working in the kitchen and invited me to sit there. Immediately became good friends with the two-year-old daughter, overcoming her reservations to such an extent that she was soon sitting in my lap while her mother prepared coffee.
>
> We began to discuss Don, her son of ten (fifth grade) who was out playing, permitting us to talk freely. Mrs. Clark first showed me his report card which displeased her, even though most of his marks were above average, mainly because his marks on deportment were not as favorable. She said she realized Don was a problem at times, attributing it to his mixed-up life, upon which she soon enlarged.
>
> She had married a man of a different nationality which caused her family to disown her. Her marriage failed, and she and her husband separated after three years. The baby girl was of illegitimate birth. When she discovered herself pregnant she decided to give the baby away when it was born, but at the time of the birth she immediately changed her mind and kept the child.
>
> Receiving no support from her former husband, she worked to support the children while they were boarded out. After the boy started school, she let him take care of himself as best he could after school. Arriving home tired and irritable, she found

herself yelling and getting angry at Don quite frequently. During this period Don tried to run away once, stole minor articles twice. With the second theft, she realized she wasn't being fair to the boy, so she quit her job, devoting full time to care of the children, subsisting on Aid for Dependent Children. Since then Don's schoolwork had improved, he was getting books regularly from the library, and going to church each Sunday, even though she couldn't accompany him because she didn't have a decent dress.

✲   ✲   ✲

Despite the battered desks and the high ceiling with its old fashioned lights set in a decrepit brick building with floors hollowed by thousands of feet, my interview with Don's teacher was most pleasant. Miss Edson had been Don's teacher in the third grade, when he arrived from being boarded in another city, and was again his teacher in the fifth grade.

She recognized and accepted that the desertion by the father and Don's mother having to work and board him had made its mark. Nevertheless, one of her first actions had been to make Don understand she was to be obeyed, that there were some things one had to do in this world regardless of whether they were pleasant or not. Don had temper outbursts on occasion, but she made no issue of these, ignoring many of them, stepping in on occasion to help him with work when he needed it.

Asked if she thought Don lacked discipline at home, Miss Edson replied that she really didn't know. She thought the mother had made a wise decision in giving up work and caring for the children, and that she had made a tremendous impression on Don by doing it, because he was so excited and happy over the situation he had come into the classroom first thing to tell her about it. Miss Edson saw Don making gradual improvement in school and believed he had great potentiality including capacity for leadership. Older than many boys in experience, he, nevertheless, was less mature emotionally. When he would come to Miss Edson on occasion, when he was having difficulty with another child, she would let him tell her about it, then encourage him to deal with the problem himself, telling him he was going to have to learn to take care of himself.

It was evident from our discussion that Miss Edson was acquainted with the details of Mrs. Clark's experiences, and that although she didn't approve them, she, nevertheless, refrained from condemning Don. Her attitude toward Don was one of realistic appraisal of the job he faced and encouragement rather than indulgent sympathy.

These two excerpts represent a kind of situation which occurs frequently and which invites condemnation because it runs counter to approved social behavior. The teacher's attitude was that her values were her business and Mrs. Clark's her own, and that her job as Don's teacher was to help him accomplish as much as she could, whatever the situation.

SPECIFIC ACTIONS

GIVING INFORMATION

Giving direct information to the parents helps them to gain a different perspective on events. The picture which they have is often one-sided and will yield to a full presentation of the facts. In the situation described on page 175 in which the mother's verbal assault overwhelmed the teacher with its sudden anger, intercession of a colleague stopped the torrent of angry words, but no chance was to be had during the remaining minutes of the tea to do anything to remedy the situation. The next day, Dicky showed no reaction to his mother's outburst; in fact, during discussion period he told the group his mother had had a good time at the party. The teacher decided to write a letter home describing in some detail her program for Dicky, hoping to clarify her actions.

> My Dear Mrs. Arsenal:
> I am sending home by Dicky a book which he may keep during the next two weeks. I don't feel that I told you enough in our conversation last Friday to give you a clear picture of just what I am trying to do for your son in reading, nor what his troubles are that led to his receiving a failing mark.
> My purpose in having Dicky read in a third grade book is to present him with material on which he can increase his reading speed, and at the same time counteract his tendency to miscall small words such as *for* and *from*. The third grade book is not the only book in which he is reading, however. It is a tool to help him correct certain difficulties. As soon as he completes it, I will move him through more difficult material until I have him reading smoothly at fifth grade level. It may take a few weeks and much will depend on his attitude and application.
> As to his arithmetic, Dicky does not have a firm grasp of multiplication facts. I allowed him the time he needed to write them down in the "old-fashioned" way, and even by adding, it

took him two hours with many errors. I have shown him how to make a set of practice cards. He needs practice with these every night. If you will ask him about these cards for his remedial work, he will show them to you.

Dicky plays in getting started on different tasks and rarely finishes his work on time. Part of this is due to his forgetting his fundamentals and having to stop and figure out each fact as he needs it. I gathered from our conversation that you want and expect him to do better work. Up to now I've let him set his own pace, because whenever I pressured him he would start to cry and say he couldn't do it. I have been working to develop his skills in fundamentals to help him overcome this difficulty.

You see, Mrs. Arsenal, I'm interested in the welfare and promotion of all my children, including Dicky, and will do whatever I can to help him. Since you know him better than I, it may be that you can suggest a more effective means of getting Dicky to do better work. That is why it is very important that we cooperate fully. Consequently, if at any time you do not understand any assignment I give, please feel free to come and discuss it with me in order that we may have a friendly relationship that will lead me to plan Dicky's program at all times with your full knowledge.

Our conference hours are after school from 2:30 to 3:00 PM, preferably by appointment so that we can plan our school work accordingly.

Sincerely yours,
Mrs. A. H.

Approximately a week later the teacher received the following note:

Dear Mrs. H.

Please excuse Dicky for being absent Monday. He had a cold and it was raining hard.

I want to thank you for the nice letter you sent me in regard to Dicky's work. I really think that if we work together we will both notice a big difference in his report card. He has been reading to me out loud and it seems to help him. I won't be able to do much over this week-end as I am to enter the hospital for another operation.

Thank you again for taking so much interest in my son.

Sincerely,
Mrs. Arsenal

The rapport established through this letter and increased through later contacts was to stand in good stead during a period later in the school year when Dicky got into difficulty with the principal for repeated violation of traffic regulations. By not finding it necessary to indulge in the luxury of anger and hurt feelings and by using a direct informative approach to clarify what appeared to be either a misunderstanding of grades and school program or a disappointment in the fact that Dicky's grades failed to fulfill expectations, the teacher was able to create a considerable change in Mrs. Arsenal's attitude.

Information can be transmitted by a variety of procedures with as much effectiveness as with a personal conference. The report card is a time honored means of transmitting information, albeit not very effective, for unless you are familiar with the teacher's standards for grading (and no two teachers in any school have identical standards), the caliber of the group, and the program of study for the class, a grade conveys very little meaning. Percentage grades are even less meaningful, inasmuch as they create an illusion of precision which is nonexistent. Check lists, parent conferences, and letters have been substituted with greater effectiveness. Report cards, whatever their form, fall far short of being an effective communication system, because they tell very little about the work of the class and the educational program of the school. Some school systems periodically mail descriptive brochures or newsletters informing the parents about different aspects of the school program—language arts, mathematics, science, school programs, and newly employed teachers—at the beginning of the school year.

Another procedure for informing parents is to send them copies of the lunch menus so that they will have an idea of the diet of the children in school. Both of these are valuable, but both fail to consider the most vital concern of the parent: what is happening during the time spent in the classroom? One procedure used by resourceful teachers is to adopt their own newsletter—from time to time mailing, or more often sending home with the children, a mimeographed letter to the parents telling about some interesting phase of the classwork.

Another procedure is to schedule occasional after-school or evening meetings (the latter are more likely to be a substitute for PTA meeting) to describe what is occurring in their children's class. Both of these procedures are group procedures and provide little opportunity for telling a particular parent what his child is doing. In this connection, the telephone is an instrument which can be advantageously used once teacher and parent are acquainted.

Information giving is basic to the development of healthy community relations, but it falls short in many instances of bringing about needed action by the parent. Suggestion and counseling are two further procedures which can be utilized to bring about a needed change in the physical, social, or emotional environment of the child.

SUGGESTING CHANGE

The use of suggestion can be shown in regard to Roger's mother (in Chapter 5 portions of an interview were recorded). You will recall that Roger lived with his grandfather, a housekeeper, Nana, his mother and father who both worked, and his younger brother. Roger had been retained once and was still a year retarded in reading, even though he had received special assistance. The teacher had observed his lack of confidence and his reluctance to join in boys' games, preferring to play with girls. By virtue of his ability to draw, he held some status in the class. The teacher had suggested a home visit, but had been visited at school by the mother.

> Roger's reading had been difficult and without interest until, wonder of wonders, we began the unit on Indians, and the boy wanted to read about nothing but Indians. On Library Day, I noticed Roger had made no selection, but spent his time going from one girl to another taking her book from her or tickling her. I ask if I could help him. He couldn't find a book to please him. I tried to help him but each book didn't please him— wasn't the right color, didn't have pretty pictures, he didn't like animals. Finally, I asked him if he could find just what he wanted, what would it be about. He told me that he wanted to read about Indians, but they were all too hard. It was easy then to find a book for him, and while getting it I learned he had been trying to get the girls to help him find a book on Indians that he could read. (His mother told me during our interview that it was the first book he ever brought home from the library and that he wanted to read it aloud to her.) He's read others since then, drawn some beautiful pictures, and since he has difficulty with oral talks, I let him show us illustrations with a minimum of words.
>
> We entertained the parents at our Indian Unit Review and Nana, the housekeeper, came. Roger was an Indian Chief, blanket, headdress and all. Nana, a large, vigorous woman, was kind in her remarks of appreciation of Roger's interest. She asked me if I would come for tea the following Saturday.
>
> The father called for me. He was a mild man, but most

courteous. The home was Victorian, the silver service exquisite, the grandfather the autocratic ruler.

Father's comments:

> Roger is really interested in school this year; first time since he started school.
>
> It is the first year he hasn't been afraid of his teacher.
>
> He talks about the things he is doing in school.
>
> He wants to bring things to school. Shall I let him?
>
> He wants to read to us and it is so painful we nearly go crazy.
>
> He wants to write Indian stories, but it is such a slow job we haven't time to struggle with it.
>
> He is beginning to play more with children his age.

Mother's comments:

> Roger is very nervous and emotional.
>
> He likes to be by himself.
>
> He cries a lot.
>
> He whines and plagues to get his own way.
>
> He likes to play with younger children for he can be boss.
>
> His younger brother, Hal, is very aggressive and plagues Roger, who shuts himself away from him.
>
> Roger is very like me.

Nana's comments:

> Roger comes right home after school and changes his clothes.
>
> He nearly always plays here at home so I know where he is.
>
> The children come here to play.
>
> They do not play rough games like ball.
>
> We never allow him to go to the store alone.
>
> He has never been to a movie more than twice and then with me.
>
> He and his grandfather build things together, but his work is so poor, his grandfather loses patience.
>
> He has a bath every night, clean clothes every day.
>
> He has little imagination; I have to suggest things to do.

The sources of Roger's difficulties were clearer to the teacher as well as possible steps to counter them. The well-ordered regime prevented Roger's making any choices or decisions for himself or engaging in activities characteristic of his age level. The parents appeared more in the role of an older brother and sister, than that of father and mother, so definite was the authority of the grandfather and housekeeper and the vigor with which they executed it. The impatience of the father and the unhappiness of the mother made neither very capable of helping the boy to learn. His difficulty in oral expression could be traced to the complete submission in the face of adult regulation and his inability to even deal with his brother on equal terms. His preference for girls was still a puzzle, and the comments about his playmates contradictory. Fortunately, the teacher had opportunity for private conversation with the mother before departure and used this chance to answer her own questions and to introduce suggestions to the mother, however they might run counter to the prevailing climate.

> T: (teacher) I want to ask about Roger's friends, who are they, and why does he seem to choose girls instead of boys?
>
> M: (mother) We live on a street that is mostly Christian, and it has been difficult to cultivate friends of our own faith for our children. The girls are of our religion and there are no boys near us. Also, Roger doesn't like to play rough games such as the boys play so he has played with the girls. He does seem to prefer playing with younger children which concerns me. We sent him to a day camp last summer so he could be with children his own age.
>
> T: Did he like camp?
>
> M: Not at first, but by the end of the summer he liked it.
>
> T: Roger is reading much more smoothly and with real understanding.
>
> M: Yes, he is even bringing home library books, which is something he never did before.
>
> T. Did he tell you he had been a pupil-teacher in his arithmetic group?
>
> M: Yes he did, but I didn't know what he was talking about.
>
> T: (*I explained to her.*) We are trying to get him into sports more.
>
> M: He doesn't like them; he is afraid.
>
> T: Roger is being a good sport about them and is trying to learn the game and do his share.
>
> M: He got his father out to play catch last night. They have never done that before.
>
> T: (*Finally we got to this thought.*) I want very much to help Roger to make more friends among his classmates. Would you mind if he brought a boy home with him some day to play a while?
>
> M: I would be very glad to have him. They can play in the garage.
>
> T: We have some very fine boys here who are not of your religious faith but they come from fine families and are well brought up children. As long as Roger's going

> to have to be in class with them shouldn't he be friendly
> with them? As he grows older he will choose for
> himself, but now he needs some help to get started.
> We live in a democratic country and we must teach
> our children how to live better than we do and prac-
> tice democracy. Do you think maybe we had better
> help him a little more than we are?
>
> M: Miss T., I have difficult problems but I'll go along with
> you as best I can. Roger likes you and is happy and
> making progress. I'll do all I can to keep it going.
>
> We talked a little more about the boys I would like to see
> Roger friendly with and even about the possibility of Roger's
> going to visit their homes sometime. She thanked me for my
> interest and assured me she would encourage Roger in new
> friendships.

The teacher quickly learned the reasons behind Roger's preference
for playing with girls. She explored the mother's feelings about
Roger's changing before she ventured a suggestion in an area that can
be as sensitive as religious prejudices. The mother appeared amenable. The teacher thought the mother was the preferable person to
approach. She had greater rapport with the mother. She sensed a
closer identification of mother with the boy than the father had
expressed, even a hint of unhappiness that she lacked independence.
She knew from her progress with the boy in school that he responded
to the opportunities presented to him provided he received some
encouragement.

As a result of her analysis she concluded that suggestions were not
likely to meet with resistance nor were the relationships between the
boy and family so entangled that he could not profit by the suggestion. Her analysis proved accurate, for the mother responded favorably and the visit proved a turning point in Roger's progress, not only
academically but in his personal-social development as well.

CREATING OPPORTUNITIES FOR CHANGE

Opportunities for increasing in-school and out-of-school associations between children occur repeatedly. The teacher sees the children and their needs in broader perspective than parents and is in a
position to make suggestions. For instance, a sixth grade teacher,
having completed a sociogram, noted that a particular child was an
isolate. During a discussion with the parent, she learned that other
children never came to his home to play with him, he wasn't allowed

to go to night basketball games with other boys, and never saw his classmates outside the classroom. The parents were worried about his physical health and babied him constantly. She suggested that as long as they had a television set it would be nice if they allowed their son to invite some of his classmates to see selected programs. She also mentioned that most of the boys who lived near them went to the high school games and an occasional after-school movie or else just stayed in the schoolyard playing softball for a half hour or so. The teacher was happy to notice that the parents followed her suggestion and the boy began to find a place with his classmates, even though it was just a start. Suggestions by teachers which, in effect, expand the environment of the child are most appropriate.

COUNSELING PARENTS

Counseling with parents is frequently needed but seldom is the province of the teacher. Several conditions mitigate against such a role. First, the teacher's concern and focus of effort is with the child, and the relationship which evolves in counseling can easily run counter to this responsibility. Second, a teacher does not have time available for the series of sessions likely to be needed. Finally, he lacks training in counseling procedures. To some degree, however, a series of interviews with a parent may contain definite elements of a counseling relationship in which the teacher serves as an interested, impartial participant with whom the parent is able to resolve a difficulty or problem with which he is faced.

Principals, more than teachers, need skill in counseling, for in many of their contacts with parents a solution to difficulties being faced by a child cannot be reached by administrative or directive approaches. An equivalent of group counseling can be obtained, sometimes through cooperation of parent-teacher groups and child study groups with the use of a professional leader. The study program of the group may be a formal investigation of child development, or, under trained leadership, it can function as group counseling in which the mothers discuss the difficulties and problems they are experiencing with children and with their own feelings relative to children or a particular child.

The major difficulty in any attempt to change ways in which a parent is treating a child is the fact that such a change involves, directly or implicitly, an admission of error or failure. Parents, just as we all do, devise a variety of defenses to avoid the necessity of recognizing their mistakes. Three common defenses are:

1. Seeing nothing wrong with the child.

   One mother whose nine-year-old son was continually starting fights with smaller children responded to every note or telephone call to the effect that the teacher had better stop those other children from picking on her Tony, that he was a good boy who wouldn't hurt a fly, etc., etc.

2. Labeling the child as incorrigible.

   Note how Sharon's mother (page 254) says that she can't do a thing with her, that Sharon has a mind of her own which can't be changed.

   In extreme cases, the parent may unconsciously desire the child to be "incorrigible" in order to justify the parent's rejection of the child.

3. Encouraging the adjustment pattern of the child because it satisfies parent needs or inadequacies.

   One mother, unable or unwilling to restrain her child in visiting other homes, would immediately announce this by saying to the child, "Oh, I bet you'll get into that bookcase won't you," or "you're not going to want to play with those ash trays, are you?" Her announcement encouraged the child and announced to the host that the actions met with her approval.

   Over-protective parents, who feel the need to have someone to care for, are reluctant to permit the child gains in independence.

To bring such changes about invariably requires working with parents over a period of time and seldom is this possible or desirable for the teacher, for the problems need clinical skills for solution.

Using Authority

Not to be overlooked in these days of non-directive counseling is the direct demand. Curiously enough, these two approaches, opposite though they may appear, have in common commitment to change. Too often a non-directive approach is viewed by untrained persons as being a timid and irresolute approach to problem situations. The very opposite is true, and a non-directive approach should not be confused with vacillation. Both a non-directive approach and a direct demand require a commitment and an acceptance of responsibility. The non-directive approach places the responsibility for decision and action on the "client." With a direct demand the responsibility for decision rests with the person making the demand.

Both have their place, for all relationships which exist are not clinical; many are administrative.

Many parents encourage their children to remain dependent upon them. Whatever the unfilled needs of the parent, such dependency can work to the disadvantage of the child in facing the demands which are inherent in going to school. This difficulty is frequently seen at the beginning of the first grade, or at the time of transfer between schools, and occasionally at the time of entering junior and senior high school.

Few adults remember how frightening it can be to enter a large building, to spend the day with strangers, doing the tasks ordered by a strange grown-up, unable to leave for the solace that mother can give when trouble arises. If you know some of the other children, there is support available. If one has been to nursery school or kindergarten, one has gradually gotten accustomed to being away for short periods of time. If a child has grown in a large family, has heard about school from brothers and sisters, or has become accustomed to meeting strangers and trusting them, the hurdle is not as great. But in every first grade there are some children who are fearful and occasionally, a child whose dependency needs are great, or whose relationship with his parents creates a crisis with the advent of school.

Barbara was such a child as many incidents will tell. Although she was a normal, healthy, six-year-old with a ruddy complexion, clear blue eyes and black curly hair, and not an only child, having a younger sister, her first weeks in school were a trial for all concerned. All in all, there didn't appear to be any reason to anticipate any difficulty with Barbara. She lived about ten minutes from the school in a suburban neighborhood, where there were many children she played with. She had attended kindergarten at the school. The first grade teacher had made a practice of spending time in the kindergarten so the children would be acquainted with her.

The first omen occurred when Mrs. L. visited the teacher the day before school opened telling her that she was so glad Barby would have her this year and had gotten acquainted with her, because she didn't know what would happen otherwise, and she didn't know what she would do if Barby didn't like school. A few days later, the mother replied to a telephone call regarding Barbara's absence, "No, she isn't sick, she just doesn't seem to want to go. She is fine when she gets up but when it's time to go she screams and cries. I don't know what to do, I can't have her cry at school and bother everyone, can

I? I know she likes school and all she does is talk about you." The teacher suggested that Barbara be sent the following day whether she cried or not.

When Barbara failed to appear the teacher visited the home. The mother explained that she just didn't know what to do because Barbara just refused to go to school. Asked if it was due to anything that happened at school, the mother replied that she didn't think so because Barbara talks about school all the time and plays school with her little sister. She promised to send Barbara the next day.

However much Barbara enjoyed playing school, she was experiencing difficulty meeting the demands when she was there. For instance, an early anecdote of the teacher reads: About 9:45 I noticed Barbara crying and asked her what the trouble was. "I made a mistake." I explained that people often make them anyway, that is why you come to school so you won't make mistakes when you're big. A half hour later I heard loud sobs, looked up from the reading group to see Barbara sobbing and repeating with fists clenched, each time more vehemently, "I will stop crying, I will stop crying, I WILL stop crying."

Ten days later, Barbara came up to inquire about the "finish lists"—children who have been unable to finish their daily work. "What happens if your name goes on the finish list?" "As soon as you do your paper," I replied, "you've earned it off." "But what if you don't do the paper?" "If you don't know how to do it, I help you, but if you know what to do you stay after school if necessary, to do it." "Would I have to stay after," she questioned. "You always do your work and have time for lots of extra and nice things, but if you didn't you would have to do just what everybody else does."

The next week while I was busy giving a vocabulary test to a reading group, Barbara interrupted me to tell me she'd made a mistake and wanted another piece of paper. I told her to put a line through the mistake and continue with her work. "I said give me a piece of paper," Barbara demanded. "No, Barbara, go back to your seat and do your work." "Give me a piece of paper, give me a piece, give me some or I'll cry." Irked by her demand I told her I wouldn't give her a piece and go sit down. She sat down and proceeded to bellow. The more we ignored her the louder the screams and the fewer the tears, until finally I told her to leave the room until she could stop. Barbara said, "I'll go but I won't stop until I get a piece of paper." She returned in a few minutes saying, "I stopped, now give me the paper." I replied, "I didn't tell you I'd give you anything if you stopped." "I know," Barbara answered, "But I always get what I want. Aren't you going to do it?"

The climax came when after several days absence, her father brought her to school. I heard Barbara outside the door saying, "I'll go tomorrow, Daddy, I promise." When I opened the door Barbara seemed pleased to see me, running up and saying, "I missed you, Miss Teager." "Why didn't you come to school and see me?" I asked. "Oh, I had to stay home," Barbara replied. Her father started to leave and Barbara said, "Daddy, don't go." "I have to go to work." "Don't go, I'll cry and scream if you go. Call Mummy, and have her come too." The father replied, "Barbara, I can't, I have to go to work." I told him to go, that we would take care of Barbara. He headed for the door, and Barbara started after him yelling, "Daddy, wait a minute, I have something to tell you." He returned and asked, "What is it." "Nothing." With this the father said, "Barby, you promised. Now Daddy has to go to work while you stay here." Barbara's reply to this was that she'd tell her mother if he didn't do what she wanted. The father stood embarrassed and confused. I took Barbara into the nurse's office for a few minutes while I talked with her Daddy. She protested, but the nurse took the cue, and interested Barbara in the scales. I returned to the hall and asked the father to accompany me to the entrance to the building. Once there, I told him very briefly that I knew it was sometimes hard to refuse a person whom you loved very much, but that we were adults whose job it was to help Barbara meet demands, and that he and his wife were underestimating her capacity. I told him that unless Barbara was ill I expected her to be in school every day, even if he had to bring her. In the event that he brought her, he was to bring her no farther than the door, kiss her goodbye, turn and leave, regardless of what Barbara did or said. He could be sure that Barbara liked me and I liked Barbara, and that we would soon be over the difficulty. He left and I returned for Barbara and took her into the classroom. She glanced out the window to see her father departing, stamped her foot, said, "I told him not to go, I'll show him," and began to scream. I told Barbara that she was in school now, it was time she acted like the big girl she was, wouldn't she like to get to work. She replied that she was glad she was in school and could do such good things.

As she departed for home at the end of the day, I told Barbara that I expected her to be there bright and early the next morning, so she could catch up on things she had missed.

That was the last of the trouble over coming to school, although it was a while before she was ready to give up her habit of demanding and expecting to get what she wanted from the other children.

The inadequacy of Barbara's parents in imposing any kind of authority is tragic, as they cower before her demands. Her liking for the teacher and satisfaction at school was sufficiently great that the teacher could tip the balance by a direct demand on the father which helped define his function as a parent and counteract his reluctance.

As a general rule, demands should be made sparingly and with some forethought, but the fact that school attendance is compulsory leads to a concept that inasmuch as the child is required to be in school, his behavior must be suffered. Some parents believe this relieves them of responsibility, overlooking the fact that education is basically a privilege provided by the community. School officials have the authority to deny admission to any pupil on reasonable grounds. In the final analysis, the power of the school rests upon such authority and can be used to impose demands in extreme situations.

TEACHERS AS SUBSTITUTE PARENTS

An observation frequently made is that younger children respond to teachers as if they were their parent. It is a short step from this observation to the suggestion that teachers should be substitute parents for those children whose real parents are inadequate. At first glance, the suggestion appears meritorious, but only because the depth and intensity of the feelings and emotions involved between a parent and a child are underestimated. A closer look will reveal that it is a mistake for a teacher to attempt to assume this role with any child, and the more serious the disturbance of a child, the more serious becomes the error of such action.

Bettelheim explores the difficulties of attempting to enter a disturbed child's life as a substitute parent in the book, *Love Is Not Enough*.[1] He points out that the difficulties of such a child have usually originated in the relationship to the parent—a relationship which the child has been unable to manage. Why, then, use this as a basis for the relationship of a new adult who enters the life of the child—his teacher. The complexity of the existing relationship, the child's confusion with regard to it, and the teacher's inability to know the ramifications mean that such a relationship is fraught with hazard.

The teacher has a different kind of support to offer children; first

[1] B. Bettelheim, *Love Is Not Enough*. New York: The Free Press, 1950.

a degree of organization to a life which is often confused, and second, an opportunity for a different kind of relationship, one that is not arranged to adult convenience and the demands of adult emotions. Many children come to school, not so much disturbed as disorganized and confused.

Barbara is a good example. Her parents provide her with no more direction than her younger sister with whom she plays school, so great is their inability to assume any degree of direction in the child's life or responsibility for being a parent in the love relationships with the child. Her teacher angers her because she doesn't fulfill the expectations she has developed regarding adults which developed as a natural byproduct of her treatment by her parents. But her teacher offers her more, first a person whom you can approach, whom you can say you like, to whom you can give affection without immediately receiving a demand as a price for the return of affection. Barbara's parents demand, in an innocuous way, with their "Barbara, you promised . . ." and "Barbara, won't you please be mother's little darling and do what she asks?" Barbara learns she can use affection and obedience as a weapon to dominate her parents.

With her teacher, the situation is different. The teacher has organization, and direction, coupled with a caring for the children in the class, a caring that is not used as a device to manipulate individuals but an attitude that freely extends to all. These are valuable to Barbara and she finds herself responding to them, even though it runs counter to what is occurring at home. Her teacher not only introduces some external organization and regulation into her life, which is a relief, but also is a person who can be liked, who responds directly to such simple actions, and in so doing provides the base for an identification by the child with the teacher which permits emotional development, just as her lessons provide intellectual development.

Almost parenthetically, an important issue arises in connection with the matter of pupil-teacher identification and loyalty. The primary premise in this chapter has been that teacher-parent contact is desirable. There are instances in which contact is to be avoided, for example when parental expectation runs counter to teacher expectation and conflict ensues, or when a child, needing the support of an adult whom he can trust, would construe teacher-parent contact as a conspiracy to deny him needed support or to compare notes on his behavior. In these instances, contact is better initiated by a third person such as a principal or guidance counselor.

GROUP DISCUSSIONS

Finally, teachers can add another perspective to children's lives, through discussions with the class which help them to understand and accept events in their lives growing out of their relationships with their parents. This can be done with any age group, provided the subject is appropriate to the age level. For instance, a second grade teacher started by asking her children to tell what they did when their mother refused to let them go out to play or refused to let them watch television when they wished. The variety of procedures which her class of seven-year-olds utilized to gain their own way surprised her: "I cry," "I whine," "I stamp my feet," "I go upstairs and make a lot of noise until she gives in," "I make her mad and she tells me to get out of the house," "I sneak out when she isn't looking," etc. These served as a basis for informal discussions during coming weeks.

In another school, a fifth grade teacher first had her class list what they considered to be difficulties they were having at home, with friends, in school, etc. She tabulated these to determine the most frequent, then scheduled weekly panel discussions, in which she gave a group of three topics, from which they could choose any for discussion. At first she had difficulty because the panel expressed stereotyped opinions, e.g., children should obey their parents at all times; children should do chores; children should do their homework promptly, and the like. After the second panel, she asked the class to evaluate how reality-centered the discussion had been. This soon opened the discussion. Even with this breakthrough the group ventured cautiously, testing the teacher to see at what point she would reprimand them or moralize that their behavior was certainly not what she anticipated from nice boys and girls. She played a neutral role, not venturing her opinions, encouraging the expression of the varying convictions and questions from members of the class, in order that they develop their own solutions and understandings.

There are many topics which can be used for discussions about the home:

1. The good times we have at home.
2. Why it's hard to be a parent.
3. Things my brothers and sisters do which aggravate me.
4. How my parents punish me, for what, and how I react.
5. Things I do which aggravate my parents.
6. What I like most about my home.
7. Why parents see things differently than children.

8. Privileges and responsibilities for a particular age group, e.g., how late to stay up, what to do to help around the house, etc.

Similarly, many events can be dramatized, by choosing typical events in the lives of the children, assigning roles, and asking the children to spontaneously enact the situations. Such spontaneous dramatizations (called sociodramas) provide both teacher and class with insight and ideas for ways of meeting differing problems or situations.

The discussions and dramatizations help the children understand and accept the realities with which they have to live, lead them to appreciate that others of their classmates have similar problems with adults, and, from knowing this, derive support by seeing that others can face and handle the events that occur.

REFERENCES FOR PART TWO

Ackerman, N. M. *The Psychodynamics of Family Life.* New York: Basic Book, Inc., 1958.

Baruch, Dorothy. *New Ways in Discipline.* New York: McGraw-Hill Book Co., Inc., 1949.

Bettelheim, B. *Love Is Not Enough.* New York: The Free Press, 1950.

Bingham, W. V. D. and Moore, B. V. *How to Interview.* New York: Harper & Row, Publishers, 1941.

Buhler, Charlotte, *et al. Childhood Problems and the Teacher.* New York: Holt, Rinehart & Winston, 1952.

Champney, H. "Variables of Parent Behavior," *J. Abn. Soc. Psyc.* 1941, 36, 525-542.

English, H. B. *Dynamics of Child Development.* New York: Holt, Rinehart & Winston, 1961.

Erikson, Erik. *Childhood and Society.* New York: Norton, 1950.

Glueck, S. and Glueck, Eleanor. *Delinquents in the Making.* New York: Harper & Row, Publishers, 1952.

Kahn, R. L. and Cannell, C. F. *The Dynamics of Interviewing.* New York: John Wiley & Sons, Inc., 1957.

Kvaraceus, William C. *The Community and the Delinquent.* New York: Harcourt, Brace & World, Inc., 1954.

Symonds, D. M. *The Psychology of Parent-Child Relationships.* New York: Appleton-Century-Crofts, 1949.

Watson, R. I. *Psychology of the Child.* New York: John Wiley & Sons, Inc., 1959.

Part Three

HEALTH AND
PHYSICAL
DEVELOPMENT

Chapter 8

HEALTH EXAMINATION

THE IMPORTANCE OF HEALTH

What do you know about the health of the children in your class?
What do you know about your own health?

Within the answer to these two questions lies the well-being of
your class and, in no small degree, the success of your efforts as a
teacher. If it is important to the aviator to check out the mechanical
functioning of his aircraft before flying it, and if it is important to
the dairyman to insure production of milk by safeguarding the health
of his herd, it is fully, even more important to the teacher to check
and safeguard the health of her pupils. Their achievement is dependent upon their capacity to learn, and this capacity waxes or wanes
with good or ill health.

None of us can avoid slipping in our performance of our duties
occasionally from loss of sleep, improper food, or accumulated fatigue. We have times of discouragement and depression during which
we fail to perform as well as we should. Some of us have experienced
hearing difficulties, eyestrain, chronic health difficulties, or other
conditions which prevent our doing our best. Many of us neglect our

health and physical condition, for example, by failing to meet with the dentist over so long a time period as to jeopardize our well-being.

Children are subject to the same deficiencies.

If we are alert to the observable clues about ourselves and the children, we can not only prevent and correct much ill health, but, most important, can contribute to the improved health of the class and the community.

Statistics have a way of being impressive but meaningless because we fail to think of the meaning of the unit of measurement being expressed. Thinking about the health statistics of the nation's children impresses one with the need for concern. More than a million children in school have hearing defects, and over four million have visual defects, many of these correctable. The equivalent of over 200 classrooms of elementary school children were killed last year by accidents, most of which were preventable. The achievement loss due to absence from school and irregular attendance is unmeasurable, and, all told, the loss to accident, physical defect, ill health, and malnutrition is staggering. Much of this can be prevented if teachers perform the key role available to them as health detectors.

The term "health detector" aptly describes the function to be performed by the teacher, for essentially her task is to screen out the children who have defects needing correction or who are showing signs of illness or communicable disease, and refer them to responsible sources of treatment. In most states the treatment of any child, except for first aid, is forbidden to lay persons and confined to those licensed to practice medicine. The procedures described in this chapter are designed to indicate to teachers observations to be made as a part of their daily practice of teaching. Once observed, the child will be referred to the proper individuals for diagnosis, treatment, or correction.

Many states have laws requiring that children be examined at one, two, or three year intervals by licensed physicians. As important as such provisions are, they are only a partial safeguard for two main reasons. The limited funds available to the school oftentimes fail to provide sufficient medical services to permit more than a brief examination. Often a complete medical history, essential to thoroughgoing diagnosis, is not available; hence, some less obvious or borderline conditions escape observation. The second reason is that illness, infection, or injury can occur at anytime, not just when the medical examinations are due. It is the teacher and the school nurse, if available, who must accept the day-to-day responsibility for the health safeguards.

Fortunately, we can be fairly certain of the adequacy of such a screen. Sufficient experience has been accumulated with the Astoria Plan, a procedure whereby teacher and school nurse systematically review the health of the class for purposes of identifying children whose physical functioning appears below par for referral to doctor, to know that the combined judgment of teacher and nurse is adequate to detect nearly all instances of poor health.

THE ROLE OF THE TEACHER IN HEALTH OBSERVATION

The teacher doesn't need expensive equipment. Eyes and ears are her chief tools, amplified by a thermometer, a vision test, a watch, a tape measure, and a scale. The importance of systematic observation cannot be over-emphasized. It is the teacher and the parent who see the child daily and are able to observe variations in appearance occurring in the child. Even though we accept a temperature of 98.6 as "normal," few, if any of us, maintain a constant, normal temperature.

A recent study with a group of college students disclosed that all of them had daily fluctuations in temperature, which was not surprising, but, more interesting, each showed fluctuations around his own normal temperature. Although all were in good health, some students never reached a "normal" temperature of 98.6°. Aware as we are of individual differences, it is not surprising that individual variations in average temperature occur. Some children appear more flushed, others more pallid, and consistently so. From daily contact, the teacher is aware of each child's typical appearance and can detect abrupt changes signalling the advent of illness.

It isn't essential to form a line of children and have a daily inspection of hands, face, tongue, and hair, but it is necessary to do more than casually observe the children. We're accustomed to noting general appearance of others—the dress, hairstyle, or attitude, the height, size or general appearance. But health observation requires more system.

OBSERVATIONAL HEALTH CHECK LIST

The following Observational Health Check List itemizes various aspects of physical appearance and behavior to be checked. As each section is discussed, relevant examination procedures will be described.

1. *General condition and appearance*
   a. underweight—very thin
   b. overweight—very obese
   c. does not appear well
   d. tires easily
   e. chronic fatigue
   f. nausea or vomiting
   g. faintness or dizziness

2. *Growth*
   a. failure to gain regularly over three months period
   b. unexplained loss of weight
   c. unexplained rapid gain in weight

3. *Posture and Musculature*
   a. asymmetry of shoulders and hips
   b. peculiarity of gait
   c. obvious deformities of any type
   d. anomalies of muscular development

4. *Eyes*
   a. sties or crusted lids
   b. inflamed eyes
   c. crossed eyes
   d. repeated headaches
   e. squinting, frowning or scowling
   f. protruding eyes
   g. watery eyes
   h. rubbing of eyes
   i. excessive blinking
   j. twitching of the lids
   k. holding head to one side

5. *Ears*
   a. discharge from ears
   b. earache
   c. failure to hear questions
   d. picking at the ears
   e. turning the head to hear
   f. talking in a monotone
   g. inattention
   h. anxious expression
   i. excessive noisiness or quietness of child

6. *Nose and Throat*
   a. persistent mouth breathing
   b. frequent sore throat
   c. recurrent colds
   d. chronic nasal discharge

    e. frequent nose bleedings
    f. nasal speech
    g. frequent tonsillitis

7. *Skin and Scalp*
    a. nits on the hair
    b. unusual pallor of the face
    c. eruptions and rashes
    d. habitual scratching of scalp or skin
    e. state of cleanliness
    f. excessive redness of skin

8. *Teeth and Mouth*
    a. state of cleanliness
    b. gross visible caries
    c. irregular teeth
    d. stained teeth
    e. offensive mouth
    f. mouth habits such as thumb sucking

9. *Glands*
    a. enlarged glands at side of neck
    b. enlarged thyroid

10. *Heart*
    a. excessive breathlessness
    b. tires easily
    c. any history of "growing pains"
    d. bluish lips
    e. excessive pallor

GENERAL CONDITION AND APPEARANCE

Children who are healthy reflect it in the tone of their behavior. Their eyes and skin are clear, appetites are healthy, their muscle tone is firm, and they have abundant energy. They carry themselves with some vitality, seldom with perfect posture, nevertheless with active and reasonably well-coordinated movements. They are not fussy about food, although they may have certain specific likes and dislikes, and they get along well with other children. They grow consistently in height and weight.

Deviations from this general appearance caused by the onset of acute illness are immediately apparent. A temperature increase above 99.5 degrees Fahrenheit, often immediately apparent by a flushed face, watery or glassy appearing eyes, skin rash, running nose, repeated sneezing or coughing, blueness of lips, fingernails, and pallor of skin, are all signals that a child may need immediate help, including separation from the other children for their protection.

Less apparent are more general conditions of poor health. Tiring easily, slow recovery from fatigue, or a general condition of fatigue suggest limitations in energy or body functioning needing careful examination. Failure to show gains in height or weight over a three month and especially a six-month period, or sudden losses or gains in weight should lead to a check to make certain that nothing is wrong.

Physical Growth

Consistent gains in height and weight can be expected in children, and regular checks on such gains is one of the best gauges of healthy development. Awareness of growth is most appealing to children, and seeing evidence of their gains in weight and height is evidence to them that they are "growing up." An increase in height has a tangibility to it that appeals to children, a note of change that is often missing in the more abstract aspects of learning. Knowing their body, gaining control of it, and feeling that it is fulfilling its promise of growth are basic to children's concepts of themselves. Most are eager to be weighed or measured and enjoy discussions on health and growth developing out of such measurements.

Children should be measured and weighed two to three times a year. Many schools have a stand with a pole calibrated in inches and a sliding horizontal bar to facilitate measuring height, but, lacking this, an ordinary cloth tape measure can be taped to the wall, or a yardstick can be hung so that the beginning is three feet above the floor (making it possible to measure any child up to six feet in height without having to continually shift the rule).

A book or a chalk box can be placed horizontally on the head of the child as he stands in natural posture, in stocking feet, with heels, hips, back, and head against the wall. Height can be recorded to the nearest half inch, in view of the fact that day-to-day fluctuations can be this great. Children tend to be taller in the morning, shrinking a little during the day (not because they feel defeated at school) as a result, probably, of compaction of cartilage during the day. Both boys and girls can be expected to grow, on the average, approximately two inches per year between the ages of six and twelve. Growth in height and weight proceeds at a more regular rate during this six-year period than it does in the first or third six-year period. Individual variations about this average occur. During the fifth and sixth grade, some of the boys and girls will show spurts of rapid growth resulting from their reaching puberty. Some children will be consistently below the average in gains, others above, in accordance with their individual patterns resulting from hereditary and environmental factors. Yet each child should show some gains.

The scale used for weighing should be checked for accuracy, either by seeing that it balances at zero pounds or by weighing a known weight on the scale. If no scale is available, either a store scale or borrowed scale are possible solutions. Disregard fractions of a pound in recording weight. Each of us show enough variation in weight during the day—we generally weigh more in the afternoon—that it suffices to record the weight to the nearest whole pound. Gains of roughly six pounds per year can be expected for both boys and girls during primary grades, although, again, it must be emphasized that individual variations in weight gains occur, just as they do with height. Between ages 9-12, boys and girls show even greater gains, averaging 8 pounds per year. If a child fails to gain in weight over a period of three months, the failure should be reported to the school nurse or physician in order that they may make certain nothing is wrong.

POSTURE AND MUSCULATURE

A great deal of valuable information can be obtained regarding the orthopedic disturbances of elementary school children by observation of the child. There is no one posture which can be termed the correct one, but it is desirable that children develop a posture that aids physical efficiency and general well-being. In the early school period, children are round-shouldered and this posture is influenced little by exercise. With the advent of adolescence, the more erect posture is usually attained.

Early recognition and treatment of postural defects is important because the greater plasticity of the bones of younger children makes orthopedic correction easier, and second, because poor postural positions become habitual and once firmly established are difficult to correct. Particularly where the cause is infection or faulty nutrition, the earlier the detection, the more possible correction. Observation should be made of head and neck, shoulders and arms, chest, hips, and spine, legs and feet. The common postural defects which demand attention at all ages are:

1. Kyphosis—rounded shoulders
2. Lordosis—hollow back
3. Scoliosis—one sidedness
4. Chest deformities
5. Knock knees

6. Bowlegs
7. Flat feet
8. Cramped toes

Many defects are such that little can be done for them except accommodation of the school program to the child's limitations. But where the causes are nutritional, external as in the case of poorly fitted shoes, or psychological, remedy is often possible.

It is no accident that maladjusted children show a higher incidence of postural defects than well-adjusted children. Their posture reflects their feelings. In such instances, correction involves consideration of the causes, but corrective actions aimed at improving posture in the form of exercise, movement, stance, and proper fitting of shoes contribute to both physical and psychological health.

VISION

With the exception of touch alone, the eye is the most valued of our special senses. Yet it is not uncommon for poor vision to pass entirely unnoticed, in spite of the fact that an hour cannot pass in a classroom without a child having to use his eyes in a learning task assigned him. At least one-eighth of the school children in this country have defects of vision. A teacher can expect three or four children in her class to have defective vision. Since most of the instruction given in schools is based upon visual impression, it is well to examine the efficiency of the visual functioning.

Tests of vision in the school should be made by the teachers or school nurse. This not only results in a great saving of school funds, but it is the only plan which gives the teachers the intimate knowledge regarding the visual capacity of their pupils. By linking this knowledge with the daily observations regarding possible eye-strain, teachers are better able than the school physician to single out children who need intensive ocular examination.

The following symptoms noted during daily contacts with children may be indications of eye difficulties:[1]

Appearance of eyes
    Red-rimmed, crusted, or swollen eyelids
    Frequent sties
    Watery or bloodshot eyes

---

[1]Ralph V. Merry, *Problems in the Education of Visually Handicapped Children.* Cambridge, Mass.: Harvard Univ. Press, 1933, p. 5. Material used with permission.

Crossed or protruding eyes

Discharge of pus (indicates need of immediate medical care)

Behavior

Walks with extreme caution, looking closely or feeling with the foot for a step up or a step down or for small obstruction; trips or stumbles frequently.

Holds reading material or other types of fine visual work close to face or at a greater distance from the eyes than is normal.

Attempts to brush away blur; rubs eyes frequently; frowns, squints, or distorts face when using eyes for either distant work (chalkboard) or close work.

Shuts or covers one eye; tilts head to one side or thrusts it forward.

Fails to see distant objects readily visible to others.

While looking straight ahead, fails to place objects in appropriate location.

Unduly sensitive to light.

Unable to distinguish colors.

Complaints about eyes

Dizziness

Headache

Nausea

Blurring of objects or letters

Double vision

Burning or itching lids

Pain in eye (indicates need of immediate medical care)

Types of Visual Defects. The most common form of visual defect is error in refraction, characterized by faulty focusing of light upon the retina. In nearsightedness, myopia, the eyeball is too long from front to back so that only near objects can be focused properly. The nearsighted child can see his book fairly well, especially if he holds it closer to his face, but may be unable to see the chalkboard clearly. Myopia is rarely found in young children but appears more frequently in the middle grades. Its seriousness lies in the fact that it is often progressive, with the danger in some cases of detached retina. Hyperopia, or farsightedness, is a condition the reverse of myopia, in which the eyeball is too short so that only distant objects are clearly seen. Late afternoon headaches can be a sign of hyperopia. This defect is common among young children but appears less frequently in the upper grades. The most frequent kind of refractive error is astigmatism, in which irregularities in the curvature of the lens or cornea of the eye cause indistinct or distorted images. Many youngsters suffer from a combination of astigmatism with either near- or farsightedness. As a matter of fact, exacting tests of school children made with a telebinocular show that less than 20 per cent are free of any defect, but fortunately most of the defects are so minor as to not affect visual efficiency.

A second group of visual difficulties result from muscular inco-ordination. The convergence of the eyes on the object to be seen is controlled by a set of muscles surrounding the eyeball. Inadequate coordination makes it difficult to fuse the two images from the eyes into single vision. This may lead to the suppression of the image from one eye and eventual loss of sight in that eye. This problem is acute with children having strabismus or crossed-eyes. If the teacher holds a pencil before the child, instructing him to watch it, then moves the pencil sidewards, she can observe that only one eye focuses and follows the pencil, the weaker eye looking in a different direction. In one study[2] of 350 poor readers, difficulty in coordination at a reading distance was found in half the cases.

A major cause of blindness and defective vision is the atrophy of the optic nerve, which may be partial or total, resulting from con-genital causes or certain diseases or infections such as cerebro-spinal meningitis, diphtheria, scarlet fever, measles, syphilis, or diabetes. Two less frequent visual anomalies are aniseikonia, in which the ocular images are unequal in size or shape, and cataracts, an opacity of the lens.

The simplest test of vision available to the teacher is the Snellen Test, a card printed with rows of letters of different sizes or rows of different size E's pointing in different directions.[3] The latter is for children who do not know their letters, but can be used with any age children. Each row of letters indicates the distance at which the normal eye can read it, starting from the largest letter which would normally be read at a distance of 200 feet and progressing through 100, 70, 60, down to the smallest row of letters which would normally be legible at 10 feet. The card should be placed at eye-height in good light from the side in such a place that the child can stand 20 feet from it. It is best to test children singly to prevent memorization. Have the child hold a stiff card in front of one eye (not against it) and read the rows of letters with the others, starting with one of the larger rows. Children wearing glasses should be examined without them for the condition of the eyes changes and glasses which were once suit-

[2]T. H. Eames, "The Ocular Conditions of 350 Poor Readers," *J. Educ. Res.*, 1938, 32, 10-16.

[3]Snellen cards may be purchased from the National Society for the Prevention of Blindness, 1790 Broadway, New York City, N. Y.

able may no longer be. Occasionally, one will find glasses which were not initially suitable. Glasses should be checked to make certain they are not bent, twisted, or cracked.

If there is doubt as to the accuracy of the test, another card may be substituted, the child can be asked to read the lines backward, or the test can be repeated on another day. In recording the test, a fraction is used which indicates first, the distance at which the child stood, and second, the size of the line. 20/20 vision means the child stood at a distance of twenty feet (the numerator) and read the line marked 20 feet without error (the denominator). If the best the child could do was the 40 foot line without error, his vision is recorded at 20/40 meaning he can read at twenty feet what is normally read at a distance of forty feet, hence, he is nearsighted. This does not mean his vision is only half as good as it should be, instead the meaning of the numbers in terms of visual efficiency follow:

Distance	Percentage Visual Efficiency
20/20	100
20/30	92
20/40	84
20/50	77
20/70	64
20/100	49
20/200	20

By definition, a child is classed as blind if he has less than 20 per cent vision, or if his vision after correction and treatment is 20/200 or less. Children falling between 20/200 and 20/70 after correction are classed as partially sighted. Children who are measured at 20/30 or worse should be examined by an oculist. This does not mean they will automatically need glasses, for, as can be noted, the loss of efficiency is not great. The decision and diagnosis rests with the oculist. The teacher has served her purpose in identifying those children who may have visual difficulties.

The need for more effective screening than provided by the Snellen Test led to the development of the Massachusetts Vision Test and the Eames Eye Test,[4] which include not only the Snellen Test but additional tests.

The additional tests—refraction, farsightedness, coordination, and

---

[4] Information on the Eames Eye Test may be obtained from Harcourt, Brace & World, Inc., New York. Information on the Massachusetts Vision Test can be obtained from the Massachusetts Department of Public Health, Division of Maternal and Child Health, 73 Tremont Street, Boston 8, Massachusetts.

binocular vision—provide a screening for the other visual defects described earlier. The advantage of using either of the latter two tests is their more effective screening. The Snellen Test can be expected to detect approximately 40 per cent of the children requiring attention. The wider range tests can conservatively be expected to double the proportion. In either case, careful observation by the teacher of daily use and condition of the eyes and of symptoms of eye defects is as important as the use of a test.

Tests of Auditory Acuity[5]

Hearing ranks in importance with vision as an avenue of acquisition of knowledge. In certain respects, deafness is more damaging to mental development than blindness. Without sound, one cannot hear words; without words one cannot think. Although the blind child, uneducated, may grow up ignorant, he seldom gives the impression of being mentally defective. The uneducated deaf child nearly always appears stupid. All too often a deficiency in hearing is not recognized as such. In anecdotal reports it is quite common to find that a child has been typed as antisocial, mentally retarded or a behavior problem when later it was discovered through tests that he had a hearing problem.

Between 10 and 20 per cent of school children have defects of hearing. At least one-fifth of these cases are serious. The danger of permanent loss of acuity is great, instruction is difficult, and retardation likely.

In a few instances, the cause of the hearing difficulty may be hereditary as in congenital deafness, but the majority of cases result from three main causes: (1) infectious diseases, (2) diseased conditions of nose and throat, and (3) stoppage of the outer canal of the ear. In children, a major cause is a middle ear infection which sweeps up through the eustachian tube from an infection in the throat. The fact that infections of the middle ear can cause progressive destruction of hearing makes regular and careful observation by the teacher of prime importance.

The following symptoms noted during daily contact may be indications of hearing difficulties:

Appearance
   Discharge from ear
   Cotton in ear

---

[5]Information on the Massachusetts Hearing Test can be obtained from the Massachusetts Department of Health, Division of Child Health.

Excess wax in ear
Blank facial expression or confused expression generally
Behavior
Failure to move head in response to sound
Difficulty in locating source of sound
Pointing one ear towards sound
Listens very intently
Asks for questions to be repeated or repeating question to self
Unconscious loud talking or whispering
Ignores verbal directions
Mistakes in pronouncing common words

Complaints
Earaches
Noises in ear
Spells of dizziness

Hearing acuity is most frequently tested with a pure tone audiometer,[6] which is an instrument designed to produce sounds of different pitch and loudness.

Children may be tested singly or in groups. Each child wears an earphone and indicates responses either by marking a record sheet or raising a finger. A series of tones from low to high are tested separately with the volume for each tone being varied in intensity. The intensity at which the child consistently responds correctly is considered his threshold for that frequency sound. Each ear is tested separately. Earlier models of the audiometer used phonograph and records repeating number or word combinations.

There are three limitations to the audiometer as far as the teachers' use of it is concerned. First, it is a complicated machine which needs periodic checking for the accuracy of its calibration. Second, it requires training for operation. Third is the limited nature of the test. Although it informs as to what level pure tones are not heard, it does not tell us what the child can hear. Our concern is mainly with what speech the child can hear, with the functional effectiveness of his hearing. Many individuals can suffer some hearing loss without its affecting their comprehension of language. So our concern is with how well the child hears the usual sounds relevant to daily life rather than pure tones. Our uncertainty regarding the physiology of sound, and the capacity of humans to compensate and dissemble makes the detection and evaluation of hearing loss difficult.

---

[6] Information regarding the audiometer can be obtained from the American Society for the Hard of Hearing, Washington, D. C.

Several rough gauges of hearing efficiency are available to the classroom teacher. Two of the simpler tests are the whisper test and the watch test. A fairly loud whisper should be heard at a distance of about 20 feet; consequently, a quiet room of this length is needed. Several children can be tested at one time, or, if a large room or gymnasium is available, the children can be placed in a circle with the teacher standing at the center. Each child should stand with his back to the teacher. If one child is being tested he can be asked to repeat number series, such as 297, or words spoken in a loud whisper. If a number of children are being tested the teacher can call out a number from 1-10 which can be indicated by the fingers of the children held behind their back. When testing a group the teacher keeps making her voice quieter until about a fifth of the children are missing answers, and repeating this several times, she notes the children who consistently miss. When testing a single child, the teacher can keep her voice at a level most children can hear. Then for those who cannot hear at the 20 foot distance, she can move closer, until she determines the distance at which he can hear. Those children for whom the teacher has to move within seven feet should be referred for examination. Each ear is tested separately, with the child holding his hand over one ear.

A second test requires the use of a watch having a fairly loud tick. Standing behind the child being tested with the watch in the palm of one hand, and a card to prevent the child's seeing the watch as it is moved towards him, the examiner holds the watch at the level of the ear and directly sideward from the ear. By holding the watch at different distances from 1-4 feet from the ear, and asking the child to tell when he can hear and cannot hear it, a measure of hearing acuity can be obtained. Normally, the watch should be heard as far as four feet distant. Children who can't hear the watch beyond a third of that distance should be referred for hearing examination.

Children's eagerness to please, combined with the fact that all of us occasionally think we are hearing things, prompts children to claim they hear the watch when they do not. The teacher can check this by turning the palm holding the watch away from the child, muffling the sound, and asking if he hears it. The distance and the muffling will make the sound inaudible. The child who answers promptly that he hears the tick either misunderstands or is too eager to please. Another explanation and trial is necessary. One should be certain that no other watches are in the vicinity, e.g., the child's own wristwatch.

CHECKING OTHER ASPECTS OF HEALTH

The consideration given to general condition, vision, and hearing has been detailed due to their immediate relationship to learning. Still, the condition of nose and throat, skin and scalp, and teeth and mouth are fully as important to the well-being of the child and his classmates. Recurrent colds and sore throats, nasal discharge and chronic swollen glands point up health problems. Common skin diseases are ringworm, impetigo, and scabies. It should be kept in mind that any eruption of the skin is abnormal. Allergic reactions can cause sudden skin eruptions. Ringworm begins as a reddish, scaly spot which spreads into a reddish, scaly ring with a pale center. Impetigo occurs as brownish or yellowish, crusty spots, usually fairly thick, appearing on the face or hands. Scabies shows itself in small red punctures and lines, often beginning around hands and wrists, and setting up an intense irritation which the teacher notices through the repeated scratching by the child.

Hair and Scalp. Many teachers may never see lice in their entire career, but in school districts where the living conditions are unfavorable, lice are frequent companions of children. The nits of lice are most noticeable, being small, gray eggs attached to strands of hair especially on the back of the head. The child who has lice is continually scratching, not in perplexity at a school task, but with vigor because of the itch. One infested child in a class is likely to cause as many as a third of the class (not excluding the teacher) to have lice. Ridding the child of the creatures usually involves ridding the family of the infestation, for it is rare when other members of the family do not have them also. Hence, the assistance of public health officials is often needed.

Needless to say, the best defense against any of these conditions is cleanliness, and the measure of the effectiveness of the health education in a school is the degree to which children apply their knowledge to their own body care. Yet such conditions are likely to occur on occasion, and the speed with which they spread in a group of children necessitates preventive action, even segregation if needed, by the teacher.

Oral Hygiene. The incorporation of oral hygiene and dental care as parts of the school program has been a response to a major national health problem, that of dental decay. The percentage of children free of dental problems is quite small. Estimates from surveys indicate that during the school years children are likely to acquire one or two decayed teeth per year. Children acquire their permanent teeth during the elementary school years, yet their limited capacity for self-care requires adult checking on dentition. Teeth that are unclean or decayed, gums that bleed, malodorous breath, and sensitivity to hot, cold, or hard-to-chew foods indicate need for referral to a dentist.

The Heart. Before closing this section, reference should be made to heart and nutritional problems. Most of the techniques for detection of difficulties require special equipment or training for use and are not within the ken of the teacher, but a few warning signs are available.

When the heart is functioning normally, the child gains weight, the color of the skin and the mucous membranes are normal, the subcutaneous tissues are firm, and development proceeds at a normal rate. Heart murmurs are frequent during childhood and the distinction between those which indicate a cardiac problem and those of little concern takes the special training of the physician. Throughout childhood, the pulse rate is more rapid than in adults, is unstable and increases rapidly in response to muscular activity or emotional stimuli. The average rate is higher in the afternoon than in the morning and more rapid after eating than before. Slow pulse rates are rare in children until adolescence, and a pulse rate slower than 60 per minute is indication of organic disturbance of the heart.

Rheumatic fever is the most important chronic disease of childhood. It is responsible for more deaths among children and adolescents than any other disease. The disease is more prevalent in the northern areas of the United States, especially during winter. It is more common in the poorer economic areas and in cities. Symptoms are listed at the end of Chapter 9. First attacks commonly occur at 6-8 years of age. A common symptom is complaint of aches or pains of the joints, particularly wrist, elbows, ankles, and knees. The recurrent nature of the disease and the damage to the heart resulting from recurrent attacks makes early detection and treatment most desirable.

NUTRITION

Nutrition is of utmost importance for the normal development of a child during his period of growth. The food requirements will vary considerably among growing children, however, a well balanced diet rich in certain minerals is essential for the development of good bones and teeth, good skin condition, complete physical development, and other conditions that contribute to healthy growth. Fresh air and sunlight are also important.

In spite of improvements in nutrition in the last few years, there is evidence that the diets of a large percentage of children are still inadequate. Poor dietary practices may be found in homes where the weekly expenditure for food is ample, however, nutritional inadequacies are more often found in families that are on relief, rather than among those in better economic circumstances.

It has been found that some of the greatest deficiencies exist in connection with the eating of green and yellow vegetables and fruit; whereas one of the least deficiencies is in the use of meat. The nutritives that are commonly deficient are riboflavin, calcium, thiamine and ascorbic acid. Vitamin D is also found lacking in the diets of some children. They do not get enough sunshine either in the winter or the summer and, without vitamin D, children vary greatly in their ability to use calcium and phosphorus. Calcium is an important mineral requiring attention during a child's time of growth and development and, as milk is the only good and constant source, it is seldom taken in sufficient amounts. The problem of thiamine can be solved by better food selection, rather than in thiamine medication. The enrichment of flour and breads has done much to overcome this deficiency. Inadequate diets occur in all socio-economic groups, and it is the responsibility of the school to help each child who is suffering from any nutritional deficiency.

Malnutrition is not painful enough to demand immediate attention, but it does bring about conditions that aid in identifying children who are suffering from nutritional inadequacies. Some of the symptoms of malnutrition, usually occurring in combination, are:

Appearance	*Behavior*
Bad posture	Restless and inattentive
Poor muscle tone	Forgetful
Rough skin	Fatigues easily, little stamina
Sores at edge of mouth	Lacks appetite
Serious dental abnormalities	Irritable
Pallor	Abnormal crying
Failure to gain steadily	Abnormal intolerance to light
in weight	Aversion to normal play
	Backwardness in school

A technique used by many teachers in conjunction with health education and particularly diet is to use questionnaires of check-lists to obtain information regarding diet. A series of foods can be listed and children asked to check the ones they like or dislike. The teacher can read the list aloud to prevent errors due to inability to read the list in the lower grades. Children can be asked to keep a record of their meals for a week as part of their work in health education. Care has to be observed that children are not afraid to be honest. They may fear a loss of face if they indicate they didn't have breakfast, or that their supper consisted of a peanut butter sandwich. The numerous possibilities of incorporating such projects are beyond the scope of this text, but texts in health education for the elementary school have many such suggestions.

Questionnaires may also be used to obtain health histories of children. No medical examination is complete without an accurate health history. In addition to the items listed in the Health Check List, the health history includes a record of any diseases (Figures 1-3, Chapter 3), injuries, accidents, operations, and chronic disturbances of the organs and systems of the body. In the main, such histories are the province of the school nurse or physician rather than the teacher, but the latter can make a significant contribution to an accurate health history by maintaining the school record with respect to absences, communicable diseases incurred, and any other health information which comes to her attention.

COMMUNICABLE DISEASES

The chart at the end of Chapter 9 lists the common signs of the most frequent communicable diseases. The use of a thermometer is important in checking temperature. Before using be certain to shake the mercury down below the "normal" temperature of 98.6. Place the thermometer under the tongue, instruct the child to close his lips (not his teeth) and hold it there for two minutes. Inasmuch as the healthy child can have a normal temperature as low as 97 and as high as 99.5, temperatures within this range do not necessarily indicate presence of fever. If the child cannot breathe through his nose, shake the mercury below 97 and place the thermometer in his armpit with arm held at the side. Temperatures taken by this technique will read one degree below those taken by mouth.

At this point in development, it should be evident that the main requirement of the teacher with respect to the health and physical well-being of her pupils is alertness, rather than technical skill. Knowing what to observe, being systematic in observation, and sensitive to change in the child are the essentials. The physical well-being of a child is basic to his learning. Trying to teach an undernourished or chronically ill child is like driving an automobile with flat tires. One goes nowhere rapidly.

Chapter 9

HEALTH AND PHYSICAL DEVELOPMENT

GENERAL DEVELOPMENT

It is certainly of importance that the average child triples his weight and adds 50 per cent to his stature during the years from six to sixteen, but the mere increase in size is by no means the most important feature of the growth process. Such striking physiological changes occur that he becomes a different being. Every proportion of his body alters; there are also changes in the internal organs, in the processes of digestion and metabolism. The sex organs mature, the lymphatic system grows and then decreases, and there are subtle changes in the composition of all the tissues. The organism not only enlarges; it is transformed.

During the school years there are internal changes in every system of the body: muscular, digestive, circulatory, genital, nervous. The nervous system has acquired most of its final growth by the age of twelve, the lymphatic system grows with great rapidity at first and then becomes actually smaller, and the genital organs grow hardly at all until after the twelfth year.

Whereas in the new-born child the muscular system constitutes about 23 per cent of the weight of the entire body, in the adult the muscular system is 43 per cent. And the nature of the muscular tissue is different in child and adult. Moreover, muscular growth is not uniform; nor is muscular growth always perfectly coordinated with growth of the skeleton so that there may be, especially at the adolescent age, embarrassing awkwardness of movement. Rapidly growing children may have so much difficulty in sports that they are not willing to participate.

The circulatory system of the child is definitely different from that of the adult; his heart is smaller in proportion to the arteries; during growth the width of the aorta increases only three times but the size of the heart twelve times.

The lymphatic circulation is chiefly dependent upon muscular activity, and, for this reason, the need for vigorous childhood activity is emphasized. Metabolism is more rapid in children than in adults. Accordingly, appetite is greater. And especially is adolescent appetite marked, and often peculiar. Because of changes in internal chemistry involved in the physiological transformations of adolescence, plus the injudicious diet usually resulting from the adolescent's own selection of foods, the boy or girl is likely to have periods of indigestion, unhealthy skin, and headaches.

As the child moves into adolescence there are strikingly rapid increases in the length of the long bones of the arms and legs, a change which produces most of the marked increase in height. Another skeletal change that is a repeated source of irritation to the organism during school years is the development, then the discarding, of one set of teeth, with the final dentition being completed only during adolescence, or even later.

Sexual maturation occurs between the fifth and tenth grades, occurring in boys about one and a half years later than girls. The majority of the children reach puberty during the seventh and eighth grades, yet approximately 20 per cent of the girls, and a smaller portion of boys reach sexual maturity in the fifth and sixth grades.

Two terms characterize growth and development especially during adolescence: asymmetry and asynchronism. Asymmetry indicates that all parts of the body do not grow in equal proportion, asynchronism that they grow at different rates during different time periods. Each child has his own natural rate and rhythm of growth and development. Adverse circumstances such as disease or abnormal conditions can interfere with and delay these normal processes. Factors affecting the process are his living conditions, diet, health habits, recreation, emotional adjustment, and physical functioning. No single arbitrary standard can be established for any child.

AGE DIFFERENCES

Gesell's longitudinal studies[1] of children provide general descriptions of the motor development and activity of children in the 5-13 year range.

Age 5. Posture is predominantly symmetrical and closely knit. May walk with feet pronate. Control over large muscles is still more advanced than control over small ones. Plays in one location for longer periods, but changes posture from standing, sitting, squatting. Likes to climb fences and go from one thing to another. Jumps from table height. Runs, climbs onto and under chairs and tables. Throws, including mud and snow, and is beginning to use hands more than arms in catching a small ball. Alternates feet descending stairs and skips alternately. Attempts to roller skate, jump rope, and to walk on stilts. Likes to march to music. Coordination has reached a new maturity. He approaches an object directly, apprehends it precisely and releases it with dispatch. Builds with blocks usually on the floor. Likes to color within lines, to cut and paste simple things but is not adept. Likes to copy simple forms. Paints on the floor with large brushes and large sheets of paper. Can "sew" wool through a card by turning it over. Can manipulate those buttons on clothes which he can see, and can lace his shoes. Places fingers on piano keys and may experiment with chords.

Age 6. Activity is sometimes clumsy as he overdoes and sometimes falls in a tumble. Body is in active balance as he swings, plays active games with singing or skipping to music. He is often found wrestling, tumbling, crawling on all fours and pawing at another child, and playing tag. Large blocks and furniture are pushed and pulled around as he makes houses, climbs on and in them. Balls are bounced and tossed and sometimes successfully caught. He tries skates, running broad jump, and stunts on bars. Some boys spend much time digging. Handles and attempts to utilize tools and materials. Cuts and pastes paper, making books, boxes, and likes to use tape to fix things. Hammers vigorously but often holds hammer near the head. Can join boards and make simple structures. Begins to use pencil crayons as well as wax crayons for coloring and drawing.

Age 7. Activity is variable; sometimes very active and at other

---

[1]Modified from Arnold Gesell and Frances L. Ilg, *The Child from Five to Ten.* New York: Harper & Row, Publishers, Incorporated, 1946.

times inactive. The child repeats performances persistently. Has "runs" on certain activities such as roller skating, jump rope, "catch" with a soft ball, or hop scotch. There is a great desire for a bicycle, which he can ride for some distance although he is only ready to handle it within limits. Beginning to be interested in batting and pitching. Boys like to run and shoot paper airplanes through the air. Likes to gallop and to do a simple running step to music. May desire dancing lessons. Manipulation of tools is somewhat more tense, but there is more persistence. Pencils are tightly gripped and often held close to the point. Pressure is variable but is apt to be heavy. Child can now print several sentences with letters getting smaller toward the end of the line. Boys are especially interested in carpentry, and many can now saw a straight line. Girls prefer to color and cut out paper dolls. Several show marked interest in the piano. Usually both hands are used with unequal pressure.

Age 8. Now aware of posture in himself and others. Likes to play follow the leader. Learning to play soccer and baseball with a softball and enjoys the shifts of activity within the game. Girls are learning to run into the moving rope and can run out, but cannot vary step while jumping. Stance and movement are free while painting. Very dramatic in activities with characteristic and descriptive gestures. Many enjoy folk dances but do not like rhythms unless of a spontaneous dramatic nature. Increase in speed and smoothness of performance. Holds pencil, brush, and tools slightly less tensely. Enjoys having a performance timed but does not compete with time. Likely to be a gap between what he wants to do with his hands and what he can do. Writes or prints all letters and numbers accurately, maintaining fairly uniform alignment, slant and spacing. Beginning to get perspective in drawing. Draws action figures in good proportion. Girls can now hem a straight edge in sewing.

Age 9. Plays hard. Apt to do one thing until exhausted, such as riding bicycle, running, hiking, sliding or playing ball. Better control of own speed but shows some timidity of speed of an automobile, of sliding, and of fast snow when skiing. Interest in own strength and in lifting things. Frequently assumes awkward postures. Boys like to wrestle, and may be interested in boxing lessons. Great interest in team games and in learning to perform skillfully. Can hold and swing a hammer well. Garden tools are used and handled appropriately. Builds complex structures with erector set. Handwriting is now a tool. Beginning to sketch in drawing. Girls can cut out and sew a simple garment and can knit. Can dress rapidly. Some interest in combing own hair. Interest in watching games played by others.

Ages 10-13. Most rapid improvement in complex and gross motor skills. Shows ability at definite motor tasks. Relationship between strength and muscular coordination increases. Shows better posture because of better muscular control. Shows improvement of endurance. Strength of grip, resistance to fatigue, improvement in accuracy and steadiness of motor control increase steadily.

Body becomes less flexible after age twelve. Enjoys swimming, bicycling and skating. They show skill in games, physical education, rhythms and dancing. In general boys are better than girls in activities involving large muscles and requiring bodily speed, strength, and endurance. Team ball games and other competitive sports are popular. Girls excel boys in eye-hand co-ordination and in body-balance (dancing and fancy ice-skating). They like to skip rope.

Gang-age reaches its fullest flower at age twelve. This period for boys is marked by restless activity, thirst for locomotion and a desire to make things. They delight in stunts and daring motor performances. Boys like wood-work and hand-work. Girls like sewing, knitting, cooking and handwork. There is a decline in all track and field activities for most girls. Boys show a preference for the companionship of older boys. Still like to play games with coaches, uniforms, and schedules.

NORMS

Hereditary and environmental influences interact to produce wide individual variations in both height and weight. Consequently, average figures should not be used as standards, but rather as landmarks for interpreting data. One should be aware of the fact that height-weight tables get out of date. Selective service data from the two world wars show the recent generation to be taller and heavier than their father's generation. As diet and health improve, the children become taller and heavier. Continued deficiencies produce losses. One has only to travel in countries where the mass of the people exist on submarginal diets to see the effects of prolonged malnutrition on an entire nation.

Two sets of data are provided for height and weight. The first (Tables 1 and 2) is the typical height-weight table for each age and sex; the second (Table 3), the 10th, 50th, and 90th percentiles of height and weight for boys and girls by age from 5-14. A percentile indicates the percentage of the population falling below a given point; e.g., 50 per cent of eight-year-old boys weigh less than 60

TABLE 1—HEIGHT-WEIGHT TABLE FOR BOYS, AGES 5-13

Height Inches	5 yrs.	6 yrs.	7 yrs.	8 yrs.	9 yrs.	10 yrs.	11 yrs.	12 yrs.	13 yrs.
39	35	36	37						
40	37	38	39						
41	39	40	41						
42	41	42	43	44					
43	43	44	45	46					
44	45	46	46	47					
45	47	47	48	48					
46	48	49	50	50	51				
47	. .	51	52	52	53	54			
48	. .	53	54	55	55	56	57		
49	. .	55	56	57	58	58	59		
50	. .	. .	58	59	60	60	61	62	
51	. .	. .	60	61	62	63	64	65	
52	. .	. .	62	63	64	65	67	68	
53	. .	. .	. .	66	67	68	69	70	71
54	. .	. .	. .	69	70	71	72	73	74
55	. .	. .	. .	. .	73	74	75	76	77
56	. .	. .	. .	. .	77	78	79	80	81
57	. .	. .	. .	. .	. .	81	82	83	84
58	. .	. .	. .	. .	. .	84	85	85	87
59	. .	. .	. .	. .	. .	87	88	89	90
60	. .	. .	. .	. .	. .	91	92	93	94
61	. .	. .	. .	. .	. .	. .	95	97	99
62	. .	. .	. .	. .	. .	. .	100	102	104
63	. .	. .	. .	. .	. .	. .	105	107	109
64	. .	. .	. .	. .	. .	. .	. .	113	115
65	. .	. .	. .	. .	. .	. .	. .	. .	120
66	. .	. .	. .	. .	. .	. .	. .	. .	125
67	. .	. .	. .	. .	. .	. .	. .	. .	130
68	. .	. .	. .	. .	. .	. .	. .	. .	134
69	. .	. .	. .	. .	. .	. .	. .	. .	138

pounds. In general, a child is expected to be no more than 7 per cent under or 15 per cent over average weight for his age, height, and sex. Ten per cent underweight and 20 per cent overweight indicate defective nutrition.

A convenient and simple procedure for graphically recording the growth of a child is shown in Figure 1 (page 224). The three lines indicate the 10th, 50th, and 90th percentiles of height and weight for boys taken from Table 3. The advantage of such recording is the im-

TABLE 2—HEIGHT-WEIGHT TABLE FOR GIRLS, AGES 5-13

Height Inches	5 yrs.	6 yrs.	7 yrs.	8 yrs.	9 yrs.	10 yrs.	11 yrs.	12 yrs.	13 yrs.
39	34	35	36						
40	36	37	38						
41	38	39	40						
42	40	41	42	43					
43	42	42	43	44					
44	44	45	45	46					
45	46	47	47	48	49				
46	48	48	49	50	51				
47	. .	49	50	51	52	53			
48	. .	51	52	53	54	55	56		
49	. .	53	54	55	56	57	58		
50	. .	. .	56	57	58	59	60	61	
51	. .	. .	59	60	61	62	63	64	
52	. .	. .	62	63	64	65	66	67	
53	. .	. .	. .	66	67	68	69	69	70
54	. .	. .	. .	68	69	70	71	72	73
55	. .	. .	. .	. .	72	73	74	75	76
56	. .	. .	. .	. .	76	77	78	79	80
57	. .	. .	. .	. .	. .	81	82	83	84
58	. .	. .	. .	. .	. .	85	86	87	88
59	. .	. .	. .	. .	. .	89	90	91	92
60	. .	. .	. .	. .	. .	. .	94	95	97
61	. .	. .	. .	. .	. .	. .	99	101	102
62	. .	. .	. .	. .	. .	. .	104	106	107
63	. .	. .	. .	. .	. .	. .	109	111	112
64	. .	. .	. .	. .	. .	. .	. .	115	117
65	. .	. .	. .	. .	. .	. .	. .	117	119
66	. .	. .	. .	. .	. .	. .	. .	119	121
67	. .	. .	. .	. .	. .	. .	. .	. .	124
68	. .	. .	. .	. .	. .	. .	. .	. .	126
69	. .	. .	. .	. .	. .	. .	. .	. .	129

mediate comparison possible with normative data provided by being able to compare the height of the boy at any point with the trend lines for the group. Similar lines can be plotted for weight, and for girls as well as boys.

If you look closely at Figure 1 you will observe that it records height in relation to age, but height alone. Further it compares the boy's height to the norm of the group. A separate graph is needed

TABLE 3—PERCENTILES FOR WEIGHT AND HEIGHT OF AMERICAN CHILDREN[2]

Percentiles, Boys			Age—Measurement	Percentiles, Girls		
10	50	90		10	50	90
			5 yr.			
36	41	48	weight, lb.	35	41	50
41	43	45	height, in.	41	43	45
			6 yr.			
41	48	56	weight, lb.	40	47	54
44	46	49	height, in.	44	46	48
			7 yr.			
46	54	64	weight, lb.	46	52	61
46	50	51	height, in.	46	48	51
			8 yr.			
51	60	73	weight, lb.	49	58	70
49	51	54	height, in.	48	50	53
			9 yr.			
56	66	81	weight, lb.	53	64	79
51	53	56	height, in.	50	52	55
			10 yr.			
61	72	90	weight, lb.	57	70	90
52	55	58	height, in.	52	55	58
			12 yr.			
72	84	110	weight, lb.	70	88	112
56	59	62	height, in.	56	60	63
			14 yr.			
87	108	137	weight, lb.	91	108	133
60	64	68	height, in.	60	63	66

for weight. Yet nowhere are height and weight shown at the same time.

THE WETZEL GRID

The Wetzel Grid, however, does record height and weight together (Figure 2). At the left of the Grid, age, height, and weight are recorded. The middle of the chart has weight shown on the vertical axis, and height shown on the horizontal axis. The combina-

---

[2]Modified from data of H. C. Stuart and H. V. Meredith in E. H. Watson and G. H. Lowrey, *Growth and Development of Children.* Chicago: The Yearbook Publishers, 1954.

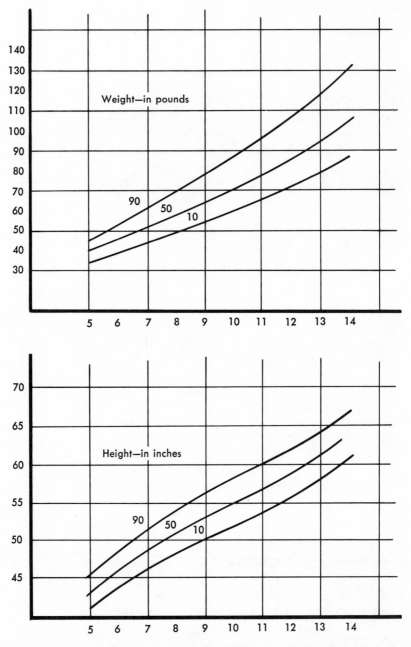

Figure 1. Graph of weights and heights (10th, 50th, 90th percentile) for boys—ages 5-14.

tion of height-weight is plotted together on the Grid and will generally fall in one of the diagonal channels running upwards in mid-page.

Wetzel based his Grid on two principles: the first that each child grows at his own pace and should, therefore, be his own standard of comparison; the second that healthy growth progresses along a channel corresponding to a child's natural physique and at an average over-all rate of one-level-per-month for all children regardless of age, sex, race, and other factors. Channels A_4, A_3, A_2, A_1, M, B_1, B_2, B_3, and B_4 range from the obese channel, A_4, throughout the center channels, A_1, M, B_1, indicating medium build, to the slender body type in B_4. A series of lines crossing the channel system is marked by numbers 30, 40, 50...180. These lines represent developmental levels at which all children falling at a given level have the same body size, the same body surface, and hence the same fuel requirements.

Many comparisons are possible with the Wetzel Grid. One is whether or not a child's growth in height and weight is progressing consistently, i.e., maintaining physique by following a given channel. According to Wetzel,[3] healthy children will remain in the same channel true to their body type and not deviate more than half a channel within a ten level advance. Any child showing greater deviation should have special attention for health problems. Another comparison can be made at the right of the chart which permits a child's developmental level *(body size)* to be correlated with individual norms of progress *(auxodromes)*, e.g., 1, 2, 3 shown in Figure 2, and with further information as to caloric needs of boys and girls. Although the Grid offers a comprehensive method for analyzing and evaluating child growth, in application it is actually simple to use.

Maturity ratings can be made at any and all points on the Grid, not necessarily at maturity alone. In this connection it should be remembered, however, that height and weight are variable at all points of a child's life. High intercorrelation of measurements of physical growth provide the Grid a satisfactory operational basis. However, the critical question is whether maturity can be gauged by height and weight.

---

[3]The reader will find an interesting and more detailed discussion of this subject in Dr. Norman C. Wetzel, *The Treatment of Growth Failure in Children.* Cleveland, Ohio: Newspaper Enterprise Association, 1948. Grid used by permission of Newspaper Enterprise Association and Dr. Norman C. Wetzel.

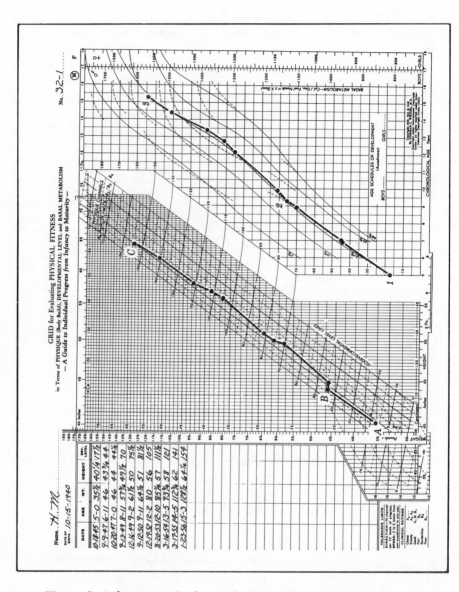

Figure 2. A long-term Grid record of "good" over-all physical growth and development as shown by consistent channel course *(BC)* and steady progress along the 67 per cent standard auxodrome (1,2,3). Minor deviation at *B* (placement in foster home) was readily compensated for after return to own family (2). This boy excelled in competitive scholarship as well as swimming and hockey for which his body type (A_1A_2) favored him.

226

Reverse side of The Wetzel Grid, illustrated above, provides a complete health record entry-form for pre-school and school children from kindergarten through senior high school.

NUTRITIONAL NEEDS

Table 4 shows certain nutritional needs of children of elementary school age.

TABLE 4—NUTRITIONAL NEEDS OF ELEMENTARY SCHOOL CHILDREN

Nutrient	6-7	8-9	10-12
Calories per pound of body wt.	34-35	32-35	26-30
Total calories needed	1700-2000	1900-2250	2100-2400
Percent of total calories from each class of food:			
Milk	35-45%	33-42%	32-38%
Cereal grain	18-22	18-22	18-24
Veg. & fruits	16-22	17-23	18-24
Eggs, meat, cheese	5-7	6-8	7-9
Fats (butter, cod-liver oil)	10-15	15-18	15-18
Sugar	3-5	4-6	6-8
Recommended daily allowances:			
Protein-gm.	50	60	70
Calcium-gm.	1.0	1.0	1.0
Iron-mg.	8	10	12
Vitamin A-Iu	2500	3500	4500
Thiamin-mg.	.8	1.0	1.2
Riboflavin-mg.	1.2	1.5	1.8
Nicotinic acid-mg.	8	10	12
Ascorbic acid-mg.	50	60	75
Vitamin D-Iu	400-800	400-800	400-800

HEALTH TRENDS IN ELEMENTARY SCHOOL

The general characteristics provide some clues to the health and susceptibility of children of different ages to particular dangers, and, consequently, to needed attention on the part of parents and teachers. Variations naturally occur in accordance with the health of individual children and differences in exposure to communicable disease.

5½ years: Complains that his feet hurt. Some have frequent colds. Headaches or earaches beginning. Stomach aches with some nausea and vomiting in connection with school. Somatic symptoms may appear after a week or two of school. Whooping cough, measles, and chicken pox are the most common communicable diseases. Hypersensitivity of face, head, neck region to washing, hair combing, etc. This child may endure great pain yet fuss about a splinter or nose drop installation.

6 years: More susceptible to diseases and sicker with illnesses than earlier in life. Frequent sore throats, colds, with complications (lungs and ears). Increase in allergies. Communicable diseases include chicken pox, measles, whooping cough, diphtheria, scarlet fever, German measles, and mumps. Stomach aches and vomiting in connection with going to school. Toilet accidents with too much excitement. Hypersensitivity of face, neck region if washed or touched. Arms most frequently broken in falls.

7 years: Fewer illnesses than at 6 but colds persist longer. German measles and mumps are frequent. Chicken pox and measles may occur. Complains of headaches with fatigue or excitement; complains of muscular pain. Extreme fatigue. Minor accidents to eyes, eye rubbing common—may be due to eye disorders or not.

8 years: Improving health. Fewer illnesses and of shorter duration. Less absence from school because of illness. Increase in allergies and otitis media (middle ear infection). Headaches, stomach aches, and need to urinate in connection with disagreeable tasks. Accidents frequent: from falls, drowning, and in relation to automobiles and bicycles. Legs most frequently broken in falls. Rheumatic fever reaches its peak between 6 to 8 years.

9, 10, 11, 12, 13 years: Improving health and few illnesses, but marked individual differences in relation to disease. Some have prolonged illness or show marked fatigue. Very few general somatic complaints, but many minute ones related to the task at hand (eyes hurt when tested, hands hurt when gripping); often can be heard saying a task makes him feel dizzy. Diseases common to this entire age group are the communicable diseases, rheumatic fever and poliomyelitis.

Communicable Diseases

The pre-school and elementary school years are periods of high incidence of communicable diseases. As children come into extensive contact with other children in school and at play, they are exposed to a variety of diseases. It is not unusual to have a quarter to a third of some classes absent at the same time when an epidemic of measles is in full swing. Table 5 lists the characteristics of the common communicable diseases to which teachers should be alert.

TABLE 5—CHARACTERISTICS OF COMMUNICABLE DISEASES OF CHILDREN

	RESPIRATORY			
Communicable Disease	Common Cold Pharyngitis Tonsillitis	Bronchitis	Diphtheria	Whooping Cough
Causation	Virus, Lowered resistance due to fatigue, chilling, chronic infection	Associated with colds, influenza, measles, etc.	Klebs-Loeffler bacillus	Pertussis bacillus
Incubation	1-3 weeks duration	2-6 weeks duration	1-7 days	5-16 days
Symptoms	Fever 100-104 Vomiting Running nose Inflamed tonsils Yellow spots on tonsils Intestinal upset	100-104 Non-productive cough, becoming productive "Rattling" in chest as child breathes Fever gone in 2-3 days	Moderate Flushed face Sore throat Swollen glands Harsh, croupy cough Rapid pulse	Ordinary cough becoming more persistent, occurring in spells, worse at night "Whoop" occurs in 1-2 weeks
Quarantine of Patient	none		1 week	
Quarantine of Contact	none		none	
Complications	Secondary invasion by various bacteria can cause pneumonia, diphtheria, sinus and ear difficulty		Pneumonia Paralysis of muscles of throat, heart	Pneumonia Bronchitis Sinusitis Hernia Encephalitis

SKIN				GLANDS	OTHER	
Scarlet Fever	Chicken Pox	Measles	German Measles	Mumps	Poliomyelitis	Rheumatic Fever
Strepto-coccus Scarla-tina	Virus	filtrable virus	filtrable virus	Virus	Virus	Uncertain Familial occurrence
2-7 days	14-21 usually 17	fever— 10 days rash— 13-15	14-21 days usually 16	12-26 days usually 18-21	7-14 days	Frequent age 6-8 years
Fever present Headache Vomiting Nausea Sudden onset Bright, red rash occurring within 24 hours on neck, chest, arms	Slight eruption of small, watery blisters in crops on both exposed and covered parts of body	Moderate Running nose Sore throat Sneezing Puffy, red, watery eyes Hyper-sensitive to light Rash appears 3 days after first symp-toms	Moder-ate, if any Symp-toms of head cold for 1-2 days followed by raised deep pink rash on face, then body	Swollen gland on neck, in front and below ears Painful to swallow	Headache Vomiting Sore Throat Stiff neck Digestive upset Drowsy Irritable for 3 days followed by paralysis or muscle weakness	Fever 100-102 Malaise, fretful nose & digestion Variable head symptoms Inflamed, red tender joints, knee, ankle, hip, wrist, elbow "Growing Pains" Abdominal pain Skin lesions Subcutaneous nodules on hand, wrist, scalp
4 weeks	1 week	2 weeks	5-7 days	2 weeks	2 weeks	
1 week	none	none	none	none	none	none
Heart & kidney damage Middle-ear inflam-mation	Infected skin lesions	Chronic inflam-mation of eyes, ears Pneu-monia	none	Inflammation of other glands, tho' rare in 5-13 yr. group	Paralysis of affected parts	Permanent heart damage

Chapter 10

PROMOTING HEALTH

The promotion of positive physical health in children can be and should be a source of much satisfaction to teachers. Living as we do in a health conscious era in which one can scarcely find a popular magazine without an article on health, and certainly not without health advertisements, and being bombarded daily by radio and television exhortations regarding digestive regularity, gastric acidity, dental deterioration, and vitamin deficiency, we become misinformed, superstitious, fad-prone health addicts. There are few adults who don't, momentarily at least, rise to the tempting bait of a vitamin advertisement guaranteeing to get rid of that "fatigued feeling." We should not be surprised then to learn that children in grades four-six have many misconceptions and believe many superstitions regarding health, and that seventh and eighth grade students identify physical health as an area of major concern.

With a little attention and effort, each teacher can make positive contributions to the health and well-being of the children in her class, contributions that are fully as important as any multiplication table she might teach. Four areas of action are open to the teacher:

1. The provision of a healthy environment.
2. The identification of physical defect or illness and referral for appropriate treatment.
3. The prevention of illness and the promotion of health through education.
4. The management of the environment in a treatment program.

A HEALTHY ENVIRONMENT

The capacity of humans, including children, to accommodate and survive in the most miserable conditions makes it necessary to inquire into the most obvious aspects of the school environment: the physical facilities in which children are educated, and the health of the principals and teachers who conduct the education. Few parents will take the time that one conscientious father did to measure the available light in different portions of the four classrooms in an 1870 school building still in use. He discovered that in certain rooms during the winter the light available to the children for their school work was less than pale moonlight. His one-man campaign resulted in the installation of suitable light fixtures. Such actions are unusual.

In the main, any unsuitable conditions will continue as long as the classroom teacher tolerates it. Unsanitary drinking fountains and toilet facilities, hazardous stairs and equipment, inadequate heating, lighting, and ventilation, unhygienic kitchens and lunchrooms, and dangerous traffic conditions should not exist in today's schools. Each child has the right to work and learn in an environment assuring him of adequate safety, health, and development. More than anyone else, the teacher should be conscious of aspects of the physical plant which are not conducive to the healthy well-being of the children.

An important part of the physical environment in which children are to learn is the physical health of the teacher. Beautiful buildings, varied equipment and materials, and spacious playgrounds go for naught unless the teachers who work in them are physically, mentally, emotionally, and socially fit.

Ill, worried, fatigued, or irritable teachers are incapable of creating or providing the classroom atmosphere needed for efficient learning or healthy development. Failure to have periodic physical examinations or maintain lives in which relaxation and recreation appropriately balance work inevitably leads to unhealthy classroom atmospheres. A simple check that a teacher can make is to keep a record for two or three days—over a period of a fortnight—of all her positive and negative responses to children in the classroom, by tallying a mark in one column every time that she encourages or praises, criticizes or blames a child. Some surprising pictures develop from such tallies.

The health and happiness of a teacher is contagious. Not only is it a model for the behavior of the children, but also a stimulus to children to like and respect each other, to understand themselves and each other, and to enjoy the opportunities which school presents. For many children, especially in cities, school is the nicest place they know, a place of pleasant surroundings and pleasant people.

IDENTIFICATION AND REFERRAL

Repeated emphasis has been made of the fact that teachers are not expected to diagnose illness or prescribe remedies, but that their main function with respect to the health and physical development of children is to be alert to signs of illness and physical defect, both through the use of regular observations and simple screening devices for faulty hearing, vision, and the like. Detection of disability is the first step, and referral to the appropriate source for treatment the second. Most parents appreciate the interest of teachers or school nurses in advising them of health problems of their children, but this reaction is not universal. The neglect which some parents show for their children springs from hidden motives which cause them to resent the efforts of school authorities. In many instances, financial duress limits capacity of parents to provide adequately for the child.

PROMOTION OF HEALTH THROUGH EDUCATION

If many of the learning tasks which are presented to children in elementary schools appear puzzling and meaningless, certainly the phases of the curriculum devoted to physical development and health should not. Alphabets and arithmetic are abstract in their very nature, but health education need not be. The present and future lives of many millions of children now attending school will be affected by the health education programs in which they participate. Experience shows that children can be helped to live healthfully, to understand themselves as living organisms, to develop favorable attitudes toward health and health practices, and to make use of professional health services.

The American Association of School Administrators holds that the major responsibility for health instruction in the elementary school must be carried by the classroom teacher and should center around the formation and extension of desirable practices, attitudes and understandings associated with the daily life of the child. Possible areas of study are: food and nutrition, exercise, rest and sleep, eyes and ears, body functions, cleanliness, clothing, safety and first aid, communicable disease control, mental and emotional health, and community health. Health education in the elementary school cannot be limited to a certain time of day nor to a particular portion of the curriculum.

At certain grade levels specific courses in health are advocated, and even in the lower grades specific health units may at times occupy the attention of the teacher and the class. However, the health education program must be considered as much broader than the presentation of formal lessons. Throughout the child's entire life at school, all his experiences shape his attitudes and viewpoints concerning health.

Probably no phase of the school curriculum offers greater possibilities in the development of the "whole child" than adequate, well-coordinated, well-directed, and appropriately adapted health education. Planning a program requires that the teacher study his pupils, their homes, and their community (using techniques for obtaining information previously described) to determine the pupil's health needs and interests; that he prepare or at least carry in mind specific health aims; and that he be familiar with health education guides, courses of studies, and teacher aids and resources. The answers to the following questions suggest specific needs and interests:

1. How many have adequate diets and nutrition?
2. How many need dental care?
3. How many use desirable health practices in school?
4. What difficulties in adjusting to classmates, teachers, and school routines are noticed in the group as a whole?
5. How suitable are their play activities?
6. How many fail to follow recommended safety practices?
7. What misconceptions and misinformation do they have about health and body functioning?
8. What particular health problems interest them?

TEACHING PROCEDURES

Teaching is a continuous process of planning, experiencing, and evaluating. The exact procedures will vary somewhat from teacher to teacher and from grade to grade and from one school to another. They will depend on the teacher's general philosophy of education, on the curriculum pattern of the school and on the teacher's own concept of the best ways to help children grow and develop. In all situations, however, opportunities for incidental health education should be grasped. Units of health instruction can be used when appropriate. In the guidance of pupils in relation to personal health, the teacher must be able to see the situation as the child himself sees it and lives it. He must mobilize knowledge to work in terms of practices possible for the child to adopt.

The development of health units is no different than the development of units for other areas of study. Timing, however, may be important. In the fall, interest in control of communicable diseases may arise from a center of interest. In the winter, when the incidents of respiratory disease are highest, a unit may take its start from inquiry as to why so many children are absent from school with colds. In the springtime, when children are thinking ahead to their summer vacations, inquiry as to their projected plans may lead to a teaching unit in safety education—traffic safety, water safety, camping safety, and the like. Health units may develop informally by capitalizing on a particular occurrence that has health complications.

Problem-solving activities based on health problems in the school, home, or community are all valuable learning experiences. Several specific suggestions for teaching can be offered:

1. *Consider individual differences.* Children vary tremendously in health, in health interests, and in mental and physical capacities. It should not be expected that all children will go to bed at the same time, gain the same number of pounds, or grow the same number of inches each year, be equally proficient in physical and mental activities, have the same interests and hobbies, or react alike to similar social situations. Each child is as unique as his own fingerprint.

In the primary grades the children are working at gaining control of gross body movement. Their learning experience and their growth are complimentary. Improvement in motor skills cannot take place without ample opportunity for experience and practice, particularly for opportunities of the trial and error nature. Failure to learn new motor patterns as the body matures will retard a child's progress in school and restrict his opportunities to establish himself on equal footing in the play groups. Subsequent low status in class groupings is associated with physical awkwardness.

Motor activity not only provides a means to group status but, equally important, is a wholesome outlet for tensions. No matter how able a child may be, school causes tensions. The necessity for working persistently, the difficulty of the learning tasks, adapting to the requirements of others, are all sources of tension. If physical activities, instead of being an outlet for tension, become another source of frustration, not only does the tension increase, but another outlet, often undesirable, must be found.

In the upper grades, where some girls and a few boys are reaching puberty, many become keenly aware of the physiological changes occurring and suffer some anxiety. Acquiring an understanding of the physical and emotional changes occurring is essential, yet far too few schools provide such opportunities.

A wise teacher will avoid making rigid health rules which all pupils are expected to follow to the letter. Health behavior should be flexible, based on principles rather than rules.

Children need to learn the basic concepts and accepted practices, rather than being regulated by dogmatic rules.

2. *Discourage self-diagnosis and self-medication.* Pupils should be warned against attempting to diagnose abnormal conditions themselves or expecting the teacher or nurse to do so, particularly in this day of televised medicine men. Health education is concerned with the positive aspects of health and the preventative aspects of sickness, not with the specific diagnosis or the details of treatment. It is true that modern medicine knows more of how to correct illness than of promoting health, but our focus as laymen is on how to be healthy.

3. *Avoid embarrassing pupils.* Children should not be held responsible for conditions over which they have little control. Accidents involving disruption of bladder control and vomiting are frequent in primary grades, especially during the afternoon from excitement, tension, and fears. A rigid schedule for toilet lines is most undesirable during this period. Some children have not been trained to take complete charge of themselves in the bathroom, others do not understand the need of washing hands after use of the toilet.

Families differ considerably in their degree of modesty with respect to exposure of the body, and children reflect their family's attitude. Girls in the fifth and sixth grade become self-conscious about their sudden growth. Some attempt to offset it by slouching. Short boys in the same classes feel inadequate in the presence of taller and stronger girls. In the middle grades many youngsters develop a slouch while sitting or walking. The children should not be ridiculed, embarrassed, or made unhappy because of these events or because of shortcomings in the care they receive at home. A health education program which helps children to understand and accept their bodies —its structure, functioning, and needs—will support children in their efforts to master their bodies. Good general health, adequate diet, plenty of activity and rest, the development of feelings of adequacy, and the emotional support of the teacher will do more to correct physical and postural difficulties than all the criticism and ridicule in the world, whether from the teacher or from classmates.

Moriarty and Irwin[1] have shown that children with poorest posture are significantly more fatigued, self-conscious, restless, and timid, and have more illness and physical defects than children possessed of good posture. Children's posture is a reflection of the way they feel. Improve their feelings, physically and emotionally, and their control, posture, and attitude improve. Basic to our feelings about ourselves and to our feelings of being worthwhile is the attitude we develop about our bodies, its appearance and capacity for functioning adequately.

Health is not a subject for competition. If children are asked to record their health practices, the information they supply should be considered personal and confidential and of interest solely to the teacher and the particular child. Children should not compare records. Competition encourages them to lie in order to maintain the appearance of doing what they think the adult desires.

4. *Adapt teaching to pupil's interests, needs, and capacities.* Progress in health instruction is obtained through adapting teaching materials to the needs, interests, and capacities of children. At the five-seven age level, when large muscles are better developed and coordinated than small, and eye-hand coordination is improving, and there is short attention span but high activity level, there should be ample opportunity for free bodily movement, use of space, games suited to large muscle control and development of rhythm involving running, jumping, skipping, marching, hopping, chasing, and throwing and catching balls from a stationary position.

Abstract topics such as health are meaningless, but growing strong bodies has meaning; bacteria and germs are too abstract, but tallying reasons for absences and discovering how to protect oneself from illness are not. The nine-year-old, prone to exhaust himself in running, bicycling, sliding, and ball playing can be helped to see the value of

---

[1]Mary Moriarty, and L. W. Irwin, "A Study of the Relationship of Certain Physical and Emotional Factors to Habitual Poor Posture among School Children," *Res. Quarterly*, 1952, 23:2, 221-225.

rest and less active pursuits such as handicrafts. At this age with the increase in accidents, particularly fractures of arms and legs, the need for safety is self-evident.

5. *Base teaching on real problems and real people.* Effective health teaching does not transport the child into a world of fantasy and make-believe; it is concerned with real problems, real people, real situations, the here and now. Health education is not a series of facts to be memorized but a program for the improved health of child, family, and community. Progress is obtained slowly, but if children are expanding their views of themselves, their families, and their community, if they are incorporating their knowledge into their daily life, they are developing healthily.

Special events offer one source of real problems. At the time of the national campaign for vaccination for prevention of poliomyelitis, a natural topic is provided. The role of science, the experimental use of animals, the transmission of diseases, the protective devices the body uses to ward off illness, and the discovery and development of vaccines are a few of the avenues of learning opened.

For all ages, adult demands for cleanliness appear arbitrary and purposeless, especially to boys. There is fun to be had in dirt, mud, and messing. A developing understanding of the functioning of the skin, of the kinds of waste products of the body, of the elimination needs of the body, of the spread of germs by contact, brought about through visual demonstrations, gives some sense to the importance of cleanliness. Even with such understanding, adult supervision will not be eliminated, but the demands may be possibly less frequent, and certainly appear less arbitrary.

6. *Use a variety of teaching methods.* Variety is the spice of teaching. Any teaching method, no matter how good, can be overdone. We teachers certainly overdo with words. Group assignments can be mixed with individual assignments; charts can aid in the study of some problems, and motion pictures or film strips another; children can perform simple experiments, teachers can offer more complex demonstrations; one topic can be developed for an assembly program, another in conjunction with the class across the hall; visits, projects, dramas, the list is limited only by imagination.

In no manner are the foregoing suggestions intended as an outline for health education in the elementary schools. The intent is to call attention to the fact that health education can be an integral part of a program designed to encourage the wholesome personal and social development of children. Several adequate sources available for suggestions as to content, procedures, and resources in health education, are listed in the chapter bibliography.

NUTRITION

If good health is essential for favorable growth and development, good nutrition is basic to both. The importance of adequate diet has support from three types of studies: observational studies of the effects of malnutrition on large populations during depression and war, the effects of dietary supplements with given groups of children, and controlled studies of the effects of dietary change.

The food crisis caused in certain countries during both world wars produced observable effects on growth and development. In Greece in 1943, over half the children were underweight, this proportion growing to two-thirds by 1944. In Holland, during the famine period at the end of World War II, most children had lost weight and stopped growing. In addition to delayed growth, marked retardation in learning occurs. Children fatigue easily, comprehend more slowly, find it difficult to concentrate, and forget more rapidly when they are undernourished. They become increasingly restless and irritable and discipline is more difficult to maintain. Although learning and performance are affected, intelligence as measured by test does not appear affected.

During World War II a group of conscientious objectors volunteered to participate in a controlled study of human starvation. The men were fed diets amounting to semi-starvation, and the effects upon the body and physical functioning were observed. Fat disappeared, muscles decreased, bodily processes slowed, basal metabolism lowered, blood sugar decreased. Anemia developed, and work capacity decreased. When full diets were restored recovery was not rapid, but slow. Seven to eight months were necessary to recover full strength.

Similar results have been obtained with undernourished children. Noticeable gains in height and weight occur but optimal functioning comes slowly. More rapid response occurs in instances where a simple deficiency of a given nutrient such as thiamin, riboflavin, or vitamins exists, than occurs where a total and prolonged deficient diet has existed. It has been observed that if the deficiency does not continue over too long a period of time, children can recover from the effects without permanent harm. Extensive post-war studies of dietary habits of children in the United States show that the diets of two out of three children can be improved, and that the diets of forty per cent are inadequate.

Observable signs of the undernourished child have been pointed· out previously in the Health Check List—underweight, pallor, blue circles under eyes, poor posture, undeveloped muscles, loose or flabby flesh. In children of adequate size for age, restlessness, inattention, irritability, and forgetfulness can be signs of malnourishment. Occasionally behavior thought to result from perversity of maladjustment is the simple result of hunger or vitamin deficiency.

The value of a school lunch program is apparent. For many children such a lunch is often the only well-balanced meal of the day. Studies show the school lunch increased the number of children having adequate diets by a third. But its value goes beyond mere nutrition, for children observe a well-balanced meal, are encouraged to taste new foods, develop better food habits. The lunch program provides a basis for classroom learning related to foods needed for body growth.

The story of Diane illustrates many of the points which have been discussed with respect to the importance of teacher alertness to health problems and of adequate nutrition to desirable school performance.

Diane, a 14 year old, eighth grader, weighed 84 pounds and was five feet two inches tall. She was blonde, very pretty, attractive to the boys in her class, very careful of appearance, well-groomed. She was generally quiet, shy, and reserved, but, nevertheless, was friendly and accepted by her own set. To the teacher she lacked animation and seemed perpetually tired. Diane gave every promise of being a top student but constantly missed out because she failed to do the extra little things which distinguish such students. During the first half of the school year, she missed 19 days of school, never more than a day at a time, excused by the mother "because Diane didn't feel well." On the afternoons she returned for make-up work Diane always complained of feeling tired and never did more than the bare minimum. Her answers on essay questions revealed her keen mind and confirmed her IQ of 130, yet she failed to complete her mid-year exams. When the teacher discussed this with her, Diane said that she was tired that day. Questioned why, Diane replied that she was always tired, even though she never went anywhere or did anything to make her tired. It was on this occasion that the teacher noticed that Diane's lips, bare of lipstick at the time, were almost white with a faint purplish tinge. Thinking

it presented a possible heart problem, this prompted the teacher
to speak to Diane's parents.

Both parents were graduates of exclusive colleges, the father
a successful businessman, the mother prominent in social events,
both active in community affairs. Both were interested in Diane's
well-being. When the teacher first broached his concern about
Diane's lack of energy, and her underachievement, the mother
dismissed it as "growing pains," but the teacher pressed his
point that he thought that something more drastic than "growing pains" existed and suggested a medical examination.

The doctor discovered that Diane was eating little besides
potatoes, canned corn, bread and cake, and was well on her way
to having pernicious anemia. With the parents often not home
at mealtime, Diane ate many meals alone, but even when the
family dined together, the parents didn't pay attention to what
Diane left on her plate. The effects of treatment were almost
immediately apparent. In the second half of the year Diane
gained over 15 pounds in weight, no longer complained of
fatigue, developed a healthy appetite for well-balanced meals,
no longer missed school and showed sharp improvement academically, achieving the honor roll.

In this instance, the results were dramatically favorable; in others,
however, change comes more slowly and sometimes not at all.
Several important considerations stand out in this situation just
described: the teacher's day-to-day observations of the girl, his
relating the facts he was obtaining, with the other information available on attendance, intelligence, actual-vs.-expected achievement,
and the like, concluding with his final observation of her pallor that
medical attention was needed, and impressing this upon the parents.
Equally interesting is the fact that the teacher's guess as to the nature
of the problem (heart ailment) was wrong, which reinforces the
distinction between detection and diagnosis. The teacher's function
is detection of a problem, not diagnosis, for the medical knowledge
available to teachers is so limited as to make diagnosis dangerous.

THE MANAGEMENT OF THE
ENVIRONMENT IN A TREATMENT PROGRAM

If the lives of children proceeded evenly without deviation along
their given paths, the need for remedial action would not exist. Our
practice of comparing children makes it immediately apparent that
some differ more greatly than others. These differences are not only
as apparent to the deviate as to the observer, but they become a

source of concern. We then face the task of acting to reduce the difference or make it acceptable to the possessor and the beholder. Such actions can be thought of as remedies or treatments, not in the medical sense of the words, but rather as procedures undertaken to ameliorate or modify undesirable conditions. In the broad sense, medical treatment would fit the definition, but not in the specific sense, for the purpose here is to restrict the discussion to the kinds of actions available to teachers. In line with the preceding chapter, the discussion should foster a definition of the professional role and responsibility of the teacher as well as the limit of such responsibility in the treatment program.

The best treatment for many so-called adjustment or behavioral difficulties is to ignore them, trusting to the growth forces in the child and the self-correction possible in the face of natural pressures to produce the desired change. If every momentary aberration of behavior necessitated action on the parts of parents or teachers, the task would be impossible. While judicious ignoring is suited to many minor behavioral problems, it is seldom an appropriate course of action in the area of health and physical development. The most significant action, of course, is the early detection of health or physical problems and referral for appropriate medical care. But beyond this there are several avenues open to the teacher: to provide emotional support, to make accommodations in program, and to exert influence to produce change. Whatever the specific action the teacher takes, it can usually be included in one of the foregoing categories.

All human beings need help at one time or another in facing the reality of living. An adult, by definition, is a person capable of facing reality independently, and yet all adults encounter moments of stress and distress when they need some emotional support or encouragement in meeting the events of life. Sickness, a death in the family, loss of a job, are but a few events in which a person's capacity may be overtaxed were it not for the emotional support and encouragement provided by relatives, friends, and others.

Children stand in greater need of help in learning to meet reality effectively, not only to prevent their being overwhelmed by events or situations too great for them, but also to help them develop their capacity, the ego-strength, for coming to grips with events as they are. This is especially true with physical appearance and with physical handicaps.

Each of us acquires an image of how we would like to appear when grown. From the adults around us, from motion pictures and advertisements, from subtle impressions of approval, we build a model of how we'd like to look. At first we may gauge it by the clothes or the cut of our hair, as we grow by our strength, grace, or athletic skill, and ultimately by shape, size, manner, or other socially established standard. Judging by our cultural models of Miss America and Mr. All-American, most of us are doomed to disappointment, for too few of us emerge with the shape and size to which we aspire.

Maturity and the attainment of adult values helps us to reconcile ourselves to our limitations, even to accept ourselves as we appear. The stages of growth, and their discrepancies, cause much disturbance in children, and for those who are handicapped, considerable anguish. There is a never ending function that teachers can perform in helping children to accept themselves as they are, and, without doubt, succeed where parents fail. Children expect their parents to minimize such concerns, with the result that they often discount parental reassurance, but teachers are representatives of the outside world, impartial in their judgment. Assurance and support from teachers can count more in facing the reality of oneself.

The second form of treatment available to the teacher is to accommodate the child's needs or capacities. The simplest form of accommodation is a shift in the physical environment, such as moving the seat of the near-sighted child closer to the front of the room.

A somewhat more difficult accommodation is to shift our standards of expected achievement, performance, or deportment. To illustrate: we find a child who fidgets, or squirms, or slumps in his seat annoying, and admonish him to "sit up straight." Yet the tall, slender child is more likely to find himself uncomfortable in school chairs, in any chair for that matter, for they are designed to fit the average; hence the child tips his chair, or twists his legs, or slumps his shoulders, or sits with his foot under him.

Another form of accommodation lies in the suitability of the program we offer. Perhaps in no single area is opportunity for development denied more children than in physical education. The competitive stress that exists in most programs from elementary schools on soon eliminates the unskilled from participation. Not that the children would not like to have the sport skills, for to have them is to gain prestige with their classmates, but they give up in the face of their own incompetence and their rejection by the more skilled, and soon avoid the activity. The result is that the undersized, the uncoordinated, and the unskilled do not get opportunity to develop skill in the competitive group sports, nor does the school offer any accommodation through a diversified program. The emphasis remains on baseball, basketball, and football. And to make matters worse, the recreational programs of the communities which emphasize Little League and (rue the day) Little Lassie competition, exaggerate the problem rather than provide an alternate avenue of activity.

The third form of treatment lies in the influence that can be brought to bear on the child's development. Teachers can influence the nature and the direction that children's feelings and attitudes take in their development. In Chapter 4 the problem of Wilma, the tall girl, was described. The most important thing the teacher did was convey a sense of understanding to the girl by relating some of the events she had encountered as a child, sharing experiences, laughing together at tactless comments, essentially to help the girl learn that height did not prevent a girl from having fun unless she let self-pity overcome her.

Through deed, word, and attitude, the teacher influenced the girl's feelings about herself, her height, and her relations to others. In this instance, the influence bore directly on the girl's attitudes—in others it may be the effects upon the attitude of behavior of the class—but in any event the teacher can be a central influence if she is willing, or she can relegate herself to the periphery should she prefer to disregard such needs and opportunities.

THE ATYPICAL CHILD

Although we speak extensively of individual differences and the need for providing for and encouraging them, many of our practices consistently deny them. Children find themselves constantly being compared with other children in dress, manner, intelligence, size, weight, school achievement, possessions, and other aspects of appearance. The result of such comparisons is to make many children unduly conscious of ways in which they differ. Our administrative organization of school based on age groupings accentuates these differences. Differences in age, size, weight, structure stand out and become sources of concern to some children.

In working with such children, one should remember that children are valued by the contribution they make to the class. It is impossible to make a boy or girl popular, but a teacher can help a child to accept himself as he is and to become more acceptable to his classmates. Many examples of atypical children can be given: the bright boy, pushed ahead by ambitious parents, unable to cope physically with others in his grade; the early maturing, tall girl; the overage, retarded boy who vents his resentment in tyrannizing younger children; the tiny girl who becomes the class pet; the crippled child, the freckled child, the stutterer, and the stumbler.

UNDERAGE CHILDREN

Underage children find it difficult to compete physically with older children, but not scholastically. These youngsters need more opportunity to develop the large muscle skills in order to develop the physical proficiency necessary to the organized games such as baseball, which becomes increasingly prominent in the middle grades. Games requiring fine motor coordination present more difficulty. Emotional control is often less stable than with the older children.

OVERAGE CHILDREN

In schools which retain children at the grade level at which they are working in preference to a policy of social promotion, most classes contain one or more children who are older and more mature than most of the class, even though less advanced academically. The administrative procedures adopted by a school should not be a source of embarrassment to such a pupil, yet this is usually the case. Evidence shows that the non-promoted student is accepted and looked to as more experienced only at first grade, where the naivete of the first graders finds them innocent regarding the expected standards of performance. At all grades above the first, the classes believe that non-promotion is shameful and look at the non-promoted student as undesirable company. Such castigation helps make him undesirable company. Inability to find acceptance in the new class, shame at his own stupidity, and antagonism toward the school, combine to create adjustment difficulties.

Suggestions for Working with Overage Children. Many avenues are open to the teacher in working with these children, but all are based on her ability to accept the fact that the child can do nothing to change the degree of intelligence with which he was born, but he can fail to use what he has if he conceives of himself as stupid. Teacher anger and aggravation are wasted energy.

1. If a child is to be retained, steps should be taken to help him see and acknowledge the value of retention. (If there is no advantage to the child, i.e., a specifically planned program for remedial action, the retention is questionable.) For example, close to the end of the school year, a second grade teacher who decided it would be wise to retain Bobby at the second grade

level for another year, began by talking to her class one afternoon about what a wonderful class they had been, cooperative,
helpful, kind, and how much she wished she could have one or
two of them to help her get started with her new class the next
year, one or two like Bobby, Jean, Bill or Margaret. The children
were not all candidates for non-promotion, rather they were
children recognized for their helpfulness. Three of them, including Bobby, responded that they would stay and help her
next year. She replied that she thought that would be wonderful, maybe it would be possible for one or two of them. The
essence of her approach was not that she obtained volunteers
from naive second-graders but rather this became an opportunity to fulfill a purpose.

Another quite different but equally successful approach was
that of a fifth-grade teacher who talked directly with a boy about
the difficulties he was having in mastering basic skills, gave her
reasons as to why she thought he could benefit by staying another year at that grade, suggested he decide what he thought
would be best for him. He didn't decide immediately, but in a
subsequent discussion decided he agreed with her. In both this
and the former instance, the teachers then discussed the planned
retention with the parents to gain their acceptance.

2. Try to make parents and child see that readiness to learn school
   subjects is important, that all children do not learn to walk or talk
   at the same age, nor do they progress at the same rate in school.

3. Help pupils discover and evaluate their own strengths, abilities,
   and weaknesses, and plan constructive action to meet difficulties.

4. Help pupils select goals, specific goals, to meet given subjects or
   skills, and plan a course of action to achieve them. Progress
   towards goals, and their actual attainment provides a sense of
   accomplishment needed to maintain self-respect and to see the
   value in continued effort.

5. Show regard for the overage child, especially during the early
   weeks of the new term. Generally he enters a class partially a
   stranger. Our consciousness of age difference makes it difficult
   for the older child to find a place in a younger group unless jobs
   can be pointed out in which he can be helpful and use his
   maturity to an advantage—on safety patrols, running audio-
   visual equipment, participating in minor aspects of room management.

6. Utilize instructional situations in which children help each
   other rather than compete with each other.

7. Teach him to be proficient in some one thing so that he has a specialty which gives him status. (This applies to all children equally well.)
8. Broaden children's view as to how they can be worthwhile besides "being smart." Classroom discussion of what makes boys or girls popular, what we like in a friend, shortcomings to be faced, etc., is a useful device, particularly if the teacher plays a minor role in the discussion.
9. If an overage child becomes a passive participant in the large group, provide situations where he can work with one or two children. Avoiding participation is more difficult with smaller numbers. Where the overage child has become dominant, this can sometimes be counteracted by having him work with a smaller group of active, aggressive pupils who, though individually at a disadvantage, can combine to hold their own.

SIZE DIFFERENCES

Very tall children can appear very awkward and uncoordinated. At puberty, during periods of growth the clumsiness can be real because the youngster has to learn to manage legs and arms which have changed lengths, and muscle-bone ratios. However, much of the so-called awkwardness comes from adults having higher expectations for larger children, overlooking the fact that there is no reason for them to be better coordinated than other smaller children of the same age.

The evidence shows that adolescents as a group are better coordinated than younger children. But, being larger, they tend to be judged by adult standards of performance. Social activities in which the tall child is paired with a short are to be avoided because of the embarrassment caused. Games such as volleyball and basketball are well-suited. Physical changes at puberty are a source of concern and embarrassment to many children. The rapid physical changes, which are internal as well as external, mark a period of physical and accompanying emotional instability, as the body re-regulates itself. Listlessness, restlessness, momentary emotional upset, and increases in irritability can be expected to occur.

Short children easily develop feelings of physical inadequacy. They are more apt to be petted and overprotected by parents. Larger children sympathize with the smaller child who is appealing and make a pet or mascot of him, but brush aside the not-so-appealing small child. Activities depending on strength, such as hockey or football, place this child at a disadvantage. Activities are needed where the emphasis is on skill rather than size: ping-pong, checkers, gymnastics, etc.

Essential to both the extremes in size is an understanding that each individual grows at his own speed and to his own pattern. Understanding the relationship of hereditary factors, nutrition, and experience to growth makes it easier to understand and accept oneself.

WEIGHT DIFFERENCES

The activities for overweight students are limited. They do not succeed at games of speed and tire quickly, sometimes presenting a ludicrous picture in their attempts to compete with more agile children. Some phases of games are available which do not place the obese child at such a disadvantage—goalkeeper in soccer, guard in girl's basketball, center in football or catcher in baseball, swimming, horseshoes, or sedentary games. An overweight student may find much satisfaction in substituting mental exercise for physical tests—being spelling champ, or some other kind of recognized success.

Whenever we are able to achieve competence in one area, it helps compensate for deficiency in another. Thinking of and providing training in skills and accomplishments for children which makes healthy compensation possible is a desirable solution, particularly where the deficiency is inescapable, as it usually is with the crippled child, for instance. Nevertheless, it is not enough to substitute one activity for another, mental success for physical success. If the satisfaction is an unconscious one, then the medium of success becomes an escape mechanism for the failure in the other activity, and fails to provide a sense of worthy accomplishment, however useful it may be as a safety valve. Bruce's experience points this up:

> Bruce is an attractive, alert, intelligent boy who has always been much too large for his age. When he was younger his mother had difficulty finding clothes to fit him. In the second grade he weighed 75 pounds, came home from school to proudly tell his mother that he weighed more than anyone else in school except the teacher.
>
> Bruce's father, once the star of his college basketball team, had decided to teach Bruce the fundamentals of basketball at the age of four (slightly impossible) and when Bruce couldn't perform as anticipated and ran to his mother crying, the father criticized the boy for being lazy. In the first grade, the school doctor detected a serious heart murmur, told Bruce that under

no circumstances was he to play any sports or do any running. The boy, an active youngster, was upset for days.

Bruce lost many of his former playmates because he couldn't compete in their physical activities. He became a drudge in school, worked hard for top achievement, and was upset when he fell short. His father, though disappointed at his son's inability to participate in sports, started Bruce learning the piano, and by twelve he had become quite skilled.

Yet Bruce's accomplishments provide him limited genuine satisfaction as these excerpts from an interview with a guidance counselor show.

C: How do you get along with your classmates in school, Bruce?

B: They don't like me because I can't play sports. They make fun of me when I try to throw or catch a ball, so I just don't try anymore.

C: What do you do during recesses?

B: Oh, I just stand around and watch the other kids, or sometimes I go over to the girls' side and talk with them. The girls like the way I play the piano.

C: How do you get along with the boys in your class?

B: They laugh at me because I can't do the things they can.

C: Do they like your piano playing?

B: No, they think I'm a sissy.

C: Why did you change from the public school to a private school?

B: I guess so that I wouldn't have to take gym (i.e., be in attendance). They used to make me take gym when I was in the other school, and I didn't like it at all. I didn't feel as if I was as good as the other boys, because I couldn't do anything.

C: Do you like school?

B: Yes, I think I do. I like to take tests in math. The teacher says I am the smartest boy in the class.

C: Do you like to play the piano?

B: Yes. People like me when I'm playing; they say I play real well. Sometimes I come home very sad and sit down at the piano, and it makes me feel good again.

C: Which would you rather do, go to a concert or attend a baseball game?

B: I think I'd rather attend a good symphony concert.

C: Wouldn't you rather be playing baseball and football with the other children in the neighborhood?

B: No, they don't know any better. They've never been taught anything else. They're much too juvenile for me. I'd rather stay in and read a good book. I get a lot more out of that than making a fool out of myself with those *children*.

C: What other hobbies do you have?

B: I sing, but only when I'm alone.

C: Why not in front of people?

B: I'm afraid they'll make fun of me, so I just sing when I'm around home.

Bruce's comments make it evident that his musical prowess and scholastic achievement don't offset his feelings of inadequacy. Partially reflecting his father's desires and partially reflecting the values of the age level, he infers that his achievements aren't masculine, and hence, for him, are second-best. His "sour-grapes" attitudes and other comments reveal this.

Bruce's real achievement in other areas can only be satisfying compensation if he has faced and accepted his limitation. As long as he denies the wish to join the activities of the other boys and to fulfill his father's ambition, his feelings of personal worth will suffer. Needless to say, taking this step could be easier if different attitudes existed among his classmates and with his father. Bruce's large size and healthy appearance make him more subject to ridicule, however undeserved.

An additional complication enters with overweight children, for their obesity is, more frequently than not, compensatory behavior, symbolizing frustration in other spheres. Some instances of overweight result from faulty diets and metabolic disturbances, but more stem from psychological factors in development. It is not easy to unravel the meaning of overeating, for the possible causes are many: early food deprivation, insufficient affection, displacement in affectional relationships by a younger child, offsetting drained emotional energies, compensating for unhappy experiences, confused love relationships with parents, reactions to training demands of parents or verbal criticisms often associated with meals, and others. Certainly the glib interpretation that overeating is compensating for lack of parent love is too easily and too frequently given as an explanation. It is not the teacher's function to interpret the symbolic meaning of overeating in a child, but to help him attain more adequate direct satisfaction of need, and/or healthier compensations.

Some of these problems are apparent with Sharon, a nine-year old, third-grader. Though of average height, Sharon, 89 pounds, outweighed the typical third-grade girl by thirty pounds. Her unkempt hair and slovenly appearance were enough to make her unappealing, but add to these disadvantages her whining voice, her refusal to join group activities, and her constant effort to attract the attention of any audience, and one found a most unpopular girl. The anecdotal reports of the teacher, gathered during October and November not only reflect the behavior, but suggest some of its origins.

School Work

Sharon is able (IQ 115), reads fluently and easily, and draws well, but rejects all other work saying, "It bores me." She often takes out the wrong book, opens to the wrong page, or drops everything.

Sharon completed only her reading workbook during the entire day, so (the teacher) kept her after school to finish her work. Asked her if she disliked school and why she didn't finish her work. Sharon replied, "Yes, I like school, but I guess I'm just slow. I like to think about things. I like to make believe I'm a horse and having all sorts of adventures." I instructed her to take one paper home and finish there. She cried, saying, "I don't want to." When I insisted she screamed and cried. When she realized I meant it, she said, "All right, I'll take it home but my mother won't make me do it."

A few days later, Sharon was late for school, which is not unusual, excusing it by saying, "I just dawdled along. If I'm slow I don't have to drag my brother with me." During morning exercises she interrupted everything by tipping over her chair. When work began she just sat there. Asked to start, Sharon replied that she didn't have a pencil. Given a pencil, she started to work.

Five minutes later I looked up from a reading group to see Sharon staring out the window. Several reminders were needed to keep her working. During phonics, she said every word wrong. Bobby turned to her and said, "Oh, Sharon, you're doing that on purpose. Don't be such a show off." The next time she was called on she gave the right word. On her way back to her desk, she held her chair as if she were sitting in it, walked backwards to her place, bumped into my desk and fell. All the children laughed and Pam said, "It serves you right for being so silly."

During oral arithmetic, she paid attention, went quietly to the board to do an example. Returning to her seat she said loudly to the girl beside her, "See, I told you I could do it if I wanted to."

Group Relations

During recess Sharon came up and held my hand. Asked why she wasn't playing with the children, she replied, "I don't like to play with them. They don't want to play what I want." One little girl who had come up said to Sharon, "All you want to do is play horse."

A few days later we were talking about the farm we were going to make in class and what we would make for it. Someone suggested a farmer and his wife, to which Sharon interjected, "Don't put those in, they'll just have lots of kids." While we were talking about work on the farm, Sharon remarked, "My mother doesn't make me do anything I don't want to." During the choosing of different tasks Dorothy suggested that Sharon make the horses because she made beautiful horses. Sharon smiled at that and said she'd like to make them.

Days later when the class was being divided into four groups for physical education, Ralph whispered to Jack, "I hope Sharon doesn't get on my team, she's too fat to run." Sharon overheard and said, "I don't want to play this old game. I'd rather be a horse." She than galloped off imitating a horse's whinny. When she came back I asked her if she would like to be scorekeeper. She smiled and said, "Yes, they can't win unless I say so." She kept score carefully for the rest of the game.

One afternoon I was called outside the room to speak with a parent. When I returned everyone was laughing. Sharon was posing along the window seat like a model at a beach. When she saw me she said, "Look, I'm a bathing beauty. Everyone likes a bathing beauty." She then walked quietly back to her seat.

Family Relations

Sharon has two younger brothers, one in the first grade, and two younger sisters of pre-school age. She resents them saying that she can't go anywhere in the house without bumping into one of them. She loves the two-year-old sister best because "she sleeps a lot and isn't always around." She rejects any responsibility towards them, refuses to take her brother to or from school.

Concerned about Sharon's overweight and her school work, I visited the home. As we entered the living room, the mother, who was extremely obese, apologized for the disorder saying, "With so many small children I don't have time to do much more than feed them and try to keep them clean." There were clothes, magazines, papers, and toys everywhere. In discussing Sharon, I suggested that something might be done about her weight. The mother answered, "Sharon may be a little over-weight, but I don't think that has much to do with her problems. The poor child can't help being untidy because she shares the room with the two little children and doesn't have any room. I can't force her to take care of her things."

At this point the youngest child started to cry. The mother excused herself saying that she'd give the baby something to eat because that always quiets her. When she returned the other two children had started yelling for something to eat. At first she refused the children because it was so close to supper, but when they started to cry, she said, "All right, take some chocolates out of the bowl." Turning to me she said, "I can't refuse them when they ask for food because I know how much I like to eat myself."

We agreed that Sharon was capable of doing her work, but as I was telling the mother how Sharon refused often to even try, Sharon came into the house to ask her mother if she could take her new doll outdoors. When the mother refused, Sharon started to beg and tease. The mother continued to refuse and told Sharon to take one of her old dolls and go outside and play. The girl started to stamp her feet saying, "I won't, I won't, I won't." In a few seconds the mother said, "Oh, all right dear, go ahead and get your doll." Sharon immediately stopped her commotion and rushed off, whereupon the mother turned to me and said, "You can see Sharon has a mind of her own." Returning to the question of Sharon's not working, the mother said that she thought the reason was due to Sharon's grasping the new material so quickly that the routines bored her.

At the PTA meeting two weeks later Sharon's father stopped to talk with me. During the conversation he said, "I know Sharon is a difficult child but I don't know what to do. I don't have much time with the children because I work at two jobs in order to support the family, in fact I took time off from work to come tonight. My wife always allows Sharon to do anything she wants. She's a wonderful woman, but she has absolutely no control over her."

Almost a month had passed since my visit, when Sharon's mother came to see me at school. She said she had been think-ing about her daughter's weight and that maybe that had some-thing to do with her attitude. She asked for my suggestions. When I suggested taking Sharon to her doctor the mother rejected the idea, "No, I want to see an expert." I then suggested the Children's Hospital. The mother accepted this suggestion saying that she'd make an appointment as soon as she got home.

Interpretation

As far as her functioning in school is concerned, Sharon's excessive weight leaves her unable to compete in active games. Her defense seems to be, "I don't want to play your silly old games anyway." She performs her work satisfactorily when the task appeals to her, but her consistent day-dreaming, and her fantasy of being a horse (a swift and graceful animal) interfere with her completing her work. Worse, she finds that refusal can gain her the attention of the class which she seldom receives otherwise. Sharon is not accepted as a member of the group, however, and she is sensitive to the responses of the group to her actions.

Even without a home visit, some clues to disturbed relationships at home appear, although verifications are essential before jumping to conclusions. These clues are Sharon's statements about having her own way at home, being late to school to avoid bringing her brother, her comments about the farmer's children, and her overweight. The home visit adds further to the picture. Certainly Sharon's result of overweight is not simple compensation for lack of affection, but a result of reaction to thwarted affectional needs, parental inadequacy, and hostility toward her brothers and sisters.

The questions the teacher faces are what steps can she take at the educational level to help Sharon develop more adequate behavior patterns, and whether or not the success of such steps is dependent on parental action to solve the basic problems.

The teacher decided that inasmuch as her expressions of disapproval had proved ineffective she would limit them as much as possible, particularly before the class. She hoped the class would sense this attitude and follow suit. She utilized Sharon's strengths by having her help some of the slower children with different tasks. Sharon appeared to enjoy this and began to do more of her own work. When she finished her work, Sharon was allowed to stay after school and help straighten the classroom, a privilege reserved for children who were doing their best. The teacher used these occasions for informal chats with the girl. Occasionally she would ask Sharon to come to school early to do special jobs. She suggested extra reading assignments in books about horses on which Sharon wrote reports. The girl soon branched out to read about other animals.

Finally, the teacher introduced some less active games during physical education period which gave Sharon a chance for some participation in play activities. She took no direct action about the girl's weight because she thought the problem beyond a simple matter of diet.

In spite of her limitations, the mother was interested in Sharon's well-being and followed through on the suggestion for medical examination. This led to psychiatric referral which proved beneficial, for Sharon established considerable faith in the psychiatrist and gained vital assistance so that in the course of a few months definite gains were observed in Sharon's acceptance of responsibility, her give and take with the other children, and her general attitude, but some time was to elapse before any difference in weight was noticed.

The underweight pupil faces much the same problems as the overweight child or the underage child. His physical limitations require that he exert himself toward attainable goals, and avoid the frustration inherent in establishing the same standards of performance for himself that larger, stronger pupils adopt. Where the energy level of such a child is adequate, he may be well-coordinated, speedy, or agile, and hence capable in many situations. Success in individual sports is greater than in those requiring body contact or strength.

HANDICAPPED CHILDREN

The busy streets of our cities appear singularly free of crippled children, possibly as a result of the limitations of movement imposed by orthopedic handicaps, but perhaps as much out of sensitivity to the reactions of the able-bodied. Many of us reflect a mixture of aversion, pity, and curiosity—aversion stemming from fear of the impact that deprivation of physical wholeness would have on our own lives, pity of the fortunate for the unfortunate, and curiosity regarding the strangeness of being handicapped. Heart ailments, diabetes, and other limiting physical conditions are the more tolerable for being hidden.

Orthopedic difficulties, in contrast, subject one to the continual reaction of other persons. Adults, understanding cause and effect relationships more fully, can be more objective about handicaps, but children, learning to control their bodies, understand its functioning, and accept its differences from those of others, are deprived of such protection, find themselves threatened or at least uncomfortable in the presence of such disabilities.

The personality of an orthopedically handicapped child is molded by the reactions of other people toward him. Studies of such children disclose that a handicap need not make a child maladjusted, although it does predispose such development. The body-image that develops has a basic influence in the self-concept of children, and for the handicapped strong emotional feelings develop in both child and parent due to the existence of the physical deformity, amplified by rejection received at the hands of other children. Unless the child receives support in facing the handicap and assistance through provision of special opportunity for adequate development, unwholesome personality characteristics develop. The pity, sorrow, and guilt felt by the parents leads them to overprotect the child. Instead of having opportunity to develop, the handicapped child is sheltered and kept dependent upon others. He needs love and support in coming to grip with his disability, but, even more, he needs greater opportunity for practice and encouragement of effort to develop skills which permit him to gain independence and the security of knowing that in some or many respects he is as capable or nearly so in thought as his non-handicapped friends.

The teacher can use all of her treatment techniques with handicapped children. Support is repeatedly needed so that they don't give up in the face of difficulties and lapse into dependency. Accommodation of program to eliminate impossible tasks and provide special opportunity is essential. Expectations regarding rate of progress should be geared to the child's capacity. Enforced absences often provide repeated disruption in program and need a teacher patient in retracing her steps.

> The need for flexibility in accommodating to the needs of the handicapped can be illustrated by John, a thin, short, 12½ year old boy in the fifth grade. Although able in reading, spelling, and music, John was retained twice during the primary grades because of repeated shifts in boarding homes following his parents' divorce. Barely accepted by his classmates, he was often the scapegoat, getting blamed for misdemeanors perpetrated by others. His small stature reaped ridicule from the other boys. Most aggravating to his teacher, however, were John's repeated requests to go to the toilet. In John's school a fairly rigid time schedule was followed, with specific times set aside for toilet lines for boys and girls. Repeated punishment by being kept after school did not deter his requesting permission four or five times a day to go to the toilet. Finally a report on John's intransigence was sent home to his aunt, with whom he was living. Taken to the doctor, examination disclosed an unusually high concentration of sugar in John's urine with a resultant diagnosis of sugar diabetes, the physical basis for his need for frequent trips to the toilet.

Teachers can help handicapped children develop compensations through the exaggeration of desirable traits to offset inferiority feelings developing out of the handicap. If the child has an interest that can be fostered, so much the better, but if not, the fact that interests are acquired calls for exposure to hitherto unknown fields of knowledge or skill. Finally, the attitude of the class has to be molded along similar lines to those discussed, to provide an atmosphere that is friendly and helpful without being overprotective. The need for such an atmosphere can be observed in the description at the end of this chapter of Richard's difficulties with speech.

In making accommodations in program, medical advice is helpful. One should not assume, for instance, that a child who has had rheumatic fever automatically incurs cardiac damage. About one-third of such children recover completely, another third incur sufficiently slight damage to permit them to lead almost normal lives, and only the final one-third need long-term accommodation in program. Hence, it is advisable that any plan of action, whether restricted activity during recess and physical education, rest periods, reduced climbing of stairs, dietary restrictions, or special transportation should be based on medical advice.

VISUAL DISABILITIES

Teachers should check on the vision of all members of the class prior to or early in the school year in order to familiarize themselves with the eye conditions of their pupils and to understand and anticipate difficulties which may arise. The near-sighted child is often too avid a reader to the exclusion of other activities. The teacher's responsibility to these children includes attention to good eye focus and increased emphasis on oral work, correct position for work, careful selection of materials, adaptation of methods of teaching, and encouragement of children to join in suitable games and other activities. The far-sighted child requires great patience because he tires quickly when using his eyes at close range. Tasks must be adapted to short periods of concentration. A child with astigmatism finds it difficult to discriminate between letters such as m and n, c and o, etc. Several specific suggestions for working with such children are:

1. Know what the doctor's recommendation is and see that it is followed.
2. If glasses are recommended, see that they are used, are clean, and worn properly, i.e., the child should look through the center of the lens at all times.
3. Permit child to sit where he has good light and can see class

work. He should not be facing light nor should there be glaring surfaces within line of vision. Surface glares from chalkboards are commonly overlooked because the teacher does not check to see how the boards appear from various seats. All chalkboards, work, charts, demonstrations, should be visible.

4. Light should be good and from the left for right-handed writers. A common defect in older school buildings is inadequate light, particularly in rooms with northern exposure during winter. Often the electrical lighting is insufficient. A light-meter, in common use now with photography, can be used to check amounts of light available.

5. Whenever possible use a movable, adjustable, tilt-top desk. If the desk top is flat a prop or copyholder can be used for a rest for books in order to keep reading material at eye level and at uniform distance.

6. Child should sit erect and place work at suitable level and distance.

7. Avoid excessive or unnecessary reading. Rest eyes by having child close them or look away from work momentarily.

8. Plan work so that the child's schedule alternates eye work and eye rest. A change of focus, from desk work to chalkboard for instance, constitutes an eye rest.

9. Where impairment is severe, child should be excused from detailed work such as sewing, mechanical drawing, reading work-books (which in the interests of economy of use of paper and inadequate spacing cause reduced legibility). Essential work can be done orally. For instance, one child may ask the questions orally of another.

10. Materials used should be especially selected for suitability. Blackboards should be clean, soft chalk used, pencils with thick, soft, heavy leads provided, books with large clear type (18 or 24 point simple design without many serifs).

Excerpts from a teacher's report on Susan show some of these steps in effect:

Susan, 12, entered my fifth grade class in December, transferring from another school . . . large girl. Although she wore glasses, I noticed she had difficulty seeing the board . . . suggested a front seat but Susan told me she could see better from where she was . . . Not wanting to embarrass her, I concurred but came to regret it.

Cumulative record . . . health good, grades poor, conduct poor, reading retarded, repeated grades one and four.

A nuisance in class, running about . . . marking up the papers of children sitting near her, taking lunches, books, balls, anything of others that appealed to her . . . excitable, talkative. The attitude of the children was to reject her, calling her dumb-bell, making unkind remarks, excluding her from games. Susan in turn treated them with indifference, working well alone but antics when in a group.

After two weeks sent for the mother, who worked every day . . . two weeks before she came . . . learned she dreaded the visit, she'd had them at the other school and was at a loss as to how to cope with the situation. Susan an only child . . . worn glasses since she was four . . . discipline problem at home . . . temper tantrums, crying, restless at night, quarrels with other children. When scolded or punished, Susan would scream, then a nosebleed. Mother most cooperative in desiring to help.

Decided to check her hearing . . . good, then her vision using the card with symbols because she wasn't sure of the letters. Tested with and without glasses . . . had difficulty seeing even the largest . . . perhaps she was fatigued . . . repeated next day with Principal helping me . . . same results. Very poor vision . . . referred to school nurse who reported back that immediate referral to oculist needed. Advised mother . . . surprised . . . asked if any recent check of glasses . . . none, only replacement of broken lenses. Mother related an incident in which Susan, having an argument with another girl who wore glasses, grabbed the glasses and stepped on them, smashing them . . . expensive replacement for the mother. Wondered why Susan hadn't pulled hair, or slapped or scratched, came to the conclusion that she knew how damaging it was to be unable to see unless one had glasses. Mother took Susan to oculist.

Susan out two days with examination. Took advantage of absence to tackle children's attitude, hoping to create some acceptance for Susan. Didn't mention Susan by name but talked about ways each of us could improve in the way we treated others.

Had to overcome the feelings of inadequacy which led to her withdrawing from all tasks and refusing to try to avoid failure . . . Started with remedial reading . . . gave her as much time as possible. Mother reported the doctor had said her eyesight was very poor, restlessness, irritation, and temper tantrums a byproduct. Susan came back with new glasses, came up to my desk and showed them to me, proud of them . . . gave me a look . . . surprised at the strong correction. Wanted to change her to front seat without embarrassing her . . . borrowed a new front desk from another room telling Susan if she sat there she could do many things to help me, being older and more mature . . . her behavior didn't change overnight, but the books with large print, varied activities to prevent eyestrain, and the steady gains in achievement contributed to steady improvement. Gradual adapting to group demands . . . gradual acceptance by group . . . often elected a leader in organized games now.

HEARING DISABILITIES

Examinations show that poor hearing is not, as most people believe, an inability to hear. Most deaf children have some residual hearing. The disability lies in inability to understand and to make sense out of sounds. Some children lack acuity, others hear well but are unable to discriminate between similar sounds, others hear and discriminate but fail to retain the sound in memory. Specific suggestions which can be offered are:

1. Know the extent of any hearing loss which exists. Learn any recommendations made by attending physician.
2. Seat the child in an advantageous spot in the room. The shape and equipment of rooms cause them to vary in the quality of sound being heard at different points in the room. The quality is usually poorer at the margins. The child should be seated so that he sees the lighted rather than the shaded side of the teacher's face.
3. Encourage him to turn best ear toward the speaker.
4. Talk normally, slowly, and articulate distinctly. Do not shout, mouth words, and most important don't stand in front of the window while talking. The child has to learn to use his eyes to supplement his ears. When speaking to the child look directly at him. Stand near him when presenting new materials or giving directions.
5. Exercises designed to teach children to listen and discriminate initial consonants, initial blends, etc., useful for all children in word training, are especially desirable for the hard-of-hearing child.
6. If a child has difficulty understanding what was said, ask him to repeat the question or direction to you.
7. Encourage the child to recite, and to enunciate words distinctly.
8. Visual training aids are an important addition in helping the child perceive and relate sounds.

SPEECH DISABILITIES

The speech problems of school children fall into four types: voice, articulation, stuttering, and symbolization. There are many causes of defective speech. The subject is so extensive and complex that only the barest identification can be attempted here, and the interested and concerned teacher will have to check specialized texts for essential details. Defective hearing and mental retardation can be causes of speech defects. Physical handicaps or neurological injury, such as malformations of mouth and teeth or cerebral palsy, produce speech defects. Criticism of speech errors by parents or teachers during the language learning process produce their share. Many speech problems derive from emotional disturbance and maladjustment. The complexity of possible causes means that diagnosis and recommended treatment call for specialized skills.

Voice. Effective voice usage requires adequate volume, pitch level, pleasing voice quality, and tone duration in order to express meaning through appropriate variation. Volume defects range from too little to too much. Timidity, hearing loss, over-compensation, or family background may be contributory. Dramatizations of stories, especially fairy tales, and choral speaking are effective means of teaching variation in volume of sound.

Pitch and quality are closely related. The child must be able to raise and lower the voice to convey meaning. The differences in the way the two words "white house" can be pitched and stressed to distinguish between a house painted white, a house owned by Mr. White, and the President's dwelling reflect the importance of minor variations. Elementary school children, particularly in the primary grades, tend to be monotonic. They need help in first being aware of pitch differences, then of making sounds at different pitch levels. Demonstrations of differences in voice quality to express feelings, such as being happy, sad, excited, imitations of different characters or animals in stories, television, and the like, are helpful. Having children talk like different cartoon characters helps.

Articulation. Articulation refers to the production of specific consonant and vowel sounds. Faults of articulation include additions of sounds, omissions, distortions, and substitutions. Teachers play an important role in assisting children in acquiring appropriate articulation due to the fact that many of the faulty sounds which children produce are the product of faulty learning.

The basic principles of correcting articulatory inadequacies are to make the child aware of the difference (hear it, feel it, see it), develop motivation for change through lessons possessing enjoyable and appealing features, teach the child to make the sound, and encourage him in his efforts. As a child listens to correct and incorrect sound production, he begins to hear the difference. Then he can be taught to pronounce it in different positions in words, initial, medial, final, starting with whichever he can do most easily. It is often fairly easy to teach a child how to make the sound; the problem lies in getting him to adopt it as an everyday part of speech. This necessitates opportunity to use it in routine activities.

The greater habituation of the older child to the use of the faulty sound creates a need for formal drill, whereas younger children can make the change with only incidental practice. Teaching requires auditory presentation by the teacher to assist the children in recognizing the sound, drill on discrimination between given sounds and similar sounds already known—particularly with those which are substitutions—practice in producing the sound in isolation, then in different positions in words, finally in prepared sentences and conversational speeches.

Stuttering. Stuttering derives from many causes: learning, parental pressure in learning speech, illness, emotional disturbances, to name a few. Stutterers show a history of family stuttering, are inconsistent in the times at which they stutter for the blocks or repetitions occur on only a small fraction of the words, and then, in greater frequency, during times of emotional stress, excitement, or high motivation. There is no definite or complete cure for stuttering.

Two primary objectives occur in working with stutterers: the first is improved personality adjustment, the second improved overt speech behavior. The starting point is accepting stuttering as the child's natural way of talking, listening attentively without correcting the child when he speaks, and listening sympathetically so that he has no fear of ridicule, which only exaggerates the disorder. Talk slowly, calmly, and in a relaxed friendly voice. Tension or displeasure is too easily communicated in your voice and manner. Observe the child's behavior and environment, observe the sources and situations in which stuttering results and alleviate or remove these disturbances. Give approval to his accomplishments in other areas to develop feelings of competence.

If there is one piece of advice to be given the classroom teacher about stutterers, it is to get them to a speech pathologist. Do not assume responsibility on your own initiative for treating the stutterer. Given adequate diagnosis, the teacher plays a key role in rehabilitation.

Encouraging Adequate Speech in the Classroom. The significance of adequate speech to human communication lends emphasis to the importance of creating a conducive classroom environment. This can be illustrated in the instance of Richard, a victim of cerebral palsy, with hearing classified as marginal, whose greatest handicap was his retarded speech. The report of the second grade teacher describes him as a pleasant looking child, the youngest of three children of cooperative, helpful parents. Unaccustomed to normal group activity he had difficulty in adjusting to the first grade routines, was highly dependent on the teacher for help and attention and given to temper tantrums when he could not have his way. His speech was so poor that the first grade teacher had him do all his reading after school. His progress was deemed sufficient to justify promotion. The second grade of thirty-three children was a mixed group from the two first grades plus several newcomers, and was in a different school building, requiring adjustment to a new group and a new physical setting. The teacher describes the first days, and some of the difficulties in part:

> The first few days were difficult for Richard. To get acquainted, each child was asked to tell his name, address, and telephone number. When it came to Richard, he eagerly jumped up and tried to tell his name, but the children kept prompting and interpreting his words so that he became cross and sullen. I noticed some of the children snickered and giggled, and made a mental note of the ones who did so as to check later to learn if they were familiar or unfamiliar with his speech. On checking, I discovered that they were from his last year's class. Apparently they had been used to treating him like a toddler, speaking for him, and jumping to do anything that he tried to do, thinking this was being "kind" to him.
>
> I'm sure the children knew I found it very difficult to understand anything that Richard said (though I tried very hard to cover it) and they would immediately interpret (correctly and incorrectly) every word he said. This made him very angry. I reminded the children that everyone should take turns and that it was polite to let everyone speak for himself.
>
> We had a little discussion about what each one had done during the summer. Richard was very eager to join in and do just as everyone else did. He was very excited when he walked to the front of the room. He had never had a chance to participate in group discussion before. He looked around the room and then began to act silly, laughing, making faces, making spastic movements, and encouraging the class to join in.
>
> I waited patiently, and by motion encouraged those whose attention I could get without speaking to wait also. Then I reminded Richard that we were waiting to hear him. He became

serious, told us of a visit to a zoo. The children started to speak for him, guessing what he was going to say. When I reminded them that it was Richard's turn, and that we had agreed to be good listeners, he finished without further "help." (Because I knew what animals were to be found in a zoo I think I understood him.) He beamed and when he was going home said that he loved the second grade and loved me too. I realized why. He had told his story, too.

This experience made me feel that I must do something about having the class accept Richard, not as someone to baby, but as a classmate who could share in the group activities as an equal member.

I later sent him on an errand and spoke briefly to the class, telling them how proud I was of the way they helped Richard by letting him take his time and tell his story. Later I took the children who had been his classmates the preceding year for a chat while the student teacher worked with the rest. We discussed how we were growing up, how some had lost first teeth, some not, some were tall, some not, some were heavier, some could run faster, play ball better or jump higher. One child said it didn't matter—we would all get big someday—it didn't matter as long as we were good citizens. Another child said "Some kids can't even walk yet and they are as old as we are. I saw it on television." One by one they pieced the whole story together of how lucky they were, and how they should be kind to people like Joe's little cousin and the little girl that Ann's mother knew. As we talked I told them I knew a little boy who was like the children they had seen on television that he tried so hard to do the things that they all did, run, play, climb, draw, read, tell stories. Robert said that he should just keep trying. Then I told them that the trouble was that his muscles were very slow and that it took him longer to do things. They thought he should just take his time and everyone should wait. Leslie said it didn't matter if it took longer, it was like her teeth. Ann got hers quicker. Peter said that he went to camp so his muscles would get strong because he couldn't play ball as well as his cousin, but he was learning.

We then brought out that we must give everyone a chance even though we sometimes had to wait for those who did things slowly. I then told them that Richard was the little boy I knew who was trying so hard to make his muscles work. This surprised them. They had not identified Richard as one of "those children" they would like to help. They began to offer suggestions how they could help him by waiting for him to have his turn and by letting him have a chance to do things himself.

Subsequent anecdotes recorded by the teacher disclose the value that creating the proper group atmosphere had in his development. (It should be noted too that close cooperation in Richard's development existed between physician, parent, speech therapist, and teacher.)

Classroom. Richard enters room noisily with small toy in hand. Teacher greets him. He smiles, continues to seat. Goes to join two boys reading together and pushes one off chair. Boy pushes back.

Cafeteria. Richard starts to talk at table interrupting others. His voice is loud. Children tell him to be quiet, they are talking. He leaves table, marches back and forth until instructed to take his seat, gradually joins conversation.

Speech Lessons. Therapist reported it was difficult to get him to work, as he was noisy on leaving room, teased, laughed, avoided getting to work. The next time he was scheduled for speech therapy I reminded Richard of his lesson and asked him if he'd like to play a game. I asked him if he thought he could get out of the room and back into it after his lesson without any of the children knowing it, just as quietly as Ann had with the attendance slip. Richard asked if he could take the slip, and I replied that if he could go and come from the room quietly, I'd let him take it tomorrow. When the therapist came, Richard was very excited, but left the room quietly, watching all the time for my approval. On return he opened the door with a shout, but when reminded of being quiet, he immediately became quiet and took his seat. One girl remarked, "Richard is growing up a lot." Richard beamed.

Classroom. Richard entered classroom, took his chair and noisily went over to a small group reading at a table in the rear of the room. He took a book and loudly demanded to know the page and said he wanted to read. The children acted disturbed, said he spoiled the fun, and could not read with them. At that moment it was time for the class to go to gym. When the class returned the children went back to the table to continue reading. Just as they got settled, Richard joined them. I noticed two of the children look at each other. Richard cautiously put down his chair and stood looking at one of the children. Polly said, "If you're not going to be silly you can play too." He smiled and the group helped him find the page. They were so busy quietly reading to each other, Richard taking his turn with the others, that I delayed calling them. Later I heard Polly say that Richard had grown up a lot and that it was fun to play reading with him.

Classroom. This morning when Richard arrived he was crying. He was wearing a hearing aid and a boy from the third grade had pulled it out. We went to the third grade but couldn't find the boy. A classmate said Richard had been showing off with it. He was very proud of the device, when I asked if he would like to show it to the children and tell them about it he beamed. He labored throughout the explanation of the aid and showed the case with the batteries. They were very interested and patient. They tested his reaction to voices, whispers, and loud tones. Richard said loud voices hurt, and he would cover his pocket. The boys said he was lucky. Richard takes remarkable care and responsibility for the aid, taking it off in the gym and on the playground.

A word is needed here about what has been described as desirable group atmosphere. Prior to the teacher's actions with the class, the effect of their helpfulness had been to deprive Richard of opportunity for his trials at a task and to force dependence on others, which he resented. It would have been just as unhealthy for Richard had the effects of the teacher's actions been to give him special privilege in the sense that the class so restrained itself where he was concerned that he could override them. It was changing the group reaction so that Richard had a chance to participate as an equal, with the same give-and-take as other children, that proved an essential element for his development. Of course, the other children make some allowance for his being less skilled and slower of movement in specific tasks. This did not give him the privilege of aggressing against them.

Another feature of the teacher's actions worth noting was her capitalizing on the incident involving the hearing aid. Children commonly react to such devices as glasses, hearing aids, braces on teeth, and other appliances and prosthetic devices with embarrassment or shame and will avoid wearing them, lose them, or "accidentally" break them. The teacher actually enhanced Richard's status with the class by her treatment of the situation. Many such subtle turnabouts can be created through a moment's ingeniousness.

REFERENCES FOR PART THREE

American Association of School Administrators. *Health in Schools,* Twentieth Yearbook. Washington, D. C.: National Education Association.

Breckenridge, Marian & Vincent, E. L. *Child Development.* Philadelphia and London: W. B. Saunders Co., 1960.

Board of Education of the City of New York, *Helping the Physically Limited Child*. New York: Board of Education of New York City, 1953.

Byrd, O. E. *Workbook for Health*. Stanford, Calif.: Stanford University Press, 1948.

Chenoweth, L. B. and Sellkirk, T. K. *School Health Problems*. New York: Appleton-Century-Crofts, 1947.

Cruikshank, Wm. *Education of Exceptional Children and Youth*. Englewood Cliffs, N. J.: Prentice-Hall, Inc., 1958.

Ewing, A. W. G. *Educational Guidance and the Deaf Child*. Washington, D. C.: Volta Bureau, 1957.

Gesell, A. and Ilg, Frances. *The Child From Five to Ten*. New York: Harper & Row, Publishers, 1950.

Johnson, Wendell, et al. *Speech Handicapped School Children*. Revised Edition. New York: Harper & Row, Publishers, 1956.

Jordan, Thomas E. *The Exceptional Child*. Columbus, Ohio: Charles E. Merrill Books, Inc., 1962.

Kephart, Newell C. *The Slow Learner in the Classroom*. Columbus, Ohio: Charles E. Merrill Books, Inc.

Lowenfeld, B. *Our Blind Children*. Springfield, Ill.: C. C. Thomas, 1956.

National Educ. Assn. *Health in the Elementary School*, Twenty-ninth Yearbook. Washington, D. C.: NEA, 1950.

Wallin, John E. Wallace. *The Education of Mentally Handicapped Children*. New York: Harper & Row, Publishers, 1955.

Ward, Virgil S. *Educating the Gifted: An Axiomatic Approach*. Columbus, Ohio: Charles E. Merrill Books, Inc., 1961.

Watson, E. H. and Lowrey, G. H. *Growth and Development of Children*. Chicago: The Yearbook Publishers, 1954.

Part Four

PERSONAL DEVELOPMENT

Chapter 11

PERSONAL INFORMATION

A wide range of techniques is available to the teacher for obtaining information about the personal development of children:

Observational

Time sampling
Rating scales
Role playing
Play expression
Behavioral tests

Verbal—structured

Interview
Check lists
Interest finders
Questionnaires
Adjustment inventories

Verbal—unstructured

Autobiography
Story completion
Sentence completion test

Diary
Creative expression
Open-ended questions
My wishes and fears
Picture projection test

Each technique will be described in sufficient detail to permit its adaptation to the classroom use, but before doing this, attention should be called to the fact that many of these activities require no further work of the teacher and that several can be provided for without interfering with daily classwork by making slight alteration in the usual tasks presented children. For instance, given a convenient time of recording so that repeated reference to the cumulative file is not necessary for recording (see forms in Chapter 3), many opportunities occur every day for what may be termed "fringe" interviews — a few questions asked incidental to another ongoing activity, e.g., discussing corrections on an arithmetic or spelling paper. Recess periods provide ready-made opportunities for time samplings and observation of play expression.

Slight modifications in the art program will yield rich material for interpretation without interfering with the creativity of the children. Too often the themes for the art work, repeated year after year in invariate monotony, are to draw, paint, or make some object relevant to the holidays — Easter, Decoration Day, Columbus Day, Halloween, Thanksgiving, Christmas. Autobiographies, diaries, and story completions can easily be incorporated as phases of written expression. Slight shifts of subject matter will provide for double-barreled performance, satisfying both curricular needs and information needs regarding personal development.

Demonstration of Various Techniques With A Well-Adjusted Child

By way of demonstration of this suggestion, a number of the techniques will be shown in the context of study of a well-adjusted child made by a third grade teacher. This study is interesting not only because it illustrates the various procedures used, but also because it shows their widespread suitability. Too often, because the discussion in texts such as this centers around the children having adjustment problems, the impression is given that the various techniques don't apply to "normal" children, and that the lives of these children are something apart. In the material to follow, the healthy development of the child is most evident.

Betty: 8 yrs. 9 mos., younger of the two children of upper middle class family. Father employed as personnel manager, both parents college graduates; older child a brother age 10. Physical examinations at kindergarten and third grade show excellent health. IQ: 123. Measured educational achievement one year above grade norms. Classroom deportment ratings: adequate to excellent.

Written expression

(The teacher had the children write a storybook for practice in creative expression. The children wrote their stories at will on subjects chosen individually).

1. MY DOLL. I have a new doll. Her name is Helen Russell. She has real hair that you can wash. She has roses on her dress. She can stand up. She has little black shoes. I like her.
2. DADDY'S BIRTHDAY. Yesterday was my father's birthday. We all gave him presents. He had a good time.
3. SCHOOL. I like school. It is fun. I like my papers. They are fun to do. I like my teacher. She is good to me. I have good friends too. They are good to me. I have fun.
4. MAKING COOKIES. My mother was baking cookies. I asked her if I could help. She said I could help with the cookies. I baked some cookies for dinner. Mother bakes some cake for dinner. I washed the dishes.
5. MY CHRISTMAS PRESENT. I got a coat from my mother for Christmas. It is nice and warm. I like it.
6. THE BASKETBALL GAME. My mother took me to a basketball game. I saw Forest Street play. It was a good game. My brother played on the team. He made one basket. My brother's friend made two baskets. He was bigger than my brother was.
7. SKATES. I have a pair of skates. I got them for Christmas. They are nice. I have been skating five times. Skating is fun. My mother went with me once. We had fun.
8. PAPERS. I got some papers Saturday. My brother and my father and I tied them all up and my father is going to take them today. I am going to buy my Brownie uniform.

Observations

(Only a few of the anecdotes are reported here)

Nov. 21. At recess today, Betty had a bag of candy. She stood talking to two other girls and myself. She offered each of us a piece of candy. Two or three other girls who noticed that Betty was passing out candy moved over to join the group. (Betty did not realize the motive in their moving and would have been able to give each of them a piece and still have one or two pieces left for herself. But evidently she decided that she rated more than one or two pieces since the candy was hers.) She smiled at the newcomers and said, "I wish I could give everyone a piece," then started to eat her candy.

Nov. 29. Betty told me that she prepared the supper all alone last night. She seemed very pleased. I asked her what she had. She said they had cold meat so she only had to boil the potatoes and cook the vegetables. Then she added, "Everyone liked the supper. Mother said the mashed potatoes were not as good as they might be but the rest of the family said they were all right."

Dec. 11. Betty said she was popping corn at six o'clock this morning. I said, "Oh, Betty, not popcorn for breakfast." She replied, "I didn't eat much of it. I put it in a bowl, put a sign on it, 'For Mother and Dad' and laid it on the table beside their bed."

Dec. 13. When we were making the Christmas decorations for our room, Betty said that she was making decorations for her own house too. She and her brother do most of the decorating. (I learned from another teacher that the two children do take over that part of the Christmas festivities and that the house was decorated plentifully, but not meticulously, both inside and out.)

Jan. 3. Today, Betty tended the Cracker and Cookie Store for the primary grades. After she had closed the store, she counted the money. She did it in the classroom and called to me, "I've got two Canadian pennies." I replied, "Don't tell me. Why did you take them?" "You gave me one," she remarked, quite pleased.

Feb. 6. The proofs arrived for the class pictures. Betty's pictures were not good. She brought back the proofs and said her mother would not buy any, that she was going to buy a group picture with her own money.

Feb. 15. One day early this month Betty was passing out notes on the back of discarded tickets, inviting all the children to come to a party. The novel invitations and the number of children being invited made me skeptical, but I said nothing. The day of the party, the mother came to school at noon saying she had just heard of it from another mother. I told her that I realized the affair was imaginative, and thought the children didn't take it seriously either, but that I would tell anyone who was planning to go that it was all a joke. The mother said, "No, I prefer to come in and tell the children myself, to be sure to embarrass Betty." She told the class that Betty was sorry that there wasn't to be a party. She added that it was wrong of Betty to have acted this way. Betty hung her head all the time her mother was talking.

Early this week, Mrs. Brown called saying that she would like to make some cookies and send them to the Valentine party to compensate for the disappointment that the children had had. I made some punch, the mother brought the cookies, told the class that this was Betty's pay-off for the joke she had played on them. Betty was pleased that she was the hostess for the occasion.

Mar. 11. Betty missed by a single vote being one of ten children chosen by the class to have their picture in the weekly newspaper because of the Rhythm Band record they are making for the Junior Red Cross. Betty looked a little disappointed when the list was read off, but not deeply hurt or sulky as some. One of the children brought the newspaper picture to school after it was published. Betty was interested in seeing it and remarked that it was a good picture, but a few who were not in the picture actually turned their backs on the whole procedure.

Picture Projection Test

(The teacher collected a box full of pictures out of magazines, illustrations and advertisements, without any captions, however. She suggested to the class that they select the pictures which appealed to them and write some little stories about them.)

PICTURES CHOSEN	BETTY'S WRITTEN RESPONSE
Young girl, sitting on chair, ribbon in curled hair.	This looks like me when I was three. I was just going to church. I was cute then.
Family of four, evening, mother sewing, father reading paper, children on floor coloring. All turned looking towards door in background.	I am about five years old. I am coloring, my brother is too.
Smiling girl in bathing suit, splashing feet in water, smiling.	I am about seven. I am sitting on water.
Smiling girl sitting on Santa Claus's lap. Smiling woman in background.	I am about six. I am sitting on Santa's knee. I am happy.
Parents and boy at breakfast table, smiling.	Here is my mother, father, and brother. They are eating. They are very happy.
Man pointing into open refrigerator. Girl standing looking at him.	This looks like me right now. My father is showing a refrigerator. He is happy.
Two couples, one much older, in kitchen. Men are cooking.	I think my mother and father are having a party. The men are doing the cooking.

The teacher purposely showed Betty some pictures showing undesirable traits and asked her if she should put them in her book. She said "No" and gave the following reasons:

PICTURE OR CARTOON	BETTY'S RESPONSE
Glum man reading in chair. Woman talking bitterly on telephone.	My mother doesn't like to talk on the telephone. It makes her cross when anyone keeps her on the phone.
Mother and daughter putting clothes into washer and dryer.	The only work I do at home is make my bed and wash the dishes.
Squalling child being carried upstairs to bed by maid.	I sometimes fuss a little about going to bed but not to this extent.
Woman kneeling at tub at bathing girl.	My mother doesn't help me take a bath anymore.
Man complaining about food woman is cooking.	My father doesn't complain about his food, when mother asks him what he wants, he says "I'll take anything."
Angry girl has broken toy, kicked man, in act of kicking woman.	I wouldn't do that to my mother.

Word Association Test

The teacher dictated the following list of words to the children, asking them to write their spontaneous response. Betty's follows:

STIMULUS WORD	BETTY'S RESPONSE
happy	smile
sad	cry
read	story
tired	bed
alone	play
eat	dinner
play	dolls
father	work
school	fun
friends	play
dark	night
brother	Donald
cry	hurt
mother	good
red	blue
sister	none
food	good
dog	cat
many	ten
cross	bear

My Two Best Times

The best time I ever had was last summer when I went to my Aunt Maude's house in Ill. because she had invited me for five weeks, and then we went back on the train. We had lots of fun. Do you like to go on the train?

Another good time I had was when I went to my camp one summer. First I was playing on the beach. Then I decided to play in the water, and all of a sudden I started really swimming. Now I know how much fun it is to really swim.

Sentence Completion Test

(Betty's response to the stimulus words are in italics)

I wish	*I had a pony.*
My father	*wants a new car.*
When I'm alone	*I play house.*
I hate	*to do the dishes.*
I feel marvelous when	*I play house with my mother's things and have on lipstick.*
I don't know why	*I always wish it was summer when it is winter and winter when it is summer.*
My mother	*lets me stay up late and listen to the radio sometimes.*
My greatest desire	*is Christmas.*
I fear	*that my dog will get killed.*
Home	*because I don't know and I like my home.*
I am worried	*because I don't know if I can go to girl's camp.*
When I grow up	*I want to be a teacher.*
I do not like	*beans.*
I like	*to swim.*
I am afraid	*of a bear.*

My Three Wishes

If I could wish for three things I would wish for:

a pony
a cat
a baby

A News Story About Me

I have traveled by:	bus	x	car	x
	boat	x	airplane	
	train	x	bicycle	x
I have visited	circus	x	airport	
	hotel	x	farm	
	dairy		factory	
	zoo	x	fire station	x

The usefulness of the information obtained about Betty by the several techniques illustrated is self-evident; one obtains a picture of parents interested in their children and finding time to participate in activity with them, able to allow Betty independence commensurate with her level of maturity, permitting freedom for performance gauged by child standards, and yet maintaining well-specified limits. Betty can accept disappointment and tolerate frustration. She thinks well of herself and reflects the happiness resulting from her family relationships. More could be said in the same vein, but it would only add to what is already apparent. Looking at each of the techniques used, amplifying on them, and suggesting others is more pertinent.

USE OF WRITTEN EXPRESSION

Almost any form of written expression will reflect the personality of the writer, provided sufficient opportunity for individual variation is possible. In Betty's class, the children were allowed to select their own topics and write as they chose. The topics chosen reflect the daily life and interests of the child, and the manner of expression shows her feelings toward them. Betty's themes reflect a positive feeling towards persons, objects, and activities. To her, life is fun, at least as reflected in the stories. However, more than fun, participation with family and friends in varied activities is seen as important.

It is possible to correct such stories for the grammatical and spelling errors evident, but, in the present instance, the teacher's purpose was to stimulate creative expression wherein the uncorrected spontaneity is more important than minor errors in form. A single sample of work can be highly selective as it represents a single episode which may not be at all characteristic of the child's life. Several variations are possible.

AUTOBIOGRAPHY

The higher the grade level and the more fluent the children, the greater their capacity to handle an assignment such as writing "The Story of My Life." It is desirable to have some preliminary discussion as to what constitutes an autobiography, perhaps even reading a sketch or two. Another approach is to list topics which might be covered in an autobiography, such as: where I've lived, friends, family, interests, important experiences, etc. Failure to do so usually results in a restricted output of information by the child. The major significance of an unstructured autobiography is the revelation of the happenings which the children recall as most important. In using this technique for the first time, an ample time allowance is needed because the novelty causes children to work slowly. A preferable arrangement is to fragment the autobiography into sections by instructing the children to write one day on "My Family," another day on "The Nicest Thing That Ever Happened to Me," etc.

STORY COMPLETION

Another modification of written expression is to have the children complete stories started by the teacher. Opening lines may be given the children, e.g., "Susan ran in the house crying," or "the boy sat alone on the school-bench," or "Jeannie was mad." Giving the lead line, the teacher can instruct the class to write a story, telling what happened, how the child feels, what the outcome will be.

In such instances, the children draw upon their own experiences and feelings and project them into the story situation, portraying their experiences, feelings and expectations. The kinds of events reviewed, the emotional tone of the story, and the optimism or pessimism regarding the outcome can be quite revealing. Again, a series of stories will disclose consistent response patterns suggestive of individual need.

SENTENCE COMPLETION TEST

Simpler to use because of the briefer responses characteristically given is the Sentence Completion Test. Commonly known as a test, it should not be so construed by the teacher, who creates her own instrument. Sentence completion tests have been partially standardized for use with adult populations, permitting more refined interpretation. The classroom teacher, however, uses such a device for suggestions and clues regarding attitudes, which will be subject to further verification. The child is presented with a series of incomplete phrases, which can easily be mimeographed on a page so that spontaneous responses are quickly possible. The class or child is asked to finish the sentences with whatever first comes to mind. The phrases given to Betty are typical. Phrases such as "it seems," "there are times," and "sometimes I think" are provocative because they are sufficiently vague as to permit wide variation in response and encourage an emotionally toned response. In contrast, a phrase such as "my dog" or "my bicycle" or "I play" is so specific as to elicit objective and descriptive responses.

Looking at Betty's responses for a moment — her future time perspective is shown in her response to "I feel marvelous," suggesting the appeal of being grown-up; her reflection on past and anticipation of future satisfaction are seen in her wishing for summer and winter, her anticipation of Christmas, and her going to camp. Usually, the longer the cue given, the more restricted the response, and, hence, the less useful. The length and content of the form can be varied to suit the teacher. The items as given are limited to the person and the family. Items relating to friends and other experiences can be included.

Quite a contrast is evident in the sentence completions of Jack, a seventh grade boy:

I dislike	*school.*
I like	*to go away.*
I hate	*people in general.*
My brother	*hates me.*
I love	*my dog.*
I would like	*to kill my sister.*
I wish	*I didn't have to go to school.*
I like	*nothing.*
When I grow up	*I want to be a bum.*
My mother	*doesn't care what I do.*
School	*I like arithmetic but get all the wrong answers.*
Girls	*giggle too much.*
I prefer	*to fight.*
Sometimes	*I want to run away and see the world.*
My father	*whips me for nothing.*

DIARIES OR LOGS

Personal or classroom logs may be kept of daily activities, and leisure time activities on an individual or group basis. The advantage of an individual log lies in its revealing the different perspective by which each child may view the same events. Particularly, logs of leisure time activity are helpful not only because they disclose sharp variations in the duties, activities, companions, bedtimes, and family relationships of individual children, but also because the combination of such data points up group needs and attitudes of the class as a whole, permitting the teacher to incorporate needed activity to provide for well-balanced experience. The approach may be unstructured or structured, either by asking the children to record their activity for the preceding afternoon and evening or weekend, or by providing them with a form which lists in separate columns: Time — What I did — With whom — Where. The advantage of a more structured format lies in the opportunity to associate activity with participants in order to determine the basis of choice of companions and activities. Which dictates the other? How do the activities or companionships contribute to wholesome development? What lacks exist in the recreational time of the children?

In submitting such proposals for class action, care is necessary to avoid their appearing as just another assignment. A class discussion can point out how interesting it would be for each member of the class to keep a record of his outside activities. If the sense of privacy that goes with their diary is desired, the class may choose to think of it as their individual diaries. The opening period can suitably be used for recording four or five lines describing the activity of the previous day while it is still fresh in mind.

A diary activity can be a welcome change from the oft-used oral report period. Suggestion should be made by the teacher of the importance of respecting the privacy of other diaries. The teacher should, advisedly, respect this admonition herself. If the teacher has rapport with her class, she will find the children trust her and want her to read their diaries. Nevertheless, too frequent a perusal runs the risk of the children's writing what they believe will please the teacher. A reading by the teacher once in three weeks is enough to inform her regarding the out-of-school lives of children. Avoid making comments or criticisms of style in order to keep the expression from becoming artificial or suggesting that some activities are preferable to others.

Two series of entries, taken from the diaries of fourth grade pupils, show the kinds of differences which appear:

Roberta, Age 8

Nov. 11. Yesterday I went to Brownies. We had a lot of fun making telephone books. When we finished we played some games. Then we went home. Jean ate over at our house.

Nov. 23. Yesterday I went out to dinner. I had a good time. When I came home my grandmother was there. Then we went to my aunt's. When we came home we watched TV.

Dec. 3. Yesterday I went to Hebrew School. When we had finished the lesson I went to my friend's house. We played games, then I came home.

Dec. 5. Yesterday I went to my piano lesson. I had a good time. When I came home I had dinner and then I talked to my father.

Dec. 7. Yesterday I went to Hebrew School. When my friend and I got home we went to a magic show. We had a good time. When I got home I went to my grandmother's. Sharon had a party.

Connie, Age 8

Nov. 17. Yesterday afternoon, when I came home I watched television. After supper I read.

Nov. 20. Yesterday after school I went to the library. When I came home I read. After supper I watched TV.

Dec. 1. Yesterday after Hebrew School, when I came home, I had supper. When I was done I had a bath. Then I read.

Dec. 3. Yesterday after Hebrew School when I came home I read. After supper I played with my sister.

The records indicate sharp differences in the leisure and recreational activities of the two children: Roberta is a member of the highly chosen group on a sociogram (see Chapter 14 for description of sociogram), while Connie is an isolate in class. Roberta's afternoons and evenings are active, Connie's passive. One girl is in constant interaction with adults and children, the other, though a member of the same ethnic group, makes rare mention of any other person.

When the teacher combined the records of groups of highly chosen children and compared them with the underchosen, she found the former had:

1. Some organized and directed club life such as Brownies, Cub Scouts, church choir, Hebrew school, Sunday School.
2. Some informal clubs initiated and directed by the children themselves.
3. Sports and outdoor games with other members of the family and friends.
4. Indoor games with family and friends.
5. Some creative work, either with clubs or family, including construction, cooking, science projects, and various crafts.
6. Some television and radio.
7. Reading books and children's magazines.
8. Responsibilities around the home.
9. Just talking with parents and other family members.
10. Finding interesting things to do alone.

The least accepted children had social lives entirely of their own making. These were of the "go out and play" variety. Hence, they often found possible playmates otherwise engaged, and so wandered about aimlessly or resorted to play with such younger or older children that their interests varied greatly and, psychologically, their needs went unmet. With this group much watching of television was evidenced.

WISHES AND FEARS

A simple procedure which can provide a stimulating beginning for class discussions is to have children list their three wishes and three fears. It is helpful to have the children list them individually rather than publicly to reduce the element of suggestion which leads one child to repeat another.

Children's wishes can be classified — many texts on child psychology describe typical wishes and fears of children at differing age levels. Most frequent wishes, particularly during primary grades, will be for desired objects, with the gradual emerging (with increasing age) of desires for association with particular persons, self-improvement, a change in environmental circumstances (often avoiding school!), and with the greater time perspective that develops in the intermediate grades, wishes regarding one's personal future or improved conditions for others.

Fears tend to follow patterns characteristic of given ages, but occasionally morbid fears and feelings of guilt are observed indicating mental health problems. The itemization of wishes and fears is a natural introductory activity for group discussions on such topics, which can become fruitful personal experiences leading beyond the formal academic discussion to provide insight and understanding.

PICTURE PROJECTION TEST

Thematic Apperception Tests have been developed for both adult and child subjects. The test consists of a series of pictures, half suitable to one sex, the other half for the other, about which the subject being tested is instructed to tell what is happening, what led up to the situation, and what the outcome will be. The pictures are deliberately ambiguous to make it easier for the respondent to construe and respond to the picture in any way he chooses. The usefulness rests upon the observation that individuals project their own personal feelings and perceptions of the world into the scenes provided by the pictures, frequently identifying with one of the persons involved in the picture and investing that person with the feelings and perceptions they personally hold but which they would find difficult or be reluctant to express directly.

The term "thematic" describes the fact that each story often represents a theme involving the interplay of the person's needs and the environmental pressures he sees existing in the picture. From these themes, the predominant needs or drives of the person being tested can be inferred, especially by the total analysis of the twenty pictures provided. Interpretations may range from simple tallies of needs and pressures, analyses of emotional tone of the stories, and favorable or unfavorable outcomes to the created stories, to elaborate and sensitive constructions of the psychological dynamics revealed.

A *word of caution* is required at this point. The formal administration and psychological interpretation of such test instruments is the purview of the clinical psychologist. The administration of such projective techniques as the Sentence Completion Test, The Children's Apperception Test, etc., requires special training and supervised experience. The administration is time-consuming and the interpretation depends upon clinical insight rather than objective scoring keys. Nevertheless, the modification described here can be used by the elementary school teacher with useful results. The procedures are essentially extensions of teacher observations and are used to provide the teacher with clues which may help her to greater awareness of the child and understanding of his behavior.

Questionnaires which inquire into personal family relationships, particularly those that ask children to express their opinions, judgments, and feelings about their family and parents, can provoke strong parental reaction.

Looking back at the use Betty's teacher made of pictures, you may see two approaches — the first to take a number of pictures from which the child may choose those which appeal to him, the second, to select the pictures to be exposed and systematically ask for a response to each. The first procedure reveals differences in the pictures which appeal to a child. Betty, for instance, chose two types of pictures, one of a young girl engaged in various activities, the other, family pictures. All the pictures she chose had in common the happy theme, both in the pictures chosen and the responses given. In many of the stories, it is noticeable that Betty identified with the girl in the picture, ascribing to her experiences and feelings which were Betty's. In addition to the happiness, and the pleasant family association, Betty reveals a feeling of satisfaction with herself. She sees herself (the girl in the picture) as attractive and competent, revealing the concept she holds of herself.

A disadvantage in letting a child choose the pictures is the difficulty in comparing responses of different children. To make an assumption that the response is characteristic, one must know that all children don't give the same or similar response, i.e., the response observed is a function of the picture rather than the child. Letting all children respond to the same group of pictures, as the teacher did in the second phase, offsets this disadvantage.

Two limitations to the picture projection technique when used with younger children are the shortness of their responses and the tendency to merely describe what they see in the picture. Descriptions of the picture reveal nothing of the personality or needs of the child. Again the warning needs to be made to avoid over-interpreting the responses. As far as classroom teachers are concerned, the child's responses provide the teacher with an expanded range of behavior and yield clues subject to confirmation through observation.

CREATIVE EXPRESSION

One of children's most natural forms of expression is art. Drawing, like singing and dancing, is a natural means of expression. By drawing in a situation where the task isn't prescribed, e.g., coloring forms which have been run off on the duplicating machine, a child will express his likes and dislikes, his emotional relationships to his own world, and to the world which surrounds him. The drawing combines his knowledge of things and his individual relationship to the persons and objects of the world which surrounds him. Paintings and drawings can be full of significant content of which the child himself is often quite unaware. It should be noted that to interpret the child's artwork as related to his personality, his art products should be observed over a period of time to determine if there are recurrent or persistent events that have become patterns in the child's pictures. A stereotyped repetition is a sign of rigidity and suggests the existence of emotional problems.

One fifth grade boy, no matter what the art medium being used, persistently drew a picture of a grave with a large cross for a tombstone around which thorns were twined. Occasionally, he would add a dagger dripping blood to the scene. Investigation disclosed a seriously disturbed foster child whose parents had been killed in an accident. His only immediate attachment was to his pet dog, which he extremely feared might be accidentally killed. To all appearances, he was not maladjusted, but rather a quiet unassuming child who managed to struggle through most of his work in school. He revealed his fears and his deep anxieties in his drawing, and fortunately so because he was able to have the specialized help he needed.

To use art work effectively for purposes of personal growth and development, not only should a range of work over a period of time be observed, but also care must be taken to avoid the influences of suggestion on expression. Young children are quick to sense what expression is permissible, what will find approval. They seek hints as to what to draw and how to draw it. The presentation of drawing or art should be such as to encourage individual expression. Topics may be suggested to avoid the stereotyped drawings which characterize different age levels.

For instance, the teacher might relate a short dream, then ask the children to draw or paint a dream of their own. She might ask them to draw a map of their head or paint what they think about. A drawing of "My Family" frequently reveals interesting aspects of how the child perceives himself in relation to members of the family. An abstract line may be presented as the beginning of a drawing for the child to complete. Any thing that an imaginative teacher can devise may be used. Different media should be utilized, inasmuch as some children draw more freely with one medium than another. Some media offer so much resistance or require so much technique or control that they impede expression. Hence, fingerpaints, chalk, and watercolors, as well as crayons, should be used.

OPEN-ENDED QUESTIONS

A number of minor procedures can provide fruitful information for analysis of group attitudes and provide useful material for class discussion. The approach may be made either in written or oral form. For instance, the class can be instructed to write a theme on one of several topics: things I like about myself, things I dislike about myself, things I would like to improve (the last named would tap the same feelings as the preceding item and have the advantage of a constructive approach), what I do when I get mad, what I do when my mother refuses me something I want. The teacher will be amazed at many of the attitudes and behavior patterns revealed and will see opportunity for class discussion of methods used to solve such difficulties.

Questionnaires

Questionnaires are useful in obtaining a broader range of information with comprehensive ease. They are particularly useful for surveying the needs of the entire class with a view to identifying problems, attitudes, or attributes and characteristics common to many children in order to plan a program designed to provide specific opportunities. Questionnaires can be discussed in relation to many topics, with variations to be suggested on each, but in the elementary school classroom, three major types can be identified.

The first is intended to obtain factual information, which can be provided with either a short answer or a yes or no answer. The questionnaire obtaining vital statistics about children — their age, brothers, sisters, address, etc. — is an example. Similarly, children may be asked to indicate their favorite sport, best friend, favorite television program, books read, places visited, food eaten, and so forth on whatever topics information is desired. The primary characteristic of this type is that the information desired is generally factual, with little or no emotion feelings associated which would make the child reluctant to respond or inclined to distort his reply.

The second type of questionnaire involves topics about which a person may be sensitive, or tempted to modify his answer in a direction which he thinks may please the person asking the questions or may provide a more favorable picture of himself. Personality and temperament inventories are good illustrations of pencil-and-paper questionnaires which depend for accuracy upon the willingness of the respondent to give an honest reply. The tendency to conceal information or to distort it in a favorable direction is perfectly commonplace. There are aspects of each person's life about which he may be reluctant to respond, not necessarily because of any shame or guilt, but often because of a desire for privacy or sensitivity on the topic. A second tendency we all have is the desire to give the best impression or account of ourselves to those about us. Both factors tend to introduce some bias or distortion into responses. The bias varies with the nature of the questions being asked and the attitudes of the respondent. For instance, when asked about fears, many children will deny having any. For some this may be true, but others either do not understand the question or feel they must deny fears rather than admit them and be forced to face them for what they are.

The following questionnaire is an illustration of one that may be used in obtaining information about aggressive feelings, shyness and fears. The questions are mixed, although they could readily be presented separately. The questions, which are multiples of three (3, 6, 9, etc.), deal with fears, the preceding one with shyness, the following with aggressive feelings.

1. Do you become angry when your work is criticized?
2. Do you feel people are unfriendly to you?
3. Do you worry a great deal about your schoolwork?
4. Do you get mad when somebody teases you?
5. Do you sometimes feel that nobody understands you?
6. Have you ever been afraid of your teacher?
7. Does it make you angry to have somebody play a joke on you?
8. Do you worry about little mistakes you make?
9. Do you dread getting your report card?
10. Do you get angry when you don't get your own way?
11. Are your feelings easily hurt?
12. Do you lie awake thinking at night when you go to bed?
13. Do you cry when you can't have your own way?
14. Do you usually prefer to have someone else be the leader?
15. Do you often have frightening dreams?
16. When your team is losing, do you quit and go home?
17. Do you often feel sad for no particular reason?
18. Are you afraid of dogs or other animals?
19. When your friends won't play the game you want, do you get mad and go home?
20. Do you wish you could stay home instead of going to school?
21. Are you afraid when you are alone?
22. Do you feel hurt when adults favor other children?
23. Do you wish that you never had to stand in front of the class and give a report?
24. Are you afraid of any particular thing? What?
25. Do you get mad if your parents don't give you a toy or a game you want?
26. Do you wish you could take part in more things with other children and have more fun?
27. Are you afraid of any particular person? Who?
28. Do you get angry if you have to go someplace when you don't want to go?
29. Do you worry about terrible things that might happen to you or your family?
30. Are you afraid of dark places like attics, halls, or basements?

A quick survey of the entire class can be obtained by listing the names of the children on a piece of graph paper and placing the numbers of the questions across the top, one column for each question. A check may be placed under each question that each child marks indicating anger, shyness, or fear. The predominant problems present in the entire class, as well as those of individual children, are immediately apparent.

The third type of questionnaire is the open-ended question, to which the child is expected to respond in some detail, rather than with a brief factual response or a yes or no answer. Illustrations have already been given.

Both questionnaires and check-lists will be easier to handle if no more than one question is asked on a single line, and the answers, the markings of yes and no, are placed uniformly down the right hand margin of the page. When this is done, the tally work on graph paper is not essential unless a single, comprehensive tally is desired. Instead, the questionnaires can be arranged in alphabetical order, laid on a table and spread (as a deck of cards would be spread) so that the right-hand margins with the marked answers are visible. By keeping the papers aligned, an immediate total count of the yes and no answers can be obtained for each question.

Check lists are closely akin to questionnaires and serve similar purposes. They have the advantage of ease of organization and administration in making quick surveys of the class. Their disadvantage lies in the lack of detailed information provided. Consider the following sample check list:

Put a check in front of the words or phrases which you feel describe you.

x	often lonesome
x	shy
	make friends, easily
x	find it hard to make friends
	most people like me
x	a few like me but not many
	most people dislike me
	like to come to school
	think school is boring
	find the work at school hard to do
	prefer to be alone most of the time
	a leader
x	not as smart as most
	more intelligent than most

The phrases presented are a potpourri without a particular frame of reference. The phrases could easily be grouped around a single topic. For instance, a section of phrases could be related to health —

get tired easily, have frequent headaches, worry about my health, find it hard to read the blackboard, etc.; another section could be concerned with school — like school, school is boring, school work is too hard for me, etc.; further sections could include items on getting along with others, getting along at home, about myself, and so forth. These can be duplicated in single sections, one to a page, permitting easy tallying for obtaining a picture of problems or attitudes common to a number of children and possibly serving as a focal point for attack. Or they may be all included in a several-page check list to be completed at one time. Commercial forms are available, such as the Mooney Problem Check List and the SRA Youth Inventory for comprehensive surveys. The commercial forms have the advantage of providing certain normative data for making comparisons, but it should be made clear that such normative data does not have the same value as norms on standardized achievement and intelligence tests.

Check lists can be especially useful early in the school year when broad general information is helpful in organization of the class, but the limits of such information are easily seen. The check marks provided on the foregoing list would identify a child's perception of himself without giving clues as to the underlying factors creating such an opinion. Further exploration would be needed before any attempts could be made at correcting the opinion, assuming its accuracy. Standard recipes for overcoming shyness do not exist. Nevertheless, after analyzing the responses of the class, the teacher would have identified the kinds of needs existing in the group and could plan major approaches.

Another effective use of check lists is surveys of leisure time activities. Lists of interests, hobbies, and recreational activities can be prepared and duplicated. It is desirable to group the items under common headings such as Collecting, Going Places, Games, Building and Making, Clubs, Watching and Listening, etc. Under each heading a list of possibilities can be arranged in a column:

Collecting:	*Have Done*	*Do Regularly*	*Would Like*
Stamps			
Coins			
Rocks			
Matchbooks			
Butterflies			
Flowers			
Dolls			
Etc.			

Going Places:	Have Done	Do Regularly	Would Like
Motion Pictures			
Zoo			
Aquarium			
Theater			
Parks			
Science Museum			
Planetarium			
Hockey Games			
Baseball Games			
Football Games			
Fishing			
Hiking			
Etc.			

A series of columns can be arranged in which the child checks those things he has done at some time, those he does regularly, those he hasn't done but would like to do. Thus, the list provides an inventory of experience the child has had and an indication of activities in which he has demonstrated some consistent interest. It also is a guide to possible interests which can be developed. Similarly, lists of the television and radio programs being broadcasted in the area can be listed and the class asked to check off the programs which they watched during a given period of time. They can check not only those they watched, but those they started to watch but changed, the ones most liked, etc. For the purposes described, check lists can be most useful in providing surveys of class interests and activities.

THE INTERVIEW

Any question which can be asked in a questionnaire can be asked directly, often without the risk of misinterpretation or inability to understand the wording of the question. The best interviews, from the standpoint of reliability of information obtained, are in fact those for which the interviewer has prepared a standard list of questions to be asked and a consistent order for asking the questions. This has the advantage of providing a uniform approach for controlling in degree the effects of the interviewer.

There are specific disadvantages to standardized interviews with children. Foremost is the fact of the teacher's being in a position of authority which makes the child reluctant or fearful to respond in any way he anticipates will displease or anger the teacher, however true the response. Couple this relationship with the fact that the teacher is customarily asking questions of individual children as part of her instructional technique, at which time the answers are judged as right or wrong, and a situation is created which seriously restricts the child's feeling of freedom of response. It is not unusual that an interview serves to obtain information which subsequently is used to reprimand, punish, or, at a minimum, point out what should have occurred.

With primary grade children, a further hazard ensues from their lack of objectivity and their tendency to seek to provide what they think is the information or response that the teacher needs. It is not unusual to see young children completely reverse themselves when, having related the information that they thought answered an inquiry, they sense an expressed doubt in additional questions as: are you *sure* that is what happened? . . . etc. This reversal does not stem from a brazen disregard of the "truth" but from the indistinct line in children's thought between reality and fantasy and their desire to please adults or to avoid punishment.

For these reasons, the teacher is more likely to make successful use of the interview if she makes it incidental to some other activity rather than a direct, face-to-face approach. This approach can be considered a fringe interview, which is not to imply that it is unimportant, but that the interview is incorporated within, and apparently secondary to, the activity in which the child or the group finds itself engaged. During the school day the teacher can find occasion to talk with a youngster when he's standing on the sidelines waiting his turn in a game, or at lunch time, or while engaged in any of the many activities during which conversation is possible without disrupting attention. Children may be asked to help on some work or projects before or after school. During any of these situations, opportunity can be provided for the child to talk about himself, his attitudes, his feelings, or his experiences, by casual questions seemingly entered as asides to the activity. In such situations, the child doesn't feel that he's "on-the-spot" and is less likely to maintain defenses to protect himself.

Even the successful use of fringe interviews necessitates a warm-up period, during which the child develops a feeling of being at ease in the presence of the teacher. He has to develop a feeling that the teacher is a person whom he can trust with confidences. Several conversations will often ensue on neutral or impersonal topics — trips taken, favorite sports, hobbies, etc. — before the child will respond freely with his feelings. Adults are no different. We respect adult privacy yet often make the error of assuming that children will respond freely to any inquiry by an adult.

The following interview with an eight-year-old boy, taken during a week-end visit depicts this approach:

> I noticed that whenever the parents did not pay attention to the boy, Rick would get rough with his younger brother, and once, when the parents left the room he became even more arrogant, jumping on the younger boy and saying, "We are just playing. I did not hurt you. Don't cry." When the parents came back in the parlor Rick was behaving like a gentleman. The doorbell rang, the grandparents came in, and I saw the light of joy in both boys' eyes as they rushed to them. The grandparents said hello to Rick, slightly patted him, and then over-showered the younger brother with affection. Ricky retreated, turned his back, and ran upstairs to his room.
>
> I excused myself and ascended to his room. "What are you doing here?" was his first reaction. "Oh, I got bored downstairs. Can't I keep you company for some time?" "O.K.," he replied continuing to construct a plane.
>
> I let him play and browsed around the room, commenting about different things I saw, asking a question, giving him credit. Little by little his ignoring attitude decreased. His eyes that were formerly absorbed in the airplane turned now from time to time to size me up. At this stage he began to discuss his interests, pulling different articles he had created from a trunk: puppets, boats, model plane, paintings. I talked about some of my interests which were similar, then turned the conversation to his brother, asking if he did any such things, following that with a question regarding what he thought of his brother.
>
> "He is pretty," Rick said, "And he's my mummy's and father's pet, but I hate him. He just makes me feel like beating him up sometimes. He is a nasty little brat. He has no sense of humor, and he always likes to be petted and hugged, and I hate all that."
>
> While conversing, he told me that he wants everyone to call him "Ugly," and that most of all he hates clean and pretty clothes, and that he can't stand seeing his little brother look pretty. Rick told me he liked school very much but was only the second smartest boy in the class. He loves his school teacher, and has many friends in school. He likes to tell and listen to jokes, and enjoys playing with his friends, but often likes being by himself to read, build, paint, etc.

Personality and Adjustment Inventories

A variety of personality and adjustment inventories are available for use at the elementary school level, and brief descriptions of those accessible for use by school personnel are provided, along with a listing of personality tests which require the trained services of a specialist for use. The major advantage that an adjustment inventory or personality test can provide is in normative data which represents a gauge for appraising the seriousness of adjustment problems. Against this advantage, several disadvantages must be counterbalanced. The first is that the limitations in reliability indices restrict the value of the tests as far as individual diagnosis is concerned. Second, children are prone to misinterpret the questions because of their limitations in vocabulary and concept development and their inexperience in being objective about non-objective events. Third, in younger children, their inclination to confuse fact and fantasy leads to erroneous responses. For instance, in a study of the responses of second grade children to *A Book About Me,* the investigator found that children (asked to check toys they possessed) would check toys they wished for as often as they checked ones they possessed. Similar distortions occurred in other areas. For these reasons, personality inventories should be used with caution in the elementary grades.

PERSONALITY TESTS—TEACHER EVALUATION						
Name	*Author*	*Publisher*	*Cost*	*Time*	*Validity*	*Reliability*
Winnetka Scale for Rating School Behavior and Attitudes (K-6)	Van Alstyne	Winnetka Public Schools Illinois	.10		r.71 w. Haggerty-Olson-Wickman	Sections .72-.82 Total .87 Test-retest

Scale is based on classroom incidents, consists of 13 situations each with 5 or more levels of behavior. Situations permit ratings with respect to co-operation, social consciousness, emotional control, leadership, responsibility. Norms based on 1200 pupils. Instructions advise obtaining ratings over two-year period.

A Book About Me (K-1)	Jay	Science Research Associates	.43			

Designed to permit kindergarten and first grade children to communicate about their life situations, the booklet presents sketches of many home, family, school, and play situations, from which the child chooses those which portray his life—what his family is like, the toys he wants, etc. Subject to inaccurate response due to the child's non-literal perceptions.

Haggerty-Olsen-Wickman Behavior Rating Schedules (K-12)	named in title	World Book Co.	.07			.86

Schedule A is a Behavior Problem Record listing common problem behaviors to be rated in terms of frequency with which observed. Weights are assigned in terms of frequency with seriousness of given problem. Schedule B is a Behavior Rating Scale consisting of 5-point graphic scales for 35 traits falling in four groups: intellectual, social, physical, and emotional. Originally published in 1930.

Name	Author	Publisher	Cost	Time	Validity	Reliability
Teacher Rating Scales for Pupil Adjustment (Ages 5-8)	Baker	Univ. of Chicago Press	1.20			

Five scales: intellectual characteristics, work and study habits, emotional adjustment, social adjustment, scholastic achievement, each with a five-step scale. Entire class rates on each scale before starting next scale to reduce halo effect.

Detroit Adjustment Inventory (K-12)	Freeman Kawin	Pub. Schl. Publ. Co.	.13			

Designed to discover problems of children during primary years. Rates four types of reaction: habits, social, emotional, ethical in each of four environments: school, community, home, self. Parents help needed on home sections. Sixteen remedial booklets available providing suggestions for work with children having adjustment difficulty in specific areas. A self administering form is available for grades 3-6 requiring 30-45 minutes.

New York Rating Scale for School Habits (4-12)	Cornell Coxe Orleans	World Book Co.	.04		.55-.75 r with high school grades	

Teacher rating of pupil traits: attention, neatness, honest, interest, initiative, ambition, persistence, reliability, stability, based on class observations. Completed record constitutes profile group of traits.

Personality Evaluation Form	Buhler Howard	Western Psych. Serv.	.12			

Provides for systematic evaluation of test materials, observations, cumulative records, and other data by counselor, teacher, and specialist in order to develop personality picture and evaluations.

PERSONALITY TESTS—ADJUSTMENT INVENTORIES						
California Tests of Personality (K-3, 4-8)	Thorpe Clarke Tiegs	Calif. Test Bureau	.08	30-40		.92

Primary and Elementary grade forms which consist of two groups of components: (1) self-adjustment—self-reliance, sense of personal worth, sense of personal freedom, feeling of belonging, freedom from social standards, social skills, freedom from withdrawal, freedom from nervous symptoms; (2) social adjustment, social skills, freedom from anti-social tendencies, family relations, school relations, and community relations. Objective scoring via hand and machine methods. A carefully constructed instrument which gives evidence of students feeling and attitudes in wide variety of situations. Its limitations are those of personality questionnaires in general —it provides a measure of the pupil's attitude about himself rather than as others see him, is dependent upon willingness to reveal one's feelings.

Name	Author	Publisher	Cost	Time	Validity	Reliability
California Behavior Preference Record (4-6)	Wood	Calif. Test Bureau	.08	30-40		.77-.88 Alt. Forms

Consists of a series of problem situations with alternate choices possible designed to (a) determine understanding of democratic ideals, (b) preferences for various types of behavior, (c) provide base for discussion. Trait scores on cooperation, friendliness, integrity, leadership, and responsibility.

Name	Author	Publisher	Cost	Time	Validity	Reliability
SRA Junior Inventory (4-8)	Remmers Bauernfeind	Science Research Associates	.10	40	.43-.56 $r_{bis.}$	.80-.90

A problem checklist permitting children to indicate degree of intensity of problem in six major areas: things in general, health, about myself, getting along with others, school, home. Items were developed from free response statements of pupils. Excellent norms.

Name	Author	Publisher	Cost	Time	Validity	Reliability
Mental Health Analysis (4-8)	Thorpe Clarke Tiegs	Calif. Test Bureau	.08	50		.89-97 K-R

20 items for each of five mental health liabilities—behavioral immaturity, emotional instability, feelings of inadequacy, physical defects, nervous manifestations, and five mental health assets—defects, close personal relationships, interpersonal skills, social participation, satisfying work and recreation, adequate outlook and goals. Norms based on 1000 or more cases on each of four norms.

Name	Author	Publisher	Cost	Time	Validity	Reliability
Aspects of Personality (4-9)	Pintner Loftus Forlano Alster	World Book Co.	.08	30	.30-.50 $r_{bis.}$	.52-.92 ½ x ½

114 items adapted to experience of school child provided at fourth grade vocabulary level. Measures ascendance-submission, extroversion-introver-

sion, emotionality. The individual responses provide valuable clues if supplemented by observation or interview.

Name	Author	Publisher	Cost	Time	Validity	Reliability
Ohio Guidance Tests for Elementary Grades (4-6)	Fordyce Yauch Raths	Ohio State Dept. Educ.	.13	120		

Test consists of five parts: (1) 360 items, forced-choice interest inventory classifying into 18 areas—sports, school, music, movies, etc. (2) modified sociometric technique based on committee selection: (3) a social acceptance scale: (4) a modified Guess-Who technique: (5) The Ohio Thinking Checkup involving caution or imprudence in interpreting data.

Interest Inventory for Elementary Grades (4-6)	Dreese Mooney	Geo. Wash. Univ.	.05	40		

250 items, interest inventory eliciting reaction to movies, radio, reading, games, and toys, hobbies, things to own, school subjects, occupations, activities requiring response of life, indifferent, dislike, unknown to each.

TESTS REQUIRING SPECIALIZED TRAINING FOR ADMINISTRATION AND INTERPRETATION

Name	Author	Age Range
Children's Apperception Test	Bellak	3-10
Horn-Hellersburg Test	Hellersburg	3-up
Kahn Test of Symbol Arrangement	Kahn	3-16
Michigan Picture Test	Mich.Dept.Ment.H.	8-14
Rorschach Inkblot Test	Rorschach	3-up
Rosenzweig Picture Frustration Test	Rosenzweig	3-13
Szondi Test	Szondi	4-up
Test of Personality Adjustment	Rogers	6-10
The Blacky Pictures	Blum	5-up
The Five Task Test	Buhler-Mandeville	all ages
Thematic Apperception Test	Murray	7-up
The Paper and Pencil World Test	Buhler-Manson	all ages
Vineland Social Maturity Scale	Doll	0-30

OBSERVATIONAL TECHNIQUES

TIME SAMPLING

Early in the book, procedures for objective observation were discussed. Time sampling is a method whereby the faults of selective observation are avoided. We tend to see only that to which our attention is directed. This means that unless we have some procedure whereby we systematically direct our attention to children, we are likely to see only the events which are dramatic, the quarrels, accidents, outbursts, etc. Time sampling insures the obtaining of a broad sample of the behavior of any child or group. It involves establishing an observational schedule. For instance, a teacher could determine to observe all the behavior of a particular child or group during a two minute, or ten minute, or any length, time period. She could set the ten minutes between 10:10 and 10:20 a.m. every morning for a week or alternate mornings and afternoons. A few of the observations made during a ten minute period follow:

> *Observed:* Seymour Nims   *Date:* 19 October
> *By:* Miss Johnson   *Time:* 10:00-10:20 a.m.
> *Class Activity:* Spelling period
> 10:10   Walks to pencil sharpener, sharpens pencil, stops and whispers to Sunny Davidson on return to seat.
> 10:12   Looks at spelling list on board, starts to copy, stops, looks out window, turns back to work, writes a word, opens desk, can't find what he looks for, pokes girl ahead and asks to borrow eraser.

The observational report would continue during the ten minute period, describing the various actions of the child. Such procedures guard against distorted impressions based upon faulty samplings of behavior. Teachers find it difficult to be this systematic in the face of all the time demands and activities to be met. Nevertheless, an arranged program of observation in which the child to be observed is specified, and persistent attention paid to observing that child over a period of days, even without a rigid adherence to a set time schedule, will provide better balanced observations, particularly of those children who tend to go unnoticed because their actions occur quietly. Internes and student teachers can often function effectively in the role of observer, providing useful information for the teacher as well as obtaining valuable training.

RATING SCALES

A common component of many cumulative records are rating scales which obtain a rating by the teacher on different aspects of a child's attitude and behavior. Characteristics such as interest in school work, attitude towards authority, control of emotions, work habits, and others may be rated. The ratings may classify the child simply into one of three categories or may provide a more detailed range:

Attention to Classroom Regulations

———Usually conforms to and accepts regulations.
———Needs frequent reminders about classroom regulations.
———Unpredictable in response to regulations.

Acceptance of Authority

Defiant	Critical of Authority	Usually Obedient	Respectful and Compliant	Resigned Never Challenges

There are so many difficulties in the construction and use of rating scales that they are not especially informative. The frame of reference within which teachers interpret the meaning of point on the scale; the ambiguity of terms such as usually, occasionally, sometimes; and the influence of hearsay (his former teacher thought well of him); stereotypes (his father is a doctor—he's a nice boy); and halo effect (he's a good student so he must be a good leader), are all factors which limit the effective use of rating scales.

ROLE-PLAYING

Given dramatic situations to spontaneously enact, children will draw on their own experiences in creating their parts. The actions disclosed in such situations can provide valuable insight into the attitudes and personalities of children. Because role-playing and sociodrama are useful in changing attitudes, greater detail is provided in Chapter 16. The essence of the skill lies in choosing typical situations from children's lives and using these as the substance for spontaneous drama. Two children may be having an argument which started out of range of the teacher's attention. Instead of asking the children to tell what happened, ask them to show what happened. Usually a child will start by saying, "I said to him ... and then he said to me." At this point, shift from narration to re-enactment by instructing the child to say what he said as he said it and let the other reply as he had. Very quickly and easily the children will re-enact the event.

Situations can be created by first starting a discussion with a leading question: "Have any of you ever been picked on by an older child?" Several children will start to tell of an event. After one has started to tell his experience, ask him to come to the front of the room and choose some other child whom he feels could act the other part and spontaneously enact the event. Or the question introduced by the teacher: "Have any of you had quarrels or gotten angry with your brother or sister?" Again, as the child starts to relate the event, ask him to choose another child to be the brother or sister and act out the situation. The child who experienced the actual event should be given the part of the instigator of the event, and the other child instructed to respond by whatever occurs to him, however he feels. After the scene has been run through once, the roles can be reversed, with the instigator now becoming the recipient of the action.

One may ask how can a fictitious enactment of a scene be of any value. The first feature of such situations lies in the fact that in the spontaneous enactment, one acts as one is, revealing attitudes, motives, behavior patterns which are true to oneself. It is much easier to talk differently from oneself than to act differently.

The second feature lies in the similarity with which many of the common roles of life are portrayed. Most quarrels between brothers and sisters have a similar ring to them; most fathers use similar tones of voice and manner when disciplining a child. By choosing situations which are typical of the experiences of children, being blamed or punished, having quarrels, making a mistake, experiencing the loss of a favorite toy or the death of a pet, having a minor accident and being afraid to tell about it, being embarrassed, hurting someone's feelings, etc., one obtains a ready insight into the child's reaction and his adequacy in handling such situations in reality.

An alternate procedure for introducing role playing is to use a photograph or picture which shows children having a quarrel, or one child crying, with another standing nearby or perhaps holding an arm around the child, in short any picture which contains some conflict or opportunity for emotional response. Show the picture to the class, ask them what they think is occurring, then ask certain members of the class to act out their ideas. Motion pictures can be used to good effect in this procedure by interrupting such a scene by stopping the film before the solution is presented and asking the class what they think will happen and having them act out their ideas.

Play Observation

Akin to dramatic re-enactment of situations is play observation. Too often adults are inclined to dismiss the play of children as merely an avenue for release of energy in activities which are governed by chance, instead of recognizing play as a means whereby children come to grips with the world and try to work out possible solutions to problems. Careful observations of children in play situations alone or in groups, will yield much valuable information on the major concerns of children. When children in a home for crippled children were given materials from which they could construct playthings and small dolls to play with, it was significant to note that nearly every child in the small group reproduced an image of himself. If the child's legs were in traction, he would put plaster casts around the legs of the doll and rig strings over a frame representing the traction assembly. If his back was in a cast, the child duplicated this with the doll. One child, who had one leg shorter than the other, made a brace out of a bobby-pin, built up the sole of the shoe with small pieces of wood, and made a crutch out of tongue-depressors.

Providing children with games, dolls, clays, paints, and other assorted toys which he can manipulate in any fashion he chooses, has long been an important tool for the child psychologist. The child is allowed to select the toy which appeals to him from the assortment available, for his choice in itself is significant, and then to manipulate it as appeals to him. Anything which inherently has no set use can be employed to discover the child's feelings. While the individual time and the assortment of toys is not ordinarily available to the classroom teacher, she, nevertheless, has ample opportunity to observe children in unstructured play situations, and, through the observation, can gain further understanding of the child. Sometime, particularly in solitary play, the child literally recreates episodes from his life:

> Laura (age 7½) is playing with her doll on the front porch of the apartment house. I (student observer) sit beside her and she asks me if I will play doctor with her. I open my book and pretend to read. She turns to her doll and after a few minutes seems to have forgotten that I am there. She speaks to her doll sometimes soothingly and in a sweet voice and then she changes abruptly, becoming harsh, and speaks to her doll in tones similar to those her mother uses when she speaks with the child. She slaps the doll savagely and uses words of punishment that could scarcely be in the vocabulary of someone so young. She repeatedly warns the doll that, "Your daddy is coming home soon and you'll catch hell then." After about a half hour of this play she asks if there are any pictures in the book I'm reading.

Two weeks earlier the observer had recorded the following observation:

Laura has just returned from school and is standing dripping rain in the middle of the kitchen. She is watching a television show standing behind her sitting mother. Mother turns about and sees her for the first time and asks if her feet are wet. Laura ignores the question intent on the drama before her. Mother arises from chair, sees the wet floor and screams shrilly, "Laura, this is the last goddamn time I'm telling you, take off your wet clothes this minute." Laura with her eyes still glued to the TV set, starts to fumble with the buttons of her coat until her mother twists her around and roughly takes the wet clothes off her. Laura, still ignoring her mother, has her head twisted and still looking at the show. Free of her wet clothes, she slumps into her mother's vacant chair and fairly screams at the mother, "I'm hungry, what is in the house that I can eat?"

In this illustration, the behavior of the child in the play observation literally re-enacts the events of her life, in that her treatment of the doll is that of her mother towards her. Many times the play is not literal, but, instead, is a symbolic representation of the child's concerns. In such situations, interpretation grows more difficult and requires greater clinical understanding of the symbolic connotation of behavior. In spite of this limitation, the alert teacher will discover many significant clues in the play and creative expressions of children.

BEHAVIOR TESTS

In the broad sense, every situation in which a child finds himself constitutes a behavior test inasmuch as it presents choices or opportunities for different kinds of behavior. In this sense, observation depends upon behavior tests. In a more restricted fashion, teachers can contrive behavior tests for children. One teacher checked her class (in addition to a number of others in the school) on their honesty in correcting their own papers. Spread over a period of several weeks, she had the children correct a number of their papers. With three of the tests, one in spelling, one in arithmetic, the third on social studies, she collected the papers from the children, made a record of the errors, then returned the papers to the children the following day saying she hadn't had an opportunity to get all the papers corrected, so the class could correct this paper. After the correction, she compared the child's corrections with her own. She found many instances in which the answer given had been changed to the correct answer. She anticipated this as a possibility, being aware of the desire for "good grades" which we induce in many children instead of a desire for learning. The result of such a test was knowledge of how great a problem the matter of cheating was and which children were having particular difficulty with it. Her purpose was not to detect cheaters in order that she would know whom to trust and whom not; it was to learn the degree with which this constituted a problem for the children.

Objections can be voiced to such procedures contending that they are unfair to the children because they tempt them to cheat. Similar objections can be voiced about a teacher who would leave small amounts of money lying on the desk, with the presumption that the teacher should keep temptation out of the paths of the children. An opposite viewpoint is that teachers can help children acquire the capacity to restrain themselves in such situations, and to learn the meaning of private property. Learning what they can or cannot use, with or without permission, is a complex task for children, but it can be dealt with directly. One does not have to be caught in the act of the theft to be made honest, but one can learn more clearly in definite situations than in abstract situations.

Contrived behavioral tests can serve such useful functions. In general though, enough events occur in the regular life of a class that one does not have to contrive a situation, unless a measure is needed which isn't normally obtained. The mechanics of such arrangements are often too elaborate to be of general value. However, teachers should not overlook the obvious: each field trip, each visit to a museum or other point of interest, constitutes a behavioral test of sorts. Too often we are so busy restraining and inhibiting that little in the way of a test of the spontaneous behavior and controls of children can be observed.

Chapter 12

PERSONAL DEVELOPMENT

Case histories and cumulative records provide a longitudinal view of a child's development which permits the viewing of present behavior in historical perspective. A well-prepared case history or a cumulative record which is sensitive to personality development as well as to academic achievement yields an impression of the unity and uniqueness of the individual and the development and persistence of character and personality traits in time through the historical view of development which they provide. The cross-section studies of children which provide word pictures of the typical six-year-old add a different frame of reference, that of "normal for age level," permitting a judgment as to the degree of deviation from the typical as well as an identification of the level at which the child is functioning, irrespective of his age.

Projective techniques such as sentence completion tests, picture completion tests, analyses of creative work, and the like, add a third dimension of depth for they yield clues regarding the dynamics of the motivation behind the observed behavior. Clinical judgment is the capacity to appraise the information available, interrelate perspectives provided, and make valid assessments regarding the source, significance, and probable outcomes of the personality development as shown.

Everybody is continually making inferences and judgments regarding the meaning of the behavior of the people with whom we are in contact. In the flow of child behavior, which a teacher experiences daily, she makes judgments regarding the significance and meaning of the actions observed, and acts on these.

Whether the teacher's decision is to ignore, to divert, or to suppress the observed behavior, it rests upon a judgment of its significance. Such inferences may be made consciously or unconsciously. Nevertheless, their validity depends upon the degree of clinical judgment possessed by the teacher. Some teachers may operate upon a series of naive or discredited assumptions about human behavior: children can't think for themselves; children will be destructive unless regulated by adults; human nature can't be changed, it can only be controlled; like father like son, and so forth. Others operate intuitively. Not that their response is innate or instinctive, but rather that the experiences which they have incorporated into themselves provide a foundation for judgment which is not dependent upon conscious analysis. Still others function more analytically, consciously assessing the known facts, evaluating them in terms of experience and knowledge possessed, and arriving at interpretations which provide the basis for judgment and decisions.

The vast complexity of the human organism makes the development of clinical judgment a slow and difficult task. One needs to be informed in many of the sciences of man—anthropology, sociology, psychology—and within these sciences possess thorough knowledge in several aspects—motivation, learning, the family, child-rearing patterns, etc. In addition, knowledge of physical and mental development, patterns of growth, aberrations of behavior, and the like, need to be known. In short, there is a limitless field of knowledge available for anyone who would attempt to understand and influence the behavior of others. The teacher, moreover, needs to be master of her own special field of instruction.

As seriously as one would study, errors are inevitable.

PATTERNS OF DEVELOPMENT

Several important long-term trends are in effect during childhood, influencing the form that behavior takes at different age levels. Children move from a comparatively undifferentiated state, psychologically and socially, to a highly differentiated state, from simplicity to complexity. Just as the physical organism grows in size and develops in complexity of functioning, so does the personality. The primitive rage and fear patterns give way to finer gradations of emotional expression—disgust, jealousy, joy, elation, affection. The concepts which a child can grasp steadily increase in complexity and difficulty. Temporal and spatial concepts of which the seven-year-old cannot conceive are conceivable to the twelve-year-old. Social relationships expand beyond the family to a friend, group membership, and finally to larger organizations such as school, community, and nation. With these associations comes a variety of values and attitudes which regulate the behavior of the individual towards a wide range of persons and objects. Paralleling this process of differentiation is a shift from an egocentric to a socio-centric person. There is a shift from initial awareness of self to awareness of others, from concern with self-satisfaction to concern for satisfying others. The degree of change, like the degree of differentiation achieved, varies from individual to individual, but those who fail to make adequate shift or move more slowly are thought of as immature. Both differentiation and socialization progress steadily during childhood.

In contrast, the shift from dependence to independence is likely to be discontinuous. In infancy, the child is completely dependent upon the adult for all care and protection, but gradually he develops his capacity to manage and care for himself, to clothe and feed himself, to master various intellectual and motor skills which make it possible for him to assume greater and greater responsibility for his actions. The negativism of the three-year-old, the explorations of the seven-year-old, the seclusiveness of the eleven-year-old, are all stages in the achievement of independence. Discontinuity occurs when society fails to provide opportunity for a steady increase in responsibility and authority. This becomes especially noticeable during adolescence, when youth is expected to act maturely and responsibly yet be quietly obedient and unobstructive.

There is small place in the reality of the adult world for the adolescent. His voice seldom has a place in decision-making, work is not available until a given age, and money must be accounted for to parents. Rarely is opportunity provided equivalent to his capacity or energy. Even student government is conspicuously controlled by the teaching staff of the school. Thus, independence and self-regulation are not gained gradually but often abruptly.

Somewhat similar in pattern is sexual status. The steadily lengthening training period required for entry into adult status in the complex society of today necessitates deferment of marriage (or early marriage with dependence on parents) for many individuals and inhibition of sexual impulses. Prevailing adult attitudes restrict the information about sexual matters which is available to the maturing youth. The subject is one which is seldom discussed.

In spite of the prevailing social attitudes, sexual development proceeds in children. Irrespective of the degree of first-hand experience, children obtain information and develop concepts, often grossly distorted, of sexual differences and function. Equally important is the steady development of concepts of masculinity and femininity and identification with appropriate sex role. A steady stream of experience shapes their concepts of what are appropriate behavior patterns for each sex and the degree to which they satisfy such socially determined roles. Physical structure influences behavior, boys with athletic builds tend to be more dominant and assertive. In turn, they prefer competitive group activities in contrast with submissive boys who prefer individual and less competitive activities.

From early childhood, children of each sex are offered different games, toys, and activities in which to participate. As they begin to play with other children of their own sex, they adopt a group standard of what is appropriate behavior for a boy and girl. By the middle grades in school, an aggressive boy is admired while an aggressive girl is thought to be "bossy." The kind and thoughtful boy, however admired by adults, does not receive the approval from his peers that the aggressive boy does. The interplay of physical development, the social significance attached to certain kinds of behavior in relation to a given sex role, the nature of games and activities played, the development of group standards which reinforce the socially determined concepts of masculine and feminine, all coalesce in the stream of steady pressures shaping personality in anticipation of ultimate sex role, irrespective of the degree of privilege allowed.

STAGES OF DEVELOPMENT

Within the matrix of forces which shape the development of children—the biological, psychological, and sociological pressures—certain characteristics of given stages of development are noticeable: the pre-school age from two until six; middle childhood between six and ten; pre-adolescence from ten until fourteen; and the adolescent years after fourteen. In each of these stages, there are intellectual, social, and emotional steps and each has its particular significance for development.

The important task in the pre-school period is building confidence in the adult world, in parents and in family, and in conceiving of the world as having some order and dependability. From this comes the sense of trust which permits the child to reach out into the world during the next stage. At six he enters school, a broader social world in which the emphasis is on skills—reading skills, number skills, and social skills. He has to gain the approval of his playmates, find his place with them, and learn to influence them. His major task is to find a place with his peers and establish confidence in them.

In the years between ten and fourteen, the child enters a transitional period from which he will hopefully emerge with a sense of his own competence, and accommodation to the dramatic physical changes coming with sexual maturation, and an acceptance of the changes and of his appropriate sex role. With the adolescent period, the child must complete his independence, establish his sense of identity, and attain confidence in himself.

During the pre-school years, the child changes from a person with rudimentary skills to one who is fairly adept. His growth in motor skills is consistent with his physical growth. Intellectually, the pre-school years are ones of rapid development—in sensory discrimination, in language growth, in imagination. His conceptual development is limited and he has only rudimentary knowledge of cause and effect; however, he is posing imaginative explanations.

The social life of the pre-schooler is primarily home-centered with even his playmates determined by his parents. Within this context he is testing his power, testing new words, testing techniques of getting his own way, testing to see how much self-assertion and aggression is safe. He is learning how far he can go, where the limits are, how the world is organized, what is real, how others will react. The child has begun to develop a notion of different social roles— of father, mother, husband, wife, etc.—and to understand that consistent differences in behavior can be expected from each. He has established the fact of sex difference but has far to go to comprehend its significance.

Up to this point, his emotions have played a prominent role, dominating his perceptions and directing his reactions. Yet, just as he has been acquiring skill in body control, so is the pre-school child acquiring skill in the control of his emotions. He discovers the possibilities of aggression and disobedience. He learns that aggression leads to different results—directed against another child it can often have advantages, but directed against adults it can draw swift punishment. He learns that he must control his aggressiveness for fear of punishment. Here the practice of the parents plays a vital part, for it determines the degree to which the child is able to master and channel his emotions. Hopefully, the outcome of the child's experience in learning to manage his emotions will be the beginnings of conscience—the adoption of adult prohibitions which permit him to pre-judge the behavior appropriate to a given situation. With appropriate management, the child will acquire the needed balance between self-control and self-assertiveness.

Going to school introduces a dramatic shift in the child's life, for now he turns from mastering himself to mastering the world. These are the years of acquiring the skills he will need to live in our world. Physical growth is consistent during this period, but the difference in opportunity and interest begins to show with a wide range in sport skill, in academic skill, in emotional development, and in interest, emerging by the age of ten. The child's vocabulary will double, but his growth in capacity to conceptualize is even more significant. When he enters school, he relates words to specific experiences. By age ten, he will be able to generalize and see similarities between events and objects where previously the differences were more significant to him.

The pace of social development parallels intellectual development. In group games, he no longer rotates, as in tag, but begins to stabilize. Certain youngsters are consistently the pitcher or catcher. Their role becomes defined in terms of a skill in which one is better than another. Social differentiation is also occurring. The child is learning the customs, the traditions, and the prejudices of his society. The aspects of his life, the neighborhood in which he lives, the kind of work his father does, his church and his friends acquire new meaning derived from social attitudes and status.

The "other kids" come to exist as people of significance, people with whom the child must find his place and attain his own status in accordance with the standards they establish. Clubs emerge. Rules are no longer something to be changed by the whim of the group or the command of the powerful. Concern about competence increases. The school, with its objective and comparative standards of performance, is inescapable, and in the classroom or on the playground, performance is constantly being measured. Increase in control and organization of emotional and personality development is equally evident. By ten, the cleavage between boys and girls is almost absolute.

Identification with the group appears to dominate his social relations. By the age of ten and, increasingly thereafter, the child values the opinions of his peers more than those of his parents and teachers. He seems to isolate himself more from the family, being more critical and negative towards many family activities. In some ways, this is more apparent than real, more of a ritual protest than actual, for, apart from the family, the youngster generally depends on and reflects the standards, values, and prohibitions of his friends. Partially, this may stem from his own need to establish himself as an independent, organized person, a self to be realized; partially it may come from the fact that he must begin to look for satisfaction of his need for love outside of his family. Nevertheless, the shared values of his peer group and the support derived from it provide a basis for lasting values, for they replace the sharply defined black-and-white value judgment characteristic of ten-to-twelve-year-olds with the more flexible standards of the adult.

Between the ages of ten and fourteen, children experience the rapid growth which accompanies sexual maturation, the rapid growth in height and weight, and the shift in physical structure to manhood or womanhood. The outward change in appearance tells only part of the shift, for complex changes are occurring in every physiological system. The extent to which physical changes and disturbances in physiological equilibrium will be accompanied by psychological stress will be dependent upon the timing of the disturbance in relation to other adolescents, upon the duration of the disturbance, and upon the understanding and consideration of adults and peers.

Usually, the stages of development are closely correlated with age, particularly with children of similar social and economic backgrounds whose experiences are much alike—having similar toys, entering nursery school at the same age, attending kindergarten, going to a day camp, etc. This makes it possible to expect given behavior patterns to occur at particular ages, to view it as "normal" and to plan programs with these expectations in mind. The following sections present certain of the descriptive information characterizing children at different age levels. It is worth noting that as the experiences of individuals differ, so will their pace of development. The advantage of such information is that it permits an identification of the level of development achieved by a child in a given area, rather than his being labelled "abnormal." One does not need descriptive data for different age levels to single out the children who are different.

The topics around which the data are organized are: self-concept, emotional development, fears, independence, and interests.

SELF-CONCEPT

Age Five. The child is serious about himself and is much impressed with his own ability to take responsibilities and to imitate grown up behavior. Is aware of the relationship of his acts to people and the world around him.

This is a rather stable period of growth. He is eager to learn. He wants to do what is expected of him and can be counted on to cooperate.

He has learned to perceive his own identity as a physical unit and as a social entity identified by a name. Combined with this perception is his growing awareness of the realities of his physical and social worlds. An increasingly difficult task for him is handling his growing need to share his emotional world with other people, for as yet he is somewhat impersonal.

Age Six. He is the center of his own universe and master of the family. The six-year-old lives so much in a field of magic he feels himself mixed up in it and actually thinks things take place because he himself wills them to take place. His self-concepts, attitudes and behavior are influenced by our culture; he accepts it unthinkingly. He is interested in difference in body structure of own and opposite sex, and in origin of babies.

Age Seven. The seven-year-old is becoming increasingly aware of both self and others. He is aware of his body and is sensitive about exposing it. He begins to criticize himself and will avoid doing things in which he feels incompetent. The feeling of inferiority begins at this age, in part an outgrowth of the inevitable companions in schools, in part because of deeper emotional reactions resulting from a concept of the disparity between himself, his size and capacity, and the world and the adults.

Age Eight. A transition period from early childhood into pre-adolescence. Child becoming more conscious of self as a person. Begins to recognize individual differences between himself and other people. For this reason he is becoming more conscious of his own personality traits, e.g., I am shy, I am slow. Shows a tendency to belittle self, both directly and in humor, e.g., the moron jokes.

May seem to consider himself the center of the stage. Tries hard to live up to the adult standards set for him.

Interest in sex remains high but exploration and play is less than at six. Asks for and should receive exact answers to questions about birth. Girls begin to ask about menstruation, father's part in procreation, etc.

Age Nine. Is becoming aware of self and his environment. Beginning to acquire new found feelings of confidence and as a result becomes more independent in his actions. Feels he is able to take part by himself. May be self-critical, but this is due to the fact he may make excessive demands upon himself.

Feels success is important and will work for a reward. Sensitive to praise and criticism from others. Beginning to worry and become apprehensive about certain things.

Interested in details on organs and body functions. Seeks pictorial information; discussion with friends. Increased self-consciousness on exposure of body.

Age Ten. Sex differences become pronounced. Girls are becoming more aware of their own persons, their clothes, their appearance. Individual differences between children becoming more apparent.

Beginning to lose self-consciousness characteristic of nine. Great interest in environment. More content with himself, more confident and as a result feels much happier. Feels more mature and is a much more responsible person.

Age Eleven. Often describes self as changing for the worse. "Now everything I do seems wrong." Engaged in an active search for self and finds it in conflict with others. Responsive to outside forces. Seems egocentric and selfish. Supercritical of self and others, but resentful of others' criticisms.

Increased identification with parent of same sex, in processing of learning appropriate sex role. Interest in knowledge or physiological functioning on explanations of written and unwritten roles covering sex behavior.

Age Twelve. Search for self by trying to win approval of friends and assuming new roles of more mature behavior. Does not want to be treated "as a baby." Can view things more objectively. Not the center of the world in all things. Less egocentric and a smoothing of interpersonal relations. Enthusiastic and impatient. Very uneven; very childish then very mature. Very critical of self and his own appearance.

Age Thirteen. Seems to search for self within himself; tries to understand himself. Interested in his own personality; wants to be similar to others. Plays roles; dreams; withdrawn; thoughtful.

Age Fourteen. Searches for self by comparing and matching self with others; wants to be just like others. Anxious to be liked; to be "normal." Preoccupied with activities, friends, life; interested in "freedom." At same time around this age level girls and boys become very conscious of their looks and they tend to primp in front of a mirror. A comb becomes an essential part of their wardrobe and is used a great deal.

Despite essential continuity in development, adolescence demands considerable reorganization in ego structure. The individual must himself assume responsibility for aspects of living previously assumed by adults. He must learn to take full responsibility for full operation of his own control system, and develop an awareness of himself as an adult with a social and emotional identity of his own.

As the child grows into adolescence and adulthood, he becomes more and more able to behave according to adult standards thus the difference between self-concept and self-ideal usually diminishes. Individuals who have difficulty accepting themselves also have difficulty accepting others.

EMOTIONAL DEVELOPMENT

Age Five. The five-year-old's emotions are brief, frequent, and transitory. Laughing occurs in connection with general physical activity, such as rolling, tossing, bodily activity opportunities for self assertion, feelings of well being. Everything considered, the five-year-old is in excellent equilibrium, self contained, and poised.

The child of five plays imaginatively with simple objects and at games requiring little organization. Such play is often solitary, even in the presence of other children. He imitates many activities of adults.

Listen to the five-year-old and you will find him full of fantasy and imagination. They imagine and create and eagerly respond to any opportunity for painting, modeling with mud or clay, constructing with tools, and building with blocks.

They are highly dramatic and strive to get inside experience and understand them by taking the role of a bus driver, pilot, postman and others.

Age Six. A transition age, an up and down sort of time when tears and tantrums are frequent, and they quarrel and argue a lot. Their moods shift often.

He has a new environment as he enters school. He faces anxieties and conflicts. Psychosomatic symptoms such as stomach disorders, speech defects, skin irritations appear.

He is more or less in a constant state of emotional tension. May be domineering and argumentative, noisy, boisterous and easily excitable. Resents authority and punishment. Wants to show off to company.

The child of six lives in a world which is entirely different from the adults. His world is a mixture of reality and sheer magic. He lives between fantasy and reality. He forms all sorts of fantastic notions and ideas about things around him and then checks them against the ideas of other children of his own age, of older children, and finally of adults. He discards many of these ideas but it is amazing how many fantastic ideas the child retains. They personify inanimate objects, which is entirely normal.

Age Seven. The seven-year-old fights and contradicts but can be motivated toward self-restraint. Cries less but will sulk, pout or fight with words. Less aggressive behavior. He tattles or blames others. He cries less but screeches more.

Age Eight. An eight-year-old child has a well developed imagination. He engages in pointless laughter, rough-housing, and practical joking. He is often careless and argumentative, but also friendly and interested in people. He is sensitive to criticism. His feelings are hurt if he is wrongly accused. Paralleling the demands made by a child of this age on his parents are occasional negativeness and resistance. An eight-year-old child outlines projects far beyond his scope of action and when this happens, does everything possible to meet his commitments. He does have the counter-characteristic of running off on tangents and proceeding to something else. There is, however, a general continuity of action which was lacking before in the child. A child at this age has, to some extent, a sense of guilt incorporated into his personality structure.

The eight-year-old child is less sensitive, less within himself, and less apt to withdraw. He is ready to tackle anything and shows courage in his attack. He also likes to argue. The eight-year-old child daydreams to some extent. These daydreams are about adventures and physical conquests.

Tension outlets characteristic of the eight-year-old child: eye blinking; stomach aches; crying with fatigue; and thumb sucking (for some).

Age Nine. A nine-year-old child tends to be less rowdy, less quarrelsome, and less willing to fight without a definite purpose. He is less susceptible to persisting flare-ups, to continued or intense anger, and to recurrent bitter feelings and attitudes. The nine-year-old child also possesses a sense of guilt.

For the nine-year-old, aggression is chiefly verbal. He objects to what people say or do in the form of criticism. He exhibits the following tension outlets: stamping feet, feeling dizzy, and picking at self.

Age Ten. The ten-year-old child is pleasant and conforms to adult roles. He cries or explodes when he is angry but the anger is short lived. He cries less because he feels he is too old to cry. He does not harbor grudges or nurse hurt feelings. He shows affection towards his parents. The child this age has a tendency to tell corny jokes and generally has a good sense of humor. With opportunity and encouragement, the ten-year-old child presents a well rounded personality. He tends to alibi and project blame on the smaller sister or brother.

Age Eleven. In general, the emotional behavior of age eleven is described by parents as presenting a penetrating, sensitive, competitive, unco-operative appearance. Response to anger is frequent, violent, physical and emotional. Physical violence is a common response: fight, hit, slam doors, cry. Violent speaking back, or pouting, verbal retorts, yelling, swearing, sarcasm, sulking, planning revenge. Displays many worries and fears dealing with school, homework, money, health, and family friendships. Often they are afraid of snakes, bugs, the dark, and high places. The boys seem to be afraid of being alone or being shut in. The girls are more fearful of physical pain, of infections, and that someone might hurt their mother. They also express concern about not being liked.

Age Twelve. In general, it is an expansive outgoing, enthusiastic, over-generous age. Often they are good company; friendly, understanding, thoughtful, likeable, and more reasonable. It is a relatively uncomplicated period. They do have many fears, but fewer worries than at eleven. Their worries are more concerning social behavior such as, "People won't like me." There is far less boiling over. They still fight occasionally, or strike out physically, but it begins to take a more verbal response at times on anger such as name-spelling and calling or muttering under breath.

Age Thirteen. In general, the thirteen-year-old is thoughtful, quiet, self-contained; may become withdrawn, moody, lethargic, and seclusive. He is extremely sensitive and easily hurt. On the whole, thirteen is not a fearful age. He might say he has the "usual, normal fears that everyone has." Thirteen is trying to convince himself he is not afraid. He is very sensitive to criticism, and keenly perceptive of the emotional states close to other persons. Boys and girls may withdraw from close confidential relationships with parents. He is more discriminating than he was at twelve in his estimation and acceptance of companions. Boys, as well as girls, make good use of a looking-glass to see how they really look to themselves and to others. He has more worries about school grades and his appearance, social fears of people, performing in public, etc. The most characteristic response to anger at this age is to leave the scene. There is less shouting and screaming; he will usually say something mean or sarcastic. Sulking is a common response, or crying, scowling, frowning. There may be a deflected response; projecting his anger by taking it out on someone else. There is a reduction of tensional outlet: fingernail biting, hand to face gestures, or scratching scabs persist in some.

Age Fourteen. In general, this age is expansive, outgoing, energetic, and enthusiastic. It is much happier and less withdrawn than thirteen. It has the fourteen-year-old love companions.

Anger is less frequent and is manifested verbally rather than physically or by withdrawal. Humor is greatly appreciated. School is the chief source of worry, and now also world conditions, personal and social worries. He is afraid of making a bad impression. At fourteen, he will often "sit and take it." He will make verbal retorts (and seldom use physical violence) or he will leave the room and slam doors. Fourteen is not really a fearful age, though quite a variety of fears is reported. It is almost as though each child has his pet fear; bugs, spiders, bees, moths, etc. A fairly larger number of boys and girls are afraid of snakes, high places, deep water, the dark, being lost in the woods. They are afraid of being embarrassed, afraid of people, of being left out, of social gossip, of "just what's going to happen, or how things will turn out."

FEARS

Age Five. His fears are likely to be much influenced by the fears he sees exhibited. There tends to be a high degree of correspondence between the fears of a child and those of his mother.

In frightening situations, reactions of fear tend to be influenced by the degree of fright or composure manifested by his elders.

Not a fearsome age, fears receding in intensity; outstanding fear is that he will be deprived of his mother. Night time heightens fear, sleep is often broken with dreams. The fears that a four- or five-year-old voices or indicates at the time are a reflection of his desire for comfort and reassurance.

There is less fear of animals, bad people, bogeymen. They have concrete down-to-earth fears, as bodily harm, the dark, thunder and sirens. Many have nightmares, and difficulty returning to sleep.

Age Six. His outstanding fear is that of being deprived of his mother. At this age he is afraid of the dark (11%), people, animals (27%), being late, of the cellar, and not knowing how to read. Behind most fear is that of threat to security.

Very fearful especially of auditory fears as: doorbell, telephone, static, ugly words, flushing the toilet, insect and bug noises, bird noise.

Fear of supernatural (20%), ghosts, witches, something hiding under the bed. Fear of being lost, fear of the woods, the elements as fire, water, thunder, and lightening. Fears little cuts, splinters, blood, and nose drops. Roughly two-thirds will show fear of imaginary or supernatural dangers. Few children are free of fears.

Age Seven. The seven-year-old does not want to experience new situations by himself. He worries. He fears the dark, the cellar, the attic and the closet. He fears and interprets shadows as ghosts and witches. He fears going into the second grade; fears he won't know how to do his school work. He is afraid he won't be liked and that he will be laughed at. He is afraid of physical punishment, going to the dentist, etc.

Age Eight. The eight-year-old child has a number of unresolved fears which are left over from the time he was seven. He tries to be brave in spite of his fears. Prevalent at this age are fear of the dark, of falling, of fighting, of someone finding fault with him, of being different in dress, speech, and behavior; of not being accepted by the group, of being a failure, of being ridiculed, and of parents. He worries about another war, about personal adequacy, and about failure in school. Nightmares have disappeared.

Age Nine. The nine-year-old child may publicly announce that he is not easily frightened. However, any of the above fears may exist. A nine-year-old child exhibts the following fears: fear of lightening, of thunder, of high places, and of snakes. Greater readiness to attack or explore feared experience.

Age Ten. The ten-year-old child often laughs at his "childish" fears. He begins to integrate fear responses into more acceptable forms of behavior. The ten-year-old child fears fire, snakes, high places, being different, criminals and burglars, not being accepted by the group, and some still fear the dark. He worries about the health of members of his family, personal adequacy, and another war.

INDEPENDENCE AND RESPONSIBILITY

Age Five. The child is beginning to be quite independent and to enjoy doing things for himself. If he has not had too many demands made upon him in the past years, he is independent. He wants to feel and rely on his own powers and should be encouraged, never pressured in this desire. He can take personal care of himself: wash, toilet needs, feed, dress, etc.

The five-year-old is usually able to attend kindergarten without an escort. Takes care of self unsupervised outside his own yard. Can manage roller skates, sled, wagon, scooter and other play vehicles.

Can be trusted with small sums of money to make purchases at the store. Carries out the directions in getting the purchases, but he may not be able to make change.

Age Six. Child is able to carry a tray with plates or bowl, use a fork, wipe up spilled things without aid, and wipe the dishes. Does a fair job at caring for personal needs. Wants to do things for himself. Baths are resisted and washing the face often means just around the nose.

Cuts, folds, pastes and draws. Sews crudely if the needle is threaded. Enjoys making simple figures in clay. Goes on familiar streets alone.

Decisions are difficult as choice between vanilla and chocolate ice-cream cone; it often tears him apart. Resists changing mind once made up. Suggestion is more effective than reasoning.

Performs bedtime operations without help. Goes to bedroom alone, undresses, attends to toilet, turns out the light according to routine. May be tucked in as a matter of sentiment but requires no assistance.

Age Seven. The seven-year-old wants to be independent, but doesn't quite trust himself. He wants to grow up and be a part of the adult world, to leave behind the manners, dress, and behavior of the little child. He is able to assume some responsibility. He likes to have a "job" at home and help the teacher at school. He can take care of his physical needs. He may worry about being late for school, but he cannot yet take full responsibility for getting there on time.

Age Eight. The eight-year-old begins to realize adults can be wrong. Identification with adults becomes weaker, and identification with age-mates increases. Begins to exercise a right to discriminate between alternatives and make decisions. Rebels against suggesting of adults, but not from playmates. Isn't really ready for independent group decision, nor impressed or aided by formal conduct of meetings. Prefers own rules in games to official rules. Great interest in property and possessions, hoarding and bartering.

Age Nine. The child likes to make rules and regulations for himself, and making and executing plans on his own initiative. Wants some freedom of choice at home. Senses his increasing capacities and seeks greater personal direction. Is indifferent to social conventions, avoids adult supervision because he wants to work out social relationships for himself and be accepted by the group on his own merits.

Age Ten. The child of ten wants the independence of making his own choice about what to wear, how to spend leisure time, how to arrange or disarrange room, how to spend money. Is ready to make his own decisions and face the consequences when the issues aren't too serious. Greatly concerned about right and wrong.

Age Eleven. Rude and resistant especially towards mother. Argues about everything, just to prove that adult is wrong. Often thinks of father as a "disciplinarian."

Often resentful and rebellious against teacher. He describes teacher less by appearance and more by behavior characteristics.

He thinks of the ideal teacher as being fair, patient, impartial, understanding, humorous, and soft-spoken.

Age Twelve. Seems to have emerged from battle with parents. Seems more reasonable and co-operative with adults and less demanding of adults. Cares more about their opinions and approval.

Less dependent on teachers. Great enthusiasm for those he likes. Criticizes a teacher who fails in techniques and knowledge or lacks ability to discipline.

Age Thirteen. Withdrawal from mother; doesn't want to be close to anyone; just wants to be alone. Feels father criticizes too much.

Can now recognize a teacher as a good teacher even though he may not like her personality. Usually prefer a strict teacher. Often very critical of the principal.

Age Fourteen. Feels parents restrict him too much. Often embarrassed by them. Tolerant of teachers. He gives a detailed evaluation of teachers. Critical of many aspects of the personality.

INTERESTS

Age Five. The five-year-old's interests are as wide as experiences have permitted. He is interested in many types of group play and in verbal guidance as "tell me what I'm supposed to do," he wants to know how things work, likes to experiment with things.

Very fond of cutting and pasting and working on a specific project. He has a definite interest in finishing what he has started.

He is primarily interested in things and articles which are in the immediate environment. Interested in seasons and holidays. Interested in words and their meanings. Finds pleasure in pictures, in books, and rethinks the story.

Likes to play primarily with blocks. Girls makes doll houses, boys houses for fire engines, airplanes, tanks, bridges and tunnels. Likes to go on expeditions with father, boys like to help him make repairs. Likes to play simple counting games and alphabet games. Likes to get into boxes and pretend they are houses, or play with chairs draped with a blanket for a tent. Likes his own record player for music as he can play it over and over, likes repetition.

Age Six. At six it is expected that interests will shift and vacillate. Today he may be interested in horses, tomorrow airplanes. Likes to do things on a game basis. Keenly enjoys short fantastic stories in which animals and fairies are the dominating characters.

Boys wish to become firemen, policemen, soldiers, and sailors.

They play with ball or wagon. Run about in active but unorganized games such as tag.

Girls play dolls. Play group games: London Bridge, Farmer in the Dell, and Drop the Handkerchief.

Age Seven. At seven there is an increasing interest in money, and expanding interest in the community. The seven-year-old likes to do things with his hands. He enjoys painting, clay-modeling, and carpentry. He wants to know how things work, what electricity is, and all about trains, airplanes, and cars. He likes to listen to stories, radio and watch television.

As children enter the upper grades of elementary school, their interests steadily diversify, making it difficult to describe the person's interest by the level of age. Not only interests but differences in the level of skill become quite noticeable. With the advent of puberty, the interests of the early maturing children differ sharply from the majority of their classmates. There is a marked decrease in the proportion of children interested in material objects and an increase in those who are concerned about self and self-improvement.

In the 6-8 year range, 85% wish for material objects, only 10% for self-improvement. The wishes are evenly divided in the 8-10 range, but by age 12 two-thirds of the wishes expressed are for self-improvement in the nature of: playing a musical instrument, being promoted, being famous or pretty, getting along better with people, going to college, being good. Another change is the increased wish for benefit for others.

The interests in these middle years have been classified by activity, with age difference noted:

INTERESTS

Sports and Games

9　Both boys and girls enjoy all types of activity such as bicycling, roller skating, swimming, sliding, and coasting.

9　Children's play interests tend to settle on fewer activities and become stronger in them. Baseball, which is highly competitive team sport, is a good example.

9　Girls' interests are likely to be folk dancing and dramatization; also cooking and sewing to lesser degree.

10-11　He likes to race on foot or on bike, ride horses, climb, ice skate, swim and row a boat, go for walks, play with pets.

11-12　Likes secret clubs, scouts, organizations.

12　Card and table games, jig-saw puzzles.

13-14   Boys develop keen sports interests: basketball, baseball, football. Girls are less interested than boys, more likely to show interest in volleyball or ping-pong.

Hobbies

8-10   Children of this age find satisfaction in meaningful and useful activities such as arts and crafts.

9-14   Interests in collecting are prevalent among children of this age. (Match covers, airplanes, dolls, stray pets, rocks, stamps, coins and shells.)

10   Boys at this age tend to show more interest in collecting than do girls.

12   Boys have strong interest in how objects work, taking them apart. Hobbies grow fewer and more intensive. Boys have mechanical and scientific interests—radio, photography, midget cars and planes.

13   Girls like to read, listen to records, telephone, daydream. For hobbies, girls like to knit, sew, paint, and draw.

14   Greater separation of activity of sex noted. Girls: draw, clothes, diaries; boys: models, carpentry, interest in automobiles. Jazz is popular with both.

Entertainment and Amusement

8-10   TV and movie interests for this group are cowboys, cartoons, and some types of comedy.
There is a tendency to watch TV as long as parents permit.
Many children of this age group will avoid the horror type of TV program.

10   This may be said to be the best age of Educational TV.

12-14   Many like to "hang-around," talk, listen to radio, attend movies.

Academic

8   Most children are developing a wider range of interest. Interest is no longer limited to their immediate environment, but extends out into the world. Implications for teaching are: Place more emphasis on industries, products, travel and transportation.

8-10   Children at this age show more interest in arithmetic and spelling due to the concrete words of those subjects. Boys and girls are interested in factual information about the building of a culture and the adventure that has gone into the building of it. (Not the political history.)

9   At this age a child may pour over reference books, collecting facts for their own sake as well as because they throw light on a problem.

9-11 Boys in particular at this age often have accurate and extensive knowledge and interest in airplanes, automobiles, out-board motors, and various principles of practical science.

12-14 Boys particularly interested in science; girls in English. Both develop greater interest in vocations.

Literature and Reading

8   Interest in fairy tales, myths, fantasies and legends still runs high.

8-10 Interest in comic books is usually high at this age level, though it may be waning somewhat by age 10 if a child's reading achievement is high.

This has been coined "The Big Injun Age." This is because of the popularity of campfire stories, scouting, hunting, etc. Incidentally, this accounts in part for the Cub Scout and Brownie movements in this country.

10   Interest in adventure and mystery stories should be noted and may be related to school activities.

Children of this age are more apt to read books in which the words "secret" or "mystery" or "horse" appear in the title.

Their desire for facts leads them to books on travel, mechanics, science, biography, and invention.

At this age boys become interested in literature that tells how to build things and that has to do with science, while girls still like fairy tales and animal stories.

9-12 Stories with underlying aspects of humor, sportsmanship, and bravery are of great interest to this age group.

12   Mystery, sport, adventure stories popular with boys.

13-14 Interested in science, biography, adventure, and history.

INTERPRETING NORMATIVE DATA

The advantage of normative data on child development is that it provides a basis for determining when and with what children may need special help. Its disadvantage lies in that often they are used as absolute scales for judgment. All children display some undesirable behavior. Often it occurs as children try different kinds of behavior in attempts to find solutions to problems they are encountering. It is not the occurrence of such behavior over a short period of time which differentiates the problem child from the non-problem child, but rather the re-occurrence or persistence of the behavior to the point that it becomes habitual. Most children steal at one time or another. In fact, if one is to judge by percentages, it would be called normal. For the great majority of children, it is a step in learning the meaning of honesty and respect for the property of others. For a few who fail to develop the needed controls, the theft becomes part of a recurrent pattern.

A further restraint needed in the use of normative data lies in the recognition that each child is his own best norm. That is, he is bound to deviate in some ways because of his own individuality, and his particular differences and his own rate of progress are individually determined. One may list symptoms of maladjustment, but in the final analysis it is not the number of symptoms present but their significance for individual development that counts. Norms provide a gauge by which to measure deviation, but the explanation of the deviation and its significance can be found only in the child's personal history.

In appraising the significance of given deviations in behavior, several considerations must be kept in mind. The first is that any behavior observed in a child, normal or abnormal, is shaped by a variety of factors simultaneously in operation. The age of the child, his level of personality development, his previous experiences, and the present interplay of child and environment, combine to determine behavior. Second, the child is much more dependent upon and subject to his environment than is an adult. The adult's drives, his habit patterns, his personality organization, and his adaptive reactions are more fixed than those of the child, which tend to be fluid and unstable in comparison. The child's immaturity, physical, mental, social, and emotional, makes him much more susceptible to external influences and, hence, to change. In fact, it is usually the perseverance of behavior, its fixity and resistance to change, which is the most useful gauge in determining the seriousness of symptomatic behavior.

Normative data then provides broad descriptions of typical behavior for children of a given age. They provide the means whereby a teacher can establish realistic expectations of children, and know, as a rule, what kind of behavior she can overlook as being "typical" rather than deviate. Symptomatic behavior can only be interpreted in terms of its relationship to the total functioning of the child, not simply in terms of its overt form. This fact adds difficulty to discriminating between behavior patterns which call for specialized assistance and those which can be expected to respond to environmental manipulations by the teacher.

General signs of maladjustment are:

1. Withdrawal, shyness, timidity, fearfulness.
2. Difficulty in forming social relationships, particularly with own age level; unsociable, solitary.
3. Low frustration tolerance—temper outbursts, poor loser, giving up quickly.
4. Hyperactivity, persistent restlessness or tension.
5. Hostile, defiant attitude; resistance to authority; suspiciousness.
6. Rejection of school routines; truancy.
7. Extreme docility; overdependence on adults or routines.
8. Over-diligence and perfectionism in school work.
9. Confusion of fantasy and reality; persistent daydreaming.
10. Hypersensitivity to criticism; feelings easily hurt.

Usually, the general classes of behavior listed are seen as representing extreme forms of behavior. This is not to suggest that children should be expected to maintain a constant balance in all behavior. Moments of anger, hyperactivity, unsociability, frustration, and being upset are typical. Variation in mood and feeling tone are not inconsistent with adjustment. When the non-adaptive behavior persists, behavior which falls in any of the categories listed, careful studies and possible referral are indicated.

Ackerman[1] presents a scheme for classification of symptoms which contributes to an understanding of relationships and severity in psychiatric disorders in children.

Disorders with Organic Base

Such disturbances are associated with impairment of central nervous system, endocrine inbalance, abnormal body functions, and physical illness occurring as defects of intellect, memory, or judgment, poverty of association, inadequacy of concept formation, limitation of imaginative capacity, defective organization or instability of emotions. This includes mental retardation and associated limitations in learning ability, poverty of association, impairment of perception, defective judgment and memory, inadequate motor coordination.

---

[1]N. M. Ackerman, *The Psychodynamics of Family Life.* New York: Basic Books, 1958, pp. 204-205. Material used with permission.

FUNCTIONAL DISORDERS

Functional disorders include a wide range of behavioral disturbances not associated with organic impairment of the types described above. Two main categories may be distinguished: character disorders and behavioral disorders. Character is a term by which we identify the characteristic quality of the habitual reaction patterns adopted by a person in reconciling or integrating inner needs and external demands. Terms such as hostile, anxious, submissive, reflect patterns and social demands which have become stabilized and are non-adaptive. Infantile, obsessive-compulsive, phobic, neurotic, and psychotic disorders can be considered disorders of character. Diagnosis of such disorders in children is complicated by the fact that often the behavior observed is a mixture rather than clearly distinguished. Psychoses are rare in children, psychosomatic symptoms and neurotic traits can exist without indicating a basic character disorder. The fact that the children's character is still being formed, their experiences are still being absorbed with attendant change in personality, the lack of fixed identifications and the responsiveness of the child to environmental pressures, suggests considerable caution is advisable in the analysis of character disorder, and that it is best left to the specialist, the child psychiatrist in particular.

Most of the aberrant behavior that a teacher will meet may be classified as behavior disorders. Ackerman groups the primary behavior disorders into three subdivisions according to the stage of development with which they are associated. Habit disorder—feeding disorders, sucking, biting, vomiting, crying, picking, scratching, masturbation, enuresis, rocking, and head-banging are considered as tension-reducing forms of behavior emerging in the earliest stages of development before the psychomoter maturity of the child is sufficient enough to permit him to counter the frustration of his needs. In a sense the child has turned to himself and his body as a means of expressing the aggression arising from frustration.

The second grouping is conduct disorders—defiance, tantrums, rebellion, destructiveness, cruelty, overactivity, negativism, lying, stealing, withdrawal, asocial behavior, deviant sex activity—which are seen arising from the stage in development when the child has sufficient psychomotor maturity to counterattack an environment which deprives him of the satisfaction of his emotional needs. Lacking the emotional acceptance and the social rewards which make it desirable for the child to learn to manage and control his impulses, and aggravated by the associated frustration, the child rebels against

TABLE 1. FUNCTIONAL DISORDERS IN CHILDREN

Primary Behavior Disorders
  Habit Disorders —
    feeding disorders
    biting, sucking, vomiting
    picking, scratching
    masturbation, enuresis
    rocking, head-banging
  Conduct Disorders —
    defiance, rebellion, tantrums
    destructiveness, cruelty
    overactivity
    negativism
    lying, stealing
    withdrawal, asocial behavior
    deviant sex activity
  Neurotic traits —
    jealousy
    inhibition of play, imagination, curiosity
    inhibition of aggression
    sleep disorders, night terrors, sleep-walking
    enuresis, masturbation
    speech disorders
    fear of animals, darkness, thunder

Character Disorders —
    infantile, narcissistic
    isolated, inhibited, schizoid
    neurotic
    paranoid
    psychopathic, psychotic

Psychosomatic Disorders —
    colic, vomiting
    constipation, diarrhea, enuresis
    skin eruptions
    asthma, hay fever

Psychoneurotic Disorders —
    hysteria
    phobias
    obsessive-compulsive
    hypochondriacal

Psychotic Disorders —
    undifferentiated psychosis
    schizophrenia
    affective psychosis

parental denial and counterattacks against parental hostility. Essentially, the child is in conflict with his environment.

The third grouping—neurotic traits—includes jealousy, inhibition of play, imagination, and curiosity, sleep disorders, enuresis, masturbation, speech disorders, and excessive fears. At this stage, the conflict is partially internal, partially external. Identification with parents and internalization of parental standards is partially complete, and the conflict between need and standard finds expression in fear of punishment from some external sources.

The primary behavior disorders include a wide range of behavior of varying degrees of duration and severity. Rarely will the teacher be in a position to know the causation of any given set of reactions or behavior patterns observed in a child, but she is in a position to appraise the more severe and deep-seated as representing a need for specialized assistance, and so encourage such action. Second, she can aid children to adopt more adequate patterns of behavior. The responsiveness of children to their environment makes it possible to induce them to give up non-adaptive behavior if they sense they can obtain greater satisfaction from some other response. This can be done directly through the interpersonal relationships which a teacher establishes with a child and which she helps children to establish among themselves, and, indirectly, as she helps children to discover competencies in school which contribute to ego-development and, hence, to more adequate adjustment.

Symptoms of abnormal behavior commonly occur in clusters rather than singly, and it is the pattern of symptoms which provides a basis for diagnosis of degree and kind of adjustment problem by the clinical psychologist or child psychiatrist. Nevertheless, the listing of symptoms in Table 2 may be of value to the teacher in helping her to recognize their seriousness at given age levels. A + in a given column indicates behavior that is symptomatic of tension, maladjustment, or abnormality. In a few instances, the symbol * indicates that it may be either normal or abnormal depending on whether or not good reason exists to justify it.

AGGRESSIVE AND WITHDRAWING BEHAVIOR

Aggression has a sinister implication of a hostile, attacking, disagreeable person or group, and is usually thought of as an undesirable quality because of this negative connotation. It is important to remember that aggression has a positive function with respect to the development of human personality, and that, in our society at least,

Table 2. Symptoms of Abnormal Behavior

Symptom	Pre-School	Elem. School	Adolescence
1. High suggestibility	+		+
2. Excessive timidity		+	+
3. Impulsiveness with poor judgment		*	+
4. Morbid fears, phobias	+	+	+
5. Excessive shyness	+	+	
6. General instability		+	
7. Anxiety	*	*	*
8. Untidyness			+
9. Depression	+	+	+
10. Sulkiness	+	+	
11. Suicidal tendency	+	+	+
12. Overboisterousness		+	
13. Suspicious attitude	*	*	*
14. Consistent breech of rules		+	+
15. Language defects		+	+
16. Illogical schemes		+	+
17. Sluggishness			+
18. Hysteria	+	+	+
19. Compulsions	+	+	+
20. Feelings of persecution	+	+	+
21. Inability to learn	+	+	+
22. Withdrawal from environment	+	+	+
23. Loss of memory	+	+	+
24. Inability to get along with others		+	+
25. Inability to stay with problem (inattention)		+	+
26. Indifference to social demands		+	
27. Dishonesty		+	+
28. Fire-setting habits	+	+	+
29. Loss of sense of feeling in any part of body	+	+	+
30. Scars on tongue, face, and head	+	+	+
31. Episodes of dizziness	+	+	+
32. Spasms	+	+	+
33. Inability to control bladder		+	+
34. Sudden emotional outbursts		+	+
35. Inability to learn to read		+	+
36. General sense of insecurity	+	+	
37. Hatefulness		+	
38. Morbid concern about own health	+	+	+
39. Consistent butt of other's jokes	+	+	+
40. Resentful of discipline		+	
41. Lonesomeness	+	+	

a person lacking in aggressiveness does not function well. In the broader sense, aggression can be a constructive and motivating force toward progress and fruitful accomplishment, whether it be the innate expression of aggressive energy in seeking food or the adult striving for major accomplishment. Whether negative or positive, one of our basic problems in being alive is learning to control and direct our aggression.

The infant is born with an undifferentiated potential for aggression. In most descriptions of infants, they are not conceived of as aggressive, instead emphasis is laid on their dependence upon others, particularly the mother, for fulfillment of their needs. It is important to recognize the infant as more than a passive receiver of the essentials of life. From the beginning stages of life, aggression is an element of considerable value to growth and learning. In the face of frustration or privation, the child reacts with rage and aggression directed at eliminating the source of the frustration or controlling the environment to relieve the privation. The infant very quickly makes demands in relation to his privations and the mother responds. With this interaction, the process of expression and management of aggression begins, not to end, for the major part, if not the remainder, of life. The roots of aggression lie in the very quality of being alive and the significant question is how this force shall be organized.

Highlights of the development of aggression can be seen as excerpted from Gesell and Ilg's[2] studies of child growth and development.

> *Age Four.* Physically aggressive: bites, hits, kicks, throws. Verbally aggressive: name-calling, boasting. Rough and careless with toys.
>
> *Age Five.* Physical aggression not as great. May stamp feet, slam door, occasional temper-tantrum. Verbal aggression: I'll kill you.
>
> *Age Five and a half.* Transition period from calmness of five to aggressiveness of six. Calls names: "Stinker," "Dope," uses verbal threats, contradicts, argues, resists direction. Temper tantrums; slams doors; strikes parents or other children.
>
> *Age Six.* Extremely aggressive, both physically and verbally. Calls names, uses threats, contradicts, argues, resists directions and orders. Hits and kicks adults and playmates, may be cruel towards animals and insects, destructive of objects.

---

[2]From *The Child from Five to Ten*, pp. 293-4, by Arnold Gesell and Frances L. Ilg. Copyright 1946 by Arnold Gesell and Frances L. Ilg. Reprinted by permission of Harper & Row, Publishers, Incorporated.

Age Seven. Less aggressive behavior—fewer tantrums and less resistance to adult instructions. May threaten to "beat somebody up," throws stones, fights with siblings, objects verbally that something isn't fair or quits in anger.

Age Eight. Aggression verbal rather than physical—argues, alibis, calls names or makes disagreeable remarks. Responds to attack or criticism with hurt feelings.

Age Nine. Aggression chiefly verbal, objects to behavior of others, criticizes. Fighting common (with boys) but more likely to be in the nature of play.

Age Ten. Sudden, explosive, short-lived anger. Aggression expressed in verbal name-calling. Crying when angry; girls more, boys less.

Age Eleven. Aware of his disposition, but sudden, occasional, outbursts of anger. Characteristic, individual patterns for expression of anger observable.

Age Twelve. Attacks by hitting, chasing, throwing, more common than withdrawal. Covert responses such as mumbling inaudibly. More aware of feelings of others. More effort at self-control.

Here we see the long term struggle to gain control of aggressive impulses in a society which encourages aggression, particularly in males, but which desires its expression to be in constructive effort. Aggression is a normal part of the socialization of the child and arises as an inherent feature of the child's general activity, as he moves about, explores, encounters obstacles, and protects himself. The more sociable children and more active children are observed to express a higher frequency of aggressive behavior, as an inherent part of their greater activity and personal contact. Because activity and aggression frequently interfere with the smooth execution of teaching plans, and perhaps because of sex, age, and socio-economic differences, teachers are prone to disapprove strongly and attempt to suppress such behavior. Instead, their efforts should be directed at harnessing and channeling the energies.

It is when the pattern of aggressive acts in a child is persistent, and the frequency and intensity become marked that the teacher is warned that emotional needs are not being met and the aggression should be viewed with concern.

Aggression is revealed in a variety of behavior:

Language: name-calling, swearing, yelling, domineering talk, teasing, statements of how they will treat other people or expressing resentment of authority, adults, family members, age-mates, minorities.

Topics of discussion among children: war, torture, cruelties, killing, murder, mysteries.

Overt acts towards others: pushing, pulling, hitting, slapping, kicking, throwing things, punching, carrying knives or other weapons, scapegoating.

Overt acts towards objects: property destruction, cutting desks, writing on walls, soiling or tearing clothes, breaking toys, suspiciousness.

In general: aggression which is consistent and uncontrolled or unchecked, aggression which is displaced on an object or person and aggression which is basically retaliatory or revengeful are forms which require attention and the concern of responsible adults.

Withdrawal is a kind of behavior, observable in many forms, which is fully as significant with regard to mental health as aggression. Although it provides the temporary gratification of tension reduction, avoidance of failure and disapproval, and elimination of problems of competition and cooperation, the ultimate result of withdrawal can be more damaging than aggressive behavior. In withdrawing, the child isolates himself from social participation and fails to develop necessary social skills which then augments his reasons for withdrawal, producing even greater inadequacy in coping with the environment. Withdrawal manifests itself in many forms, commonly, shyness, timidity, excessive blushing. Avoiding games and sports, making excuses for non-participation in social activities, procrastinating, forgetting, oversleeping, being aloof or refusing to comply, are means of avoiding contact with the environment.

Children avoid the company of other children of their own age or compensate for their inability to find a place in the group by preferring younger children or adults, reading voraciously, watching television or attending movies excessively, preferring animals to humans. In the classroom, withdrawal and avoidance behavior is observed in apathy and lack of interest, daydreaming and staring out windows, absence and tardiness, frequent trips to lavatory, water, or sharpener, doodling and picture drawing, taking a back seat or speaking only when spoken to. In extreme forms, withdrawal leads to regression or escape into fantasy.

In gauging the significance of such behavior, consideration has to be given to the consistency and the range throughout which it appears. All withdrawing behavior is not symptomatic of maladjustment. Many times such behavior can be desirably protective. There are many events within a classroom which are dull and boring for some children. There are occasions of excessive fatigue to which the child responds with lassitude. There are various occasions in which the child finds himself uninterested, incapable, or ill-at-ease, and his natural response on such occasions is to avoid or withdraw from the activities of the group. Withdrawal constitutes a problem when it becomes a characteristic behavior pattern occurring in the various segments of the child's life. When he withdraws from class activities, avoids participation in play groups, becomes overly dependent on a single form of stimulation, e.g., reading or television, persistently daydreams, or manifests other persistent forms of withdrawal, there is cause for concern.

Withdrawal manifests itself in a variety of ways and is often accompanied by one or more associated conditions. Table 3 lists a number of such indicators.

TABLE 3. CHARACTERISTICS OF WITHDRAWAL AND ASSOCIATED CONDITIONS

Behavioral manifestations	*Associated conditions*	*Psychological*
Habitual avoidance of	Physical defects	Marked feelings of
interpersonal contact	body deformities	guilt
group activities	hearing defects	unworthiness
authority	visual defects	inferiority
reality	malnutrition	inadequacy
Attitudinal-emotional	obesity	Rationalization
frequently depressed	skin defects	Denial
or unhappy	Neurological	Projection
resentful, jealous	poor motor co-	Self-pity
negative	ordination	Fantasy
marked fears, shyness,	general nervousness	
timidity	Emotional	
marked submissiveness	inaudible speech	
sensitive, easily	stuttering	
embarrassed	avoidance of eye	
Other responses	contact	
lacking initiative	Social	
truancy	rejection by peers	
extreme fatigue	racial or religious	
persistent infantile	prejudice	
behavior	economic status	

CREATIVE PRODUCTS OF CHILDREN

The several creative and projective devises described in an earlier chapter offer means for obtaining deeper understanding of difficulties that children may be experiencing in their lives. The wishes and fears which children express, the form and content of written and artistic creative products, and the other spontaneous creative acts of children provide useful clues to children's needs. Children's art work can be an avenue of understanding between teacher and child, by means of which she can gain insight into intellectual, social, emotional, and perceptual growth. But if it is to be so, children have to be allowed to express themselves freely in their art expression and not be constrained by convention. Unfortunately, we treat children's art work like any lesson, as something to be graded and evaluated.

In reading, arithmetic, or other aspects of academic achievement we can gauge the accuracy or speed or volume of information recalled, and by virtue of these measures can appraise achievement with some degree of objectivity.

In art, unfortunately, we can only impose our own, usually inadequate standards of aesthetic judgment upon the creative work of children. I say inadequate because most teachers recognize art and music as areas of limited attainment and skill. The aesthetic training provided them in teacher training programs, whether in teachers' colleges or liberal arts can rarely be called adequate, much less exciting or imaginative. Worse, we tend to treat the creative endeavors as experiences to be avoided, or, at most, something to be handled as conventional subjects. The imposition of our conventional standards of aesthetic judgment and preference for representational art acceptable to adult levels of perception denies us access to the child's perceptual and emotional world as it may be expressed in creative products. Whether we are concerned about art for art's sake, art as a means of developing creative expression, or art as a means of learning something about the emotional development of a child, I'm tempted to suggest that, in the majority of instances, the educational approach adopted is most inadequate. The overworked device of using holidays as themes for the art programs becomes progressively more boring. The stereotyped room decorations leave little room for imaginative expression. It is strange indeed how we labor to make difficult experiences which with less direction could be stimulating.

Drawing, to the child, is primarily a language, a form of expression rather than a means of creating beauty. In drawing a picture, a child expresses his likes and dislikes, his emotional relationships to the world in which he lives. He draws what he knows rather than what he sees. He exaggerates the size of items which are interesting or important.

There is an order which is remarkably constant in the development of children's drawings, even among children from different backgrounds. Their drawings parallel their concept development and provide a useful gauge of the intellectual maturity of the child. At the beginning of the 2-4 year age range, the child's drawings are little more than a disorderly scribble, for the two-year-old is easily distracted and does not always watch his hand movements. He paints for the joy of motor activity. He may paint several colors over each other. Gradually, with experimentation with lines of different length and direction, he gains greater control and the scribblings take on a more orderly appearance, the lines running more uniformly in a given direction and of a given length. Finger paints are usually more satisfactory than brush or crayons for the direct sensory satisfaction from manipulation of the paint and the motor activity available which does not require the control demanded by brush or crayons. By three, the beginnings of design emerge, the scribblings being regulated and rhythmical, often time being named by the child, e.g., mother is cooking. Although there is little resemblance between the so-called drawing and reality, the child is entering the representational stage. Between the ages of four and six, dramatic changes occur. The drawings take on form and identity. Typical objects such as horses, people, trees, animals, play things and the like are reproduced although size and space relationships are distorted. Most of the work is imaginative with only limited resort to knowledge and memory.

At first, portrayal of space is not important to the child. Figures are scattered over the page in random fashion. Beginning about the age of four, in brighter children, the items are arranged in a row, with an occasional line for the ground. Still later, the sky may appear as a line at the top of the page.

During the six to nine age, the child expands and extends his interests. About the seventh year, the base line appears along which objects are arranged suggesting that the child is aware of a definite order in space, and of himself in relation to it. Further, the relationship between color and object becomes more definite. Distant objects are placed along a line, near objects along a ground line in the foreground, somewhat in the manner of Japanese prints. This represents the beginning of perspective, which will not develop into a third dimension until adolescence. Drawings become more realistic between the ages of 9-11 as the child's observation and contact with the world expands and as the distinction between reality and fantasy becomes more sharply defined.

For the teacher to attempt a personality evaluation on the basis of children's creative work is out of the question, for even with the necessary knowledge of personality theory and psychodynamics, the margin for error is great. Most of the work which has been completed regarding the interpretation of paintings and drawing has been exploratory, and has yet to yield useful measures of personality. In addition to the maturational level, the creative work of children can be useful in three ways: first, it provides an opportunity for observation of behavior in a relatively unstructured situation. The child's manner of approaching and executing such a task has less constraint than in the more highly organized classroom lesson, and, hence, is more revealing. Second, the content and organization of the creative product can provide clues to the child's interpretation of external events and his feelings in these matters. Third, the persistent repetition of unusual themes and unchanging reproductions can be detected.

Lowenfeld[3] has developed an evaluation procedure for children's drawings during the schematic stage of development—seven to nine years of age—which provides a basis for understanding the child's growth during these years. It is presented here in simplified form.

> *Intellectual growth.* Has the child developed concepts for familiar experiences? How clearly expressed? How well differentiated? How are color and objects related?

Children reflect their comprehension and perception of the world in the objects and relationships which they attempt to produce. Their facility in expression is governed by their capacity to formulate a conceptual whole. Are there size-object distinctions? Are the parts relevant to the whole? Most children will reproduce familiar elements in the environment but with varying degrees of differentiation—for instance, a feature of the face or parts of a house. Are the parts alike in appearance, e.g., doors and windows of a house may all be identical rectangles, or are there observable distinctions? Are the colors appropriate in that they denote recognition of relationships?

> *Emotional growth.* How flexible or stereotyped are the schemes presented? Does size of object vary with significance? What degree of exaggeration or omission of significant parts?

Healthy emotional growth necessitates being able to adapt and maintain stability in the face of variable situations and changing demands. Children who feel secure in their emotional relationships are able to be independent, creative, and imaginative. Children lacking emotional security become preoccupied with obtaining it or protecting themselves and reflect this in rigid, stereotyped drawings

---

[3]Reprinted with permission of the publisher from *Creative and Mental Growth*, pp. 142-43, by Viktor Lowenfeld. Copyright 1957 by The Macmillan Company.

in which form and figure remain constant and fail to reflect variation in functions. Human figures will not show difference in position according to activity.

Exaggeration or omission are frequent. For instance, a seven-year-old drawing a picture of himself on a bicycle drew one arm five times longer than the other in order to make it reach the handle bar. But only in this one drawing did such exaggeration occur. A classmate, in each of several drawings, persistently exaggerated the length of the arms of all persons drawn, especially herself. She herself had unusually long arms, appeared at times to be "all arms," and reflected this in persistent exaggeration. Repeatedly missing parts of bodies may reflect similar concerns. Other types of exaggerations reflect like concerns, but some reflect perceptual differences. Possibly a reason for the commonly exaggerated trunks of trees in proportion to branches is that this is the predominating part of the tree seen from a child's eye-level.

> *Social growth.* How does the child identify himself with the experiences shown and with other persons in the drawing? What spatial relationships are shown? How is the environment characterized?

The development of concepts of spatial relationships and of oneself in relationship to the environment is an important step in relating to others. The introduction of the base line previously mentioned illustrates such an ordering of space. The child reflects his relationships with the important persons in his social environment in the position and function he assigns himself relative to other persons. The extent to which they detail subsidiary aspects of the environment discloses their sensitivity to and awareness of such aspects.

> *Perceptual growth.* Is the child aware of sexual differences? of distance and perspective? To what extent has he departed from geometric representation?

> *Physical growth.* How aware is the child of different body parts? Do the figures reflect awareness of motion and action? What sensitivity is shown in use of different parts of body, e.g., joints.

All writers warn against making any analysis on the basis of a single drawing. Data from different sources need to be congruent before any conclusions can be drawn. It is important, therefore, to collect varied samples of children's creative work over a period of time before assaying any appraisal.

Clues to the emotional responses of children are better inferred from the expressive qualities of color and line than from the subject matter itself. Some children consistently choose warm colors such as red, yellow, orange, whereas others prefer the cooler colors such as blue, brown, green, and black. Those who consistently favor the warm colors tend, for the most part, to have free emotional behavior, affectionate relationships, cooperation in play, and sympathetic feeling toward others. The emphasis of color suggests a strong emotional orientation. With increased emotional control, an associated shift in color usage is seen. The use of cold colors in nursery school children is associated with highly-controlled and over-adaptive behavior.

Like other aspects of behavior, the symbolic meaning of color, line and form, takes on increasingly individual meaning with age. Not only does the shift from color to line and form reflect on increasingly maturity, perception of the environment, and greater physical control, but it reflects the developing personality as a whole. Children with compulsive traits tend to make smaller, detailed drawings; rejected children to cramp their work into a fraction of the space available; timid and insecure children use weaker lines. A smeared painting or a drawing which emerged and was then obliterated can reflect dissatisfaction with the quality, feelings to be concealed, or an expression of hostility to what was represented. Sudden smearing may evidence conflicting feelings. Rigid, unchanging patterns usually reflect deeper disturbances and unresolved conflicts in feelings.

A fruitful avenue of information can be opened by asking children to tell about their drawings, what is occurring and what is going to happen. Too often the adult reaction to creative work of the child is to indicate whether or not he likes it or approves of the technical quality of the work, or, if he is unable to comprehend, to bluntly ask: "What is it?" A more informative approach is to ask the child to tell you about the drawings. His descriptions invariably provide a more detailed portrayal of his perceptions and concepts.

The stories which children create offer another source of understanding to them. Elaborate scoring systems have been worked out for interpreting various projective tests which essentially depend upon eliciting a spontaneous story from children in response to a picture or other stimulus which has been presented. The psychological dynamics of such materials should be left to the clinical psychologist, and yet, without such elaborate analysis, the teacher can achieve some helpful insight.

Does the child present himself in the story or identify with the hero of the story? What qualities does he attribute to the hero–

strength, courage, resentment, fearfulness, etc.? What difficulties does the hero encounter, what problems does he experience? Do these reveal or parallel problems experienced in reality? What means are adopted to obtain solutions—direct effort, magic, superhuman talents? What relationships exist between the persons described—affectionate, supporting, helpful, or antagonistic, injurious, punitive? Who possesses what power and authority and how it is exercised? What is the general outcome of the plots—favorable, successful, optimistic, or unfavorable, unhappy, defeatist? It will be noted that the answers to these questions concern themselves with the observable attributes and relationships existing between the principal characters and the themes portrayed in the story and do not depend upon inferential analysis regarding the needs, drives, defense mechanisms, or other psychological considerations.

Chapter 13

ASSISTING PERSONAL
DEVELOPMENT

We are so accustomed to children's doing what is expected that we take their compliance for granted, instead of appreciating the miracle of self-management that is demonstrated by most children. We take it for granted that children will come to school, beginning with kindergarten or first grade, and from the first day fall into the school routines.

Not long ago, a six-year-old, entering a Boston first grade, decided after several days that school didn't appeal to him. He wasn't afraid of the teacher nor was he afraid to have his mother leave; he just decided, after looking the situation over, that it didn't interest him and he didn't see any reason for putting up with it. So he walked out to the playground. The teacher, cajoling and admonishing, got him back for short periods. His mother began to bring him to school, but, as soon as she left, out he went to the playground where he would sit on the fence waiting for recess period when he'd wholeheartedly join in the fun, always being quite cordial to the teacher. When we consider the millions of children who enter school each year and accommodate to the demands in contrast with this rare youngster who balks, we can appreciate children's capacity for self-regulation in accordance with social expectations.

If we think of the temptations which accidentally and systematically (deliberate adult efforts to exploit children's desires) confront each child each day, his success in controlling his behavior has to be admired. Every supermarket has its special seduction-sections for children with its books, candies, and breakfast food, brightly packaged in eye-appealing colors to trap the innocent passer-by. Television commercials serve as constant exhorters to join the infant bacchanal. The toy departments in the emporia and the counters in the notion stores present their charms. And successful though they are in selling their merchandise, children manage to resist the impulse to take the objects. In the same manner, children meet numerous disappointments and frustrations—the cancelled motion picture, not being allowed to go out to play, having a favorite toy broken—and in meeting them control the impulse to sulk, get mad, or cry. These few examples point up the constant task of behavioral control being met by children. They are not always successful. They have temper tantrums, they steal a toy, they fight and sulk, they need adult support to help restrain impulses and reinforce their controls, but, on the whole, they succeed at the task.

MAJOR DEVELOPMENTAL TASKS

Each child is engaged in three major developmental tasks: mastering skills, ego development, and social development. Teachers are concerned with all three. Personality development is, essentially, the development of an ego capable of self-direction and self-regulation. When we speak of a mature person as being one who is responsible, goal-directed, independent, and able to work, love, play, and function effectively in groups, we describe a person whose ego is sufficiently well-organized to control his impulses, to achieve satisfaction of his needs, and to meet life's realities without breaking under the burden. The achievement of an ego capable of such self-management is a task consuming years and one in which teachers play no small part. It is also a task in which the complexity of demands in relation to ego capacity can become too great, resulting in breakdown of ego functioning. The task of the adequately functioning ego is to strike a balance between a series of conflicting forces, determine an objective, and select appropriate courses of action of attaining it.

Recognizing the fact that repressed desires exist which are beyond the scope of consciousness, nevertheless, the ego must be aware of and appraise internal needs, desires, and fears—both physical and psychological—what one wants and what one thinks one ought to want. Second, it must appraise the outside reality, the life space in which one exists, both physical and social, for its opportunities, dangers, and pressures. Next, it selects a course of action which is consistent with the perception of the forces and, in their appraisal, appears most likely to provide a satisfactory outcome, yet finally musters and directs the energies towards the chosen goal. This procedure occurs with small events and large, with child and adult.

An eight-year-old girl was called to the telephone by her mother one Friday afternoon and learned that a friend wanted her to come spend the night. Arrangement had been made earlier in the week for another friend to come spend Saturday afternoon and Sunday with the girl. Responding to the telephone invitation, the girl said: "Wait while I ask my mother." The mother, thinking of excitement and loss of sleep which accompanies such over-nights decided that spending Friday night out would result in too much fatigue when Saturday night and Sunday had been added. The girl, wanting badly to go, began first to beg, then argue, then complain that her mother wasn't being fair. The mother explained her position several times without mollifying the girl who quickly began to storm. The mother was adamant. In the midst of her tirade and tears, the little girl ran back to the telephone, calmly asked her friend to wait a few moments because she wasn't sure if she could come or not and then returned to storm the mother with more tears. The mother held her position. With the telephone call terminated, the little girl didn't subside but continued her crying, deploring her mother's unfairness. The father, who had overheard the events, particularly the telephone conversation, sat down with the girl and attempted to show by the sequence of events how she had purposely attempted to pressure her mother and now was trying to make her feel unhappy. The girl listened, but rejected the procedure, continued to fuss, and was sent to her room until she could straighten up. The volume of her crying mounted until finally, precipitated by an act of her younger sister, she had a temper tantrum. At this point, the father ordered her to stop, telling her he could understand her wanting to go, being disappointed and angered at not going, but that she was to stop the tantrum and whenever she felt better she was free to come downstairs. A few minutes later the father returned, inviting her to rejoin the family.

The situation illustrates the several elements in ego functioning:

the girl's desire to spend the night with a friend, the appraisal of the external world, the determination of a course of action which seemed likely to overcome the parent refusal, the marshalling of energies to that end, and the breakdown of emotional controls in the face of failure. Several aspects of the adult role in relation to ego development are also seen: in this instance, an error in program management by the mother who could have avoided the situation by refusing the invitation when she answered the telephone, a failing attempt by the father to interpret the girl's behavior toward the mother, the imposition of limits on behavior, and the final support of the child's ego by bringing her back into the group. Although any adult (including the parents in retrospect) could suggest several actions which would have been more effective, nevertheless, the role of adults is clear in providing support to children in their course of developing the ego strength to manage and control their behavior.

THE TEACHER'S ROLE

BECARING

Teachers have a special role which they can play. The hazards of attempting to be a substitute parent were noted in an earlier chapter. But there are several important aspects to the role of a teacher who would provide a guidance-oriented environment. The first of these is to "becare" children. Bettelheim[1] quotes the distinction that a disturbed child made between her parents and her counselors in a treatment home in which she was living. The child said that her counselor "becares me, she doesn't love me. . . . Love means to hug and kiss me and carry me and put me down. Parents do it. . . . My parents don't becare me, they're not counselors."

Bettelheim adds,

> With the exception of love at first sight, an adult's immediate love for a child can only be due to emotional starvation and keeps the child from one of the most maturing experiences—that of a slowly developing, mutually satisfying personal relationship. Immediate loving or mothering of a child implies the obligation to return such love, a response which is beyond the disturbed child's emotional capacity at first and results only in feelings of worthlessness and guilt.

[1] B. Bettelheim, *Love is Not Enough*. New York: The Free Press, 1950, pp. 18-19. Material used with permission.

It might be added that if a disturbed child shouldn't be offered such a relationship, a normal child doesn't need it. Instead, both can benefit from being becared.

CONSISTENCY

The second aspect of the teacher's role in a guidance environment is consistency. This oft-extolled essential of parental discipline is too often interpreted to mean uniformity of action, especially by teachers. There is the notion that all children should be treated alike—given the same reward or the same punishment for the identical act, allowed exactly the same privileges, and judged by the same standards. Teachers fear that variations in such routines will incur the resentment of pupils and encourage them to challenge their actions. Yet, children's perception of fairness is determined more by how they are made to feel than by uniform rules. Consistency involves both internal and external aspects. Children sense conflicts in teacher attitudes: the teacher trying to be permissive when she fundamentally believes in an adult-ordered world for children; the teacher who encourages group-planning provided such plans coincide with teacher decisions; principals who "encourage democracy" by having student councils whose sole function is to rubber-stamp administrative plans. Children will feel uneasy and anxious in the presence of teachers having such internal conflicts in philosophy.

Second, consistency implies that events within the classroom are reasonably predictable, and that a child knows where he stands, that he will not be denied opportunities and privileges permitted others, and that he can count on the adults for support as he needs it. A classroom which satisfies these conditions has a structure (see Figure 1) in which certain kinds of actions are forbidden, e.g., striking one another or destroying another's possessions; certain kinds of actions are subject to rules and regulations, e.g., leaving the room, recess times, etc.; and a certain area for freedom of choice exists, e.g., choice of companion, talking with a neighbor, choice of assignment, etc.

This last aspect of the classroom environment is vital if children are to grow, for it is in this area that they manage their own lives and develop the strength to control their own behavior. It is by providing this freedom of choice that adults show they have confidence in the abilities of children to develop independent responsibility, both alone and in groups. The area of rules and regulations is to help provide a structural framework which gives direction and support, and the scheme of the two cuts across all activities. For

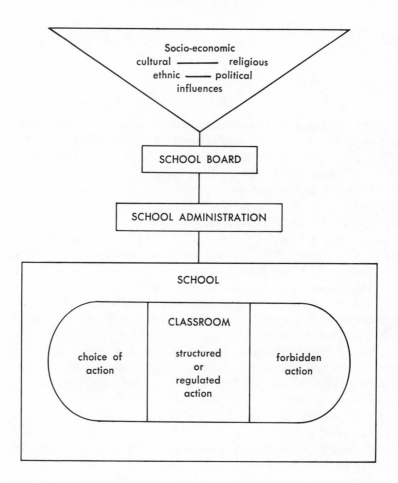

Figure 1. Diagram of socio-psychological factors influencing class structure.

instance, the teacher may designate the arithmetic assignment for the day or week, establish a rule that the assignment has to be completed before leaving school, but allow freedom of choice in the number of problems to be completed; or she may determine the daily schedule but allow the children a 45-minute period for which they work out their own plan; or the entire class may spend Friday afternoon planning individual and group schedules for the following week. A variety of arrangements are possible which combine the two areas of choice and regulation.

A classroom program which does not include an area of choice denies children the opportunities they need for learning self-management; it is instead no better than a prison. The outstanding characteristics of a prison are rules and schedules. Prison officials propagate long lists of rules which prisoners are expected to obey under penalty of loss of privilege (privilege being synonymous with being human— having visits, correspondence, access to library, recreation, etc.). All phases of life are regulated—sleep, awakening, eating, working, playing, talking, bathing, reading, smoking, et al. Instead of having the opportunity to develop self-respect through increased capacity to accept and discharge responsibility and increasing degrees of freedom under the direction of a staff which treats them with respect, the opposite is the case—apathy, loss of skill, discouragement, and self-hatred or self-centeredness.

PROVIDING A STABLE ENVIRONMENT

A third aspect of the teacher's role in assisting the ego development of children is that of director of affairs. She provides children with a program and an organizational structure which gives the children the feeling that they live in a world which has some order, some stability, and some purpose. Many children arrive at school more disorganized and confused than maladjusted. The main contribution that the school can make to the lives of many children is a sense of organization and coherence, which comes from a sound program, routines that lend comfort, assurance, and predictability to life, and practices consistent with principles. The uncertainty, stress, and anxiety to be faced in today's world requires an ego that can take some blows, can stand some tension, and has some resilience. Children will develop such personalities if they find a stability and a meaning to their world which they can internalize.

PERMISSIVENESS

One of the most misconstrued aspects of modern education has been the doctrine of permissiveness. This has been equated with laissez-faire classroom leadership in which the adult resigns from his managerial role and permits children to determine their own course of action. The idea is often directly implied that to set limits, to prohibit, to order, or to direct is to damage developing personalities, which, to flourish, need the everwarming indulgence of a passive leader. The opposite is the case. If anything, a domineering, punitive adult is preferable to an indifferent, submissive one as far as personality development is concerned. A child at least builds some ego strength resisting the former, whereas he ends confused and hapless with the latter. Adults are responsible for directing the course of development and protecting children from harmful and overwhelming experiences (including their own impulses). Permissiveness is permitting and encouraging the child to try his wings and to test his strength, not run the show.

Another aspect of permissiveness would better be thought of as tolerance for error and deviation. Variation in children's behavior is inevitable. The same little girl of the temper tantrum mentioned previously had on an earlier occasion on her own initiative refused an overnight invitation because she and her mother were planning to work together on a Halloween costume (which the mother would have made more easily alone). Tolerance of variation in behavior is essential, especially with children who are experiencing adjustment difficulties because of their reluctance to give up their symptomatic behavior easily.

DEVELOPING EGO STRENGTH

With these aspects of the teacher role identified, the essential elements of a program for developing ego strength can be examined. Basically, the total environment should be appropriately designed. The school, with its curriculum and its guidance program, its materials and methods, and most of all, its staff and its practices, should be designed as an environment which provides optimal opportunity for individual and group development. All schools have some such elements; few have been consciously designed to fulfill such needs.

Redl and Wineman[2] (whose thoughtful writing has contributed much to the identification and application of techniques of ego-support) found a complete "vacuum in the area of specific educational tools" in the area of ego-support. The secondary schools have a jury-rigged guidance program tacked on an academic program which has grown incoherently. The elementary schools are emerging from the self-contained classroom into a diversified and flexible scheduling intended to better meet individual differences. Hopefully, the change in progress will see attention given to the psychological aspects of an emerging school program better designed for child development.

[2]F. Redl and D. Wineman, *The Aggressive Child.* New York: The Free Press, 1957, p. 277.

Within the school, each teacher is the architect of her own program and the engineer responsible for making it function. In the area of personal development, several important phases of development occur with regard to: (1) self, (2) responsibility, (3) independence, (4) appreciation of others, (5) acceptance of reality. With entry to school, the child's entire world changes. He learns to adjust to a society represented by the school which makes more and different demands than the home. The child must learn:

1. to dress independently
2. to adjust to teacher demands
3. to adapt to school routines
4. to work independently
5. to get along with other pupils
6. to share with other pupils
7. to work co-operatively with others
8. to attend to tasks until completion
9. to work as well as play.

These are major steps for a child with the first step, that of entering school, being one of the most important. The step incorporates some curious changes in the child's dependence-independence, for he has to make sacrifices in both, giving up his dependence on his family and giving up some of his concern about his personal satisfactions in deference to group satisfactions. The success in this transition is largely dependent upon the environment created by the teacher and the impact of her first contact with the child. Although the transition from home to school is more critical, the same considerations apply each time a child meets a new teacher with each annual promotion.

First Contacts

Little research exists on the kind of environments which attract children and the effects of particular environments upon their mood, morale, and behavior. The design of the modern school plant assumes that children's concepts of beauty and function are similar to adults', but seeing the divergent physical types of teachers that a child will term pretty (in his response to personality and attitude rather than face and figure), the assumption seemingly has doubtful validity.

The environment should create a mood and offer an invitation to action by the kinds of materials it contains and the organization of space. An essential difference between teachers who have "good discipline" and those who have "discipline problems" is the talent of the former in having materials "ready-to-go" and a skill in getting children speedily on the track and involved in the materials. This is the point at which preparation pays. Materials can be displayed to provoke curiosity, invite entry, and facilitate movement. No better illustration can be offered than a well-designed science-museum with its displays designed to invite attention, direct the response of the participant, and teach him something about science. At the same time, the arrangement of space is important. The traditional classroom had space for little more than a full class with individual work oriented to the teacher and/or the front chalkboard. Housekeeping was difficult due to inadequate storage space.

Effective space organization requires provision for large group and small group work, for action and for quiet space, for storage and display, for individual work, and for privacy. Most school rooms fail in the latter two items, for privacy and uninterrupted individual work which can be left and returned to is rarely possible.

Most initial meetings of class groups from elementary school to college begin with too many students present. The older student with his capacity to stand and often a preference for psychological distance has greater tolerance for the anonymity which occurs in larger groups, but younger children establish contact with a teacher better if groups are small. The first week of a first grade could see the teacher meeting with only five new children each day. The psychology of the first contacts is quickly summed up in the song from *The King and I.* "Getting to know all about you; getting to feel free and easy" — describes the essential purpose of initial meeting.

Beyond establishing personal contact, and reducing the barriers which block accessibility, the second steps in the relationship should come from the child at his own choosing. The teacher is an agent of change. The child may be hesitant or resistant. The teacher keeps in contact, is accessible and sensitive to the child's moves as he reaches into and takes hold in the new environment. In this connection it is worth noting that some children are fearful about learning. Parental attitudes and responses to the child's curiosity have led to the conviction that inquiry is dangerous and can lead to dire results. Furthermore, learning in the school setting means competing with other children, and this too can be hazardous. The result is a child who hesitantly tastes the new environment as if putting his toe into the water to see if he really wants to go in.

A child who enters the class during the year presents special problems. If no effort is made to include him he often floats on the fringe of the class, yet if a special event is made of the newcomer such as,

aren't we lucky to have X join us—the truth is ignored, for the newcomer is a threat to the status quo. The group has to accommodate
him and some are likely to be displaced in their friendship. A well-
integrated group will respond with tolerance as if saying you may
find a place on your own merits. An insecure group is likely to join
ranks against the newcomer, with a few persons on the fringe competing for his friendship while masquerading as persons really "in-
the-know." In-between groups are more likely to make a show of
incorporating the newcomer, as if to prove their own friendliness to
themselves.

In assisting self-development, one of the capacities to be developed
in children is the ability to cope with insecurity, anxiety, and fear.
Everyone has to face events which are discouraging, threatening, or
dangerous. Fear and anxiety serve as warning systems, insecurity
and frustration spur greater effort when they occur in managable
proportions. Each child varies in his susceptibility to insecurity according to the way he has responded to life's pressures. These may
occur in the form of overprotective, ambitious, or rejecting parents,
an environment which is improverished or hostile, siblings who are
domineering. The child's poise, posture, and confidence provide
clues to his level of self-esteem. For all children, secure or not, new
environments, changes in status, and exposure to failure cause the
child to feel uncertain of his position and the ground on which he
stands. The school presents all three—a new environment in which
he is not the apple of his family's eye but one of many being continually praised, criticized and evaluated on his performance. As his
anxiety mounts, so does his tendency to avoid and withdraw from the
situation, e.g., by daydreaming, increased dependence, apathy, etc.,
or to attack, e.g., by fault-finding, attention-seeking, hyperactivity,
etc. Much can be done to increase the confidence with which children
approach school and to build their self-esteem: warmup periods
which involve a game or appealing activity; instructing and encouraging children to help each other in the removal of outer clothing;
establishing closer physical proximity—a pair seated together at first
grade level, groups at upper grade levels, and a morning conversation period for recounting to friends the special events of the preceding day are all means of getting started.

Group planning is particularly valuable. By having some information about what is going to happen, children are more likely to have
a favorable rather than a negative anticipation. Knowing the schedule
for the day helps them to bridge the in-between periods and make
transitions from one activity to another. Inner control is needed to

shift from one activity to another, or one location to another, both to give up an activity in which one is engrossed and wishes to continue and second, to enter another activity which may appear strange, novel, or difficult. Children respond to such tensions and strangeness by clowning and "goofing-off", by hanging on to the old, or clinging to a dependable person. Varied procedures are available for facilitating transitions. One is to establish anticipated goals: "After we do our work we have a story"; "Jerry, will you and Bill take the game equipment out to the playground and get it ready for our game?"; "Next year when you're in the fifth grade and spend a week at winter camp"; etc. Getting several children started on the new activity, knowing that others will observe and want to join, avoids a break in continuity of events. Creating symbolic satisfaction by various props — name tags, club groups, objects from home — creates a sense of identification.

BROADENING CONCEPT OF SELF

As the child matures during the elementary school years, his responsibility increases for independent control and direction of himself. If he is to be able to accept this responsibility, he has to conceive of himself as capable of controlling his impulses, fulfilling his needs, meeting external demands, and tolerating some failure and partial success in all of these. Two aspects of ego development emerge as important in meeting the inevitable gap which occurs between desire or demand and performancè. When we speak of children learning to accept criticism and facing difficulties in learning, we imply a needed capacity to tolerate frustration and cope with anxiety and insecurity. The terms tolerate and cope indicate that we want the child to keep trying rather than attempt to avoid or escape from the situation. A well-planned program will incorporate devices and arrangements that encourage children to keep trying and learn to cope with insecurity, and these devices will be much more than merely implying by word or deed that "I expect you to persist because that is what school is for."

Help should be available as hurdles are encountered, either from the teacher or from classmates. Classroom regulations which forbid such contact and assistance deny children an important resource in learning to cope with difficulties. Many children manage to get through difficult situations by being able to depend on a beloved person who is present. Some children turn to the teacher, not so much for help as emotional support and security. Other children derive the support from the encouragement of friends and class-mates, which is one important justification for encouraging and helping children to establish friendships among their classmates. In difficulty, a child does not feel as helpless or vulnerable if there is someone from whom he can derive encouragement and support. Helping children to find healthy ways of compensating for short-comings and deficiencies, instead of using clowning or attention-getting procedures as compensatory devises, through accomplish-ment in special subjects or knowledge of special topics should en-couraged. If scholastic achievement and athletic prowess are the only ways in which status can be attained, many children are doomed to feel inadequate.

Not only must immediate frustration be faced, but also the emo-tional feelings aroused by the frustration. Teachers have to be sensi-tive to the total frustration level within a classroom as evidenced by physical restlessness, increased irritability of children, conflict between persons, amount of daydreaming, etc., and gauge the ap-propriateness of introducing a given task in relation to the immediate capacity of the children to tolerate the additional amount of frustra-tion involved. In addition, procedures are needed to siphon off feel-ings of fear, anger, jealousy, and despair as they accumulate. Physical activity, humor and laughter, discussions of how the children feel in certain situations, of events that make them angry, fearful, or jealous, of things that teachers do which they dislike, of what to do when angry — provide opportunities for displacement of the feelings, for direct recognition and understanding of them, and for learning ways of meeting them.

Being responsible involves taking care of oneself, of possessions, and of one's obligations to other persons. It begins with an appreci-ation of oneself derived from the feelings which other people reflect. If children are treated as being valued, they develop an appreciation of themselves and sense some purpose in caring for themselves. There is purpose in good health, in cleanliness, and in care of one's posses-sions. A second aspect in the development of individual responsibility is the building of inside controls. The situations, materials, and groups which a child encounters present a steady stream of temptations. It is fun to run and slide in hallways, shout in tunnels, splash water, throw snowballs, clay, or erasers, sail paper airplanes in the class-room, and shriek in the theatre with other children. Wagons can be crashed as well as ridden, animals teased as well as petted. Resistance to such temptations necessitates adequate inner controls. Organiza-tional arrangements, regulations, and routines exist not only for efficiency in operation but also to provide the outside controls which help children resist the lure and temptation of sudden impulses to act or use objects in ways different than desired. It would be desirable, physical arrangements permitting, to have all materials available at all times to any child. Such an arrangement would assume complete self-control by the children. Knowing that such is not the case, materials should be accessible in proportion to the ability of the children to manage their usage, and, similarly, regulations and routines provided to the degree that ego support is needed. A junior high school principal who required that no student move between points in the building, even to the toilets, without a pass was denying his pupils opportunity for self-regulation, well within their capacity.

The contagion which frequently occurs in group situations as excitement rises in the face of unexpected stimulation and impulses necessitates the development of group controls through codes of behavior (informally agreed upon or established procedures rather than formal codes). For example, in order to combat the inevitable outbursts of excitement which occurred when she left the room, one teacher of a group which had a reputation for being unruly, made the arrangement that they could talk as much as they wanted while she was in class, but if she had to go out they were to be quiet. The behavior pattern wasn't established as easily, but out of several instances when the opposite occurred and the teacher expressed her disappointment, and out of a growing relationship in which the group felt that the teacher was "for them," the class gradually developed a pride which was curiously double-edged—that they had more freedom (and responsibility) in class than did other classes — and second pride in their self-control when she was out of the room. This self control was achieved by the development of a two-sided picture of reality — the situations as they existed and the link of individual responsibility. Partially, this results from observing what happens to others, and also from reflecting and seeing one's own behavior in relation to events. It is the latter link which constitutes an essential step in the development of responsibility and independence. By the middle elementary years, children have the capacity for seeing their behavior with some objectivity. Given adequate gratification, this link can be established, for in the face of excessive frustration and emotional disturbance, children develop distorted perceptions of reality and are blind to their own actions.

The need to be aware of reality and to see oneself at face value is necessary if one is to deal with any effectiveness with the difficulties that inevitably have to be faced. There is no question that in many instances reality is so bad as to be overwhelming and that some compromises which permit temporary escape or partial avoidance are necessary if the individual is not to break down entirely. In most instances, evasions are undesirable because they postpone, if not prevent, the possibility of adjustment and solution. Leading children to analyze a situation and their own behavior in it leads to a recognition of reality. Awareness of their motives and various possibilities for satisfying them in given situations helps in the selection of socially constructive courses of action. Unless children are encouraged and permitted to become independent, they are unable to become responsible persons.

SPECIAL TACTICS

A gradual change occurs throughout childhood from the completely dependent but completely free infant (no self-control or self-denial required) to the independent but responsible adult. Yet with increased opportunity to do and think for oneself, some fear often occurs and with it an impulse to hold onto the dependent status. This reluctance is often expressed in over conformity to adult or group requirements. Feeling inadequate or uncertain, we recognize that disapproval and anxiety can be avoided by identifying ourselves with important adults or with the group and copying their behavior. Personal adequacy and confidence develops from ability to carry out minor tasks in childhood, gradually increasing responsibilities and the independence and inner-direction needed. This share of increasing responsibility cannot occur unless parents and adult are willing to share authority with children. Each day in each school provides many problems and difficulties — corridor patrol, behavior when visitors are present, treatment of small children by older, etc. — which can be solved through group decision participated in by children. In addition to the program elements described, teachers need a repertoire of tactics which can be used to manage and direct behavior.

Redl and Wineman[3] have described a variety of procedures which they found effective in their work with disturbed children. A number of these are familiar to many teachers:

---

[3]*Ibid.* Material used with permission.

1. *Signal interference.* Supporting the ego of a student in a moment of temptation by signaling disapproval with a gesture —a slight headshake, a raised eyebrow, a wink, a quizzical expression. Catching a pupil's eye can check the foot reaching out or the paper ball about to be thrown.

2. *Proximity control.* Standing near a pupil who is likely to disrupt helps him maintain control. Moving about the classroom, returning at sufficient intervals helps the child observe limits. The skin and touch can be important for establishing contact, e.g., a boy who displaced his anger at being rejected and beaten by his father against principal and teacher would challenge the teacher from his back seat by tapping feet, pens, ruler. Having ignored her signals, the boy responded when she would come to him, touch his arm or shoulder, talk quietly, giving him a choice, trouble or work with help thrown in.

3. *Mutual involvement.* An altercation in a playground game fades when the teacher inquires as to who is winning and whose turn is next and stands by for a few moments "talking up" the game. In the classroom, if the teacher gets around fast to those likely to have difficulty in getting started, she can work with them and get them underway. Particularly with young children, adult participation in getting started smooths progress.

4. *Unexpected affection.* In the face of frustration or difficulty an extra shot of encouragement or affection can provide the needed lift to cope with the situation.

5. *Tension release through humor.* Humor serves to make painful experiences tolerable, probably because it gives distance and perspective to an otherwise unhappy situation and counterbalances the other emotional feelings. Example: a teacher discovered a newspaper cartoon comparing her to an old Ford like a crank up front. She could have shown her vulnerability by demanding acknowledgment of ownership and threatening to retain class until the culprit confessed. Fortunately, she read it and smiled, showed it to the class after opening exercises, joining in the laugh, finally asking who had discovered the cartoon. The perpetrator, relieved of any hostility or guilt, took a bow for his wittiness. Teacher smiled and dropped the matter. At a later opportunity, while granting the boy a favor, the teacher gave a slight rub-in: "Even if you think I'm an old crank."

6. *Hurdle help.* Anticipation of or alertness to insurmountable obstacles—a boy who refuses to give an oral report before a class cooperated pleasantly when seated between friends at

a table. A slight shift in arrangements avoided the failure and frustration and provided a means to a solution.

7. *Interpretation.* Helping children understand situations or their own motives. A youngster who overly criticized his work was helped to understand that he was afraid others wouldn't like it and was attempting to avoid their criticism.

8. *Regrouping and restructuring.* Changing seating arrangements, groups, and teams creates opportunity for change just as shifting activities can avoid individual and group failure. Where progress was coming slowly on a difficult song, the good singers became bored and the poor singers gave up. Switching to an easier song before the lesson disintegrated, the teacher then returned to the difficult song for a short time each day until mastered.

9. *Tool and space restriction.* "Let me keep your ruler until you need it" or "Turn the pages this way and the town can buy us a new film strip instead of having to replace a torn book" are illustrations of avoiding undesirable behavior and gaining cooperation through limits placed on tools and equipment.

The discussion so far has been concerned with general aspects of programs designed to foster personal development in children — a strategy for such a campaign. At this point, consideration of specific behavioral problems is desirable. Four classes of problems related to adjustive behavior (see Chapter 4, Figure 9) will be considered: Aggression, low self-esteem, withdrawal, and fear, anxiety and tension. In each of these four major categories the behavior will be defined, its manifestations described, associated causes and underlying conditions identified, suggestions for treatment indicated, and necessary precautions noted. The intent is to identify a series of possible actions which can be taken by the teacher, leaving the specific selection to her judgment after appraisal of the causative conditions.

AGGRESSION

In the desire for well-ordered classes teachers are inclined to view any aggression as undesirable or symptomatic of maladjustment, particularly that which challenges their authority. The higher the grade level of the teacher, the more likely this is to be true. As our society is now organized, aggressiveness is an asset; the problem is not to suppress it but to channel it. Furthermore, aggression can be a clue to frustrating conditions in the classroom which should be changed. Often this will require adjustments of the learning tasks, classroom regulations, and other administrative aspects of the situation rather than in the children, for the aggression may be indicative of unsuitable conditions. Finally, all behavior has to be viewed with the understanding that all normal children display some problem behavior at some times, with the number of forms and frequency of symptoms varying with the age level of the child.

The kind of aggression which comes from exuberance and self-confidence is to be distinguished from that which arises from frustration, rejection, or indulgence. And even the latter is of concern only when it becomes excessive, is destructive of objects, injurious to persons, or arouses feelings of guilt. Aggression directed to overcoming the source of frustration is desirable provided it is expressed in socially constructive channels. Aggression may take both physical and verbal forms, e.g., direct attack against a condition or person, or criticism, censure, ridicule, and belittling. It may be attitudinal as well, i.e., hostility. It will take various forms depending upon the needs, goals, and emotions with which it is associated. For instance, coupled with a need for independence, one sees disobedience, defiance of authority, argument with authority; coupled with need to dominate, one sees rough treatment of others, physical or verbal attack, and, carried to the extreme, sadism, satisfaction derived from hurting and injuring. Where controls are inadequate, temper tantrums and destructiveness occur. Typical behavior evidencing aggression is fighting, quarreling, teasing, bullying, physical attacks, temper tantrums, pouting, and sulking. Generally unhealthy aggressive behavior occurs as attack against person or property, as antagonism in interpersonal relationships, or as resistance to authority.

Any one of several types of causative conditions may be associated with aggression.

1. Physical and health factors. In some instances organic factors result in the child's being unable to control his anger and aggression. Fatigue can contribute to greater frustration and anger.
2. Family relationships and home conditions. Parents who lack affection or quarrel, and those who reject, domineer, or indulge the children create aggression in them. Negative attitudes in the home, or conflict between attitudes held by home and school can create the aggression. Parent favoritism toward other children and sibling rivalry are contributing conditions. Economic deprivation or failure to satisfy material needs of child can lead to aggressive acts.
3. Rejection by age mates can be an associated factor.

4. Personal feelings of fear and inadequacy can lead to aggressive behavior.

Generally, the teacher's approach will be to

1. Reduce frustration by alleviating conditions causing aggression.
2. Reduce the level of aggression by helping the child to recognize, accept, and express his feelings and displace them in other activities.
3. Direct the aggression into useful channels.

More specifically, regarding

Teacher attitude, behavior, and relationship

1. Accept feelings—one can listen without approval or disapproval.
2. Reduce demands on child.
3. Show concern for child—get well card or telephone call if sick; walk to corner or to bus with child; etc.
4. Accept and share confidences with child.
5. Accept child's offerings or compliments graciously.

Environmental changes

1. Create permissive atmosphere in classroom.
2. Arrange party, dramatizations, or other activities permitting activity, expression, and relaxation.
3. Arrange with mothers for invitations to rejected child.
4. Give individual challenge.
5. Attempt modification of parental attitudes, demands, etc.
6. Provide parents necessary information on child development.
7. Identify the situations in which aggression is likely to occur and avoid those which trigger aggression.

Personal modifications

1. Check health record—physical examination may be in order.
2. Share in children's personal experiences.
3. Help children develop hobbies.
4. Help child develop special skill or talent which will provide him recognition.
5. Compliment children on positive actions and appearance.
6. Establish and maintain limits for indulged child's unchecked aggression.

Group influences

1. Friendly, receptive attitude towards group on daily arrival.
2. Help children establish friendships—via sociometric grouping, time for interpersonal contact, group work, etc.

3. Determine child's status in group and work to improve it.
4. Determine needed, missing skills in class and work to create.
5. Cite specific examples of aggression from literature and discuss with group.
6. Involve children in role-playing to assist them to develop more adequate behavior patterns and self-understanding.
7. Group discussion and analysis of problem situations which arise.

With these general indications of the treatment possibilities for aggressive behavior, consideration can be given to specific kinds of aggression and their treatment.

RESISTANCE TO AUTHORITY — TEMPER TANTRUMS

Temper tantrums can be resistance, insubordination, or direct disobedience expressed in word or action. They are a more violent emotional display used by younger children who have not developed more successful or specific ways of expressing their feelings. Temper tantrums manifest themselves in diffuse outbursts, having little real direction, but producing kicking, screaming, breath-holding, minor self-injury, destruction of objects, name-calling, sulking, and pouting. The older child's resistance may not be as dramatic, appearing in argumentative, antagonistic actions directed toward teacher or group, attention-seeking displays, leading group into disapproved actions and behavior.

Temper tantrums are the end result of a training process in which the child has learned he can refuse to comply with parental request and/or obtain his own way by the emotional outburst. Where a pattern of temper tantrums exists, the parents are likely to have been indulgent and oversolicitous of the child's needs by complying with his demands and failing to provide sufficient discipline to aid the child in learning to control his aggressive impulses. In some instances, the child may have adopted outbursts of temper in modeling his behavior after a parent.

Underlying Causes. Underlying causes of negativism, rebellion and associated conditions may be:

1. *Physical:* fatigue, malnutrition, illness; atypical physical development and appearance; failure to develop essential sport or athletic skill.
2. *Environmental:* rejecting, domineering or over-critical parents, rigid discipline or excessive demands in home or class room; socio-economic differences between home and school.

3. *Personal and social:* failure in school, lack of ability, rejection or scapegoating by peer group, feelings of inadequacy or rejection.

Indicated Treatment. Indicated treatment varies with the causative factors and suggests that the first course of action is identification of underlying causes through observation, and identification of situations triggering behavior through comparison of child's behavior in different areas of life.

Action during a tantrum

1. Use restraint only if risk of injury or damage to property likely.
2. Remove child from precipitating conditions and from group. Temporary isolation usually restores quiet. Presence of one person may be needed.
3. Wash hands and face and suggesting child lie down may help overcome crisis.
4. After the rage subsides re-establish friendly contact—suggest something to eat, or a pleasant activity. Do not try to re-establish the activity which caused the event. Re-establish yourself, reassuring the child of your understanding without indulging in a lecture.
5. Ignore the tantrum as much as possible; allow child graceful way out to save face. Reasoning or pleading during the tantrum is wasted effort.

At other times

1. Encourage reflection and introspection by encouraging child to explain how he feels about slights and injustices through conversation if the child is articulate, indirectly through writing or drawing if not.
2. Help the child to recognize his own tendencies by pointing out these tendencies in others as they manifest themselves. Often the anger rages so suddenly that the child is swept away by it without being able to realize what has occurred and see his behavior as it is. He may literally be blind to his own behavior.
3. Avoid situations which trigger the behavior. Move in on situations quickly at beginning, e.g., by calling child to you, by diverting attention to another event or question. Permit the child to leave the room and arrange for him to go somewhere —library, nurse, principal—when he feels he can't control himself.
4. Make it clear to the child that you understand and are willing to help him. Try to prop up or restore his ego instead of dis-

ciplining him, e.g., avoid talking about the event—this irritates, shames, and creates unnecessary guilt.

Precautions. If the child shows little gain in his ability to control his emotions over a period of time or to recognize his behavior and avoid events which contribute to it, specialized help is indicated.

A distinction should be made in the course of action to be taken with a child whose temper tantrums result from indulgent parents who have failed to teach the child to restrain his aggression or limit his demands and with a child whose anger results from excessively demanding or rejecting parents. Rejected children who feel antagonistic towards the world are likely to feel threatened by teachers who are considerate and kind. In order to justify feeling rebellious, they have to prove to themselves that the considerate teacher is really not offering love but just disguising her rejection. They prove this by provoking anger and punishment by the teacher. Therefore the teacher wants to avoid head on clashes with rebellious children. In contrast, the indulged child who has never learned to check his aggressive impulses and whose concept of the world is that all persons exist to fulfill his desires has to learn that he must limit his behavior and adapt to others. In this instance, fair but firm and fixed limits should be set and maintained.

NEGATIVISM

Negativism is an expression of the child's refusal to accept a plan of action proposed by others. Like aggression, it is a normal response during pre-school years. In the period between two and three, children are apt to show signs of balkiness and other inner tensions. The child has difficulty making up his mind. Negativism re-occurs in six- to nine-year-olds — the period when the child tries to throw off his dependence on his parents. The child reacts with contrariness and a refusal to do as directed. Rejecting demands is often accompanied by stamping and shrieking "NO." It can be manifest in behavior varying from mild irritation and resentment to violent breath-holding reactions. It may take the form of weepy submission or the doubtful hesitant reactions of a neurotic type.

Associated Conditions. Excessive negativism is apt to be present when the parents and teachers are overauthoritative, overcritical, or overcorrective. Dawdling is a mild form of negativistic behavior. Here the child fears to disobey openly and lingers over the unpleasant task.

Treatment Indicated. Negativism should be treated by avoiding opportunities for the child to refuse. When possible, he should be placed in a group and not receive any individual instruction or requests. Nagging and coaxing should be eliminated. Try to keep from interfering too much; do not hurry the child. Get things accomplished without raising issues.

Precautions. If negativism continues, it can be one of the most serious of all types of mental disturbances. The individual becomes unresponsive in terms of group participation and refuses all outlets and opportunities for cooperative expression. Negativism is harmful because the reaction is a response to situations usually accompanied by emotional feeling. It is likely that such response may lead to more serious forms of adjustments motivated by fear and frustration.

DESTRUCTIVE AND ASSAULTIVE BEHAVIOR

Resistance to authority is also expressed in domineering, bullying, destroying, truancy, stealing, and hostility.

Bullying. Occasional fighting among children is normal and should not concern adults. The child who fights more than he plays with other children needs help, particularly if the children are younger and smaller. The bully intimidates smaller children by domineering, belligerent behavior which frequently vanishes in the event of a showdown. Bullying may be accompanied by cruelty directed against animals, insects, etc.

Underlying Causes. Underlying causes and associated conditions may be:

1. *Physical:* an undersized child compensating for size, or a retarded child.
2. *Environmental:* Displacement of aggression resulting from deprivation or tensions in other areas of life; a child subject to bullying and nagging by parents, siblings, or older children; identification with admired aggressive father, or reaction to anxious or over-protective mother.
3. *Personal-social:* Reaction to general feelings of insecurity or inadequacy or rejection by parents, teacher, or classmates leading to an attempt to gain recognition by strong-man role or appearing tough.

Indicated Treatment. Efforts to increase cooperation with other children instead of antagonizing them is indicated for treatment in order to give him satisfaction from working with rather than against other children. Supervised work in play groups, YMCA, Boy Scouts, etc., can be valuable. Several popular children can also be encouraged to begin to include the bully in activities and be friendly with him. As aggressive children develop friendships and a place in groups, they adopt the group's code of fair play. Invariably, the bully's isolation permits him to avoid "playing fair."

Group discussions of reactions to being teased and picked on and sociodrama can be useful. Ask the class if anybody has ever been picked on by a bigger boy. Ask several to relate the incident. Choose one of the children, ask him to select another child and treat him as he was treated. After the enactment, ask each to describe their feelings in the situation. Re-enact several episodes, putting the bully into the recipient role to help him understand the feelings of others. If the bully can be induced to help or assist a younger, smaller, or weaker child on a regular basis, the responsibilities and the satisfaction derived may convert aggressiveness into protectiveness. It is not unusual for the bully in a class to be an older child who has been retained one or more times. Inspection of sociograms shows these children to be rejected or isolated in high frequency by their younger classmates, which induces or contributes to their aggressive actions. Further, teachers tend to reject or be highly critical of such children. Actions taken to help the child establish himself in the group and enjoy the class activities lead to a reduction in frustration and a lowering of aggression.

Destruction. Destructiveness is an ultimate form of aggression, manifesting itself in the breaking, cutting, smashing, and burning of objects as a means of releasing anger, reducing tension, relieving frustration, and acquiring revenge. In many instances, the less serious forms of destruction such as scratching paint, writing on walls and furniture, and scribbling in books, proceed almost unconsciously as tensional outlets. At such times, effective control can result from group guidance which calls attention to the action, allows for ventilation of feelings, and develops a group attitude opposed to such actions. Prompt repair of minor damage by administrators alleviates the condition or reduces it because children are more likely to expand on damage once begun than to start new damage.

Vandalism. Vandalism is a more serious and deeper-seated problem. Destruction of school property is often symbolic aggression against school or public authority and stems from cumulative frustration in school and in the community. Identification of the individuals responsible for the destruction is needed. When such events are repeated or occur on a large scale, a community social problem is likely to exist which can only be solved by concerted action of community agencies.

Truancy. Truancy could be grouped with avoidance mechanisms as readily as with aggression, for the simple unlawful absence from school invariably masks a complex behavioral problem. In effect, truants are hitting back at school, family, and community. Many truants have a history of early habit problems. As they grow older, they become more defiant and aggressive and have difficulty accepting any routine. Truancy is of major concern because of its association with delinquency. The truant child's actions indicate that something is wrong in the school or family environment. The school is the only social agency in a strategic position to take preventive action.

Truancy may arise from many causes — bad companions, poor home discipline, the attraction of the streets, desire to earn money, broken home, distaste for a particular course of study or dislike for a particular teacher. All these can play a part in a poor adjustment to school, but an unstable home life seems to be a leading cause. Physical and mental characteristics are commonly associated with truancy. Physical defects, atypical appearance, and mental retardation contribute to feelings of inferiority which leads to isolation and hostility towards school and classmates. School is a frustrating or threatening situation to be avoided. Many children, unable to do the required school work and outdistanced by younger classmates, avoid the humiliation and boredom by becoming truant. Low capacity to tolerate frustration is frequently seen.

Early action is indicated to forestall the development of a habitual pattern of truancy. Chronic absenteeism is the seedbed of truancy for it fosters avoidance mechanisms. In primary grade children, absenteeism can suggest a fear of school — an unwillingness to meet the new demands, jealousy of a younger child able to remain at home with the mother, fear that the parent will not be home on return. In such instances, continuous contact of the child with the school is important. Where truancy is associated with school failure, adaptation of tasks to the level of the child's ability is indicated. In such instances, where the child is not likely to obtain recognition or maintain status with his classmates by his academic prowess, another means of obtaining recognition and status is needed. Research has demonstrated that helping children develop individual specialties in which they are the "class expert" contributes to better social adjustment. Praise and reward granted for behavior other than sterling academic performance suggests to children that one can be a commendable person for qualities other than "brains."

A number of specific items can be listed but the main import of all is that of giving the absentee the feeling of being wanted by teacher and classmates, that school can provide satisfaction, and that failure is not inevitable.

1. Get-well notes and cards from teacher and classmates to absent pupils creates a feeling of being wanted.
2. Keep a class record of absence excuses, preferably having it maintained by one or two chronic absentees. Use this as a basis for class discussion, leading into attention to real reasons and stated reasons, and finally inquiring into events in school which contribute to absenteeism and tardiness.
3. Schedule special events for days on which absences occur in higher frequency, such as on Monday and Friday. Organizing team activities is helpful for it creates a sense of responsibility to the group.
4. Dramatize situations which contribute to absenteeism — visiting relatives, avoidance of test days, athletic events, etc. (see N.E. Shoobs, *Psychodrama in the schools*. New York: Beacon Press, 1944, monograph)
5. Where a group is repeatedly absent, identify the group leader, and make special attempt to utilize his leadership ability in classroom and school situations which necessitate his presence in school.

Stealing. Stealing is a common occurrence among elementary school children. It most commonly manifests itself in shoplifting, theft of a toy or object from another child's desk or coat, and theft of money from the teacher's or child's desk or from a parent's purse. In older children, stealing and truancy frequently occur together, and the thefts are often a gang phenomenon, thus, more resistant to correction.

A number of associated causes are observable:

1. An underdeveloped sense of the meaning of personal posessions.
2. Need or desire for an object without other means of obtaining it.
3. Inadequate social and moral standards in the home.
4. Neglect by parents, permitting child to acquire inadequate moral patterns or adopt gang code.
5. Retaliation, vindictiveness, or jealousy resulting from parental rejection or favoritism towards another child.

6. Susceptibility to suggestion by other children—often accompanied by feeblemindedness.
7. Desire for recognition and acceptability by other children.
8. Economic deprivation.

The nature of the object taken and the use to which it is put by the child are helpful indicators of the cause. Comparatively meaningless objects or thefts which appear unintelligible suggest a symbolic theft indicative of frustration or tension in other areas: need for affection, retaliation for rejection, relief of frustration from failure, and attempts to gain recognition from peers. Thefts of money or toys, particularly where the results of the theft are shared, indicate desire for acceptance and shared activities.

The actions taken to correct the problem have to be consistent with the cause indicated. Primary grade children can easily take possessions of others because of their appeal without knowledge that such action is stealing, or with indistinct knowledge of the difference between borrowing and stealing. In homes where one's toys may be taken and used by anyone, where the child does not have a place for "his" things, and where property rights are not recognized, a child's notion of "personal property" will be quite fuzzy. In these cases, the child has to be taught the concept just as he has to be taught the "place" concept in arithmetic addition. If group acceptance is needed, it should be provided, relieving the child of taking recourse to theft in order to have something to share. Where economic deprivation exists, the basic problem is that of providing a child with opportunity to earn what he needs rather than steal it. Unfortunately, our society provides less and less opportunity for children to earn money through services offered or materials sold. Even the childhood lemonade stand appears as an anachronism in these days of refreshment vending machines, but opportunities can be created in school and community and often Parent-Teacher funds can be appropriated to more useful purpose than buying school equipment.

In almost all instances protection of children especially vulnerable to such behavior is needed through reducing temptation — teachers and class being careful about leaving or exposing toys and money — and increased supervision. However, a theft should be seen as suggesting a problem to be solved by either educational or therapeutic means. An environment in which children are not exposed to temptation and which does not give them opportunity to learn to respect another's possessions and control their impulses fails to provide for the character development needed to live in this world. The task for teachers is to provide manageable amounts of temptation for children in their course of development.

Where the stealing is pathological, therapy is needed. The pathology may lie with the child or it may be social. In areas of high delinquency, community forces aimed at controlling the harmful influences are needed. Where the pathology is individual, as in the case of a child who is retaliating against rejection or sibling rivalry, psychiatric treatment of child and parent is essential. Rarely is group action indicated, i.e., talking to the class about a particular theft and expressing the hope that any one who knows about the event will tell the teacher, and admonishing the class about such actions. Children respond to such exhortation by feeling guilty and angry and prone to reject the culprit, real or fancied. It is much preferable to identify the child personally and speak directly and privately with him. Although specific group action is not suggested unless the problem is common to the group and resulting from group codes, indirect instruction regarding honesty, property, respect for person and property, etc. is in order.

SUBMISSIVE REACTIONS

Repeated failure to find satisfaction for needs can result in a sense of defeat and unwillingness to continue to strive to achieve. Low self-esteem, lack of confidence, feelings of self-pity, over dependence, and attention-seeking are results. The need for self-esteem and mastery have their origin in the attitudes of approval that parents exhibit towards the child and the concept that he builds of himself from the appraisals he encounters. Several years of effort are expended in first controlling and mastering his body and emotions, and then striving to meet and master the environment.

The school plays an important role in the concepts that children develop of themselves and the sense of competence which they develop. The school presents children with a series of intellectual, physical, and social tasks to be mastered, linked with a constant feedback of approval of performance, both through specific approval of performance by teachers and through comparison with the performance of classmates on similar tasks. Failures are inevitable. They are greater where uniform standards of performance are expected of all. Failure is tolerable where it leads to ultimate success or where it is counterbalanced with sufficient success. Continued failure produces a sense of defeat, feeling of inadequacy, and, with these, a lack of self-esteem and confidence, occasionally aggravated by feelings of self-pity.

Such attitudes manifest themselves in avoidance or fearfulness in new situations, refusal to join group activities, attention-seeking to compensate for inability to obtain legitimate recognition, and reluctance to try — in short a giving up in the face of what appears to be an inability to succeed.

In general, treatment requires massive doses of guaranteed success to restore self-esteem and confidence and increase the child's capacity for tolerating frustration. A variety of actions can contribute to overcoming feelings of inadequacy:

1. Provide differentiated assignments for class members geared to the observed level of performance and on which the success of the inadequate child is assured.
2. Praise work done correctly and avoid criticism of parts which are incorrect, avoid any reprisal for failure.
3. Give subtle encouragement during assignments.
4. Assign very little work at one time, simple enough for assured success.
5. Foster and give special instructions in development of game skills.
6. Search for any actual or potential special interests or capabilities and promote their development.
7. Have child compete with himself, not other pupils.

ATTENTION-SEEKING

Attention-seeking is an attempt to obtain recognition and compensate for failure or unfulfilled needs in other areas. In the school, showing-off and clowning are the most common forms of attention-seeking, but it manifests itself in diverse forms, many of which basically represent an attempt to obstruct or frustrate parents and teachers:

1. *Physical and emotional manifestations* — Crying, temper outbursts, vomiting, refusing to eat or sleep, and pretending illness.
2. *Social and behavioral manifestations* — clowning, showing-off, buffoonery, outspokenness, teasing, requesting help in routine situations, exhibitionism, and stealing.

Basically, the causative factors are lack of praise and affection, or events which produce a drop in amounts of affection, e.g., birth of a new child, divorce of parents, working parents.

Treatment is aimed at identifying the causative factors and instituting actions, where possible, to alleviate them. Where environmental conditions exist which cannot be affected by the teacher, her best action is to provide the child with legitimate avenues for obtaining recognition, plus ignoring the attention-seeking behavior so that it isn't reinforced through success. It should be noted that seeking the attention of teachers is legitimate and desirable activity for children. Teachers are important persons in children's lives, and children legitimately desire and seek their attention. When this is given voluntarily to all children, exaggerated efforts to seek attention are less likely. A word of caution is needed due to the tendency of many teachers to label any disturbing behavior as attention-seeking. The fact that a given sequence of behavior attracts the teacher's attention does not establish this as the primary goal of the behavior. For instance, destructive behavior may result from frustration or hostile feelings and serve to relieve those feelings. The fact that it captures the attention of the teacher does not mean that the basic motive is a desire for recognition.

OVERDEPENDENCY

Overdependency is an insatiable desire for emotional support expressed in failure to emancipate oneself from adult direction or from the group sufficiently to maintain originality, individuality, and some degree of independence and self-direction. Overdependent children find themselves feeling inferior and inadequate, threatened with failure in the face of too-high expectation imposed by self or adults. They show little initiative and lack self-direction and initiative. Socially, the overdependent child appears inept, immature and ill-at-ease, unable to express his own opinions or individuality.

Associated Conditions. Conditions which may accompany overdependency are:

1. *Physical:* Small size and stature can cause a feeling of lack of force or power with other children. Physical handicaps contribute to feelings of inadequacy and fear of rejection by others.

2. *Environmental:* Dominating, over-protective parents who deny the child opportunities for essential growth experiences, e.g., helping him whenever he encounters slight difficulties; not letting the child fight his own battles. Lacking opportunity to develop needed skills leads the child to overdepend on parents, creating a circle of mutual need. Being an only child whom the parents value highly or being from a broken home and fearing the loss of the remaining parent are contributing conditions.

3. *Personal-social:* Children too long dependent upon parents will lack ability to associate with other children, will appear and feel inadequate and ill at ease. Tendency to be withdrawn and shy for lack of experience; tending to go along with the group thought and opinion in preference to expressing his own ideas and feelings. These children, dependent upon adult direction, are likely to lack originality, imagination, and initiative, and find it difficult to adjust to new situations.

Indicated Treatment. Actions taken to overcome the dependency and foster independence include:

1. Refusing to direct child's activities.
2. Encouraging independent steps, however small.
3. Encouraging class discussions of fears, growing up, etc.
4. Avoiding unfavorable comparisons.
5. Showing interest in child and his activities.
6. Listening to and encouraging child to discuss his feelings and fears.
7. Encouraging him to imitate more adequate children in group situation.

Precautions. Don't push the child too quickly; allow him to gradually accept responsibility and become independent. Don't overpraise.

The close relationship between overdependency in children and overprotection by parents warrants some discussion of this. Overprotective parents are excessively solicitous for the welfare of their children and shield them from activity and achievement.

Associated Conditions. Associated conditions may be:

Physical: The child may have a physical handicap or illness or have experienced an early serious or long continued illness requiring constant nursing care by the mother.

Environmental: The lacks that the parents have experienced in affection, success in vocational aims, can be contributory to overprotection. Parents are likely to overdo for a child long awaited; if there were previous miscarriages; an earlier child born dead; or a difficult pregnancy. Only children are often highly valued by parents; first children are commonly oversupervised as a result of parental inexperience. Marital conflict or infidelity can lead to maternal overprotection. Parents may overdirect the child in choice of friends and in extra-curricular activities in efforts to satisfy their ambitions for their children. Overprotection may be masking real rejection (see Chapter 6).

Personal-social: A child too long dependent on his mother is unlikely to be able to take responsibility for tasks or to meet minor problems. In situations which he finds to be too difficult, the child is submissive, obedient, fearful, or withdrawn. Overprotected children are often tense and nervous, reflecting parental worries and anxieties. Such children find it difficult to get along with playmates, are afraid of rough sports, lack courage, are timid and fearful and inclined to play with children whom they can dominate.

Treatment: The actions suggested for the overdependent child apply. Such children need opportunity to have successful experiences in which some degree of independence is exercised. The child can be given increasing responsibility for increased responsibility in study and play schedule. It is helpful if the parents can be encouraged to allow the child to help at home with simple household tasks and to take more responsibility for self-care. Special tasks and small responsibilities in school which can be carried through to success are indicated.

AVOIDANCE PATTERNS

Avoidance behavior takes a variety of general forms intended to provide for escape from painful stimuli or their consequences — withdrawal and isolation, shyness and timidity, fantasy and denial, and, in extreme form, regressive behavior. In school, behavior symptomatic of avoidance pattern is:

1. Disinterested and apathetic about school work.
2. Daydreaming, doodling, staring out windows.
3. Frequent trips for water, pencil-sharpening, lavatory.
4. Participates only when called, speaking only when spoken to.
5. Frequent tardiness and absence.
6. Avoids company of other children.
7. Avoids games, sports, social situations.
8. Behaving shyly, timidly, blushes or pales easily.

Behavior seen outside of school includes:

9. Isolation from activities of other children.
10. Preference for adult company to peers; clinging to adults.
11. Oversleeping, procrastinating, forgetting.
12. Addicted to motion pictures, television, reading, or hobby.
13. Prefers animals to humans.
14. Continually playing with younger children or opposite sex.

The list of underlying causes and associated conditions is extensive, because many events can produce the frustrations which cause a person to consistently remove himself from conflict and painful events, either real or anticipated.

1. *Physical and health factors* — ill health, physical handicaps, unattractiveness.

2. *Personal characteristics* — lack of interests or aptitude, social ineptness, fear of failure, feelings of inadequacy, feelings of guilt or self-rejection, preference for reading or solitary play, ambitions in excess of abilities.

3. *Social conditions* — environmental or cultural impoverishment, excessive mobility and migration of family, minority status or ethnic differences, geographic isolation, poverty, rejection by peers.

4. *Parental causes* — rejecting, threatening, restricting, disapproving parents; demands or ambitions beyond child's capacity; overprotection by parents which restricts experience and limits independent and social activity; identification with fearful and anxious parent.

5. *Educational causes* — unsuitable, boring, or monotonous curriculum; excessively demanding and authoritarian teaching; inadequate materials and teaching; repeated failure.

Withdrawal provides for temporary gratification by reducing tension, avoiding failure, disapproval and humiliation, and escape from problems of competition and cooperation, but eventually it produces a cumulative handicap of isolation from social participation and failure to develop the social skills necessary to effective functioning in interpersonal relationships. The general program of treatment will fall into one of the following courses of action.

1. Identification of isolate, e.g., via sociogram, and of causative or contributing conditions and attempt to alleviate them.

2. Support and reassurance of child to offset feelings of inadequacy — permissive classroom atmosphere, emphasis on praise and recognition rather than blame and criticism, assurance of child of teacher regard and appreciation, repeated success experience in school, with emphasis on the present rather than past or future time orientation.

3. Action to bring child into contact and more effective operation in physical environment through identifying interests, encouraging them, development of skills. Care is necessary not to overwhelm the child with attention or recognition — e.g. begin with comparatively inconspicuous tasks, participation in choral

singing or reading, use of puppets, etc., use of interesting and varied teaching procedures and materials.

4. Action to bring child into contact with social environment — helping child make a friend, bring into small group play without having to take conspicuous role, assist child in development of social skills, encourage participation in club or group activities outside of school.

Shyness and Timidity

The most common form of avoidance is seen in shyness and timidity—being apprehensive and cautious in the presence of others, manifested in hesitant and inaudible voice; easy crying, blushing, and paling; expression of feelings of inadequacy or inferiority; reluctance to enter activities; excessive attention to preparatory acts and details; quietness, seclusiveness, and reticence; and lack of friends or playmates. Every large elementary school classroom has a few shy and withdrawn children. Most individuals are shy under some circumstances, wanting to participate but fearful about failing or not performing as well as others.

In addition to what might be considered the natural causes such as prolonged illness, geographic isolation, non-social parents, and foster home placement resulting from a broken home, the primary cause of shyness or timidity appears to be the failure of the child to develop feelings of adequacy and confidence in his ability to meet new situations. Parents who demand excessively high performance, who repeatedly criticize the child for his shortcomings, or compare him unfavorably to another child, and parents who overcare for a child, denying him the experiences he needs for growth and leaving him fearful that he can't succeed, are typical producers of timid children. Secondary and contributing causes are observed in school where the honors go to the child who is self-confident, poised, and aggressive and who monopolizes participation. The fearful child is ill-equipped for the competition. Harsh and demanding teachers, failure experiences, placement in a group with which the child cannot compete effectively, aggravate the condition.

Treatment basically consists of helping a child overcome his deficiencies, real or perceived, and building his particular strengths in behavior valued by children. A number of specific suggestions from which appropriate actions may be selected:

1. Check on physical condition and health record.
2. Be certain work and standards are suited to child's ability.

3. Give explicit directions to make starting easy for the child.
4. Let recitation take place in very small group before expanding to a larger one.
5. Discover activities and tasks in which the child can readily achieve legitimate success: music, hobbies, athletics.
6. Maintain social contact with child—greetings in hall, chatting on playground.
7. Show by manner of talking and attitude that you look upon him the same as others.
8. Freely give approval and regard, particularly in initial stages of program.
9. Permit dependence in early contacts. Success experiences, increased confidence, and a period of dependence are needed prior to "cutting the apron strings."
10. Assign inconspicuous tasks such as rearranging bookcases, getting materials ready, etc. prior to asking him to participate in more conspicuous phases of activity.

Certain precautions are indicated in working with shy children. Nagging, scolding, ridiculing, and forcing the child into social activities should be avoided as much as overprotection. However, appealing the behavior of such a child—quiet, unassuming, and pleasant—his shyness presents a potentially serious handicap in adult life and is a possible forerunner of more serious emotional illness.

FANTASIES AND LYING

Fantasy and lying are forms of relieving tension and escaping unpleasant or threatening circumstances by withdrawing from external sources and stimulation or denying their existence. Daydreaming can serve several useful purposes—rehearsal of contemplated action, experiencing events in anticipation, imaginative fancy, recreation, and escape. Nearly all persons daydream and certain common fantasies appear—social success, power, prestige—which usually are a picturing of events as we wish they were. Generally, daydreams are a harmless means of tension reduction. When the pattern becomes habitual or serves to reduce effective effort to solve problems, treatment is necessary.

Causative factors and contributing conditions include:

1. Impoverished environment—drab and uneventful home life; poverty; and dull and boring school regime.
2. Unsympathetic treatment—teacher or parent nagging; unwillingness of adults to listen to difficulties, problems, or fears of child.

3. Repeated failure experience and inability to master school tasks.
4. Excessive discipline often combined with physical punishment.

Teacher actions should be directed to providing and encouraging social contacts and satisfying objective tasks as balancing factors to beguile the child out of his dream world into the reality world. Criticism, ridicule, and punishment for daydreaming are more likely to perpetuate it than reduce it. Initially, action has to proceed on two fronts, the first being that of real success and the second that of capturing the child's dreams and causing them to lead to activity in the real world.

For instance:

1. Opening exercises may include: What I dreamed last night.
2. Teacher may start an art lesson by describing a dream she has had, then asking children to draw a dream, subsequently tell about it.
3. Give children a few moments with eyes closed to dream of something, then tell about it.
4. Start stories with a lead line or two, e.g., "Susan was crying . . ." and have children finish the story. In upper grades, each may write, then tell his ending.
5. Have children make and tell about their wishes.
6. Discussions on many related topics help: making wishes come true; adventures I dream about; my imaginary friend.
7. Have children dramatize their wishes or dreams and other children guess their meaning.

Each of these procedures has the effect of bringing the dream-world of the child into the open and permitting its association with the events in the classroom. Classroom procedures which facilitate contact between children—group work, mutual help and quiet conversation—reduce opportunities for isolation. Fantasy can sometimes be turned into a social asset by creating the position of class storyteller. In short, efforts to interrupt, channel, and reduce the opportunity for persistent daydreaming are the order of the day.

A word or two of caution is advisable—if the fantasy is symbolic of an emotional disturbance, actions directed at the fantasy will only be partially successful as long as the basic problem goes unsolved. Second, no attempt should be made to interpret the dreams. Although dreams may represent unfulfilled wishes, their significance is only ascertainable through knowledge of the private symbol-world of the individual.

Lying is an attempt to escape the consequences of actions or avoid responsibility by denial of the truth, falsification, or deception. Several forms do not constitute cause for concern because they are readily understood—the imaginative tale or exaggeration, confusion or faulty memory for events which produces inaccurate reporting, and the white lie told out of loyalty to protect a friend or at the direction of parents. Where lying occurs for personal advantage or gain, to cause injury to another person, to gain attention, or to avoid the consequences of one's action, cause for concern exists. Fear, defense, and desire for approval are major contributing factors— fear of punishment, disapproval, ridicule, and loss of affection and friendship; defense to cover up shortcomings and dereliction, to prevent loss of face, to avoid feelings of guilt and feelings of inadequacy, and to offset social and economic deprivation; and desire for approval of adults and peer group. In elementary school children, lying is usually situational rather than a general condition. Further, it is related to the severity of punishment probable and to group codes of behavior, e.g., loyalty to friends. The specificity of lying to particular situations makes it readily subject to change through modification of environmental conditions. Actions possible are:

1. Explore and understand specific causes of lying incidents.
2. Establish climate where frankness is permissible and fostered.
3. Avoid harsh punishment and reduce the threat of punishment.
4. Insure honest behavior in adult contacts inasmuch as imitation of adult behavior is common.
5. Plan so consequences of behavior give insight and stem naturally from act if possible.
6. Utilize child's imagination in socially approved channels.
7. Help child to understand it is to his advantage to tell truth because advantage rarely comes from lies.
8. Help group to develop appreciation of honesty through discussions of principles of stories.
9. Foster acceptance by classmates.
10. Establish avenues for obtaining social approval and recognition.

Care must be taken that casual slips are not exaggerated into lies by adults. Considering the extent of adult exaggeration for purposes of effective narration, latitude should be provided for children. Cross-examination and leading questions are to be avoided, especially with young children whose appreciation of objective truth is less than their desire to please adults. The resultant tendency is to shift their story to provide what they believe the adult wishes to hear.

Regressive Behavior

It is not uncommon for children on the threshold of a new achievement to revert temporarily to earlier levels of performance: a child learning to walk reverts to creeping; an older child breaks his toilet habits with the arrival of a new baby; fatigued children may engage in thumbsucking. Regression often appears as a response to a baffling problem or frustrating task.

School presents many situations where the learning task is difficult, where the child experiences a gap between his ability and the demands to be met, and where failure and frustration have to be met. In these instances, regression is a typical response. The only concern is the degree and duration of the regressive behavior. The natural physical and psychological bent of children is a desire to grow, not retreat. This impels them to strive for more mature behavioral levels. Thus, regressive behavior, which is readily observable, can be considered a normal deviation where there is observable cause and the duration is short. Within short periods of time, a child should become sufficiently adjusted to the new situation to permit him to regain previous levels of performance.

In the school environment, treatment includes planning programs of activity which enable the child to find satisfaction in daily activities. Care is needed to avoid a continuous series of frustrations. When regression appears to become the major adaptive pattern of the child rather than response to an immediate situation, psychiatric treatment is needed.

FEAR, ANXIETY, AND STRESS

Fear

All children experience stress and tension and develop fear and anxiety at one time or another. Each of these has its useful role in protecting the person from danger. The nature and form that fear and anxiety take in children is related to their developmental stage. Certain fears are characteristic at particular ages and reflect the conceptual development of children (see Chapter 12). Although children vary in their predisposition to fear as a result of differences in emotional stability and security in social and family relationships, their fears have the advantage of being specific situations, and the individual fear can be treated directly.

To discourage irrational fears:

1. Make the child feel safe, not only from bodily harm, but from ridicule and failure.
2. Provide verbal explanation and assurance. Sudden exposure to unknown situations can be frightening. Analysis and explanation reduces the unfamiliarity.
3. Confidence and calmness of adults is likely to be imitated and goes far to dispel fears.
4. Provide contact with the feared stimulus, first in small degree and then in gradually increasing intensity until it is encountered in its entirety.
5. Present the feared object in conjunction with another to which the child has a strong positive reaction. The appeal of the latter will overcome fear of the former.
6. Teach the child a skill which enables him to cope with the feared situation. Competence dispels fear.
7. Encourage the child's curiosity with respect to the feared stimulus. Fear not only contains a desire to withdraw but also a curiosity about the feared objects. Familiarity will reduce fear.
8. Utilize group situations in which the child will accompany and duplicate other children, gaining assurance from their willingness, and not wanting to appear less brave.

ANXIETY AND STRESS

Anxiety differs from fear in being non-specific, a vague state of insecurity and fearfulness which isn't associated with any specific situation. One feels threatened without apparent reason. Anxiety is usually accompanied by evidences of stress—shown by specifically induced changes in physical functioning. Both are evidenced in physical and emotion symptoms:

1. *Physical*—Nail-biting, ear-tugging, teeth clenching and other motor symptoms; complaints of diffused aches and pains; and psychosomatic disturbances such as loss of appetite, overeating, gastrointestinal disorders, sleeplessness, skin rashes, vomiting, and others.
2. *Emotional*—restlessness, impulsiveness, irritability, blushing, compulsions, phobias, and hyperactivity.

A variety of underlying causes and associated conditions have been recognized—physical, emotional, and environmental—but their primary effect is that of creating a condition of tension, fearfulness, inadequacy and insecurity in the face of environmental pressures.

The individual feels threatened by an impending catastrophe as a result of contributing factors and experiences which leave him feeling unable to cope with events.

A wide range of recommendations are to be found in the literature for reducing anxiety and stress and increasing the child's ability to cope with events:

1. Create understanding and feeling of competency.
2. Take the uncertainty out of situations by definite instructions and definition of task.
3. Encourage analysis by the child of new situations and a problem-solving approach including identification of possible solutions.
4. Encourage the child to make small or partial decisions and judgments.
5. Create a situation in which adequate performance is probable and his security and self-esteem are associated with adequacy of performance.
6. Maintain a reassuring and positive attitude toward child's performance. Positive teacher attitude towards child is a major asset.
7. Reward efforts to try to reach goals.
8. Let the child know that his personal acceptance is not jeopardized by inadequate performance.
9. Do not push a child beyond his capacity.

SEXUAL IRREGULARITIES

Sex irregularities are disturbances which include such behavior as masturbation, exhibitionism, use of profanity, sexual fantasying, and rejection of appropriate sex role. Although elementary school years have been termed a latent period of sexual development, abundant evidence from many cultures indicates that children manifest several kinds of sexuality: (1) curiosity about sex differences and reproduction, (2) masturbation for direct satisfaction itself and as a form of tension reduction, and (3) non-erotic body contacts with parents as an expression of affection. Although such actions may be carried to extremes and present a problem, a certain amount is to be expected in most children. Persistent sex irregularities are usually symptoms of deeper fear, tension, or guilt. The child may reject conventional standards of conduct to gain attention or defy authority; or he may use sexual fantasy as an escape device.

Failure to accept appropriate sex role appears with boys' playing with dolls, playing girls' games, and dressing in girls' clothes. Girls are more acceptable as "tomboys" than are boys in a girl's role. Sex deviations are more likely to be treated as serious because of the embarrassment and shock experienced by parents and teachers.

The aura of secrecy surrounding sex leaves the child uninformed by parents and misled by his peers. He can easily obtain the impression that sex is dirty and that his natural impulses and curiosity are also dirty. His curiosity leaves him feeling ashamed and guilty. It is necessary to know the underlying causes to treat sexual irregularities and deviations effectively. Nevertheless, sex education is usually an effective starting point inasmuch as removal of the mystery surrounding sex and satisfaction of curiosity about sex will do much to help a child obtain an understanding of the connotations of his behavior. The typical embarrassment which most teachers and parents feel about the subject restricts their capacity for direct action.

REFERENCES FOR PART FOUR

Allen, F. H. *Psychotherapy with Children.* New York: Norton, 1942.

Alschuler, Rose and Hattwick, Laberta. *Painting and Personality, A Study of Young Children.* Chicago: University of Chicago Press, 1947.

Axline, Virginia. *Play Therapy.* Boston: Houghton Mifflin Company, 1947.

Bettelheim, B. *Love Is Not Enough.* New York: The Free Press, 1950.

Cruickshank, William M. (Ed.). *Psychology of Exceptional Children and Youth.* Englewood Cliffs, N. J.: Prentice-Hall, Inc., 1955.

DeHaan, R. F. and Kough, J. *Teachers Guidance Handbook, Vol. II, Helping Children with Special Needs.* Chicago: Science Research Associates, 1955.

Detjen, E. W. and Detjen, Mary. *Elementary School Guidance.* New York: McGraw-Hill Book Company, Inc., 1952.

Harms, Ernest. *Handbook of Child Guidance.* New York: Child Care Publications, 1947.

Leuba, Clarence. *Personality: Interpersonal Relations and Self-Understanding.* Columbus, Ohio: Charles E. Merrill Books, Inc., 1962.

Louttit, C. M. *Clinical Psychology of Children's Behavior Problems.* New York: Harper & Row, Publishers, 1947.

Lowenfeld, V. *Creativity and Mental Growth*. New York: The Macmillan Company, 1957.

Moustakas, C. E. *Children in Play Therapy*. New York: McGraw-Hill Book Co., Inc., 1953.

Prescott, D. *The Child in the Educative Process*. New York: McGraw-Hill Book Co., Inc., 1957.

Redl, F. and Wineman, D. *The Aggressive Child*. New York: The Free Press, 1957.

Rogers, Carl R. *The Clinical Treatment of the Problem Child*. Boston: Houghton Mifflin Company, 1939.

Part Five

SOCIAL DEVELOPMENT

Chapter 14

SOCIAL INFORMATION

The focus on individual differences and methods of teaching which has characterized teacher training in recent decades has left the social-psychological aspects of the classroom the most neglected factor in learning. True, the theme of democratic atmosphere has been incorporated into many phases of teacher education, even with some confusion between democracy as a system of political organization and democracy as a form of interpersonal relationships. Yet, the so-called democratic atmosphere identifies a form of leadership by the teacher, leaving untouched important aspects of group life in the classroom. Individual human beings can develop only in interaction with other humans. Their capacity to give and receive love and hatred, to be loyal, honest, and courteous, or deceitful, dishonest, and craven, to work and function in groups toward social goals, are an outgrowth of the quantity and quality of the relationships they have with other persons as they grow to maturity. The very term interpersonal relationships conveys an aseptic note devoid of the emotional attunement in the interplay of human lives.

If anything, educators tend to ignore and leave to chance the quality and functioning of the human interplay and its effect on development and learning. Tasks are individually assigned, and graded. Reward and recognition is awarded on an individual basis. The child is taught that he rises or falls according to his personal achievements only. Yet in the complex society of today, there are few achievements which can be gained or problems that can be solved independently. Most all involve combined efforts of many individuals. The capacity of individuals to mobilize their skills and function as effectively in groups as alone is crucial to human survival.

The major problems of abuse of power, intolerance, and discrimination which confront us nationally and internationally are present in each classroom. The bullies exist, and the hostility between Catholic, Protestant, and Jew, between permanent resident and migrant, between refined and rough, occur in any community with any heterogeneity or any changing in progress. It is convenient to ignore their existence, for a direct attack on any of them can unleash forces and open feelings for inspection that are as dangerously volatile as those involved in desegregation. Yet an alternate approach is possible through systematic efforts to create relationships which can dissolve the barrier and create group relationships which provide for individual and group health.

It is not sufficient merely to mix children, for as important as physical proximity may be to contact, it does not insure an amalgamation any more than pouring cocoa in milk produces chocolate unless abetted by special stirring. The starting point is some knowledge of the existing patterns of relationships within a class. Human beings placed in groups set up some process of social interaction. Within most classes, regardless of whether they have been together for a short time, certain children occupy places of high status, certain others are outcasts, group attitudes develop which affect the work and play of the group. Cleavages between subgroups develop, some the function of teacher attitude, others the result of group relationships. The cleavages which exist in the community carry over into the classroom and affect the status and acceptance of class members.

If a teacher is to work effectively with a class of children she has to learn something of the existing relationships. She needs this knowledge not only for attaining the academic achievement she desires, but also to create interpersonal relationships between the children which will provide the setting for social group. One cannot be an effective member of an adult group if he has not had some experience as an effective member of a child group. Just as our physical skills are determined by the motor and sport activities in which we engage, and our intellectual achievements are a function of the learning experiences, so is our social capacity a result of the interpersonal experiences we have in family and child groups. What teachers often overlook is the fact that for children the functioning on a par with other children, and the acceptance and approval by other children is more significant for development than the approval of adults.

Teachers think they know the social relationships which exist within a group. They think if they let children choose their own seating and play arrangements they are providing for adequate personal relationships. They deceive themselves. Few teachers can predict more than 25 per cent of the choices which will be made by a group of children when allowed to choose their companions. These few will usually be primary grade teachers who are sensitive enough to observe children's overt approaches to each other. As the hand of conformity and etiquette settles down on child life, the impulses to seek out others for fraternization are gradually dampened; by graduate school a student may sit all semester in a classroom with persons whom he feels he would like to know better but never make the overt approach. He may even go through the entire semester without learning the name of the person in the seat beside his.

If the teacher is to manage the social relationships, she needs a map of the social terrain, just as she needs a profile of individual abilities if she is to foster scholastic development. A sociogram is a map of the social relationships existing in a group and a device for charting the progress in such relationships from time to time. Like any map, it requires skill to make and skill to read. The first step is the making of a sociogram.

ADMINISTERING A SOCIOMETRIC TEST

A sociogram is a means of presenting graphically the structure of relationships existing within a group at a given time. It portrays the forces of choice, of attraction and of group life. The sociometric test is made by asking the children to choose among themselves a preferred companion for some school activity or situation which is real to them, and arranging the result in a diagram called a sociogram. Its success is dependent on several considerations:

1. The basis for choices should be real, not hypothetical.
2. The presentation should enlist enthusiasm.
3. The presentation should encourage spontaneous choice.
4. There should be an immediacy to the choice situation.
5. Confidential nature of the choices should be insured.
6. Time limit should be set for the new arrangement.

The following presentation would be typical:

As you know, you are now in seats which I assigned to you at the beginning of school. But you also know we work better and learn better when we are with people whom we enjoy working with. So I think we could work out a better seating arrangement.

> To do it, I have to know the people with whom you would like to be seated, because each of you know with whom you enjoy working the most. I'm going to give you a piece of paper. Put your name on the top line. Then list the boys and girls with whom you'd like to be seated. Write your first choice first, then your second choice, and so on. When you have finished writing the names of the children you want to sit with, give me the paper. I will be the only person who will see it. You may choose anyone who is absent today as well.
>
> After I have all the papers, I will re-arrange the seating plan so that next week everyone will be sitting by at least one person whom he chose. We will keep this arrangement for six weeks.

The presentation should be casual rather than formal, enthusiastic rather than indifferent. The enthusiasm of the teacher is contagious, and enlists the spontaneity of the children in making their choices. If they get the impression that the sociogram is an academic exercise for the teacher or that she doesn't plan to carry it through, they will respond in similar fashion. Any connotation of a test should be avoided. By stressing the fact that the choices will be confidential, freedom to express choice is made possible.

It is important to encourage the children to make more than one choice in order to have flexibility when the time comes for arranging groups or seating plan. Sometimes this can be done by specifying that the children are to make two or three choices, but ordinarily someone will ask how many choices they can have. The teacher can respond they may make as many as they like. Most children will make two or three, few will make more than five, an occasional child will make none or only one choice. The advantage of unlimited number of choices lies in its providing a measure of the spontaneous expression of positive feelings between group members. An occasional child will be reluctant to make any choices, perhaps fearful that he may not be chosen by others. The teacher should be careful not to suggest how to choose, but merely tell the child that he knows best whom he'd like to choose and whom he'd feel most comfortable with. If the child writes nothing or "anyone," this should be accepted without further questioning. Ordinarily, it is more convenient to the teacher to pass out the paper or cards for the choices, in order to avoid the varied sized pieces which would otherwise be used. The uniformly sized paper is more conveniently handled in making the sociogram.

It is often appropriate and desirable to instruct the class to turn the paper over and on the back write the names of any persons with whom they would prefer not to sit or work. It is as important to be as aware of points of tension or conflict as points of rapport in an effort to establish groups which will function adequately. One advantage the elementary teacher possesses is the frankness of the child in this age range, and the capacity to be direct, provided the teacher can speak of such feelings without apology or embarrassment. The groups can be told that as each person knows there are some people with whom we work effectively, some with whom we don't work as well. It is perfectly natural that this should occur. They know best if there are any people with whom they feel particularly uncomfortable. If they will write those names down, the teacher will do her best to arrange the seating to avoid this.

With first and second grade children arrangements can be made so that the children tell the teacher their choices, coming up to her desk so that they are out of hearing of the other children. The choices can be entered directly onto the tally sheet. The time lost by having to listen individually to each child is gained by making a direct tally. As soon as the children can write the letters of the alphabet, they can make the choices, if, in preparation, each child is instructed to write his initials on a large card and stand it on his desk, permitting other children to write down the initials of the person they choose on their paper.

Seeking Reasons for Choices

One can do a much more effective job of grouping if one knows the reasons for the choices which have been expressed. Seldom do the persons chosen appear the same to the teacher as to the child doing the choosing. Usually children make their selection on the basis of their emotional response to the person of their choices, on the basis of common experience, or mutual interest. The teacher usually perceives a child in a different frame of reference, for she tends to see him as attractive or not in accord with his academic performance and classroom demeanor. To inquire into the reasons behind the choices made yields valuable information on the qualities behind the choices, in the persons which the children think important, and to the individual needs of children which find expression in their choices and rejections.

Two procedures are available for obtaining the reasons for the choice. The simpler is to ask the children, after they have their choices completed, to write down their reasons for choosing each person beside the name. A more time-consuming arrangement, but more instructive procedure, is to obtain the information by interview. First, have the children complete them, then on the following day report to the class somewhat as follows:

> Yesterday you chose the persons with whom you'd like to sit (or work, play, etc.) and I've been working on a new seating plan for the class based on your choices. To do a good job of this I need your help. Several of you have chosen the same persons, yet I can't give each of you that particular choice. I'm sure I could work out a satisfying arrangement if each of you would tell me how you happened to choose the persons you did. Would you come up to my desk sometime during the day and let me know your reasons, then I could pool this information and work out the most satisfactory arrangement. Whatever you tell me will be confidential, nobody else will know it.

While this latter arrangement takes more of your time (yet it is surprising how easily it fits into the flow of the day), it is more informative because children will say more than they will write. There is a hidden dividend which contributes to more effective working relationships—the fact that many children have not had the experience of telling a teacher about something of personal importance. Usually their verbal interchange deals more with school work or passing events, and as often as not they are being told more than telling. It is a new and valuable experience to discover the teacher to be a sympathetic listener, and this experience can be an important first step in establishing communication with children which makes it possible "to reach them" on other subjects.

To bring this about requires your avoiding any appearance that the children are having to justify their choices. Their choices exist. The making of a sociogram did not suddenly create the feelings of affinity and hostility between the members of the class; it is merely a means of gaining access to them. If you ask the class to tell you *why* they chose whom they did, you convey the impression that they must justify their choice. This they will do, seeking the most socially acceptable reasons, which may or may not be true. Asking the class to tell you "how they happened" to choose whom they did implies that the choices are accepted and taken for granted. Similarly, in the conversation about their choices, difficult as it may be, restrict yourself to the role of listener. Avoid being a questioner or evaluator. A receptive facial expression, a slight nodding of the head, a vocal "m-m-m-m-" will obtain more information than questions. Occasionally, the reasons for choosing which are given will not meet with your approval. Should you, at these moments, frown or reveal disapproval by your facial expression or by sound, you will shut off what the child has to say, for they are sensitive to and fearful of adult disapproval. A word of admonition to the child at this point may leave you with the feeling of having done your duty as an adult, but, unfortunately, will accomplish little more than to advise the child that it is dangerous to tell this teacher. Children receive so many admonitions that whatever their misbehavior it is not from lack of adult words, but rather from being unable to reconcile conflicting impulses and discover satisfactory channels of expression. By learning something of the attitudes and feelings which exist, one can plan a course of action aimed at a solution on a more constructive basis.

To illustrate the value of understanding the reasons behind the choices, glance at Figure 2. The most rejected person is Barnes. This came as a shock to the teacher, who anticipated his being highly chosen and with good reason. Barnes was the ablest scholar, he was athletically skilled, he was attractive and well-built physically, he had been elected by the pupils as a class-officer. He was popular. How then account for the seven rejections? Without knowing the reasons, the answer remained a mystery; with the reasons, it appeared that Barnes' seemed too capable. The class appreciated his abilities and would choose him for jobs which needed doing, but when it came to choosing a person with whom to be close, Barnes didn't appeal to them for his very capability made them more conscious of their own inadequacies.

Occasionally, after listening to the reasons given, the teacher can elicit further information, particularly about the less chosen persons in the class by inserting a declaration which appears as a question: "You didn't choose Paul?"

With both the choices made and the reasons given, the teacher has assured the class that these will remain confidential. This promise must be respected, and under no circumstances should the teacher reveal the choices made or received. A child should never be informed as to how many people chose or rejected him, nor should a parent be informed of the child's standing on the sociometric tally.

THE SOCIOGRAM

The initial step in making the sociogram is to enter the choices on a tally sheet. This is illustrated in Figures 1 and 2. Arrange the choice(✓)slips in alphabetical order. Write the names in the same

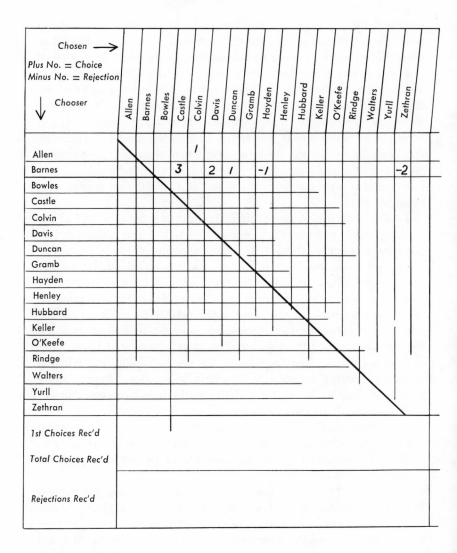

Figure 1.　First step in tallying sociometric choices.

alphabetical order (include any children absent) across the top and down the side of a piece of graph paper. In the class shown, the first slip is that of Allen, who made only one choice—Colvin. Hence, a 1 is entered under Colvin's name. Barnes made three choices and two rejections. His first, second and third choices are indicated by the numbers 1, 2, 3 opposite his name, and the rejections by negative numbers. Different colors may be used if desired to indicate the differences. Once all the choices are entered, the total number of choices received by each person is obtained by counting the number of choices in each column and recording the total at the bottom of the tally sheet (see Figure 2). With the tally sheet completed, the sociogram can be constructed.

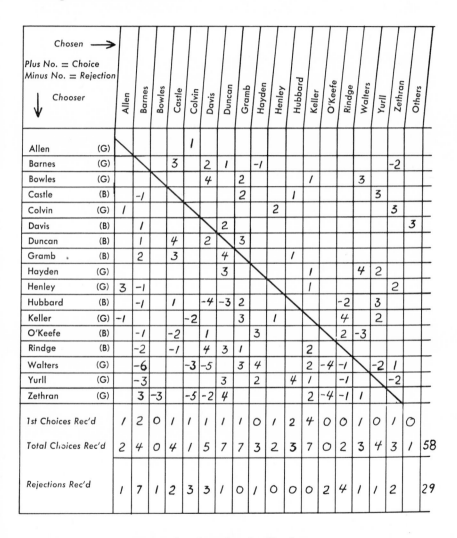

Chosen → Plus No. = Choice Minus No. = Rejection ↓ Chooser		Allen	Barnes	Bowles	Castle	Colvin	Davis	Duncan	Gramb	Hayden	Henley	Hubbard	Keller	O'Keefe	Rindge	Walters	Yurll	Zethran	Others
Allen	(G)				1														
Barnes	(G)			3	2	1		-1										-2	
Bowles	(G)				4		2						1			3			
Castle	(B)	-1					2					1				3			
Colvin	(G)	1							2									3	
Davis	(B)		1					2											3
Duncan	(B)		1	4		2			3										
Gramb	(B)	2		3			4						1						
Hayden	(G)						3						1			4	2		
Henley	(G)	3	-1										1					2	
Hubbard	(B)		-1	1	-4	-3	2								-2	3			
Keller	(G)	-1			-2			3			1				4	2			
O'Keefe	(B)		-1	-2		1		3							2	-3			
Rindge	(B)		-2	-1	4	3	1					2							
Walters	(G)		-6		-3	-5		3	4				2	-4	-1		-2	1	
Yurll	(G)		-3					3	2			4	1	-1				-2	
Zethran	(G)	3	-3		-5	-2	4						2	-4	-1	1			
1st Choices Rec'd		1	2	0	1	1	1	1	1	0	1	2	4	0	0	1	0	1	0
Total Choices Rec'd		2	4	0	4	1	5	7	7	3	2	3	7	0	2	3	4	3	1 · 58
Rejections Rec'd		1	7	1	2	3	3	1	0	1	0	0	0	2	4	1	1	2	29

Figure 2. Completed tally sheet.

It is possible, on occasion, to omit the making of the sociogram and proceed to arrange seating or groupings directly from the tally sheet, but this would occur after the teacher had developed a working knowledge of the groupings within the class derived from earlier sociograms. From the tally sheet, the teacher can detect mutual or reciprocal choices—pairs of squares equi-distant from the diagonal line and containing a number. For instance Allen and Colvin chose each other. Both squares (which fall an equal distance from the diagonal) contain the number of the choices. The choice is mutual regardless of the degree of the choices involved—see Gramb-Duncan. Three pupils stand out for the choices received—Duncan, Gramb, Keller; two because they are isolates (not chosen), Bowles, and O'Keefe. Some children are nonexistent, exciting little in the way of choice or rejection (Bowles), while others arouse strong feelings (Barnes). Some children are emotionally expansive (Walters), making a large number of choices or rejections; others are emotionally inhibited (Allen).

A blank piece of paper divided down the middle will serve to begin the making of the sociogram. By virtue of the fact that only a few choices will be exchanged between boys and girls (approx-

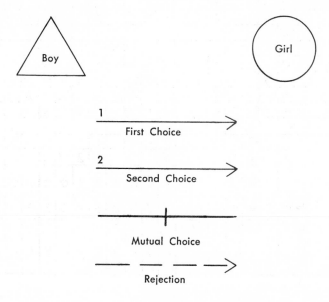

Figure 3. Symbols used in sociogram.

BOYS   GIRLS

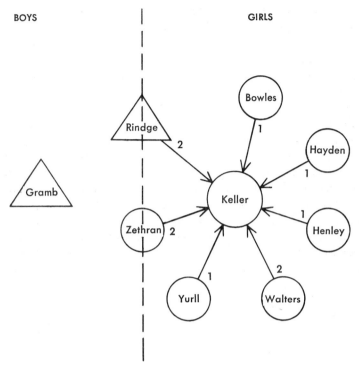

Figure 4. First stage in constructing a sociogram.

imately 25 per cent in the first grade, decreasing to 3-4 per cent at sixth grade) most of the boys will end grouped together on one side of the page, and the girls on the other. Choose the most highly chosen boy and girl, in this instance Gramb and Keller. Gramb is selected in preference to Duncan because more of the choices he received are first or second choices.

In making the sociogram, only first and second choices are used initially to avoid too complex a pattern of lines. Subsequent choices may be added later, although usually they effect little change in the appearance of the social structure of the group. They frequently are of use as possibilities in arranging seating plans or work groups where neither of the first two choices are possible. Next, draw a circle for the most highly chosen girl on the girls' side of the page and a triangle for the most highly chosen boy on the other side. Around each draw a triangle for each boy choosing that person and a circle for each girl. These choices may be found by locating the names opposite the numbers 1 and 2 in the column. For example, look in the column under Keller's name. Looking down the column one sees the numbers 1,1,1,2,2,1,2. Opposite these numbers are the names Bowles, Hayden, Henley, Rindge, Walters, Yurll, and Zethran, six girls and a boy. Around Keller's circle draw six circles each with a girl's name in it and a triangle for the one boy. The triangle is placed nearer to the boys' side of the page on the assumption that his other choice will likely be for a boy. From each of the figures draw an arrow pointing to Keller and enter a number indicating whether the choice was a first or second choice. Figure 4 represents the sociogram at this stage of development. Having one choice entered for each of seven people, the next step is to enter their other main choice. We have Bowles' first choice for Keller; we need her second choice. Finding this by looking along the row opposite her name, we see she chose Gramb as a second choice. This is entered on the sociogram (Figure 5), and we follow by entering Hayden's second choice which we discover to be a mutual choice, i.e., the two chose each other. Mutual choices are indicated by a line crossing

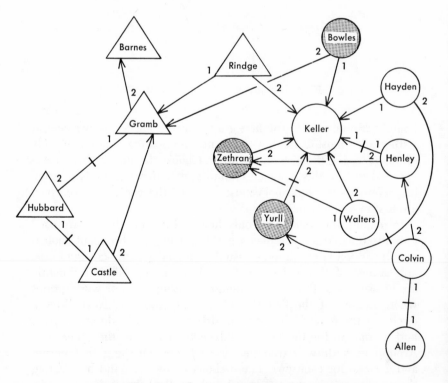

Figure 5. Second stage in constructing a sociogram.

the choice line suggesting that the choices are meeting other (see Figure 3 for symbols used).

Following this procedure, we continue until we have two choices entered for each person appearing on the page, including Keller and Gramb. When a name appears which has not been encountered previously a triangle or circle has to be added to the page and the name entered. When one gets to Gramb, neither of his first or second choices (Hubbard, Barnes) appears on the page. Draw a triangle, enter Hubbard's name, draw the arrow from Gramb to Hubbard indicating it to be a first choice, another triangle for Barnes with an arrow indicating second choice. Then proceed to enter Hubbard's choices, and Barnes'. In this way, all the names are gradually entered. Occasionally, one encounters breaks between the choice pattern. For instance, when the circle of girls was completed, a check of the tally sheet would show that Colvin and Allen had been omitted. These would be added adjacent to any person either had chosen, in this case Henley. Figure 5 shows the sociogram completed to this stage. One might think it would be simpler to enter a circle for each girl and a triangle for each boy on a piece of paper and then begin to draw in the choice lines. Appealing as this idea may seem, it usually ends in a chaotic jumble of lines.

After all the names have been entered, it is usually necessary to re-arrange the position of some of the figures in order to simplify the appearance of the sociogram and by so doing clarify the pattern of choices within the group. Compare Figures 5 and 6. The shaded figures in Figure 6 have been moved from their original position in Figure 5. The effect of the move is to shorten the lines, uncross lines, and make the network of choices more intelligible. The key spot held by Keller among the girls is immediately apparent.

The boys are divided into two main clusters and one peripheral group—Gramb, Hubbard, and Castle; and Barnes, Davis, and Duncan with O'Keefe and Rindge on the fringes—in this case, the highly skilled in sports, the moderately skilled, and the unskilled. Gramb appears as a possibility for closing this breech, but this is getting ahead of events, for later chapters will consider the use to which sociograms can be put.

THE SOCIAL DISTANCE SCALE

Closely allied to the sociometric test is the Social Distance Scale. It has the advantage of requiring each student to give a reaction to

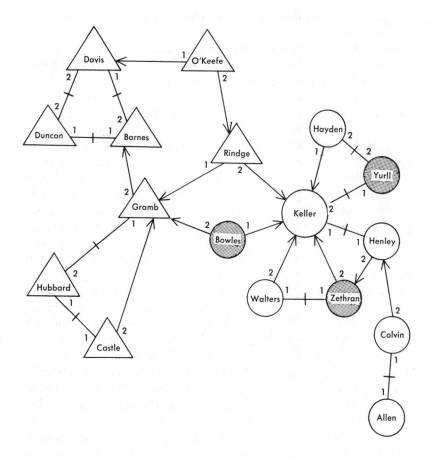

Figure 6. The completed sociogram.

every other student in the classroom. Its disadvantage, particularly
with increasing age of the group, is that it mixes the criteria upon
which choices are made. With young children, the sociogram one
obtains when children are asked to indicate their best friends, and
the sociogram when they are asked whom they would like to work
with on a project does not differ much. With the increasing differentiation that comes with age and experience, the sociogram differs
according to the basis upon which the choice is made. For instance,
in your own choices, you would choose differently when asked to
indicate the persons with whom you'd like to go on a vacation trip
and the persons with whom you'd prefer working on a curriculum
committee. Your choices would differ according to the potential of

the individuals for satisfying the demands of the particular situation. Young children do not make these distinctions. They tend to choose those who are emotionally satisfying to them. But with increased experience, one chooses differently for a task to be done than for emotional responsiveness. The Social Distance Scale has the disadvantage of combining the question of friendship and work.

Figure 7 shows a Social Distance Scale. Each pupil is provided with a sheet of paper which lists the names of all members of his class. He can either write his name in the upper corner, or circle it where it appears in the list. The effectiveness of this instrument, like the sociogram, depends upon the relationship which exists between the teacher and pupils. If she has rapport with this class

MY NAME *Judy Henley* Names of class in Alphabetical Order	5 Would like to have this person as one of my very best friends.	4 Enjoy being with this person. Would like to have him in my group but not as a close friend.	3 Would like being with this person once in a while but not often.	2 Don't mind his being in our room but don't care very much for him, and I don't want to do anything with him.	1 Do not like this person and wish he weren't in our room.
Allen				✓	
Barnes				✓	
Bowles			✓		
Castle			✓		
Colvin			✓		
Etc.					

Figure 7. Social Distance Scale.

and they trust her, she can expect valid responses. If they suspect a hidden motive in the use of the instrument, they will exhibit resistance, either through modifying their responses or resisting signing their names. The general conditions relating to the presentation of the sociometric question apply to the Social Distance Scale. The teacher, in a natural manner, attempts to enlist the enthusiasm and cooperation of the class.

> As your teacher, I not only try to help you learn the many things we study in class, but also to help you get along better with each other. I think I can do this better if I know how you feel about each other. We don't like all our friends in the same way, we like some more than others. There are some people for whom we don't care at all.
>
> This check list will give you a chance to tell me how close an acquaintance you would like to have with the other boys and girls in this room. Place a check after each name in the column which describes how you feel about that person. Nobody will see your papers but me.

Two procedures can be followed in having the class check the sheet. The first, and most effective with younger groups, is to read aloud the instruction in column (5) and then tell the class to place a check after each person's name for whom the description is suitable. Then read the phrase in column (4) and have the class check each person towards whom they hold this viewpoint. After reading each of the headings, each pupil should check to make certain he has not overlooked any names.

The alternate procedure is to read aloud all of the headings, then instruct the class to place a check after each name in the column which appropriately describes their feelings.

After collecting the papers, a social distance score can be obtained for each pupil by assigning a 5,4,3,2, or 1 for each check given, and obtaining a total score. For instance, Allen's score could be:

1 person checked a 5	5
2 people checked a 4	8
6 people checked a 3	18
4 people checked a 2	8
3 people checked a 1	3
Group Social Distance Score for Allen	42

If, for instance, Allen had checked a three after each name on her page for the group of 17 shown in the sociogram in Figure 6, her expressed social distance score towards the group would be 48 (16x3) because she would have no check after her own name. Relatively speaking, she feels more positive towards the group than they do towards her. The quickest way to obtain a score is to hold the pages evenly together and flip through the pages, adding the score as one goes.

The comparison of the two scores is not particularly significant, unless there is a considerable gap between the two, for rarely will a person get and give exactly the same score. Of greater significance is the spread in scores between the highest and lowest; are there many persons with closely grouped scores; are there clusters of scores a few high, a number moderate, a few very low; and, finally, what is the average expressed-score of the class. For instance, if the impossible occurred and everybody in a group of 21 checked a 5 for each person, the average expressed-score would be 100. At the opposite extreme, if everybody detested everybody, the average score would be 20 (20x1). One would anticipate a score somewhere between 50-70 as an average.

Before leaving the point of scores, it should be mentioned that one should not interpret them in the same manner as achievement test scores or intelligence test scores. Arbitrary numbers have been assigned. If the numbers assigned ranged from 5-9, the scores would change accordingly. There is no metric quality involved in the scores. From the comparisons made during the preceding discussion, the relative standings and the differences are the significant features to be observed. One more difference should be noted. Some authors reverse the order of the assigned scores on the Social Distance Scale, giving a 1 to the most favorable attitudes and a 5 to the least favorable. In this instance, the persons with lowest scores hold the most favorable positions, i.e., there is the least social distance between them and members of the group. The purpose in reversing the order is not to be different but to align the scores with the customary usage of higher scores being considered more favorable.

THE GUESS-WHO TECHNIQUE

A procedure which may be utilized by teachers in determining interpersonal attitudes between members of the class is the Guess-Who Technique. Essentially, this consists of providing the class with a series of descriptive statements mimeographed on paper and asking each person to insert the name of the person who fits the description. Each person is asked to indicate as well the particular phrases which he feels describe himself. By this means, a comparison of the way in which a person sees himself and the view others hold of him may be compared. The unanimity or occurrence of opinion can be compared as well as the degree of reactivity of the class to any one person.

The word descriptions offered below are adapted from Cunningham,[1] but variations for different age level or grade level may well be considered. Two types of descriptions appear, those incorporating aspects of behavior which are readily observed, and the other including expression of feeling and attitudes which involve a more subjective evaluation of the actions of a child or one's response to him. For instance, "Here is someone who is always telling on others" describes actual behavior, while "Here is a boy who would prefer to be a girl" or "Here is someone who doesn't care if he is the center of attention" requires an interpretation of behavior or an inference regarding whatever motivates a given individual. The descriptions should illustrate how a child appears to other persons, e.g., cheerful, unpleasant, attractive, etc.; how he relates to others (the roles he plays relative to the group), e.g., helpful, leading, submissive, bullying, etc., or the feelings or attitudes he reveals by word and deed. Both positive and negative statements should be included in the descriptions to provide for a range of judgment. The teacher may, if she chooses, include statements descriptive of her relationships, e.g., "Here is the person who irritates the teacher, here is someone who always wants the teacher's help, here is someone whom the teacher picks on, here is someone who the teacher especially likes." Space should be allowed between phrases in the following list for several names.

Guess Who

Directions: Here are some word pictures of members of your class. Read each statement and write down the names of the persons whom you think fit the description.

You may write as many names as you think belong with each description.

You may mention the same person for more than one description.

When you find any that you think fit you, write "myself."

If you cannot think of anyone to match a description, just skip it and go on to the next one.

You have as much time as you need.

Now you are ready to begin:

[1]Ruth Cunningham and associates, *Group Behavior of Boys and Girls.* New York: Bureau of Publications, Teachers College, Columbia University, 1951, pp. 419-422. Material used with permission.

1. Here is someone who finds it hard to sit still in class—always on the move.

2. Here is someone who works quietly without moving around all the time.

3. Here is someone who likes to talk a lot, always has something to say.

4. Here is someone who doesn't like to talk very much, is quiet even when nearly everyone else is talking.

5. Here is someone who plays active games like baseball, football a great deal.

6. Here is someone who seldom plays active games, but prefers to read or sit and play quiet games.

7. Here is someone who is always ready to take a chance at things that are new or unusual, is never worried or frightened.

8. Here is someone who is always worried or scared, who won't take a chance.

9. Here is someone who always knows how to start games or suggest something to do that others like to join in.

10. Here is someone who waits for somebody else to think of something to do and always likes to follow suggestions that others make.

11. This person always seems to have a good time wherever he is and enjoys things very much.

12. This is someone who never seems to have a good time and doesn't enjoy things very much.

13. This is someone who always is cheerful, jolly, and good-natured—who laughs and smiles a great deal.

14. Here is someone who always seems rather sad, worried and unhappy—seldom laughs or smiles.

15. Someone who is thought to be very good looking.

16. Someone who is thought not to be very good looking.

17. Someone who always tries to be neat and clean.

18. Someone who never tries to be neat and clean.

19. Someone whom everybody likes to have around.

20. Someone whom nobody seems to care much about and isn't noticed much.

21. Here is a girl who likes to read boys' books, play boys' games, or would prefer to be a boy.

22. Here is a boy who prefers girls' books and girls' games, or would prefer to be a girl.

23. Here is someone who enjoys a joke and sees the fun in it even when the joke is on himself.

24. Here is someone who can never appreciate a joke when it's on himself.

25. Here is someone who enjoys a fight; would rather fight than let the other person have his way.

26. Here is someone who will never fight but will always give in.

27. Someone who is always trying to get others to watch what he can do or tell about the things he can do.

28. Here is someone who doesn't care to be the center of attraction.

29. Someone who is always telling others what to do, always bossing.

30. Someone who doesn't mind being bossed.

31. Someone who is very friendly, has lots of friends, is nice to everybody.

32. Someone who doesn't care much to make friends, is bashful about being friends, or doesn't seem to have many friends.

After the sheets are collected, the names can be matched with the phrases on a master tally sheet as started in Figure 8 and Figure 9. The first form provides a total of the designations assigned a child by the other members of the class and himself. A check indicates the phrases which others noted as describing the child; the circle indicates those phrases which he thought described himself. Where the class and individual concur, the check and the circle fall together.

The second procedure (Figure 9) is modeled after the sociometric tally sheet and has the added advantage of revealing who thought what of whom. In this instance, the number of the descriptive phrase is written in the square of the person to whom assigned. For instance,

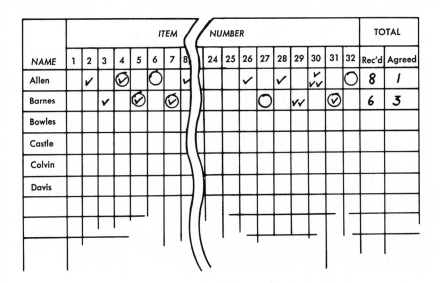

NAME	ITEM							NUMBER												TOTAL	
	1	2	3	4	5	6	7	8	24	25	26	27	28	29	30	31	32			Rec'd	Agreed
Allen		✓		Ⓐ		Ⓞ		✓				✓		✓	✓✓		Ⓞ			8	1
Barnes			✓		Ⓐ		Ⓐ						Ⓞ		✓✓		Ⓐ			6	3
Bowles																					
Castle																					
Colvin																					
Davis																					

Figure 8. Tally sheet for Guess-Who questionnaire. Check indicates what others thought. Circle indicates how person voted himself.

Allen wrote her own name after descriptions #4,6,32 (see circles in Figure 8). She wrote Barnes' name after phrase #15, Davis' after #5 and #25, Gramb's after #4. The more times she used a person's name the more numbers occur under that name, giving an indication of the feelings held and the perception of that person. Looking down the column under Allen's name, one finds the numbers assigned by five of the first seven persons tallied. Two people (Bowles and Colvin) see her as someone who doesn't mind being bossed (#30). Davis agrees with Allen's view of herself (#4) that she is not the talkative type and is quiet even when everybody else is talking. The tally form indicated in Figure 9 is more complex, but more informative, especially when compared with groups on the sociogram, for one can determine how different sub-groups of the class see each other, as well as where the perceptions are held which differ from the common, e.g., Gramb's seeing Allen as cheerful, jolly, and good natured (#13), while all the rest report Allen as quiet and worried.

Through the use of the sociogram, Social Distance Scale, and Guess-Who Technique, a wide range of useful information can be obtained about the social structure of a class.

	Allen	Barnes	Bowles	Castle	Colvin	Davis	Duncan	Gramb	Hayden	Henley	Hubbard	Keller	O'Keefe	Rindge	Walters	Yurll	Zethran
Allen	4 6 32	15				5 25		4			5	13 19 31	27				
Barnes		5,7 27 31															
Bowles	30																
Castle	8																
Colvin	30																
Davis	4																
Duncan																	
Gramb	13																

Figure 9. Alternate tally sheet for Guess-Who questionnaire. Numbers in rows indicate ratings made. Numbers in columns indicate rating received.

Chapter 15

SOCIAL DEVELOPMENT

The pre-school years provide a vital base for the social development that occurs during the elementary school years. A sense of trust or distrust, of taking and giving arise from primary social experiences. The development of speech, the replacement of grabbing, crying, hitting with verbal requests and criticisms, and the regulation of behavior by words are essential steps to interpersonal and group participation. By the age of four, short-term cooperative activities occur, although unless an adult is available to help at critical moments, the duration is necessarily short. The initial step in the differentiated roles which are essential to highly organized groups is found in the complementary role-playing by children of doctor and patient, parent and child, teacher and pupil. The acquisition of learned social motives is evidenced in rivalry and competition, in the seeking of praise and attention. Transitory efforts at group leadership occur.

From the pre-school years to adolescence, dramatic changes occur in children's social development. The first stable friendships, the development of small groups, the participation in larger-scale class activities, the shift from the undifferentiated popular games of hide-

and-seek to the highly organized team sports of baseball and football with sharply defined differences in role and function, occur during these years. The translation of moral precepts from the verbal level to the behavioral level in the observation of rules governing group behavior and group codes of ethics, and with it the parallel adoption of group attitudes and prejudices, makes the elementary school years crucial to social development.

If the sense of trust and confidence in adults is a primary product of the pre-school years, the sense of trust in peers and belonging to and acceptance by a group is an important product of the early school years. Regardless of the size of family or the range of play contacts, nearly every child finds himself one of a group of thirty children in school faced with the task of establishing his place in the group on the basis of his personal qualifications and abilities as seen by his classmates.

Several characteristics of the social development of children during the elementary school years are briefly traced to provide a descriptive norm of the general trends. These characteristics are the relationships of the child with adults and peers, group organization, and moral development.

SOCIAL RELATIONSHIPS

Age 5-7 General. The child entering school for the first time at age 5-6 begins a second stage in the process of socialization. He is expected to conform to the more formal requirements of school routines and accept the impersonal authority of the teacher, meet the demands of his age group and learn many rules and conventions for living in the larger social world being experienced. This broader experience provides them with a measure of what they can do compared to their classmates. They are susceptible to feeling inadequate when their performance does not equal that of their classmates.

Their increasing capacity to communicate verbally with others facilitates cooperative effort, but generally their sense of shared experience, reciprocated affection, and awareness of the feelings of others is limited. If one child starts an activity, the others near him may imitate him by working at a similar task, and by so doing build up some feelings of relatedness from working on a similar task. Nevertheless, their capacity for being involved very deeply with others is limited.

Children of this age love dramatic play in which they spontaneously reenact experiences and imitate adult activities.

Age 5. Relationships with adults are generally smooth and pleasant, with strong attachment for family and protective attitude toward younger brothers and sisters. The five-year-old enjoys company of his own age group and feels rejected if excluded from play with other children. He plays well with other children if the groups are small, in fact he is likely to play better with one other child rather than with more. His capacity for sharing experience and reciprocating affection is limited and difficulties are likely to arise from inability to understand another's feelings or to be aware of the impression he is making on another child.

Age 6. The shift to a full day and the task of gaining emotional freedom from parents, particularly mother, contribute to difficulties in interpersonal relationships. The child of six experiences difficulty in maintaining smoothly functioning relationships with others and reconciling his needs and external demands. He exhibits more aggressive behavior—pushing, grabbing, arguing, bickering, dissension. He is more likely to be domineering with younger children in the family. He shows marked ambivalence in his feelings for mother, now loving her, now hating her. Disobeying mother can be seen as daring and grown up. The six-year-old is sensitive to parents' emotions and tensions, however they try to hide them. Rejection by parents creates compulsive dependency, power striving, aggression, preoccupation with sex. In contrast to relationships with mother, the six-year-old seeks approval of both adults, wants commendation for his undertakings, and thrives on their praise. Friendship pairs are a noticeable characteristic of peer relationships at this age, usually lasting but a short time, with friends and group membership changing from time to time. Marked changes in control of socially undesirable behavior occur during the year, and an increased capacity to recognize and tolerate the privileges and property of others.

Age 7. A noticeable gain in social capacity is evidenced by the seventh year. They are generally much more companionable, both with adults and peers than during the previous year. Often spoken about is the difficulty of making the shift from home to school during the first grade, of leaving a protective environment. There is much more to the task, for the child is required to work a full day at difficult tasks in competition with other children. The school tasks place a heavy demand on the physical and emotional capacities of children and their assurance with respect to their capacity to meet the tasks seldom materializes before the second grade and the seventh year. Both a decrease in concern and an increase in skill contribute to the greater facility of the seven-year-old in his social relationships. As yet, he makes few discriminations along sex lines, sharing games with girls as equals. In fact, it is not uncommon for the seven-year-old to be serious about a girl friend. By the end of the second grade, loosely-formed groups of some stability begin to show up, heralding the emergence of the peer group and the coming precedence it will exert over adult requests in matters of personal relationship and behavior.

Age 8. Eight is an expansive age, physically, mentally, emotionally. He is physically healthier; he perceives contextual reference and implication where previously he saw only parts; he sees himself more clearly as a person involved in participating and responding with other persons. He is concerned about his treatment by adults and desires close, understanding relationships, particularly with his mother, for whom he often expresses strong admiration. His physical activity and noisiness often aggravates adults. Having a special friend is important, although in general, the eight-year-old is group minded, being highly sociable and ready for a wider range of contact, both with peers and other adults.

Age 9. Conceded a degree of independence and detachment, as well as the importance of his group, the nine-year-old's relationships with adults are generally amicable. He desires to please parents, enjoys helping them. He is developing and using a set of standards by which he evaluates and expresses his judgment of adult behavior. However, his scale of values is likely to be sharply black or white. A strong sense of loyalty characterizes the age, loyalty and pride in family, home, and parents, loyalty to friends and gang, even to defiance of adults. He is very sensitive to judgment of his age mates, wants to be like them in clothing and possessions. Difference in interests become noticeable in reading, TV, sports, and other activities. The cleavage between the sexes emerges and will become progressively greater through the elementary school years. Both boys and girls exhibit a strong attachment for members of their own sex.

Age 10. Gets along well with parents as a rule, generally obedient, and enjoying participation in common activity. His greater skill and stamina augmented by greater knowledge makes shared activity with parents more feasible. His capacity for friendship and group relations have been steadily expanding, and, by ten, a child can be readily inspired by group loyalties. He is interested in teamwork and makes a loyal player on a team. He is receptive to social information and able to participate in group discussions. Informal clubs are frequent but often of short duration.

Age 11-14. These years mark the advent of adolescence accompanied by the dramatic changes in physique, awareness of self, and interpersonal relationships. The need to establish independence, the need to establish an appropriate sex role and adequate heterosexual relationships, and the need to establish a meaningful explanation of one's being are all significant factors affecting social relationships during this period. By eleven, children have become aware of parental limitations. They are engaged in a wide variety of activities. Both factors coupled with growth forces exert strong pulls away from parental dependence. Nevertheless, they utilize parents as a base for emotional resources. The relationships need not be characterized by strife if parents respect the child's growing individuality and capacity for independent decision, and do not arouse his guilt feelings as he tries to find satisfaction in being independent. In urban areas the group in which the adolescent is a member is likely to be large, particularly during junior high school years; in suburban areas where propinquinty may be lower, the groups will be smaller. The capacity to function in larger groups is an indicator of increased social expansiveness which will give way to greater selectivity during high school. The seemingly bland assurance of the 13-14 year old and their confidence in their views can be quite aggravating to the adult who is not aware of their sensitivity to adult attitudes and actions even while insisting on maintaining the appearance that their actions are of their own volition and decision. The cleavage between the sexes is at a maximum during the eleventh and twelfth year, but the occurrence of sexual maturity in greater numbers of children each succeeding year up to the eighth grade presages a shift in attitude more favorable to mixed activities.

GROUP CHARACTERISTICS

At all stages of development a child's behavior is interwoven with other aspects of his development. As a child develops, there is an increase in ability to discriminate and undertake more complex activities, an increase in attention span, a better understanding of group values and the opinions and customs of others. With due allowance to the variation introduced by differences in physical environment, family backgrounds, family social activity, and parental occupations, characteristic trends in the group behavior of children are observable.

Age 5. Interested in group activity and group play but with limited capacity to tolerate frustrations, either from waiting turn, attempting performance, or in duration of activity. Interests tend to be self-centered, still very much an individualist, and not really able to cooperate with others. Wants to be part of a group and wants to do the things that merit approval, but has limited capacity to conform and be like others all day long. Will stay with group as long as he enjoys it, but then detach himself and shift to independent play.

Groups are loosely organized, usually small of two to five children. Can play in organized group for 15 minutes or more at a time in group of half dozen children; larger group activities require skillful adult leadership. Children are developing techniques for accepting and advancing ideas, for waiting one's turn, and for understanding feelings of others. Capacity for cooperative play limited, groups disintegrate easily, with individual children being excluded or isolating themselves. A few solitary children still find social satisfaction in imaginary companions. Groups are mixed.

Age 6. Much group play and enjoyment of group activities with group highly flexible and low in organization. The six-year-old is unable to work effectively in large groups, assume leadership of activities where many children are involved, or cope with complex organizational structure. Will enter a game with enthusiasm only to leave it if he does not get the part he wants, if he loses, or if his attention is distracted by another activity.

Identification is more on a one-to-one basis with a particular friend; he has little group loyalty or responsibility. Competitive behavior increases, with boasting and comparisons of size, families, possessions, etc.

Age 7. Groups are showing signs of sex cleavages, with game activities exclusively of one sex. Size and organization of group expanding, with six or seven children playing harmoniously for long periods of time. Able to solve conflicts without much recourse to tears or fighting, to use materials to greater purpose, to wait turn without uneasiness, to carry plans over from day to day.

Both cooperative and competitive behavior is more evident, with strong desire evident to be the winner in competitive games, yet increased capacity, willingness, and interest in undertaking group projects together. Prejudice makes its appearance, partially as a result of growing awareness of social, political, religious, and economic differences among people, partially as a result of growth in group loyalty and antagonism.

Age 8. Groups are short-lived, new ones constantly being formed, loosely organized and based on interests. Group activity enjoyed, isolation deplored and usually abandoned when opportunity for group play presents itself. Play is cooperative, with much rough and tumble activity in boys' groups. Groups are usually small, boys' groups possess rather rigid standards and are more highly organized and likely to function around one or two leaders. Girls' groups have less organization, fewer purposes for existence, and less dependence on leadership.

Success in establishing himself in a group becomes increasingly important, and concern for group recognition and approval is great. Greater concern about measuring up to the standards set by agemates. Prejudices are found among those who have learned it from watching and listening to adults, although in general the child at this age level accepts other children without regard to socio-economic status, color, or other personal characteristics. Adult leadership usually determines whether there is conflict or cooperation within groups.

Age 9-10. Age distinctions become less apparent. Clubs and gangs emerge, often with secret names and insignia, mottoes and passwords, rules and regulations—all evidence of established and organized, rather than evanescent, groups. The impulse to stress secrecy often causes parents to suspect unwholesomeness, but this is not the case. Agemates provide standards of speech, clothes, manners, and games, with adults and teachers providing ideology, morals, etc. The club or gang exists more to solidify a group than for any particular purpose. Generally the clubs or gangs will reinforce attitudes antagonistic to the opposite sex and serve as a basis for gaining some degree of independence from adults. Size of groups likely to range from 3-10 persons.

Comradeship is preferred to competition, boys tending to be less exclusive than girls. Club spirit and class spirit develops and with it resistance to adult direction. Group activity expands from playgrounds to include participation in various community activities—Scouts, Campfire Girls, church groups, community swimming pools, Y's, etc. Prejudices increase as children acquire attitudes from parents, peers, and others whom they admire.

Ages 11-14. Learning to be a good sport, i.e., live in accord with peer standards. Any infringements upon the rules of the game are intolerable to other children. Girls' values undergo a marked change as to their model behavior—from that of neat, quiet, gracious nine-year-old to an attitude of bouyant amicability and rather aggressive good sportsmanship with boys, plus an added touch of glamour in some girls. Boys' values shift from aggressive boisterousness to greater emphasis on personableness, grooming, and social ease. Physical skill and leadership important at all age levels.

Peer group status is so important that the individual will greatly modify his behavior in order to win approval of the peer group. The gang spirit becomes a dominant influence. Youngsters grow more and more alike in clothes, manners, haircuts, and the use of "slanguage" which identifies them as members of the same clan. The child needs this support to aid him in mastering his fears, anxiety, and guilt, as he moves forward in independence and adult responsibility. A new type of interest in the other person appears, crowds and cliques replacing the gang, except in slum areas, with congeniality of interest the main criterion for membership. The groupings gradually become more selective, with socio-economic considerations influencing choices.

ETHICAL DEVELOPMENT

Age 5. Although generally conforming to parental demands and "good" most of the time, his concept of goodness and badness is limited largely to what parents allow and forbid. Is highly pleased with his accomplishments, but will avoid responsibility for misdeeds by denying own fault and blaming someone else. Frequent fanciful stories associated with indistinct demarcations between reality and fantasy.

Age 6. Adults standards are still the predominant basis for judgment of right and wrong, and although still passing the blame to others for any misdeeds, a growing willingness to accept criticism from friends is evident. Strongly self-assertive, resistant to demands and punishment, responsive to praise. Likes to have toys and possessions but little care of them and little sense of ownership or of property. Falsehoods not uncommon.

Age 7. Through empirical experience in games and play ideas of justice and fair play evolve and the inevitable necessity to give and take helps him to understand and accept a growing concept of right and wrong. Is more aware of behavior of friends than of self. Takes better care of possessions.

Age 8. Growing capacity for self-evaluation, and with it more responsibility for acts. Is likely to deny guilt but not to blame others as a result of developing concept of fair play. Is developing standards of good and bad, right and wrong, to which he desires to adhere.

Considerable interest in possessions and money. Given to exaggeration although mainly truthful in important matters.

Age 9. Able to evaluate own performance well, may at times be too ready to take blame. Is essentially truthful. In games in which sides are equal can usually play without recourse to cheating. Particular about own possessions, treats them often as if sacred possessions with extreme resentment of anyone using them without approval. Not uncommon for children to steal coins from parents, trinkets or food from stores, but it is not likely to continue. When it does, suggests immaturity of moral teaching or deprivation in life of child.

Age 10-11. Confidence and respect for one's own capabilities develop continuously and with it regard for other person's rights. The rules of the game become very important and are appreciated as inviolate and no longer subject to individual whim. Regard for fair play, rights of others, and right and wrong at a peak. Traits such as honesty, truth, courage, bravery, begin to exist in the abstract sense as standards for regulating conduct. Loyalty to friends evident, e.g., occasionally lying to protect a friend.

Age 12-14. Increased deference to group standards and development of group standards for regulating conflict. Increased awareness of relative rather than absolute standards of morality, to the "gray" in-between areas, and to conflicts in value systems.

ANALYSIS OF SOCIOGRAMS

A sociogram is like a highway map in that its usefulness varies with one's ability to interpret it. Figure 6 in Chapter 14 presents a sociogram constructed from the data on the tally sheet shown as Figure 2 in Chapter 14. Looking at the latter for a moment, certain differences are immediately apparent, first in the expansiveness of certain children as far as the number of choices they make, and second, in terms of the status of certain children as far as number of choices received.

Walters and Zethran are quite expansive with the largest number of choices and rejections made. Compare their expansiveness with Allen who made only a single choice, or with several youngsters, who made only positive choices. Walters and Zethran have sharp positive and negative feelings for more than half of the class. Again looking at the totals, differences in the status of given pupils is evident. There is the cluster of three high status pupils—Duncan, Gramb, Keller—followed by several above average in status—Barnes, Castle, Davis, Yurll. At the opposite pole stand Bowles and O'Keefe, isolates receiving no choices, followed by the neglected persons—Allen, Colvin, Rindge who received only one and two choices each. The remainder fall in a below average or underchosen category. Moreno[1] has termed the phenomenon by which a few persons capture a great many choices and the majority receive less than an average number of choices *sociodynamic law.*

Sociometrically speaking, there are a few wealthy persons and many poor as far as number of choices received. In the elementary school, a teacher can anticipate a distribution approximately as follows:

[1] J. L. Moreno, *Who Shall Survive?* New York: Beacon House, 1953.

	Per cent
Stars	15
Overchosen	25
Underchosen	40
Neglected	15
Isolates	5

Approximately 40 per cent of a class will receive above the average number of choices, and 60 per cent less. In a class in which the average choices made by each student was three, 40 per cent would receive three or more choices. Distributions which show marked departure from this distribution, particularly as regards the number of isolates, suggest the existence of special classroom conditions in need of remedy. For instance, where a few stars monopolize the choices, a large number of isolates are likely because of the few choices remaining to be divided between many. Providing opportunity to more pupils to demonstrate and develop special talent is necessary if the wealth is to be spread.

Another index which can be obtained from the tally sheet is one of class morale. Note that in this free choice situation (this would not apply where the class was instructed to make two choices and two rejections), the group made 58 choices and 29 rejections. It is generally characteristic of groups that the positive feelings far outweigh the negative, and this finds expression in the ratio of choices to rejections. A 2:1 or 3:1 ratio indicates positive morale. Invariably, when the ratio dips as low as 1:1, low group morale will be observed—considerable interpersonal hostility will be manifest. In such circumstances, a teacher is wise to provide greater direction and management to class activities than she does where greater positive feelings exist between students.

The sociogram in Figure 6 in Chapter 14 was constructed from the tally sheet. A number of questions can be presented which, if answered, provide understanding of the group relationships and suggest possible actions to improve individual and group relationships.

1. What appears that you had expected?
2. What appears that was unexpected?

It is often interesting to attempt to predict two choices for each pupil by marking the tally sheet prior to inspecting and recording the choices made by the children. In the primary grades, where children are more overt in their behavior, teachers are more successful in prediction, but even here, their difficulty in predicting more than 50 per cent of the choices indicates that many factors unknown to teachers are operating to influence the group relationships.

There will always be the surprises of pupils whom the teachers thought would be highly chosen who apparently make little impression on their classmates, probably because teachers and pupils are attracted by differing kinds of achievement. There is the unexpected center of attraction who emerges. In the sociogram presented, Gramb, a quiet, unassuming boy who had been in the class only three months, emerges as a central figure with the boys. It is not unusual for a newcomer to obtain a momentary high status, usually from choices received from people on the fringe of the group, but after the novelty effect wears off, and this is usually fairly rapidly, the newcomer arrives as his level. In this instance, Gramb's status was stable and not temporary in nature.

There are the expected isolates and the unexpected, the latter for surprising reasons on occasion.

3. What are the characteristics of the highly chosen?
4. What are the characteristics of the underchosen?
5. What accounts for certain pupils being most chosen?
6. What accounts for certain pupils being least chosen?

The task here is to identify common characteristics. Are they from the same race, religious group, socio-economic level, intelligence level, achievement level, sex group? Do they have common attributes such as sport skill, aggressiveness, cooperativeness, leadership ability, timidity, etc.? The answers to these questions provide insight into the kinds of characteristics, attitudes, and skills held in esteem by the group. Two procedures can be suggested. The first is to briefly list the known characteristics about each of these children under his name in order to inspect the characteristics possessed by all. Another procedure is to use symbols to mark the sociogram with identifying characteristics as shown below:

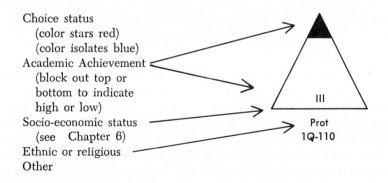

Choice status
   (color stars red)
   (color isolates blue)
Academic Achievement
   (block out top or
   bottom to indicate
   high or low)
Socio-economic status
   (see Chapter 6)
Ethnic or religious
Other

III

Prot
1Q-110

It is ordinarily easier to identify common factors among the highly chosen than among the isolates, for in addition to common social factors many of the isolates occur because of personality and problems of adjustment, which in one may be shyness, in another aggression, making the identification of common elements difficult.

   7. What are the mutual choices and what needs are being fulfilled by the mutual choice?

Approximately one-third to one-half of the choices at elementary level are mutual. Where proportions fall below this, unstable group relations are more evident and the need is for initiating person-to-person contact more than group activities. More significant is the value of mutual choice for personal development. In the primary grades choice is likely to be made entirely on the basis of emotional response, that is, on the terms of emotional needs to be satisfied. Until these emotional needs are satisfied, children find it difficult to become sufficiently detached from their person-to-person relationships to focus on social tasks. Some evidence of this is found in the fact that as children grow older they vary their choices with the nature of the question being asked. They learn that certain persons have the capacity to satisfy emotional needs, while others are desirable because of special talents which they possess. If they are asked whom they want to play with, in short, be with on their own time just for the intrinsic satisfaction to be gained in being together, they will make fewer choices and a higher per cent of mutual choices. Ask who they wish to work with and one observes a wider range of choices, fewer mutuals, and individual talent introducing itself.

If by the fifth and sixth grade similar sociograms appear from differing questions, it indicates that children are not finding satisfaction of their emotional needs and are not free to make the discrimination of choice on the basis of work-task to be performed. This distinction is readily illustrated in the oft-heard adult remark: "Oh, I can work with him all right, but I'd hate to have to live with him."

   8. How do school and classroom arrangements contribute to the choices?

A dramatic illustration of how classroom management established child status occurred in a fourth grade class in which it was discovered that all the children seated in one row appeared as isolates on the sociogram, while all the children seated in the row on the opposite side of the room were highly chosen. Puzzled by the unique event, the psychologist asked the teacher if she had any explanation. The teacher quickly responded that one row contained the poor readers, the other the best. Thinking it difficult enough to be facing inadequacy without having the event publicly branded, the next question of the psychologist was why the teacher found this arrangement desirable. The teacher's response was: "Oh, I don't. The reading supervisor insists on having the children seated this way so she can easily identify reading groups whenever she comes in." Here, adult values of human work are dramatically influencing children's perceptions of each other. Though usually less dramatic, this is often the case.

Administrative arrangements about playgrounds, types of games played, lunchrooms, formation of lines, seating arrangements, promotional policy, and the like all affect the patterns of choice that emerge on sociograms and should be evaluated.

9. What cleavages exist between subgroups?

Invariably a division will appear between boys and girls. In the primary grades, approximately 20-25 per cent of the choices will be between boys and girls, but this drops rapidly until by sixth grade level only 5 per cent will fall between sexes. A gradual rise occurs during the adolescent years to the highest level of 40 per cent by college.

Often the cleavages which exist between social groups in the community will find reflection in the classroom sociogram. For example, in a thirteen-room elementary school serving two widely separate socio-economic groups, the cleavage was evident on the sociogram from every classroom.[2] Again, in a junior high school in New York, there was almost a complete cleavage between the several ethnic groups served by the school: Puerto Rican, Negro, and white, with the first being the high status group and the last holding lowest status. A common cleavage showing up on the classroom sociograms in many New England communities is that between religious groups: Catholic, Jew, and Protestant. The degree of status depends on the composition of the particular community.

In the sociogram of the class in Figure 6 in Chapter 14, there exists a division among the boys between first-team athletes, second-team athletes, and non-athletes. A number of other social factors can be influential on occasion: bus children vs. walk-to-school children, housing development vs. non-development children, migrants vs. residents, good students vs. poor, etc. Certainly if the school cannot work effectively to overcome such cleavages when children are malleable in attitudes, the ancient prejudices will perpetuate them-

[2]Mary Dineen and R. J. Garry, "Effect of Sociometric Seating on a Classroom Cleavage," *Elem. Sch. J.*, 1956, 56, 358-362.

selves. But the cleavages cannot be overcome until the causes are recognized and understood.

10. Any groups or cliques in the entire group needing closer relation to the rest of the class?
11. From an analysis of the structure of inter-relationships what needs further developing?

Several types of structures will be observed: *chains, wheels, clusters, networks,* although not all sociograms can be classified into one of these types. The *chain* is like a school line, each child facing ahead possibly with his hand reaching out to the person ahead, and oblivious to the person behind. Few mutual choices occur and as a result the group tends to be unstable as far as continuous group activity is concerned. The first step in working with such a group is to establish pairs of children, somewhat like buddies.

The *wheel* is a pattern commonly observed where a few stars monopolize the choices. They appear as the hub of a wheel from which the many choices they receive radiate like the spokes of the wheel. Frequently, one boy will be the center of his sex, and a girl of hers. It is not unusual that these particular children receive excessive privilege from the teacher as far as acting as helper, monitor, etc. Other children in such classes need opportunity to shine.

The *cluster* arrangement characteristically presents small, separated groups of children, pairs, threes, and fours, choosing each other but cut off from the rest of the class. In some classes, this is a formative stage in the emergence of a total group. The older the children are, the more likely it is the sign of a set of cliques excluding one another. In either instance the task is to find points of contact between groups, often to be located through the third and fourth choices rather than the first and second.

Finally, the spiderweblike *network* is likely to be less evident in the elementary school, for it is evidence of a well-developed and intricate network of interpersonal relations. Sheer immaturity is one of the reasons it is less likely to occur than at secondary or adult levels.

A procedure for assisting in analysis is seen in the following:

Sociometric Analysis Form

Question: Seating	Grade: 3
Choices asked for: 3	School: Cobb
Boys: 16	City:
Girls: 9	Date:
Total Pupils: 25	Teacher:
Choices possible: 75	
Choices made: 75	

Analysis of Tally

No. of persons	Choices	Mutual Choices	Boys	Girls	New-comers	Children permanently resident
Not chosen	1	10	0	1	1	0
Chosen once	6	12	6	0	3	3
2	8	1	4	4	4	4
3	2	2	1	1		2
4	4		2	2		5
Five or more	4		3	1		3
Total Persons	25	25	16	9	8	17

Comments

Unreciprocated choices of boys for girls............................... 8

girls for boys................................. 5

Mutual choices between boys and girls.................................... 2

Chains are evident

No sharp cleavages in evidence

Newcomers moved into school district during summer vacation.

From the data presented, the proportions of under- to over-chosen is approximately as estimated—slightly higher in the under-chosen category. Fifty per cent of the choices are mutual and there are no greater number of boys than girls receiving lower high status—in proportion to the number of each in the class. It is immediately seen that the newcomers apparently start off with low status for they all fall into the under-chosen category. Given normal opportunities for association, this status would be expected to change unless there were other factors such as socio-economic status associated. The same type of analysis can be made for any variable as well as those presented here.

SOCIAL DISTANCE SCALE AND GUESS-WHO

The Social Distance Scale described in Chapter 14 requires that each pupil respond to all others on a five point scale, usually with respect to friendship for that person. One shortcoming is that the statements describing the scale frequently mix the criteria, for instance, including friendship and work. From our knowledge of sociometric results, it is known that expression of choice will vary somewhat with the basis for choice, although the highly chosen persons and the low status persons tend to fall in that position regardless of the question. The Social Distance Scale permits a rank-ordering of pupils according to status, provides information on the general level of feeling among persons and of the spread from highest to lowest. It simultaneously incorporates both positive and negative feelings, which the sociogram does not unless both choices and rejections have been sought. In this connection, it is important to note that being an isolate does not constitute rejection, only non-choice. Some pupils will incur both choice and rejection, others appear scarcely to exist for they receive neither, and some pupils receive blunt rejection.

The guess-who technique provides the teacher with a characterization of each pupil as he is seen by his classmates. It provides helpful information as to the roles held by different children and to the perception and interpersonal relations between particular children. It has the disadvantage of being somewhat cumbersome to manage as far as assimilation of data is concerned.

In general, the sociogram is likely to provide more comprehensive information not only of the person-to-person relationships but also of group structure. Where information regarding reasons for choice is requested the results are as helpful as the guess-who technique. Sociometric status correlates with rank obtained on other measures, and especially where a sequence of sociometric questions have been asked, stability of results is assured. Reliability of sociometric choice is high. Correlations on test-retest range from .60 to .90 on the average, with the length of time between administrations producing lower correlations and the older the age of the individuals the higher the reliability. Substantially stable results have been attained with kindergarten age pupils. The changes over time would appear to be less a matter of inconsistency in the selection and more a valid change in the basis for choice resulting from growth and development.

Chapter 16

FOSTERING SOCIAL
DEVELOPMENT

CHARACTERISTICS OF GROUPS

Thirty children in a classroom do not constitute a group but rather
an aggregate of subgroups and individuals with diverse interests,
needs, and goals. No simpler evidence can be offered than asking a
child to name his classmates. Even in their presence, many children
will have difficulty identifying all members of their class, suggesting
that certain of their classmates do not exist, psychologically, in their
perceptions.

INTERACTION

A primary characteristic of groups is interaction between members—interaction for purposes of communication, for expression of
feeling, for identification of goals, and for achievement of common
purpose. Until children are brought to interaction with each other,
a group cannot exist. In the classroom under teacher direction, three

types of interaction patterns predominate—teacher directs, pupil submits or rebels; teacher plans with individual pupils; teacher directs group planning. The last type facilitates group development for it brings pupils into give and take with each other as they attempt to evolve a mutually satisfying plan. Further, it is the only one of the three which helps children learn the skills they will ultimately need as adults for developing plans in groups of their peers. These facts do not imply that this type of interaction is the only desirable one, merely that it should occur just as the first two inevitably will.

GROUP COHESIVENESS

Cohesiveness implies an attraction between members of a group, a wanting to be together, a "we" feeling. The greater the degree of cohesiveness the higher the morale, the shared feelings and beliefs, and the loyalty between members. Greater effort will be expended towards group goals, and more frustration endured on behalf of the group. Classroom groups suffer as long as school attendance occurs only because it is compulsory. Not until children attend from desire do the properties for group cohesiveness exist, for such desire is an expression of need satisfaction. Reference here is to class groups as a whole. In all instances, friendship groups are likely to exist between some of the children in the class, but these are usually informal and unrelated to the purposes of the class taken as a whole. They may be utilized as elements in the development of group cohesiveness, for the attractiveness of the participants, interest in the program available and the goals of the group are bases for attraction.

GROUP CODES

For a child to function in a group, he has to share and cooperate but not exploit. He must be willing to sacrifice some of his desires for the sake of common purpose, and he must accept or tolerate the demands of others. At the same time, he must identify himself with the common needs and the goals of the group and conduct himself towards these ends, rather than attempt to exploit the group or manipulate it for his exclusive benefit. It is interesting to note the difficulties experienced by many Little League teams where the adult pressures and temptation to exploit the team for personal gain interferes with the boys' successful attainment of group cohesiveness and common purpose. Typically, in the process of give and take— literally giving up and taking from—individuals exert pressures on one another and in so doing evolve commonly accepted standards of operation, to which group members are expected to adhere.

Group Goals

Children need to know where, how, and why they are going someplace if they are not to bog down. If they are to do this in concert, group goals have to be identified and accepted by the members. Where this occurs, progress or locomotion towards group goals can be made. The younger the age of children, the more teacher help they need in establishing goals. These goals have to be consistent with individual needs and talents if effort is to be expended in their attainment.

Group Structure

In order to achieve its goals, groups arrange a division of labor, assign roles to different individuals, and evolve a structure for facilitating efficient operation. The structure has to provide for effective communication between members, identification of abilities and assignment of tasks to members, division of power and authority, and arrangement of members into compatible working groups.

The teacher plays a vital role in the several aspects of group functioning which have been identified: interaction, cohesiveness, codes, goals, and structure. The way in which she functions as a group leader determines for children the amount and kind of interaction, the degree of identification between members, the goals for which they are working either with or against the teacher, and the kinds of experiences, roles, and mutually satisfying or frustrating experiences possible.

The complexities of the teacher roles and leadership functions are readily seen in the following list:

As director—organizes groups . . . assigns leaders . . . instructs leaders . . . suggests activities . . . directs activities . . . directs group thinking by questions . . . prepares guide sheets for groups.

As instructor—teaches skills, techniques, concepts . . . teaches children how to work in groups . . . shows groups how to do research . . . how to obtain and assemble materials . . . how to prepare and give reports . . . trains leaders to perform duties.

As supervisor—checks group performance . . . observes children for individual and group difficulties . . . channels group efforts to avoid wasted time . . . corrects faulty work habits . . . encourages children's participation.

As *guide*—assists groups in identifying goals . . . suggests division of duties and responsibilities in order to provide each child a variety of experience . . . assists group in maintaining progress . . . facilitates successful completion of task . . . assists group in establishing and applying standards for evaluation.

As *advisor*—helps in planning . . . acts as clearing house for information . . . suggests sources for research materials . . . answers questions and provides information.

As *moderator*—helps establish friendly relations in groups . . . anticipates and prevents sources of conflict . . . arbitrates conflicts . . . prevents leader domination . . . observes individual and group performance . . . facilitates inclusion of isolates into groups . . . maintains favorable group climate . . . coordinates efforts of groups.

As *helper*—supplies suitable materials . . . adapts materials to interest and ability level of children . . . assists and encourages slow and shy children . . . gives individual help as needed . . . helps pupils and leaders with duties . . . assists in establishing procedures and plans.

As *evaluator*—administers tests . . . analyzes groups and individual achievement . . . evaluates leader performance . . . keeps records of individual growth and development.

The dynamic aspects of a group which have been identified and the teacher-roles can be illustrated in what, at first glance, would seem a most improbable location—a kindergarten, inasmuch as children of this age are given to parallel play and individual activity rather than group participation. Yet, the plans and activities of the teacher for the development of group experience and identification begins the first day when, after following their individual lines of play for some time, the teacher suggests that all the children join in helping to clean the room. Not only was a routine begun, but also a common purpose and accomplishment. Perhaps a familiar song will follow. The beginnings of a sense of "we" and common goals start when one boy pushing a truck along the floor, accidentally or deliberately knocks down the building that another boy had constructed with blocks, and a fight begins. All perfectly normal. The teacher intercedes, explains what happened and suggests erecting a building for the truck to go in and out. Sounds like fun; the children try and the teacher helps. It works. Side by side, the two boys accomplish something and they carry it over to the next day. Out of such experiences the following illustration becomes possible.

Children sitting on floor with teacher who asks: "What can we do to decorate the room?"

Three answers: "Everyone could make a picture and we could hang them up" . . . "We could make hundreds of snow flakes" . . . "We could make a big snow picture." The last drew most acclaim.
Teacher asks: "How do we do it?"
Suggestions: Get a big piece of brown paper. Cover it with cotton for snow. Paint it white for snow.
With a vote—painting in white won. Then: paint the sky blue. Children gather together enough jars of blue and white paint and twelve don aprons and start to work, some at the top with blue, others at the bottom with white. One boy says: "The sky is way up high, lots of it. Snow's down there—a little." Others listened, agreed, but became so enthralled with job of painting that they forgot their goal and merrily painted until blue and white met.
Teacher to the remainder still sitting with her: "What can you add to the picture?" One girl says she'll make a sled with a little boy on it, and getting permission obtained materials and makes it. Three want to make pink trees, and although the teacher raises her eyebrows at the color the children explain the trees would be "pretty," so they make pink trees. Two boys collaborate on a house. Another cuts out three jagged circles, rather immaturely, covering them with cotton, for a snow man. Two boys walk away, refuse to join the activity, preferring to play with blocks.
When all is completed, the picture is hung, and all gloat over its beauty.

In this situation, 19 of 21 children contributed to a single piece of work, the majority working alone or beside someone, with a pair and a trio working together.

Interaction was teacher directed. The task was simple enough for the children to suggest plans and it was in line with abilities. The pasted objects permitted seven children opportunity to do more intricate work of their own choosing suited to their capacity. One of the two boys who didn't participate was a leader who finds it hard to be part of a group activity which he doesn't organize. His refusal to the suggestion for his joining was polite. In part, his behavior was a reaction to the domination he experienced outside of school from older brothers and playmates. The other boy was a follower identified with the first boy.

The painting was definitely a "we" activity, with the parts seen as belonging to the whole. No one expressed the typical desire to take his product home. The group established its own goal and worked on it steadily with little teacher direction. They did not carry out the idea of snow and sky placement to which they agreed but this did not bother them.

The group structure showed excellent communication during both planning and execution stages and stable group work arrangements with little evidence of exertion of power between members. Each individual's idea was listened to and considered, accomplishment well discussed and praised, participation was in accord with personal desires, and no special status was granted or desired. The group pursued established routines in getting aprons and materials, working at tables and cleaning up. The desire of two of the boys to remain apart was accepted.

Classroom Atmosphere

The greatest need of children today is to be an important and accepted part of their society. The very nature of our society is such that children are less needed and less wanted. They are no longer an asset but an economic liability. When children feel that they are not needed, they lack motivation for constructive effort; the opposite is true when they feel needed. This very fact makes it imperative that teachers see that each child becomes a contributing and wanted part of the school society. The close link between emotions and learning points up the importance of a favorable classroom atmosphere, which is more important to the development of children than any list of techniques. The dominant role played by the teacher in the classroom makes his personality and behavior of initial importance. No single personality type can be designated as ideal for teachers, but the kinds of effects needed can be seen in the words of children describing their favorite teacher:

> "She makes you feel good at school."
> "She doesn't make a monkey out of you before everyone."
> "She helps you until you get it."
> "We do a lot of things like taking trips."
> "She smiles so much that I want to please her."
> "She likes every one of us and treats us all alike."
> "We laugh a lot but not at each other."
> "She's pretty. She has a smiling face and a nice voice."
> "She made me know that I could do the work."

With a favorable classroom atmosphere as a matrix, teachers have three main tasks to perform with groups and their success has important implications for the mental health and character development of children. Our concept of ourselves, our convictions about what we stand for, our beliefs of right and wrong, and the goals for which we strive are created and shaped by the groups to which we belong: family, friends, and organizations. Character is developed by the identifications we make and the groups of which we are members in growing up. Teachers can and do play a significant role in the process in their capacity as leader and director of children's groups.

Three main concerns and related character traits and problems are:

1. *Group belonging*

   Character traits — Identification, conformity, loyalty, obedience, patriotism, piety.

   Problems — Overconformity, ethnocentrism, integrity, individuality.

2. *Group participation*

   Character traits — Cooperation, generosity, helpfulness, fair play.

   Problems — Competition, selfishness, hostility, aggressiveness, dishonesty.

3. *Acceptance of individual and group differences, and regard for privileges of other*

   Character traits — Openmindedness, tolerance, respect, consideration.

   Problems — Prejudice, intolerance, scapegoating, stealing, gossiping.

GROUP BELONGING

In order to feel good about his life a child needs a sense of belonging. He needs to find people whom he likes and with whom he wishes to be. Moreover, he needs to find among his age mates children who like him and who want him. He wants to be part of group activities and he wants to be thought of when people he knows are deciding to do something together. Any way in which a teacher groups children has implications for their mental health. In one fourth grade class, where, strangely, all the isolates on the sociogram were seated in one row and all the highly chosen in another, investigation revealed that the isolates were the poor readers who had been seated together at the request of the reading supervisor who liked to be able to immediately identify reading groups. A child's status and his worth as a person was being established by a seating arrangement which put a premium on reading ability.

As long as it is impossible to learn without making errors, an environment is needed in which children feel free to make mistakes. When children are placed with those whom they choose, they feel a greater security, and, feeling this way, they experience a freedom and emotional release which makes them less hesitant and fearful. One way of increasing security is to utilize the natural groups that are discovered through the sociogram. In large degree, the effectiveness of the teacher in influencing the social and character development of children is determined by her skill in creating and directing group value systems.

SOCIOMETRIC GROUPING

From her analysis of the sociogram, the teacher has identified the status of each child in the classroom, the natural grouping, the values and characteristics admired by the children, and, to some degree, the problems in interpersonal relationships and group needs. She knows that the path to maturity proceeds by meeting and solving today's problems rather than by detached preparation for some remote adult problem. In re-arranging seating, work, or play groups, five conditions should be met:

1. Satisfaction of pupil *choice*.
2. Consideration of *task* to be performed.
3. Provision for *group balance*.
4. Fulfillment of *group needs*.
5. Provision for *teacher comfort*.

In obtaining the information for the sociogram, the teacher promised each child that he would receive at least one of his choices. Ideally, she would give each child his first choice or a mutual choice. Where the choices were seriously made, first choices have a special significance for they are indicative of important needs of the child which find satisfaction with that person. Other considerations which are important to individual development and group functioning have to be considered. Certain combinations of children have a contagious effect on each other, triggering impulses which are disruptive. The normal excitement, partially from the novelty of the event and partially from the joy of being with chosen people, which follows a sociometric regrouping is not to be confused here. The novelty effect wears off in a few days, especially as the groups begin to function. The triggering effect is one reason for wanting children to express several choices when the sociogram is taken in order that the teacher has the option of exercising her professional judgment as to what combinations of children will prove effective.

On rare occasions, situations occur in which some child will have to go unsatisfied. In such instances, highly chosen children are better able to tolerate the frustration and will usually adapt amiably to the teacher's explanation of why she placed him where he did and to her promise to see that his choice is granted on the next occasion for re-grouping. Every effort should be made to place the isolates in proximity to highly chosen children because their finding a place in a group is less dependent on their modifying their behavior than it is upon the capacity of other children to reach out and include them. Highly chosen children usually have a greater store of emotional acceptance than other children as well as fewer unfulfilled needs, and, accompanying these capacities, a greater tolerance for individual foibles. Hopefully, when the isolate experiences the warmth of acceptance and possibly thinks he has been chosen by the children with whom he has been placed (the teacher does not reveal the results of the sociograms, having said they would be kept in confidence), he will modify his behavior to satisfy his companions. Where the isolation results from deep-seated maladjustment, he may be unable to change without benefit of therapy. Most such children, hungering to have their social needs satisfied, respond to the opportunities presented.

Next, the task to be performed should be considered. Art, science, social studies, and other kinds of projects to be performed by groups require varied talents—research, art, reporting, leadership, library skills, organizational ability, etc. The particular talents needed for the execution of the task should be considered and care taken to see that each group has its share. If all the leaders end in one group and all the artists in another, the end products can scarcely be satisfying. In addition, appreciation for the value of the contribution of other individuals to group living and working comes from recognizing their unique contribution. Where all possess the same kind of ability, competition and quarreling is more likely to ensue than collaborative effort, such as would occur in a family if all wanted to do the cooking and none possessed the talent for other housekeeping tasks.

The third consideration needed is for the group balance. To a great degree, the teacher is going to have to proceed by trial and error and benefit of her own insight into group functioning, for research on the dynamics of the interaction of normal personalities in groups is not available. But the satisfaction of the criteria for groups identified at the beginning of the chapter requires communication between group members with the result that there is a limit to the disparity which can be tolerated within a group. For this reason, groups should not be too large, rarely more than seven (unless the activity or game require it) and preferably with an odd number to permit a balance of power.

The teacher will observe that few if any bright children choose morons or vice versa. Instead, both groups will show a number of choices of children of average intelligence, as if in order to accept their own differences they must first find acceptance in the general group. Furthermore, they have to be in communication with the main social group. Somewhat the same phenomenon occurs with respect to such traits as aggressiveness, timidity, selfishness, dependence. Where this is a concern to the child, he will be found choosing among the average and choosing persons who are what he wishes he were. Isolates choose highly chosen persons as a rule, as if sensing the person they wish they were.

These are the reasons for the analysis of the meaning of choices made by children, particularly their mutual choices, for from this analysis comes insight into the needs of individual children. In arranging them into groups, care is needed that the balance of the group is assured. If all the children in a group were shy and timid, communication would suffer, just as it would if all were aggressive and belligerent. Children at the extremes of any trait counterbalance each other, and both need children in the middle range to bridge the gap as they attempt to come into communication with each other. Were only aggressive and shy children in a group, the former would tend to dominate the latter aggravating the problem. The presence of the middle group restrains and prevents such exploitation.

Needs common to the group appear in the analysis of the sociograms. This analysis shows cleavages to be bridged and value systems to be re-oriented. In creating groups, the sex cleavage can be bridged by combining pairs or trios of boys with pairs or trios of girls. If the sociograms were duplicated in the classroom, all boys and all girls would be together. However, choice can be satisfied and the cleavage bridged by interspersing small groups. Rarely should a single child of one sex be placed with all persons of the opposite sex. A boy who chooses all girls is likely to be acknowledging his inability to succeed in a boy's role with its aggressive rough-and-tumble activity, and seek the more complacent companionship of girls. This may result from the fact that he lives in a girl dominated environment and feels more comfortable there. If he has chosen only girls, one or two other boys should be included in his group.

In a similar fashion, the teacher can arrange groups to overcome other cleavages by combining persons from opposite "sides of the fence." Cliques can present a problem where small, tightly-knit groups of four or five exclude others from membership. Usually, a mutual pair can be extracted from the clique and joined with other persons. There is likely to be some grumbling but the teacher's reply is that she kept her promise of satisfying choice, and at no time did she promise to give everybody all their choices. Occasionally, a child will grouse that he hadn't really made the choices he wanted because he didn't think the teacher was serious, to which the teacher's reply is that next time he will be more careful.

An important consideration in effective group functioning centers around a distinction which Jennings[1] has made between psyche-groups and sociogroups. The former are groups which exist primarily for the emotional satisfaction of their members, the latter to fulfill some social purpose. Each person has affectional needs which take precedence in any scale of importance of satisfaction. Satisfied in our need for love, we can be sufficiently detached from ourselves to work in groups where the primary goal is not the fulfillment of the individual need but social purpose. Faculties, curriculum committees, finance committees, boards of directors, etc., are examples of social groups which exist mainly to accomplish a specific task. In such groups, one must work with individuals with less regard for emotional compatibility than for individual capacity and effectiveness at the task. Something comparable is observed with science and social studies projects and athletic teams in school.

In order to function efficiently in a sociogroup, one's emotional needs must be basically satisfied. In school, children must have the feeling that they are approved and accepted before they can operate effectively in a sociogroup else they devote their energies to gaining acceptance rather than towards group goals. Younger children in the primary grades make their choices primarily in terms of their emotional needs and emotional responsiveness. With these needs satisfied and with growing experiences, they recognize that other qualities are important and that execution of certain jobs requires particular talents. They come to recognize and appreciate differences in talent, and this recognition influences the choices they make, with the result that sociograms begin to vary in choice pattern and structure in the intermediate grades in accordance with different sociometric questions. If the same sociogram occurs regardless of the question, it is likely that the children are choosing on the basis of unsatisfied emotional needs and utilizing any opportunity to obtain satisfaction.

Teacher comfort is not the least consideration in re-arranging groups on the basis of sociometric findings. Tempted though we may

[1]Helen Jennings, *Leadership and Isolation.* New York: Longmans, 1950.

be to pretend differently, teacher needs and motives are an important determiner of the behavior that is permissible and what will occur in a classroom. Many of the basic human motives depend upon reciprocal reactions. To obtain recognition or approval, a child finds himself pressed to act in ways that obtain approval and recognition. Such ways of acting depend in part upon the attitudes and values of each particular teacher. Thus, teacher needs are an important consideration. Still more, the teacher's mental health is of such importance to children that she should consider her own psychological comfort. Thus, a combination of children which excite each other in a manner that disturbs the teacher is to be avoided. This is not likely to interfere with the social development of children for a variety of combinations can be equally effective in promotion of social growth.

The information provided by the Social Distance Scale and the Guess Who is valuable in making the decisions and planning programs in this area. The Social Distance Scale, in addition to identifying the status differences of children in the classroom, helps identify friendship groups. More useful, the Guess-Who, with its characterizations of children, provides information on individual and group needs and problems permitting adaptation of program to such needs.

Re-arrangement of seating or grouping is not the end but the beginning of the program, for it provides the contact between children which offers opportunity for change and development. The direction of movement and the successful attainment of progress depend on continued follow-up as a regular part of the classroom program. A good portion of this will occur as a result of the way in which the teacher handles the day-to-day events that arise as a natural part of group functioning. The remainder comes from the kinds of activities which the teacher includes.

Supplementary information is usually needed and can be obtained through questionnaires or check lists. This provides a basis for class discussions. Check lists permit identification of those problems being faced by a number of children which would benefit from open discussion. A preferable procedure is to obtain information through the free-writing of children in response to questions such as:

1. What I do when I'm angry.
2. When I grow up I'll . . .
3. When I'm alone I think about . . .
4. What my parents expect of me.
5. What I like about myself; in others.

6. How I wish I were different.
7. What I dislike in others.
8. How I feel when punished; excluded; picked on; discriminated against; etc.
9. Why I felt left out (where cliques are present).
10. Things I like (dislike) about my home.
11. What I do at home; in my spare time; etc.

The replies to such free-writing (which can be evaluated for style of language usage as well as style of living) will provide topics for discussion and incidents for use in sociodrama and role-playing for the purpose of training for greater adequacy in performance of life roles.

The follow-up work and influence of a teacher in bringing an isolate into a group is illustrated in the following report:

Personal Background

Bert N., age 13, is a healthy seventh-grader. Oldest of two children of middle-class family. Father an electrician; mother at home. Family has been residentially stable, owns home.

B, IQ 95, Stanford Ach—6.0, honor marks in art and shop, average in PE, Science, Soc. Studies, Low passing in Eng. and Math. No grades repeated. Favorable attitude towards school, liked by teachers, plans to become a machinist. B. has a paper route, earns $9 a week, buys his own clothes, has household chores, avoids detention for fear of missing bus and delay on paper route. No participation in sports.

Problem:

Isolate on two successive sociograms. B chose highly chosen boys.

Group Background Information:

Peer culture in this school dictates that boys wear dungarees and plaid sport shirts. Their language includes such terms as "kiss boy" with appropriate sound effects for the teacher's pet and "fruit" for someone they reject as sissy. Athletic prowess symbolized by school award confers high status. Most of the boys do a lot of "fooling around" and "goofing off" as they term it. Stamp collecting is popular among boys and is an important homeroom and spare time activity. Copying assignments is a favorite pastime as are comic books and talking. Popular horseplay is for one boy to grasp from behind the arms of another boy who has to demonstrate superior strength by freeing himself.

B did not fit; was termed "fruit." Even the girls remarked "He isn't even a boy, he acts and talks like a girl." He had no hobby.

He did not copy assignments and apparently no one wanted to copy his. He did not remain after school for sports.

Analysis:

Isolation stems from not accepting and participating in peer group culture.

Action:

B wore shirt, tie, and slacks every day; other boys did only when no gym class or sport practice. When B was talking with me in corridor and another boy arrived I would ask: "How did you happen to wear dungarees today?" After hearing a series of replies: "Oh, we have gym today. Football practice this afternoon," B got the idea and began wearing similar clothes on gym days. As he tagged around homeroom at my heels I made a point of asking other boys—what made that stamp so valuable? Where had they gotten it? How did they get started collecting? Was it expensive? Where did they get stamps locally? Again, the power of suggestion was effective.

Placed him with a group of six boys, one of whom was his first choice, studying manufacturing occupations. He worked well with the group. Now he is working with group of six boys and girls planning a school dance. He has ideas to contribute but doesn't domineer. Encouraged him to work with business committee as part of an extracurricular activity of putting out a school paper.

Recently, have noted that he rarely follows me around, instead joins groups of boys on arrival talking about stamps, reading comics, joshing, etc. Observed him comparing homework assignments, and joining in the strength contests. Social Distance Scale recently administered shows one mutual best friend and three choices as group member. Learned he took a pretty, mature girl to an after-school movie.

Some teachers may feel that the changes in this instance were for the worse—slacks to dungarees, comparing homework, reading comics, and "goofing off." Certainly it is true that his behavior was less that of a model boy. However, the general adjustment of the boy was such that there was little likelihood of his being exploited by the group. His ego structure is such that he can resist group pressures to engage in behavior that is too far afield. What occurred was rounding out of balance in an important area of life—social belonging —to accompany his wholesome family and work adjustment.

In comparison with the actions taken by the preceding teacher to help an isolate establish a place in his peer group, the following report, including data and sociograms of one fifth grade class, describes plans carried out by principal and staff in improving the social adjustment in the school.

Procedure followed

1. Preparation of sociogram for each class by principal.
2. Discussion of results with teachers.
3. Pooling knowledge concerning children.
4. Conferences to try to learn causes for rejection and acceptance.
5. Plan to help each child.
6. Identification of group needs and formulation of plans to meet them.
7. Initiating of sociometric grouping.
8. Introduction of small group activities, creative activity, class management, assembly programs to encourage self-expression.
9. Survey of membership of Scouts, YMCA, etc. and encouragement of membership.
10. Obtaining remedial and specialized help where indicated through community agencies.
11. Continued observation of children in play situations.
12. Direct drive on developing understanding of what constitutes good leadership in order to insure effective group performance consistent with school goals.
13. Periodic evaluation of progress.

Analysis of first sociogram (27 Oct.)

We were eager to see the results. Most of the children are above average in IQ, alert, talkative (almost garrulous), interesting, cheerful, informed, and eager for new experience—a definite challenge to any teacher.

We expected to see leadership widely distributed, and less of a sex cleavage. We were aware of religious cleavages because many children attend church school at the close of school. Also, residential proximity would create sub-groups. Surprised at status of Robert A. and Ken B.—they are not ones whom teacher would select as leaders. Likewise for Robert S.

Children's values· revealed—boys admiring fearlessness, aggressive daring, sport skill, and energetic behavior. Both boys and girls show close ties. Neighborhood, church, and club groupings influencing status of highly chosen.

Sex (male) is the only common characteristic evidenced among isolates, although the number comes as a surprise.

Allan C.—inconsistent behavior evidence from year to year.

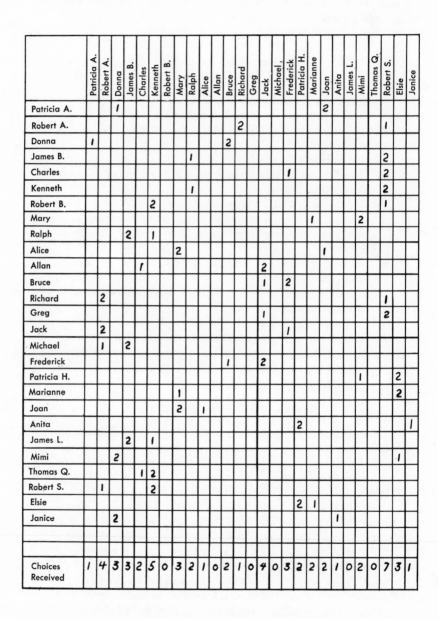

Figure 1. Tally Sheet—Fifth Grade, October 27

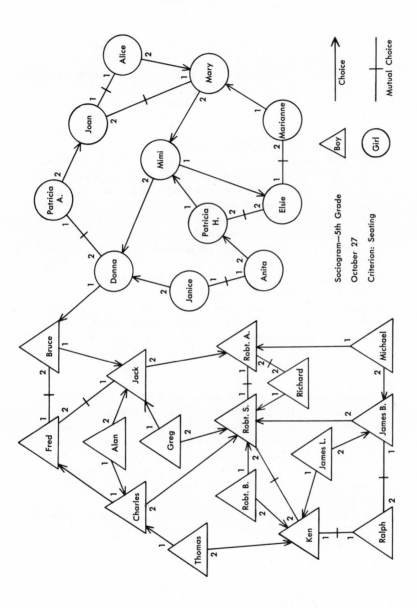

Figure 1. Sociogram — Fifth Grade, October 27.

Gregory F.—broken home, working mother is high strung.

Thomas Q.—careless, not working at capacity, underprivileged socio-economically.

James L.—father dead, mother working, underprivileged socio-economically.

Robert B.—overweight, not achieving, overbearing manner.

Michael G.—His afterschool attendance at Hebrew school takes him away from neighborhood classmates who are of different faith.

Procedure followed

The actions listed above were introduced in part. Teacher, a man, inclined to be authoritarian, teacher-directs-pupils-obey relationship, was in effect introduced to the class by the sociogram, became aware of peer group, is learning to accept and work with it, to be more friendly, to learn about children's interests and experiences, to lower his standards to pupil level, to encourage children to express interests and feelings. Tension is decreasing. Groups have worked together to prepare learning activities for assemblies, decorate for Christmas, do library research, and prepare for an instrumental concert.

Discussed qualities of good leadership and need to build up in all activities and to give Charles B., a potential leader, opportunity for development.

Capitalizing on talents to build interpersonal appreciation—Marianne and Robert B. wrote and directed a play; and Alice C., James L., Robert B., Richard F., and Michael G. play in orchestra together. Alice, shy and uncertain, is skilled in locating information and is encouraged to help those less skilled.

Special needs identified: Allan's isolation stems in part from marginal status of family which is not accepted either by religious group or "outsiders." Conference with mother.

Parent-conference with Ken's mother—attempt to get more attention to work and less to amusing class; also remedial reading help.

Greg's mother gave permission for him to join Y, also recognized his need for more time in spite of her work.

Robert A. more cooperative since father's visit, but especially since effective development of group leadership in class subgroups more oriented to productivity than play.

James L. and Robert B. encouraged in friendship; go to instrumental class together.

Bruce, Jack, and Fred, lifelong pals, encouraged to include Allan and Michael in group.

Tom Q., with help in improving work and appearance, is emerging as a leader.

The children in this class have beautiful singing voices and read music. Planning a music festival which will provide opportunity for solo and group offerings.

Analysis of second sociogram (15 Dec.)

Evidence that children are recognizing and accepting positive leadership—Bruce, Fred, Ralph, and Alice received more choices; Robert A., Robert S., Jack, and Ken fewer. The last three are doing better school work and becoming better citizens. Donna received fewer choices because two friends have moved.

Sex cleavage remains; more mutual choices and fewer isolates observed. The Richard, Robert A., Robert S. clique has opened up, but not that of Bruce, Fred, Jack.

ADAPTING INSTRUCTIONAL PROGRAM

Guidance programs in elementary schools will never be wholly effective until the instructional program is managed to foster personal-social development simultaneously with intellectual and physical development. The following illustration attempts to point out ways in which the language arts program in a sixth grade can serve the development not only of the listening, speaking, reading, and writing skills essential to communication, but also group belonging and participation.

Individual differences in ability and achievement have long been recognized. We need now to recognize individual differences in social and emotional development and to consider them in terms of pupil needs in specific learning situations. The language arts program is so broad in its scope that it offers many opportunities for cooperative experience.

Language concerns a child's relationships with others. Through language the child emerges from a self-centered to a social being; in choice and use of words he learns to show courtesy and consideration; in addressing a listener he develops interest and the ability to share points of view. Language contributes to the larger development of the child to the extent that activities are real and vital.

In utilizing the language arts curriculum to promote the goals of social development in group living, the major objectives will be:

1. To foster an identification with and a loyalty to the class as a group, having a common ground of interests and goals, recognizing a need for conformity as well as variations.
2. To achieve group participation based upon attitudes of cooperation, consideration, generosity, helpfulness, fair play, and sportsmanship.

	Patricia A.	Robert A.	Donna	James B.	Charles	Kenneth	Robert B.	Mary	Ralph	Alice	Allan	Bruce	Richard	Greg	Jack	Michael	Frederick	Patricia H.	Marianne	Joan	Anita	James L.	Mimi	Thomas Q.	Robert S.	Elsie	Janice
Patricia A.	MOVED																										
Robert A.									1			2															
Donna												2															1
James B.									1	2																	
Charles																	1							2			
Kenneth									1																2		
Robert B.																		1							2		
Mary																		1	2								
Ralph						2																1					
Alice						2												1									
Allan					1																			2			
Bruce													1	2													
Richard	2																								1		
Greg				2											1												
Jack													1			2											
Michael																	1								2		
Frederick												2			1												
Patricia H.																			2								1
Marianne								1		2																	
Joan										1								2									
Anita										2																	1
James L.						1						2															
Mimi										1																	2
Thomas Q.				1												2											
Robert S.					2	1																					
Elsie		1			2																						
Janice																	1			2							
Choices Received	1	1	1	2	3	1	3	4	4	0	4	1	0	3	1	4	1	2	3	1	1	1	2	4	2	2	

Figure 2.   Tally Sheet—Fifth Grade, December 15.

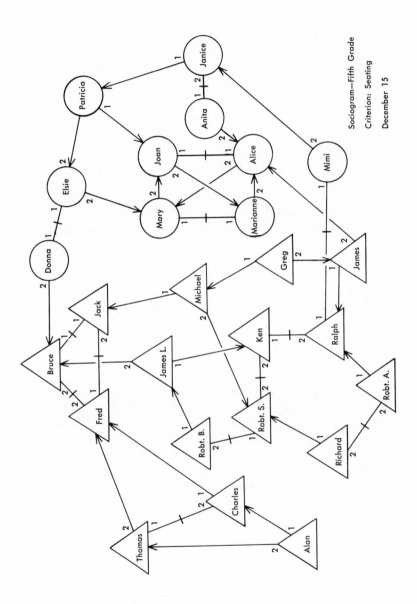

Figure 2. Sociogram — Fifth Grade, December 15.

In the modern approach to organizing the language art curriculum instead of a fixed curriculum, there is a trend towards planning for the language arts as an integral part of all classroom activities, with attention concentrated specifically on language skills only when they are needed to accomplish some other purpose. It is thus possible to develop the program around the wide range of interests and needs which are found in the sixth grade. There will be interests common to the entire class, those shared by a small group, and some individual interests and hobbies. Each type of skill is introduced wherever the need for it appears first, and it is reinforced by each succeeding experience in which it is used. To foster an identification with and a loyalty to the class as a group, the following language activities may be of value:

1. Introductions—the teacher tells a little about herself to the class, then asks the pupils to identify themselves. Match stick drawings of people can be used on the blackboard to represent the teacher's immediate family. Then suggest that the children write a few paragraphs in which they tell about themselves and their families. Tell them that their writing will be kept confidential, will not be graded, and will be returned to them in June so that they can see their growth in the ability to express themselves in writing. Some children like to attach a drawing of the family scene. These papers provide an insight into the family relationships as well as an opportunity to survey the needs in written English.

2. Discussion by the class as a group with a common interest. The questions: "Now that we know a little about each other, what are the things we can do to make this a class that we are proud to be in? What are some of the things we can do to make our classroom a cheerful, pleasant, and interesting place in which to work and play?" These questions usually evoke responses that can be drawn up as a code of acceptable behavior. This involves critical thinking as to the use of language before the acceptance of the final list. The children usually see the importance of setting and maintaining standards, rules and regulations, by which to judge their own behavior. They know what is expected, what will be considered right or wrong, what is helpful and considerate in personal conduct. The pupils understand the criticisms of classmates if group established standards are violated.

3. The children next plan for assuming responsibility for taking care of supplies, plants, pictures, books, coatroom, library table, windows, lights, attendance book, blackboards, and other class-

room chores. They will take this seriously and work out their own system for assigning responsibilities.

4. If classroom officers are to be elected, the class discusses and lists the qualities which they think are necessary to qualify for election to such offices. They recognize the need for skill in oral and written communication as well as skill in getting along with people.

5. Another discussion period is concerned with what can be done to assure absent children that they will be informed about what went on during their absences.

One arrangement which results is the setting up of a series of notebooks, one for each major subject. In these notebooks, brief notes of the daily activities are recorded along with a list of absentees for the day. For example:

Arithmetic
September 12
Review of addition of fractions with similar denominators
Written work—page 20—examples 1-10
Helen, John

The children decide who will do the recording, for how long a period, and how the responsibility will be rotated. The recording involves correct spelling and legible handwriting. Absentees assume the responsibility of checking the books and making up work wherever it is necessary.

Other activities which foster group belonging and involve skills in listening, speaking, reading and writing are as follows:

1. Planning for opening exercises and sharing time.
2. Planning for trips to museums, etc.
3. Planning for parties and holiday celebrations.
4. Organizing an assembly program.
5. Organizing a classroom paper.
6. Writing letters for information, for appointments.
7. Writing a class letter of thanks.
8. Writing, as a group, a brief outline for social studies.
9. Making a class list of places of interest in and around the community.
10. Writing, as a group, a play for a special occasion.
11. Oral sharing of experiences with the class as a group.
12. Evaluating a piece of work, a trip or an activity.
13. Giving directions to the group for playing games, for reaching a destination, or for making something.
14. Writing summaries of a class project.

The second objective is to achieve group participation based upon attitudes of cooperation, generosity, consideration, helpfulness, fair play, and sportsmanship.

1. Choral speaking has many values beyond the enjoyment of poetry and literature. It is a group activity which builds the confidence of the shy child, while at the same time it subdues the child who is excessively loquacious. It serves to improve voice quality, slovenly speech, and faulty English without singling out any one child for correction. It requires cooperation by the entire group. Children are pleased by what they can produce collectively. They will work hard to blend their voices into the tone and rhythm pattern that they want to portray.

At a sixth grade level the group can do much of the planning. They can analyze the quality of voices, and can evaluate different types of interpretation. The group chooses a selection appropriate for speaking in unison and decides upon an interpretation which will express the thought and the feeling. Voices are divided into three groups:

A. High pitched—fine and delicate
B. Heavy—low pitched
C. Middle voices—usually having a wide pitch range.

In judging voices for grouping, each child answers a question which requires some thought so that he will be less likely to imitate the pitch and quality of another child. The children stand or sit together in their own groups, but they perform as a unit.

Unity of articulation is very important. The group begins together, keeps together, and finishes at the same time. The diction of every member must be good. A skillful group member can learn to take over whatever direction is needed. There is a great deal of literature available explaining choral speaking techniques.

2. Dramatization is another activity which requires cooperative group participation. Spontaneous dramatics can result from a reading activity, a social studies unit, or can be used to emphasize and solve problems of living together harmoniously.

There is a series of seven short stories called *Little Stories on Big Subjects*.[2] They are about children who are of various racial, religious, and ethnic backgrounds. These children have problems which are common in the mixed cultural setting of American life.

---

[2]Gertrude Noar, *Little Stories on Big Subjects*. New York: B' nai B'rith Antidefamation League.

The main characters are boys; their reading level and content material is suitable for children from ten to fourteen years of age.

The spontaneous dramatizations of such stories as these can help develop tolerance and understanding of group differences.

The following is a suggested procedure:

1. Everyone becomes familiar with the story.
2. A discussion establishes what the first episode shall be, who is in it, what they do and say.
3. A cast is assembled and goes to a corner of the room for brief planning. Second, third, and possibly fourth casts are sent to the other corners for planning.
4. Each cast presents its act.
5. The class decides which cast is best.
6. Succeeding episodes are presented in like manner.
7. A final cast is assembled and a complete production is presented.

The conversation is made up spontaneously. No one memorizes or reads lines. There are variations in techniques which can be used to meet the needs of the group. The use of a tape recorder can be of great value in the evaluation of the speaking abilities.

3. Oral reading to a small group is something that a shy child can do more easily than reading to an entire class. Members of a small group can read to each other to share information, original stories and poems, scripts of plays, or to share humorous, best-liked, most interesting parts of a story.

4. Oral book reviews can be handled in small groups. Each member of a group presents to the group a brief review of a book he has read, emphasizing his reaction to the book. Sometimes the groups enjoy selecting the best review in each group. These best reviews are then presented to the entire class. Four groups can function this way, giving each child an opportunity to discuss a book. The pupils must be cooperative and considerate enough to keep their voices low. This can be an exercise in respect for the privileges of each group.

5. Panel discussions by a group of four to six children at the front of the room can be used to develop tolerance and understanding. Each child in the group reads the same book before the discussion takes place. The children talk about the book, developing the plot as they talk.

Group participation places obvious dependence on oral activities. Creative writing can be incorporated in a number of the procedures suggested, helping the development of this talent as well as assisting children to recognize and appreciate individual differences.

GROUP PARTICIPATION

Group participation exists when two or more people join forces to achieve a common goal. As social beings, we are often involved in group activities, voluntarily or otherwise, with variation in the demands that the nature of the group's goal makes on its energy.

Groups are formed in school for specific reasons which largely determine the size and stability of their organization. The kindergarten classroom is more free in encouraging children to participate. There, groups range in size from 3 to 30, depending on whether they are engaged in work-play, dramatizations, or group games. In grades 1-4, groups are formed on the basis of common levels of ability. Here, four to seven children work best together, limited by the capacity of this age child to respond to many personalities simultaneously. The majority of such groups are directed, the teacher playing a dominant role in sorting personalities and talents and setting the stage for the activity. Nevertheless, in groups of this age, the children look to one another as true contributors and expect a high degree of cooperation from each other. In grades 5 through 8, the groups can range up to nine without significant difficulty. At this level, children are aware of personal limitations and often exclude those of lesser talent, provided the latter are not friends. At this age, the children enjoy and want to have their "say" in choosing teams, captains, subjects for projects. They want to make judgments and develop authority, part of an increasing drive for self-realization and independence.

Physical, environmental, and personal-social factors determine the stability of groups. Kindergarten children are curious and inventive. The groups are easily created and the structure highly variable. In any day there can be many leaders, much sharing, and continual interaction. In the primary grades, a more formal situation develops as children are introduced to group work in academic areas arbitrarily. The limits are defined as to number, task, and time, and children in this framework test their ability to work together. In upper elementary grades, as group structure becomes more complex, stable roles emerge augmented by a new social force—loyalty.

Mutual cooperation to achieve a common goal emerges slowly during elementary school years and is initially dependent upon structured situations and adult supervision. The six- and seven-year-olds are individualistic and set on having their own way, with the result that group play is primarily for individual ends. By the age of eight, real cooperation can be observed in simple situations, and, with the emergence of club and gang interests by nine, mutual effort to achieve group goals is observed.

Thus, grouping factors that affect the degree of cooperation are: age range of children, size of group, capacity and interest of each child in the group, quantity and variety of equipment, and quality of adult leadership. However, personal factors affecting the degree of cooperation are overstimulation, excessive competition, insecurity, fatigue, poor health, poor balance of activities, and over-scheduled lives with little opportunity for relaxation.

The forms, if not the substance, of cooperation, are learned. As much as possible, children should be encouraged to work out their own techniques of getting along with others, even if frequent and often violent arguing occurs. Adult guidance enters into the kinds of situations which are created and the atmosphere in which they occur, rather than in direct interference in the group. In a society which values both cooperation and competition, the task of striking an appropriate balance between individuality and conformity is difficult, for the stress on both competition and cooperation is confusing.

Our school children are rewarded for their attempts to surpass others to a much greater extent than children in many primary cultures. Our educational system is, at least partly, a system of social relationships in which students are pitted against each other. Much of the child's perception of himself comes from comparing himself with others, in testing his strength and ability against others. In this way, he develops a concept of who he is, what he can do, what the boundaries of his abilities are.

Competition in school can give zest to many activities, encouraging children to try new experiences and discover their potentialities. The problem is to keep the competition within bounds. No hard and fast line can be drawn between healthy and unhealthy competition. Generally speaking, it may be regarded as healthy when it is spontaneous and productive, when the zest and verve of competing outweigh the bitterness of losing, and when a friendly attitude prevails rather than a desire for retaliation. Very high and very low competitive behavior requires an evaluation of causes, for both can result in group rejection or isolation. Factors in the family background are frequently contributory. Sibling rivalry in the home can influence children's group behavior. Mothers who have not resolved their own feelings of rivalry for their siblings tend to incite this behavior in their children. Children who are reluctant to compete suffer from feelings of inadequacy, have such a high level of aspiration that their fear of failure is great, or are fearful of competing because they fear the outcomes will be dangerous in terms of the consequences which ensue or the feelings likely to be provoked.

Problems in group participation are evidenced in the following types of persistent behavior:

1. Lacking social skills necessary for group participation.
2. Displaying traits which antagonize associates.
3. Uncooperative in working with others.
4. Non-participant in group activities.
5. No sharing of possessions or experiences with group.
6. Doesn't contribute ideas or materials to solution of group problems.
7. Intolerant of actions of others even when explained.
8. Refuses to abide by majority decisions.
9. Rejects right of individual to express minority opinions.
10. Unappreciative of contributions of others.
11. Receives little or no satisfaction from group accomplishments.
12. Favors suggestions detrimental to common welfare.
13. Unconcerned about improving living conditions of groups— family, play, class, school.
14. Won't share in decision affecting group or accept responsibility for carrying out decisions.

In many instances individual work is necessary to effect change in the behavior of children, but many aspects of the behavior submit to a group approach. The following illustrations are offered to indicate activities at primary grade level which contribute to improved group participation and adjustment. In each instance the objective is identified and suggested activities follow.

1. *Willingness to follow rules.*

   a. Discussion with group to make rules for halls, cafeterias, toilets, assembly. List of rules displayed. Rotate leaders responsible for seeing rules carried out.
   b. Dramatization of situations involving rule violation: Boy pushes friend in corridor; argument over place in line. Assign children to pupil roles and teacher role.
   c. Utilize games at recess or in physical education which have differential assignments and where success in game is dependent on all executing assignment.

2. *Respect for rights of others.*

   a. Dramatizations or discussions on respect for others:

child carelessly spoils work of another; property destruction—what should teacher do, etc.

b. Have children draw simple cartoons showing lack of
regard for others.

c. Have lost and found department with game to see if
owner can be found.

d. Library corner—compare damage to some books which
have been misused with new books being added. Have
children identify ways in which damage occurs. Plan
to inspect books a month later with class to see if they
have been cared for.

3. *Willingness to do share of the work.*

a. Room helpers divide room tasks, prepare list of duties,
check execution. If work slides, plan a special time of
day for doing.

b. In rhythm band rotate instruments and evaluate quality
of group performance.

c. Plan holiday program, adopt children's ideas, make
responsible for execution.

d. Projects which require different kinds of skills show
importance of interdependence as compared with situation where all children have identical assignment.

4. *Taking turns when working with a group.*

a. See items listed under #1.

b. Use a language unit to show value of taking turns. Start
discussion with small group on interesting topic but
without ground rules. In successive meetings guide
children to see improvement in discussion and conversation. This can be preparation for leaderless group
discussions on problems of concern to children.

c. Reward children demonstrating desired behavior by
assignment to preferred positions at game time.

5. *Giving and accepting helpful criticism.*

a. Read or tell a story, speaking some parts in monotone,
others more dramatically. Ask children to criticize and
from this develop basic rules for effective expression.
Have children read or give short report and evaluate
same with rules.

b. Written language—children write paper without aid—
e.g., my happiest day, what I did at the beach, etc.
Teacher reads aloud without identifying. Discuss what
makes paper interesting.

c. Discussion on giving and taking criticism, how it feels

to be criticized, how to use it, who will accept criticism from whom and who not.

6. *Increase in courteous attitudes.*

a. Buzz sessions on courtesy—likes and dislikes, advantages, disadvantages, etc.
b. Utilize opportunities—visitors, etc., to write a thank-you-note, both for individual favors and group.
c. Borrow necessary equipment from telephone company for instructions in courteous use of telephone.

7. *Habit of attention to other persons' reports and conversation as a form of courtesy.*

a. Devise rating sheet and assign two or three people as navigators to rate class on performance.
b. Use listening to music for difference in moods, rhythms, particular instruments, etc.
c. Check class attention during story telling, experience, sharing, etc., and discuss.

8. *Growth in ability to accept and discharge responsibilities.*

a. Discuss solution of hypothetical or real situation in which a person requires the help of other persons for success of a project: e.g., duties to be performed by you and others if you were chairman of a class picnic.
b. Discuss responsibilities of patrol boys in caring for safety of others.
c. Send children in pairs as messengers or work in pairs as helpers until certain of selves. Sociometric data can be used.
d. Gradually transfer responsibility for many housekeeping functions.

9. *Making plans and putting them into operation.*

a. Social studies: Project—visit to fire station. Give each of three groups a phase of trip to plan and execute: (1) letter to parents obtaining permission, (2) listing things to look for and acting as group guides, (3) arranging transportation and collecting money if necessary.
b. Any unit offers multiple opportunity for obtaining desired information by group activity.
c. Dramatization: plan holiday program for parents; select play, songs, assign parts; assign responsibility for props, scenery, costumes.

10. *Developing leadership and followership.*

   a. Divide into pairs with one pupil helping another.
   b. Allow children with special talents or hobbies to help others have similar interests.
   c. Games: Follow leader; Simon says; Giant steps.

11. *Evaluating work.*

   a. After trip to fire station or post office have each child list what he recalls and compare his list with total list compiled by class.
   b. Have each child evaluate his own health habits.
   c. Let each child prepare his own report with his own rating, then compare with teacher. Discuss differences.
   d. Use check lists daily for a week in which pupil checks off his performance, e.g., obeying rules; helping others. (The check list of rules will provide immediate evidence as to the number and reasonableness of rules in effect).
   e. Have children keep individual graphs of progress in academic subjects. Intervals should be far enough apart that progress occurs and day-to-day fluctuations don't become discouraging.

13. *Enjoyment of working and playing with others.*

   a. Organize groups on basis of sociogram. Select tasks or topics considered enjoyable and interesting. See that each child has equal opportunity for performance.
   b. Discuss games to be played during recess and ways in which most enjoyment can be had. Care will have to be taken that minority interests are served and that seasonal games played by the majority do not exclude all others.
   c. Music: recreational singing; rhythm bands; homemade instruments.
   d. Oral language: making up and producing simple spontaneous plays. Typical parent-child and brother-sister problems can be used.

14. *Helping others to carry out responsibilities.*

   a. Alternating chairman on activities so all have opportunity to lead and follow.
   b. Social studies committees each assigned a country in a given geographic area can not only develop their own project but contribute information about neighboring countries.
   c. Opportunities for children to perform real duties: e.g.,

fifth grade rotates answering school telephone. Sixth grade rotates helping in cafeteria for a week. Fourth graders act as guides to visitors. Within districts where many new children come each year, individual classes can work out arrangements for helping the newcomer, not only in classwork, but in community.

15. *Punctuality and consistency in carrying out duties.*

    a. Have groups set and check their own standards for time, neatness. Guidance in making regulations reasonable needed.

    b. Discussions of tardiness and reasons for, disadvantages of, effect on groups.

ACCEPTANCE OF INDIVIDUAL AND GROUP DIFFERENCES

The activities discussed in the two preceding sections, "Group Belonging" and "Group Participation" mainly serve to help children become aware of what they are expected to do in particular situations in school and in other parts of the community and to help them assess and accommodate to group codes—to be aware of what makes one popular, disliked and to know what goes under what conditions. Social adjustment, also, requires one to be sensitive to other people and how they feel towards us and about our behavior towards them. Many children are simply "blind" to other people and their feelings and until their "eyes," so to speak, are opened, they will persist in inadequate behavior. In some instances, the blindness results from simple ignorance. Bert, discussed earlier in the chapter, is a good illustration. There is no question here of personality maladjustment or even basic social maladjustment. He simply was out of step with the social situation in which he lived part of his day, and he was quick to see the difference and changed when he was given appropriate clues.

Some children don't want to see. As long as they see themselves being pushed around by adults who don't respect them, warfare is the order of the day. And like the soldier who shoots first and preferably doesn't think afterward, peace has to be declared before reconstruction can start. Many elements in school programs present such hazards to some children: unsuitable curricula, overcompetition, inadequate provision for individual differences, punitive disciplinary methods, etc. Then there are some children who can't see because of individual pathology which prevents their grasping reality as it is without clinical help to remove the blinders.

Four sets of conditions exist which have important effects on children's abilities to accept and respect individual differences.

1. Community cleavages, prejudices, and attitudes which are reflected in the classroom.
2. Teacher acceptance of individual differences.
3. Competition for status and security in school.
4. Pupil status systems.

By the third grade, children can be seen expressing prejudices and attitudes towards differing social groups and minority groups which they unconsciously acquire from their parents. A school in which all the highly chosen children in all classes are from a favored socio-economic group or a given religious group reflects a social cleavage within the community. Most of these problems can be approached directly or indirectly at either an informational level or an attitudinal level. Four examples of these approaches with respect to prejudices:

> *Direct informational.* Children are asked to express frankly how they feel about religious, ethnic, or minority groups (according to the type of problem existing), Catholics, Protestants, and Jews may be characterized or caricatured in the process. Follow with comparison of known persons to determine how true the stereotype is; or evaluate actual facts known and seek further facts about member of groups. Information may be sought from parents as to known facts and subsequently evaluated (anonymously).
>
> *Direct attitudinal.* Ask children if any of them or their families or relatives have ever been discriminated against. Have children relate instances. In upper grades, particular situations can be selected and acted out in a sociodrama by asking the child who had the experience to select a pupil with whom he'd like to act it out, then treating that person in the way he experienced discrimination. Preferably he should pick a person from the majority group, in order that the latter can experience the feeling and that other members of the group identifying with him, experience it emphatically. At a minimum, there are certain to be children who have been picked on by bigger children, a miniature form of intolerance.
>
> *Indirect informational.* Many social studies projects inquiring into American History have units on immigration. Usually the conditions in Europe which gave rise to the immigration are more fully discussed than the reception the immigrants met in America—the Irish in the East, the Negroes in the South, the Mexicans in the Southwest, the Japanese in the West, the Indians

in the central states (although Indians scarcely qualify as immigrants). Discussion of such topics can increase the children's understanding of and make them more sympathetic toward minority groups.

Indirect-attitudinal. Few communities exist which do not have members of minority groups who have experienced persecution and scapegoating, either in this generation or previously. Invitations can be extended to such persons to visit and discuss their experiences.

Whatever the approach adopted by the teacher, we are unlikely to make much progress in eliminating prejudice and intolerance in our communities if we take no action to reduce it in children. The teacher will find a rich source of suggestions in two publications of the American Council on Education—*With Focus on Human Relations*[3] and *Curriculum in Intergroup Relations.*[4]

The emotional capacity of highly chosen children to reach out and accept isolates was mentioned in the discussion of the use of sociograms. These children develop this capacity because of the adults around them. In the classroom, their ability to use it is directly affected by the capacity of the teacher to accept and reach out to children, however unlikable they may be. Few adults are able to like all children, but we can attempt to broaden our attitudes, to find some virtue or likable quality in most children, and by expressing these feelings encourage a similar attitude among children.

Teachers will find it a fascinating experience, if they have the patience and courage, to keep a record for a week of the classroom events that annoyed them, the events that pleased them, the behavior they rewarded (by any positive indication) and the behavior they rejected (by any negative indication). From such a log or diary of events, they will identify the actual reinforcement schedule in operation in their classroom and the kinds of behavior towards which it is directed. Children have little choice but to comply with the standards established by the teacher, or else rebel. If the only way to gain acceptance and approval from the teacher is through brilliant academic performance, then those children who care about such approval will strive for it by fair means or foul, and no love or consideration of fellow classmate will interfere. Thus, the range of behavior being actually approved by the teacher will strongly influence the behavior of children towards each other.

---

[3]Hilda Taba and Deborah Elkins, *With Focus on Human Relations.* Washington, D. C.: American Council on Education, 1949.
[4]American Council on Education, *Curriculum in Intergroup Relations: Elementary School.* Washington, D. C.: 1946.

A system of rewards which restricts success in a classroom to a fairly narrow range of human ability, as academic achievement based on grades does, creates an environment in which satisfaction of need is dependent upon defeat of classmate (until one gives up and no longer cares). In effect, a highly competitive environment is created. In homogeneous groups and so-called classes for the gifted, the dangers are even greater, for a portion of children who would normally experience success in a heterogeneous group face defeat and humiliation in a "high-pressure" group. In actual practice, it is absurd to give grades in gifted classes. The emphasis should be on satisfactory task performance. Children who don't perform return to regular groups. With the remainder, grades are irrelevant. If the gifted-class is a success, it will yield better grades in high school and college; if not, it is better forgotten.

From the mental health viewpoint, consideration should be given to several essential aspects of ego functioning if children are to survive in a competitive environment.

1. Restraint of immediate needs in favor of long range goals (difficult for young children).
2. Ability to generate aggression and channel it into socially useful purpose without allowing hostility to dominate (difficult for aggressive or highly frustrated children).
3. Ability to engage in the competition with adequate self-control, enjoyment, and necessary skill (difficult for nearly all children).
4. Ability to take defeat without disorganization and victory without crowing (difficult for insecure children).
5. Sufficient ego-strength and assuredness to neither develop feelings of superiority on success or scapegoating on defeat.
6. Ability to accept temporary frustration in hope of possible later gain (difficult for zealous perfectionists).
7. Ability to accept limits and results without recourse to code violation (cheating) or displacement of hostility (to self or others) (difficult for children with high aspiration and goal anticipation).

The difficulties posed for children in the foregoing list can be appreciated. Only well-integrated egos are built to withstand such demands. In the face of incapacity or defeat, hostile, belligerent, intolerant or scapegoating behavior is likely. It is for such reasons that mental hygienists decry the hazards of competitive environments, for the price in individual anxiety and social hostility is too great.

Attention has to be given to the pupil status system in understanding the conditions which affect regard for individuals. In the primary grades, the factors which determine status among children are largely a reflection of the adult attitudes and behaviors, but as children mature, they evolve their own scale for judging individual worth. One of the advantages of asking children on a sociogram why they chose certain persons, or interviewing them on their choices, is to obtain insight into the value system operating within a given group. Generalizations are dangerous for these standards vary from group to group (see above for anecdotes on Bert); nevertheless, they are subject to influence by teacher action. When a teacher says, after reseating a classroom on the basis of a sociogram, "I was pleased to see the reasons you gave for choosing others: being friendly; kind and cooperative; he helps me; we have fun together; she is a hard worker," she selects (and possibly inserts of her own volition—a teacher prerogative) and announces ways in which children should appreciate each other. If her actions are consistent with these values, children will adopt the model presented and respond accordingly. Often our shortcoming as adults is our tendency to pay lip-service to one kind of behavior and effectively encourage another through the systems of rewards in operation. By shaping such attitudes, the teacher literally molds the kinds of interpersonal relationships which exist in her classroom.

A final word is in order with respect to individual and group behavior concerning the authoritative "NO." The stress that guidance texts place on group planning and decision, individual and group responsibility, permissiveness and freedom, leads many teachers to a conviction that the word "no" doesn't exist in the guidance vocabulary. Quite the contrary. Unfortunately, in our efforts to change existing practices, our recommendations reflect a counteraction and an extraordinary emphasis on the direction of needed change. On occasions when children's impulses are out of hand, when they are on the verge of engaging in actions they really wouldn't enjoy, or when their actions present a real danger to themselves or others, a firm and unqualified NO is needed, which says simply and without argument: Stop.

An advantage that accrues to the principal's role is that his greater remoteness from familiar contact with children and his higher position in the authoritative hierarchy gives his edict a firmness which may not be challenged with the ease that the teacher's might. In schools where teachers and principals have developed effective working relationships, the principal can be used as such a resource. This assumes that an established arrangement exists for tapping this resource rather than its being a court of last resort. If the group feels that the principal was called as a last resort because the situation was beyond the control of the teacher, much of the teacher's management capacity has evaporated. In contrast, a recognition of the eventual progress of group mood and action with recourse to planned interference procedures can not only stop the behavior but fortify teacher authority.

REFERENCES FOR PART FIVE

Allport, Gordon W. *The Nature of Prejudice*. Reading, Mass.: Addison-Wesley Publishing Co., 1954.

Bullis, Harold E. *Human Relations in the Classroom*. I & II, Wilmington, Delaware: Delaware State Society for Mental Hygiene, 1947.

Cunningham, Ruth. *Understanding Group Behavior of Boys and Girls*. New York: Columbia University Press, 1951.

Gronlund, N. E. *Sociometry in the Classroom*. New York: Harper & Row, Publishers, 1959.

Ilg, Frances and Ames, Louise. *Child Behavior*. New York: Harper & Row, Publishers, 1951.

Jennings, Helen. *Leadership and Isolation*. New York: Longmans, Green & Co., Inc., 1950.

Moreno, J. L. *Who Shall Survive?* New York: Beacon Press, 1953.

Slavson, S. R. *Introduction to Group-Psychotherapy*. New York: International Universities Press, 1943.

Taba, Hilda and Elkins, Deborah. *With Focus on Human Relations*. Washington, D. C.: American Council on Education, 1949.

Taba, Hilda. *Elementary Curriculum in Intergroup Relations*. Washington, D. C.: American Council on Education, 1950.

Part Six

SCHOOL AND COMMUNITY

Chapter 17

SCHOOL AND COMMUNITY

To this point, our focus has been on the individual and his developing characteristics. Now we turn to the group, the class, the school, and the community, inasmuch as each child develops in the context of a given environment over which he has limited control, yet which plays an important role in his personality and character development. Generally speaking, children are not analytical about teacher and school. They can tell you whether or not they like school—some children develop quite penetrating insights into the motivation and action patterns of teachers—but for the most part, school is what it is and not until later years does one arrive at a critical evaluation of what it was or might have been.

Two impediments interfere with our gathering information about groups and school: (1) our usual focus on the individual and his characteristics makes it difficult not to see a group as the mere total of several individuals; and (2) the extent to which we adapt to our environment and accept it as it occurs obstructs our view of the school and community as it is. Groups develop particular characteristics of their own: the attitude towards authority, the morale, the degree of cohesion, and the style of leadership, to name a few. It requires some skill in observation to look beyond the characteristics and personalities of individual members and observe the common attitudes and ways of treating each other.

One can look at a community and appraise some of its characteristics objectively; the buildings may be tenements, single family residences on small lots, large homes on spacious grounds. The buildings may be well maintained or show deterioration. The streets may be in good or bad condition; recreational facilities may or may not exist. Certain conclusions can be drawn from such observations. But to know the full characteristics of a community, one would have to observe more than the physical and economic conditions. Some time would have to be given to the social, religious, and political functioning. Two communities may be similar in physical appearance, but one may be governed by an entrenched clique, the other not; one may, covertly, of course, exclude Jews or Negroes, or have marked suspicion or sharp antagonism between Catholic, Protestant, and Jew. There may be a modus vivendi, whereby the political parties have informally agreed to split the control of the school committee, or the opposite where an entrenched political group is fighting vigorously, even unscrupulously, to control all seats. In short, the social health of communities is not regulated by the physical environment.

If you spend any time in different schools, you will be impressed by the influence of the principal upon the life of the school. One school will be deathly quiet with all classes performing with solemn decorum; another will be the opposite, noisy and confused, the principal's voice resounding periodically over the intercommunication system. Some will sound like the soup-pot on the back of the stove, mildly bubbling with hidden activity in different rooms. Within a school, there are variations from classroom to classroom, consistent with personality differences among the teachers. Somehow, and this is supposition, there seems less variation than one would anticipate. Whether this is the result of process of selection or training which provides for similarity in all teachers, or the result of the principal's recruitment policy wherein he senses which applicants are more congenial to his desires, I'm not certain, although I suspect the latter. Whatever the factors, one would have to look beyond the age of the building, the height of the ceilings, the maintenance of the floors, the age of the books, to understand the attitude and morale of the school as it exists for children.

All of this holds true for classes and groups as well. Their nutrition, dress, age, cleanliness, and other conditions can be estimated. But to know the group, one has to know more than the individual children.

One must look to the ways in which they treat each other, choose their leaders, follow instructions, and other aspects in order to know how they function as a *group*. Skill in making such appraisal is difficult to attain for it requires observing what occurs *between* two or more individuals. Perhaps an illustration will sharpen the argument.

GROUP CHARACTERISTICS

A teacher, in discussing a project she wished to undertake, said that she wished to study her "clawing class." She was a junior high school teacher who had become concerned about the manner in which members of this class treated each other. She recounted how she provided for class elections of officers with an attempt to develop some skill in parliamentary procedure, and group discussion of problems that arose. Instead of her efforts to share responsibility and provide for group development proving effective, the class had subverted the arrangement to their "clawing" or fault-finding. For instance, she related that any time the class secretary would report the minutes of a previous meeting, the class would sit expectantly, like panthers waiting to spring, listening for errors in the report. The first mistake, however trivial, would be detected, then the second. Always with the second, someone would say: "That's your second mistake, you have to do the report over again." The teacher's concern was to learn how such practice had developed and how it might be changed for the better.

The following guide for group observation is quite crude, but it suggests aspects of group behavior which can be observed:

Maturity: (compared to other classes of same grades)	immature	average	more mature
	wide variation		narrow variation
Activity:	active	average	lethargic
Ability:	below average	average	above average
Interests:	narrow passive	diversified active	
Attitude toward school:	apathetic	neutral	enthusiastic
Group relations:	competitive tense cool	antagonistic cool friendly	cooperative helpful intimate

Group structure:	unorganized
	independent work by individuals
	group goal with effective division of labor
	group goal with ineffective division of labor

Group cohesiveness:	individualistic
	few sub-groups, remainder individualistic
	many sub-groups, pairs, triads, and larger
	closely knit

| *Types of group activity:* | disorganized | organized |
| | formal | informal |

Extent of participation:	few participants, many observers
	many participants, few on the fringe
	all participating

Roles played in group:	agitator	critic	leader
	teacher's	clown	helper
	pet	daredevil	little
	boss, etc.	scapegoat	mother
			tattletale

| *Reaction to teacher:* | hostile, fearful, indifferent, responsive, friendly |

Control patterns:	adult domination of individual or groups
	individual planning
	group planning

Control techniques:	suggestions: "couldn't we do this?"
	"why not try?"
	discussion of problem: "what should we do?"
	praise-blame
	appeal or threat—
	"report to principal or parent"
	"good boys and good girls don't"
	"good or poor marks"
	giving or withholding of affection
	imposed authority
	established group standards

GROUP OBSERVATION

Observation of the natural social units of children—cliques, if you will, or friendship groups—will yield fruitful information about the nature of the interpersonal relationships. Cliques or friendship groups have as their basis the acceptance of each member and the satisfaction derived from interaction with each other in whatever activities may be undertaken. The places to observe such groups are in those situations where some freedom of choice exists: where children have free choice of seats, on the playground when they group themselves for games or teams, or in the lunchroom as they group themselves for eating. Charts like a sociogram can be made, designating which children are participating in which groups. The amount of interaction between subgroups can be recorded. For instance, in the lunchroom, a group at one table made repeated exchange comments, jokes, etc., with another table, and ignored all other members of the class. The children who eat alone, play alone or are chosen last, who sit or stand on the fringe of activities, can be observed. These natural subgroups can be compared with the sociogram, both differences and similarities being noted.

Once the membership of subgroups are noted the possible factors influencing the division can be investigated.

The problem is to identify the common characteristics or characteristics which distinguish the members of one particular group from another. Possibilities to be considered are:

Age: Are the younger children excluded by the more mature?

Nationality: Is there a cleavage between groups of different nationality or ethnic background?

Religion: Is there a division between religious groups?

Transportation: Is there a division between children who bus to school and those who walk?

Sex: Are girls separate from boys?

Residence: Are the neighborhood groups carrying over into the school situation?

Intelligence: Do the brighter students group together?

Social Class: Do children of the same socio-economic background tend to stay by themselves?

These questions and their use in the analysis of social groups were discussed in Chapter 15 under the analysis of the sociogram.

ANALYSIS OF SOCIAL CLASS

Sociological studies in many American communities have shown that the natural groups in which people participate fall into a series of strata which may be ranked according to the prestige they are accorded by all of the community. Their terms—upper, middle, and lower class, or white collar and blue collar—have been used to designate these differences. These groups differ in their attitudes, value systems, procedures used in child-care, attitude toward education, and other significant characteristics.

One of the virtues of education has been that it provides equal opportunity for any individual to make full use of his talents and attain a standing in the community commensurate with his ability. This vertical mobility which education makes possible is a valued procedure in our society (other avenues for rising in the social scale are via marriage, personality, and special talent). This sorting of people into social strata which occurs by social process in the community is important to the teacher because of its carry-over into the school. Children, especially as they get older, are likely to form their friendship groups among children from the same strata, excluding those from different strata. This tends to hold children to a given strata, regardless of their talents, for their friendship groupings reinforce the attitudes and values inherent in a given social strata. This becomes especially significant when the children from the more favored strata reject their classmates.

I have observed an elementary school serving children from two quite diverse social strata in which every classroom revealed a cleavage on the sociograms wherein all the highly chosen children were from the upper class and all the isolates were from the lower class. This resulted from the tendency of the upper class children to choose each other, and the lower class children to seek acceptance in the upper class groups. Where such conditions prevail, children of talent are denied access to participation and membership in groups which permit their acquiring the values, motivations, and behavior patterns which are as essential to vertical mobility as talent.

It may develop in time, particularly under the influence of mass media, that a leveling process will occur which eliminates the social stratifications, but until such time and as long as we espouse a value system which encourages vertical mobility (any boy can be President), it is important to foster procedures in the school which reduce the congealing of these divisions along existing lines. There are other considerations fully, if not more, important to the health of a democracy than the personal success of its individuals which prompt such considerations, but which are beyond the scope of this book.

It is of value to the teacher to understand the differences in social strata and recognize their influence in the group structure of her class and school. There is a danger too, as there always seems to be, with knowledge. The value systems of teachers are derived from the social system and tend to reinforce existing conditions. Teachers "look-up" to the "better families" and disregard those of lesser status. The designation of a child as lower class can be used injuriously just as intelligence test scores have been so used. To tell a group of children that the tests show they are stupid or that they should be doing better work because the intelligence tests show them to be bright is a destructive use of information. Similar unpleasant castigating can be done with social class appellations. In contrast, to know that social class differences are a factor entering into the groupings of a class provides knowledge which can be put to constructive use.

In the investigation of social class, the discovery was made that certain common characteristics could be used to determine social class membership with approximately the same accuracy that is obtained with extensive, but time-consuming, interview procedures. By obtaining the occupation, the source of income, the neighborhood, and the house type, assigning each a rank from 1-7, and multiplying this rank by an assigned weight, a total score can be obtained which permits the designation of that family to one of several social strata.

Tables 1 and 2[1] provide the basic information needed for making a social status survey. Using the form shown in Table 1, list the names of the pupils in the left column, following this with the occupation of the parent, the source (not the amount) of income, the type of house, and the neighborhood. In Table 2 you will observe the categories to be used under each of these headings. The most difficult of the four is that concerning neighborhood. The best procedure is to obtain a map of the community, and either by inspection or with the help of a real estate agent who knows the community, mark off the map into the different areas. Following this, mark each child's residence on the map, then assign the type of neighborhood.

Once each piece of information is recorded, as shown for Dick Abbott in Table 1, the rank from 1-7 taken from Table 2 can be recorded in columns A-D. In the instance of Dick Abbott, his father is a machinist, a skilled occupation receiving a rank of 4. Care should be taken in obtaining specific titles of occupations and levels within occupations in order to distinguish between skilled and semi-skilled work. The source of income is wages ranked as 5; the family dwells in a two-family house in a mixed neighborhood both ranked 5. Ad-

[1]Tables 1 and 2 are adapted from W. L. Warner, *Social Class in America.* Chicago: Science Research Associates, 1949.

Table 1. Form for Social Status Survey

Social Status Survey

Directions: List class in alphabetical order. List information needed in Columns 1, 2, 3, 4. Using Code Sheet, assign a Rank to information listed and record it in Columns A, B, C, D. Multiply these ranks by weights shown and record under weighted ranks and total.

Name	1 Parent Occupation	A Rank	2 Source Income	B R	3 House Type	C R	4 Neighbor-hood	D Weighted Ranks					Status
								R	4A	3B	2C	2D	Total	
Abbott, Dick	machinist	4	wages	5	two-fam.	5	mixed	5	16	15	10	10	51	

TABLE 2. CLASSIFICATIONS OF OCCUPATION, SOURCE OF INCOME, HOUSE TYPE, AND NEIGHBORHOOD FOR A SOCIAL STATUS SURVEY

Rank   *Occupations*

1 Professional and proprietors of large businesses
2 Semi-professional and smaller officials of large businesses
3 Clerks and kindred workers—sales
4 Skilled workers
5 Proprietors of very small businesses
6 Semi-skilled workers
7 Unskilled workers

Source of Income

1 Inherited wealth—main income made in previous generations and passed on
2 Earned wealth—those who have earned in their own right enough money to enable them to retire—the successful man in terms of money-making
3 Profits and fees—professional men who derive income from fees for services, business owners from profits, writers, etc.
4 Salary—income received on a regular monthly or yearly basis, including commissions
5 Wages—usually determined on an hourly basis and paid weekly
6 Private relief—supported by family, friends, churches, associations, etc.
7 Public relief—receiving government aid or aid from semi-public source which reveal name of recipient. Include here the non-respectable sources—gambling

Rank   *House Type*

1 Excellent houses—large, ostentatious, in *top* shape, large, well-cared for grounds
2 Very good houses—those which don't measure up to above; lesser but perhaps newer
3 Good houses—conventional, slightly larger than needs, unostentatious
4 Average houses—conventional, 1½ or 2 story frame or brick, single-family dwellings, little or no landscape
5 Fair houses—as in #4 but not in good condition; also small houses in good condition
6 Poor houses—state of disrepair barely possible of being mended
7 Very poor houses—badly deteriorated, debris

Neighborhood

1 Most exclusive—the aristocracy
2 Less pretentious, fewer mansions, difference one of reputation
3 Nice, respectable area inhabited mainly by society folks. Streets neat and well-cleaned
4 Average neighborhood—workingman's neighborhood
5 Mixed neighborhood, frequently too close to railroad, industry or some such distracting factor
6 Semi-slum. Houses too close, no new buildings, sometimes poor streets
7 Slum area—worst in town. Distinct social stigma attached to area

joining these classifications in Table 1 are four columns under the caption "Weighted Ranks." The rank that has been given is to be multiplied by the number adjacent to the A, B, C, or D to obtain a weighted rank. The occupational rank of 4 in Column A has been multiplied by 4 (4A) to obtain the 16 shown. The 5 in B has been multiplied by 3 (3B) to obtain the 15. In C and D, the 5's have been multiplied by 2 (2C and 2D) to produce 10 for each category. These numbers are added together to obtain the total of 51 shown. It can be seen that the effect of multiplying makes occupation twice as important a factor as either house type or neighborhood in the final score, suggesting that one's work plays an important part in the particular stratum of society in which one finds oneself. The scores below give the class designation.

Score	Social Class Designation
12-22	Upper class—"Old Families" of high status and more recently wealthy families. Incomes from investment, large business, and professions.
25-34	Upper-middle class. "Solid and respectable" citizens of professional and smaller businesses.
37-50	Lower-middle class. White-collar, clerical, skilled. The "common man."
54-63	Upper-lower class. The "working class"—the semi-skilled, building trades, transportation and retail sales. The "little man" in "shirt-sleeves."
67-84	Lower-lower class. Unskilled, part-time, and unemployed, plus resident immigrants.

Having arrived at the social class designations, these can be compared with the membership of sub-groups within the class to determine the extent that it plays in the formation of groups.

COMMON GROUP EXPERIENCES

Direct inquiry can be made with upper grade classes into the kinds of opportunities in interpersonal relationships which are to be found within a given group. Cunningham[2] and her associates have developed a check list which obtains a frequency rating and an importance rating on the kinds of human relations experiences to which a group

[2]Ruth Cunningham and associates, *Group Behavior of Boys and Girls.* New York: Bureau of Publications, Teachers College, Columbia University, 1951, pp. 407-412. Material used with permission.

is exposed. The form, which is reproduced below in modified form, provides the teacher with a quick survey which, combined with information obtained from other sources, assists her in identifying the kinds of experiences needed.

CHECK SHEET OF OPPORTUNITIES IN HUMAN RELATIONS

Name_____ Age_____ Grade_____

School_____ Boy_____ Girl_____

Read each statement under the heading "Experience." Then give the following information for each statement:

1. How often? Check one of the three columns: frequently, sometimes, seldom or never. If you honestly don't know, check the ? column.

2. How valuable? How valuable has the experience been? Important? Then check the important column. If OK but not important, check the second column, if unimportant, check the third column. If you can't decide, check the ?.

Check Sheet of Opportunities in Human Relations Experience	How Often?				How Valuable?			
	Freq. Almost Every Day	Some-times	Sel-dom	?	Imp.	OK	Not Imp.	?
1. Be a member of a team for some sport.								
2. Be a member of a club or gang.								
3. Work or play with people of different religious belief.								
4. Work or play with people of different race or nationality.								
5. Work or play with people who are considerably wealthier than my family.								
6. Work or play with people who have considerably less money than my family.								
7. Work or play with people who are much smarter than I am.								

Check Sheet of Opportunities in Human Relations Experience	How Often?				How Valuable?			
	Freq. Almost Every Day	Some-times	Sel-dom	?	Imp.	OK	Not Imp.	?
8. Work or play with people who are considerably slower thinking than I am.								
9. Work or play in groups in which adults are members (aside from teachers or youth leaders).								
10. Be a member of a group which makes its own rules or elects its own leaders.								
11. Be a leader of a group my age.								
12. Be a member of a group my age where no adult is in control.								
13. Meet people who come from outside my community.								
14. Visit communities other than my own.								
15. Spend leisure time with friends of my own choice.								
16. Spend leisure time alone.								
17. Discuss with others my age what is going on in the world.								
18. Discuss boy-girl relations.								
19. Discuss questions about sex.								
20. Discuss marriage, home, family, living.								
21. Discuss possible vocational choices.								
22. Take part in community affairs.								
23. Work for pay.								
24. Work at home (do chores) without pay.								
25. Do useful work for the community without pay.								

Check Sheet of Opportunities in Human Relations Experience	*How Often?*				*How Valuable?*			
	Freq. Almost Every Day	Some-times	Sel-dom	?	Imp.	OK	Not Imp.	?
26. Work or play with people much younger (4 or more years.)								
27. Work or play with people much older (4 or more years).								
28. Work or play with persons of the opposite sex.								
29. Work or play in a group of four or five people.								
30. Work or play in a group of 10-12.								
31. Work or play in a group of 30-50.								

32. If you had a personal problem about which you were worried, to whom would you go in your family?
33. To whom could you go outside of your family?
34. How do you feel about the amount of adult control you receive from your family? (Check one) Too much_____ About right_____ Too little_____.
35. How do you feel about the amount of control over you by your school? (Check one) Too much_____ About right_____ Too little_____.
36. Check the words or phrases which you feel describe you:
    _____Find it easy to make friends.
    _____Find it difficult to make friends.
    _____Wish I had more skill in getting along with people.
    _____Well liked by most.
    _____Liked by a few, but not many.
    _____Disliked by many.
    _____Shy.
    _____A leader.
    _____Not understood.
    _____Not as smart as most.
    _____More intelligent than most.
    _____Prefer to be alone much of the time.
    _____Want to be with people most of the time.
    _____More interested in people than in things or ideas.
    _____More interested in ideas or things than in people.
    _____More interested in sports than in either.

————Wish the school would give more help in how to get
along with people.

————Wish I didn't have to go to school.

37. My three friends in school are:

Another procedure of value in determining the caliber of group
functioning is to concentrate on a specific aspect of behavior for a
period of several days or a week, noting the kinds of events which
occur with respect to the item under consideration. Several items
excerpted from a longer list under each category are reported from
the notes of a sixth grade teacher:

Self-control and self-discipline

1. Jeanne and Sue had a fight during recess. They went after
each other, wildly swinging baseball bats.
2. Julie was corrected by Seymour, a monitor, in the hall for
pushing. She then began kicking John, the boy in front of her.

Responsibility

1. The majority of the pupils fail to carry out the various room
duties assigned to them. Unless reminded in the afternoon,
many duties are neglected or left half done.
2. Judy, Sandy, and Dickie left new playground equipment out
of doors. Rule had been established that whoever took it out
was responsible for returning it. Bat and ball rained on.

Aspects of behavior such as cooperation, consideration for others,
willingness to accept newcomers, sportsmanship, attitude towards
others, care of property, can be considered. Care should be taken
to observe the full picture, not merely the transgression and violations. Adults are so prone to judge children's actions by adult expectations that they see more of the failures and fewer of the
accomplishments that children exhibit.

CLASSROOM ATMOSPHERE

Volumes have been written and will be written on classroom
atmosphere and the role of the teacher in the creating of a psychological environment conducive to healthy emotional development.
Indeed, the teacher who uses many of the techniques which have
been suggested in this and earlier chapters can scarcely avoid seeing
some reflection of herself in the information obtained: in the structure of the group, in the personal relations, the attitudes, and the
standards which evolve.

The following sociometric tally sheet (Figure 1) reflects the teacher
quite clearly. Ten of the twenty-four children in the class are iso-

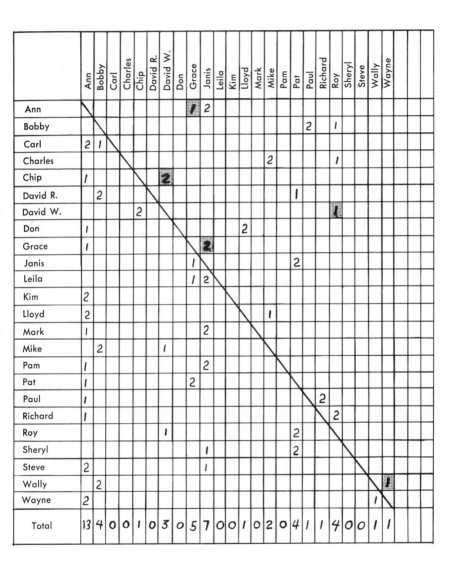

Figure 1. Sociometric tally of 3rd grade class showing high frequency of isolates and few mutual choices .

lates, receiving no choices whatsoever, and six more receive only one choice. One quarter of the class captures three-quarters of the choices expressed, with the three most highly chosen being girls. Only five mutual choices occurred with two of these within the highly chosen triumvirate. If this sociogram is a true picture of the class, the situation is most unhealthy, for the great majority of the class is not experiencing any sense of friendship or participation in mutually satisfying interpersonal relationships, with the boys especially experiencing difficulty. The three girls were good students, but more significant they were the teacher's pride and joy, Ann in particular. More than scholarship, they exhibited prim propriety in class and marked deference for the teacher. You ask: what was the teacher like? She describes herself as "strict"—but "the children are very fond of me" and "the parents like me because the children behave for me." And it was true, her principal was quite pleased with her work—"she had such a quiet, well-mannered class."

Well-subdued would more accurately describe the situation. The teacher thought that she used modern educational methods when she appointed a class captain (Ann) whenever she left the room. The class captain was, in effect, an excellent policewoman, mimicking the teacher's authoritative tone, reporting all infractions to the teacher on return.

During an arithmetic lesson, a shy, reserved boy, having difficulty adding aloud at the board in the presence of two observers, was admonished five times to "Speak up," "Face the class," "Talk louder." He was scolded for skipping the zero in adding a column. Several times during the morning, students had come to her desk to apologize with a prescribed ritual for minor infractions.

The group lacked spontaneity or enthusiasm, personalities appear dulled in the strict atmosphere. Emphasis was placed on being smart. It became more and more evident that the highly chosen on the sociogram were these preferred by the teacher, not by the class, and that so dominant was the impact of this young teacher, of three years experience, on this third grade class that they dared not express a wish of their own.

This is a striking incident, but even in less dramatic incidents, the teacher should repeatedly ask herself the question: To what extent have the classroom arrangements and administrative procedures which I follow created this effect and what change would produce what benefit?

A teacher needs feedback devices which inform her from time to time about the feelings and expectations of the class. It is generally more desirable that such feedback of information from a class be done orally, for it is a necessary step in the development of independence and self-discipline to be able to disagree with authority and have the disagreement accepted without attendant feelings of guilt being stimulated. Discussions have the advantage of bringing attitudes and feelings into the open and, in the process of discussion, assisting the group to review and crystallize its thinking.

Several simple techniques are available to the teacher for obtaining a reflection of the roles she is playing in the class. One is to ask the class to list:

The most satisfying aspect of this class
The most irritating or annoying aspect of this class
The thing most in need of change
What should I suggest be done

These questions identify the most and least favorable features of the class—the teacher can repeat this from time to time, one time designating the program, another personal relationships, and the third time, the teacher. Most important, it leads to recommended changes, which if the teacher desires, can be listed and discussed.

An approach that is effective at the beginning of the school year, or at a time when a new teacher joins the class, is to ask the class to list what they want most and least in a teacher. Items such as fairness, pleasant manner, sense of humor, knowledge of subject matter, helps the class to learn a lot, will lead the list and crabbiness, yelling, favoritism will be high on the list of dislikes. Such an inquiry provides the teacher not only with a model for herself, but with an opportunity to discuss with the class what she likes in a student— after all, turnabout is fair play—and by so doing create the foundation for the kind of relationships and attitudes to be developed.

A variation on this theme—asking a second grade on the last day of school the kind of a teacher they would like next September— produced the following wishes:

Desired	12 Boys	15 Girls
Personal qualities		
Soft voice	5	7
Pretty, blonde (1)	3	5
Young	1	3
Remain single	0	1
Woman	1	3
Man	0	1

Like boys	3	0
Like girls	0	1
School activities		
Spelling every day	2	1
Arithmetic	1	1
Write on board	3	0
More homework	5	5
Read a lot	2	2
Stay after school to help	0	1
Color	1	0
Gym	1	2
Privileges		
Eat things in school	3	0
Party every day	0	1

Fortunately, every teacher can be pretty to primary grade children, for they respond less to physical appearance than manner and attitude. The most desired personal quality was a soft voice. Whether or not this is a reaction to the preceding year is unknown. As much interest was expressed regarding the class work as the personal qualities of the teacher, although the girls were somewhat more concerned with personal qualities.

Another procedure which proves useful in appraising the tenor of events is to keep a record or diary of annoyances, disruptions, or occurrences which called for special action or attention by yourself. Many times such a record will bring to light repeated disciplinary actions or control actions being taken with a given child which are proving ineffective. The record will reveal this quite clearly, whereas the press of events erases them from memory. Oftentimes alternate methods of handling the situation, either to avoid the event, or to provide for effective action, suggest themselves. Frequently, the teacher will see herself revealed in the record as becoming unnecessarily annoyed by trifling events, which sometimes almost appear to exist specifically for the purpose of annoyance. Sometimes the solution lies in personal restraint, sometimes in other corrective action.

THE SCHOOL GUIDANCE PROGRAM

Inevitably, a teacher's efforts become vitiated unless the school program is organized to integrate her accomplishments with that of the total faculty. This is true with respect to her instructional efforts as well as her guidance efforts. In a one-room school, a teacher could carry out an uninterrupted instructional program for an individual child, but in schools with annual promotion from teacher to teacher, the effectiveness of any program depends on the coordination of the faculty effort.

The curriculum of a school is designed to provide sequence and order to the presentation of instructional experiences in order to fulfill the educational goals established. To be effective, information is needed regarding the rate of progress and level of accomplishment of each child at different points in time if instruction is to be more than an aimless barrage. The school testing program is designed to provide this information. Similar information is needed in determining a child's personal-social development and needed experiences in this area. The school guidance program serves this function. Both programs need a means of storage and transmission of information, which is the purpose of the cumulative record.

Effectively administered, the instructional program, the guidance program, and the testing program blend into a system which provides an even flow of activity with respect to each child and integrates the services he is receiving from the school. This cannot occur unless the administration and the staff have defined their objectives clearly and devised a mutually understood plan for attaining them. The extent of the program will depend upon the time, money, staff skills, and special services available, plus effective organization.

A brief review of needs can ascertain the status of a guidance program and major needs. More detailed analysis may be made with criteria specifically designed and available in texts on the organization and administration of guidance programs.

THE ADMINISTRATIVE FUNCTIONS

Planning and Organization

Time: How much time is provided in the regular schedule for guidance services—testing, counseling, parent conferences, etc.?

Materials: What is the budget allocation for needed materials for guidance tests, cabinets, space, record systems?

Procedures: What procedures are regularly planned for the guidance program? Is testing regularly scheduled? What procedures are regularly used for gathering information? What information is available, what is systematically gathered? Check the list of information and procedures. (Chapter 2.) Who uses cumulative records? With what frequency?

Delegation and Supervision

Is the execution of the guidance program left to the individual volition of staff or are specific duties assigned and reviewed? How are the separate duties coordinated to avoid duplication of effort? What assignments can teachers execute independently and which require administrative approval?

Training and Development

What in-service training is provided to develop skills of personnel to perform guidance functions? Is time and recognition provided for such developments? What recognition is given to problems and what arrangements made for solution? What portion of staff time or staff meetings is given to the guidance program?

THE STAFF FUNCTIONS

Training:

What is the background of education and experience of the staff in guidance? What is their knowledge and experience in test administration, interpretation, casework, counseling, etc.?

Skills:

What special skills are available in the staff that can be utilized in the guidance program, either for direct operation or in-service training, e.g., interviewing, testing, diagnosis of learning difficulties, etc.?

Attitudes:

What are the attitudes of the staff toward guidance services? Are they seen as an infringment on the teaching function or a desired service? What are the attitudes with respect to child development, discipline, parent relations, etc.? What are the significant contributions of each faculty member to the life of the school?

SPECIAL SERVICES

Consultants:

What services of specialized personnel are available and how often? Physician, nurse, dentist, psychologist, psychiatrist, psychometrist, guidance counselor.

Community Agencies:

What is the relationship of the school to both public and private agencies in the community? What use is made of them? What cooperative effort in individual cases?

The questions just presented fall short of a complete evaluation of the guidance program, but they do serve as guide lines to indicate the important aspects of the program and a rough measure of their adequacy. Guidance programs which depend on the volunteer effort of teachers working at their own expense on their own time can seldom rise above a makeshift level, and their effectiveness varies inversely with the level of fatigue.

THE TESTING PROGRAM

Tests are a device for obtaining a specified sampling of a given aspect of human ability which permits comparison of individuals with respect to that of the particular aspect sampled. They possess four main virtues: the trait or characteristic being tested is validly defined; the score obtained will not vary greatly on a retest; comparison of the standing of any individual to a known group is possible through the use of norms; many individuals may often be tested simultaneously providing an economical means of obtaining such information.

For each virtue there are one or more hazards to be risked in the use of tests. The test may be invalid. The author may claim a test measures sociability but offer no evidence other than his claim. The basic value of a test lies in its validity, for this determines the kinds of conclusions that can be based upon a test score. Even if valid, a test may be misinterpreted by a teacher. Two common misinterpretations are made of intelligence test scores. The first is too broad an interpretation, e.g., that an IQ is a measure of one's capacity to adapt to life, when essentially it measures capacity for scholastic learning. As a matter of fact, this latter interpretation is overly broad, for one cannot speak of *the* IQ as such, but rather of the meaning of the score obtained on a particular test, e.g., a Stanford-Binet IQ or a California Mental Maturity IQ. The second common misuse of an IQ score is associating a value judgment with it—to treat children with higher IQ's as if they were inherently more worthy than children less favored intellectually.

Another hazard lies in conditions which make a test score unreliable or inconsistent, e.g., another testing would produce a markedly different score. For instance, the required time limits may not be observed. Too little or too much time lowers or raises scores. For many reasons, one or more children may be poorly motivated to take the test—he may be ill, frightened, resentful of the test administrator, anxious, etc. The test scoring may be inaccurate, producing faulty scores. The use of a test score assumes that the test was appropriately selected, adequately administered and scored, and that the child understood the task and was working at capacity.

The norms provided by the test author may not be suitable for comparison or may be mis-used. A vocabulary test standardized on urban children has obvious limitations for rural children because of differences in experience. Intelligence tests in particular, in order to permit a conclusion that the difference in scores result from difference in basic intelligence, assume that all persons taking the test have had similar previous experiences. The degree to which a person taking the test differs from the norm group violates such an assumption, e.g., immigrants to the United States being tested on local tests.

Another hazard is that the tests used may determine educational goals. Some teachers, anticipating an achievement test at the end of the year, or College Entrance Examinations, specifically teach for the test. No achievement test can ever be more than a limited sample of knowledge, and some, by virtue of their content, are totally unsuited to a specific curriculum. A higher score obtained as a result of coaching is not a true score but a spurious score, for the coaching invalidates the test. If the achievement test at the end of the year becomes the teacher's concept of the ends of education, then education becomes a sorry mess.

With all the risks involved, properly standardized tests which have been selected for their suitability to the population being tested provide information which is useful and dependable, and, in some respects, superior to judgments of teachers. For instance, teachers can select the more able pupils in their classes, but cannot correct for age or experience differences, which an intelligence test can inasmuch as it relates ability to age.

Table 3 identifies three levels of a testing program for the elementary school. As a general rule, a suitable testing program is based on intelligence and achievement tests, supplemented by teacher-made tests and optionally used personality tests. As a systematically administered procedure, personality and interest measures are more appropriate to the secondary school level. Many of the procedures discussed elsewhere in the book provide the equivalent or greater information. Achievement tests provide information about a pupil's progress in the basic language skills and arithmetic. In appraising the results, accommodation should be made with respect to the ability levels of the pupils, hence pupils of above-average intelligence should excel grade medians. An adequate appraisal of achievement needs

TABLE 3. THE TESTING PROGRAM

Level	Reading Readiness	Intelligence	Achievement	Other
MINIMAL	Given in late Kindergarten or early first grade. Aid in determining reading groups	Two given—one in primary grades, one in intermediate grades. 10-15% given individual test to a. confirm low IQ b. check faulty scores where results do not jibe with other information	Standard Achievement Battery at end of primary and intermediate grades to determine standing in subject matter areas, analysis of weakness and instructional needs	None
OPTIMAL	Same	End of grades 1, 3, 6 or at the beginning of grades 2, 4, 7 plus a non-language test during course of school period	Reading skills during Grade 2 Teacher-made tests on units Diagnostic tests beginning of school year. Standard Ach. Test Battery annually at end of year or in October if no Diagnostic Testing	Optional aptitude interest and personality tests
MAXIMAL	Same	Same as optimal plus individual intelligence test to every child on admission to school	Same as optimal	Aptitude interest and personality tests incorporated in intermediate grade program

additional tests, usually teacher-made, intended to measure accomplishment in specific areas of the curriculum. Standardized tests do not cover a sufficiently broad range of human endeavor to be the sole criterion of accomplishment in the evaluation of the outcome of education.

The condensed guide to tests on pages 490-497 lists the details on a number of tests suitable to the elementary school. In considering the adoption of a test, the following items should be included:

1. *Validity.* What does the test measure and how has this been established—by correlating with established tests of known validity; through selection of subject-matter content from textbook series; by expert opinion; or by prediction of specific criteria?

2. *Reliability.* How consistent will the scores be? Correlation coefficients of reliability should approximate .90 for intelligence and achievement tests. How was the reliability determined—between alternate forms, by retest, by dividing a single test in half and correlating the part scores, by internal consistency?

3. *Standardization.* What norms are provided on what size groups? Of what are the groups representative? Are different forms of the test available, each with adequate norms?

4. *Suitability.* How suitable is the content of the test items? Is it antiquated? Is it consistent with the content of the curriculum? Is there continuity between the different levels of achievement?

5. *Administration.* Are detailed instructions for administration provided? Are they clear and concise or are they likely to confuse? Is the format of the test clear to the person taking it? Is it suited to age and grade level?

6. *Scoring.* Is scoring simple or complicated, rapid or time-consuming? Is the scoring objective or are interpretations of the meaning of answers required?

7. *Cost.* Are the results obtained worth the expense involved in both expenditure for materials and personnel time involved in administration and scoring? Are test booklets reasonable?

Administration of the Testing Program

1. The administrator usually has the responsibility of procurement of tests, organization of the testing program on a regularly scheduled basis, and the distribution and collection of testing materials.

2. The classroom teacher generally has the responsibility for the administration of the tests, under the supervision of principal or guidance director. A teacher who has had no training or experience in the administration of tests should not be assigned the responsibility for testing. Interchange of teachers permits utilization of skilled teachers for such duties.

3. Scoring the tests may be done by teachers, clerks, or central scoring agencies. The latter two are preferable in order as far as possible to avoid expending professional time on a clerical task.

4. The testing situation should be pleasant and encouraging. Seating facilities, lighting, acoustics, heating, and ventilation should be adequate.

5. The test group should not exceed ten-fifteen in the primary grades and twenty-five to thirty in the upper grades, without the addition of extra proctors.

6. The instructions should be clear to all pupils. Every precaution should be taken to insure the clarity of directions. Each pupil should be checked on each section of the test to make certain that he is carrying out the instruction correctly.

7. Test instructions should be given exactly as stated in the manual. Time limits required should be religiously observed.

8. Achievement tests given at the end of primary and intermediate grades are best given at the end of the year. Continuity of test programs through the use of comparable tests is desired. When achievement testing is done annually, the test may be better given in October of each year in order that the present teacher can use the results for diagnostic and instructional purposes.

9. Tests and data should be regarded as confidential information, available only to those with specific and legitimate interest.

The Community

The emphasis in this text has been on describing the techniques of guidance which an elementary school teacher can use with her class in fostering the person-social development of children. Only briefly in this section does the discussion relate the use of these techniques to the over-all guidance program of the school. Unless the guidance program, like the curriculum, is geared to the needs of children, much of the effort put forth will be wasted. Part of the needs of children is related to the economic and social life of the community and the kinds of resources available to parents and chil-

GROUP INTELLIGENCE TESTS

Name	Author	Publisher	Cost	Time	Validity	Reliability	Evaluation
California Intelligence Lang. Sect. Gr. 4-8	E. Sullivan W. Clark E. Tiegs	California Test Bureau 1957	$5.25-35	45-50 Min.	High with Stanford-Binet	.80-.94 ½ × ½ Sp.-Br.	Age norms from 9-15 years on basis of ample cases. Diagnostic profile can be used to appraise relative strengths & weaknesses although research evidence validating factors is lacking.
California Intelligence Non-Lang. Gr. K-1, 1-3, 4-8	E. Sullivan W. Clark E. Tiegs	California Test Bureau 1957		45-50	High with St. Binet	.948 ½ — ½ Sp.-Br.	Age norms for 40 months to 168 months. Power rather than speed test. Complete info in manual. Pictures clear & well designed. Does not fulfill conditions of I.Q. constancy. More evidence needed in connection with validity.
Chicago Non-Verbal Gr. 1-Adult	A. Brown	Psychological Corporation 1940	$3.45-25 Manual & Key $1.20	40	.67 with Otis Non Verbal .57 with Kuhl.-And.	.80-.90 Sp.-Br.	Age norms based on 1844 children. Good for foreign population & those children with language difficulties or who are hard of hearing. Some parts are conducive to eye strain. Some parts are ambiguous.
Detroit Beginning 1st Grade Revised Gr. 1	A. M. Engel H. J. Baker	World Book Co. 1937	$3.05-35	30	Secured by stat. select. of items showing increase in % of passes from dull to bright	.91 odd-even	Mental age norms are given on scores of 37,996 Detroit 1st grade pupils. Is standardized. Bold print outline drawings make test easy to read. Simple to admin. & score.

GROUP INTELLIGENCE TESTS

Name	Author	Publisher	Cost	Time	Validity	Reliability	Evaluation
Kuhlman Anderson Form A-Gr. 1 Form B-Gr. 2 Form C-Gr. 3 Form D-Gr. 4 etc.	F. Kuhlman R. Anderson	Psychological Corporation 1947	$3.00-25	40-60	Not Given	$.92 \pm .02$ ½ × ½	Directions clear & specific. Validity not given. Reliability satisfactory.
New Calif. Short Form Test of Mental Maturity Gr. 4-8	E. Sullivan W. Clark E. Tiegs	California Test Bureau 1957	$3.15-35 with key & manual IBM Ans. .04	Untimed Give in 1 period	Correlates high with Binet	.90 ½ × ½ Sp.-Br.	Items subjected to extensive statistical analysis. Norms based on 1,000 children in grades 4-8. Percentile norms. Grade placement. Gives 3 M.A. (Lang., non-lang., total). Scored by machine or hand. Low sub-test reliability.
Otis Classification Revised Gr. 4-9	A. S. Otis	World Book Co.	$3.95-35 with key & manual	Part I 30 Part II 30	Rational selection of items	.93-.95	Gives age & grade norms & percentile rank based on 1,800 pupils in grades 4-9. Enables teacher to classify pupils on basis of mental development & actual achievement. Can get E.A., I.Q., M.A., educational quotient & accomplishment ratio.
Pintner General Ab. Non-Lang. Gr. 4.5-9.5	R. Pintner	World Book Co., 1941	$5.50-35 with key & directions	50	Given in terms of uses of tests.	.85-.89 ½ × ½	Age norms based on 6,000 pupils (9½-13½ years old). Standard score norms. A well constructed test. Useful in testing children with language handicaps, the deaf, those who don't know English.

GROUP INTELLIGENCE TESTS

Name	Author	Publisher	Cost	Time	Validity	Reliability	Evaluation
Pintner General Ab. Verbal Gr. 4-9	R. Pintner	World Book Co., 1938	$3.95-35 IBM-.05	45	Construct. Not Given Ach—.84 Binet—.71	.94 odd-even	Adequate norms based on 60,000 cases. Gives mental ages, deviation I.Q. & percentile rank. One of best for school use. Easy to give. Scored by hand or machine. Age of test a limiting factor.
Pintner-Cunningham Primary Test Gr. K-2	R. Pintner Cunningham Durost	World Book Co., 1938	$3.25-35	25	.73-.88 with Stanford Binet	.89 $\frac{1}{2} \times \frac{1}{2}$	According to Buros Third Yearbook it is the best available for school use. Easy to give & score. Timing difficult & only 15 pupils can be tested at one time. Raw score with table of norms. Percentile norms.
Quick Scoring Mental Ab. Test-Alpha Gr. 1-4	A. Otis	World Book Co., 1939	Alpha $3.40-35 Beta $2.45-35	35 30	.86 with grade placement	.81 Form A with Form B	Norms based on 18,000 children. Gives M.A.'s & I.Q.'s. Reliable results quickly obtained. Useful for grouping children in the class. Hand scoring easy & rapid by use of perforated stencil.
Lorge-Thorndike Intelligence Test K-1, 2-3, 4-6	I. Lorge R. L. Thorndike	Houghton-Mifflin 1954-57	$3.00-35 IBM Ans. Sheet-.04	35-50	.54-.77 with Binet and WISC. .67-.87 with Ach.	Alternate Form .76-.90 $\frac{1}{2} \times \frac{1}{2}$ .88-.94	Incorporates both verbal and non-verbal material. Excellent norms based on 136,000 children in 22 states. Valuable statistical data included. Useful group test.

			INDIVIDUAL INTELLIGENCE TESTS—PREFERRED				
Name	Author	Publisher	Cost	Time	Validity	Reliability	Evaluation
Arthur Point Scale of Perf. Test Ages 2-12	G. Arthur 1952	C. H. Stoelting	$70-set	30-60	Not Given	Not Given	Materials of excellent quality & convenient & easy to use. Good directions but must be given by trained person in a clinical setting. Easy scoring. Interesting to children. Reliability believed high.
Revised Stanford Binet Scale Age 2-Adult	L. Terman M. Merrill	Houghton Mifflin Co. 1960	$31-set $4.20-manual	30-90	Progressive portion by age passing individual items	.82-.95	Widely used. Extensive standardization. The most useful and best constructed instrument for measuring intelligence of children. Simple, speedy scoring.
Wechsler Scale for Children Pre-school-15	D. Wechsler	Psychological Corporation	$24-set & manual	40-60	Not Given	.85-.92	Gives both verbal & performance I.Q. Also full scale I.Q. Interesting to children. Good norms. Convenient, easy to handle. Modern in construction. Standardization adequate. Easy to give. Takes less time than most.

READING READINESS TESTS

Name	Author	Publisher	Cost	Time	Validity	Reliability	Evaluation
Gates Rdg. Read. Tests 5 Tests Gr. Kg.-1	A. I. Gates	Bureau of Publications Tchrs. College Columbia Univ. 1939	$4.85-100	50	.70-.76 Pintner-Cunn.	.974 1/2 × 1/2 Sp.-Br.	Advantages—Conforms to acceptable standard for test construction. Comparison of abilities on sub-tests may indicate specific weaknesses of individual pupils. Disadvantages—20 cards to be made by teacher to accompany Test 3.
Metropolitan Readiness Test Gr. Kg.-1	G. H. Hildreth N. L. Griffiths	World Book Co. 1949-50	$4.65-35	60	Face Validity	.83-.89	Advantages—High correlation between test scores and IQ tests. Probably unnecessary to give IQ and Readiness Test. Adequate norms. Disadvantages—Requires 60 mins. to give. Probably not as analytic as Monroe Readiness Test.
Monroe Reading Apt. Test Gr. Kg.-1	M. Monroe	Houghton & Mifflin Co. 1935	$3.30-25	40-55	.60 Vis. .66 Aud. .50 Mot. .57 Art.	.87 odd-even Sp.-Br.	Advantages—Considered excellent test to survey and classify first grade entrants for prediction and analysis of reading abilities and disabilities. Disadvantage—Requires a trained examiner to administer.
Murphy Durrell Diag. Rdg. Read. Test Gr. 1	H. A. Murphy D. D. Durrell	World Book Co. 1949	$3.30-35 Accessories 2.35	Tests 1-2 1 hour Test 3 20 min. group. Individ. test 3 times	Not Given	Test I .96 odd-even Test II .95 odd-even	Results useful in determining readiness of pupils to undertake formal reading instruction. Excellent test to analyze causes of failures in the 3 abilities—auditory and visual discrim. and learning rate.

READING TESTS

Name	Author	Publisher	Cost	Time	Val.	Rel.	Evaluation
Reading Capacity and Achievement Gr. 2-6	D. Durrell H. Sullivan	World Book Co. 1945	Prim. test $4.90-35 Inter. test $3.70-35	Prim. 40-45 Inter. 30-35	Construct. Validity	.85 ½ × ½	Tests easy to give, to score, and inexpensive. Practical use in problem of selecting cases for remedial reading. Reveals discrepancies between understanding spoken vs. printed word.
1. Gates Rdg. Read. Form I 2. Gates Prim. Read. Form I 3. Gates Basic Read. Form I 4. Gates Adv. Prim. Forms I, II	Arthur Gates	Psychological Corporation 1958	$1.50-2.10 for 35	1-2 20 3-4 30		High	These tests have a disadvantage in not adequately proving their validity, but they provide a basis for grade placement and instructional needs.
Iowa Every Pupil Test of Basic Skills Silent Rdg. Comprehen.	H. F. Spitzer E. Horn, M. McBroom, H. Green, E. Lindquist	Houghton Mifflin Co. 1945	$3.30-35	Elem. 50 Adv. 70	Not Given	.50-.80	The reading selections are well chosen and provide adequate opportunity for checking skills. Extensive norms. Low reliabilities limit individual diagnosis.

Note: See O. K. Buros, *Mental Measurement Yearbooks* for recent information regarding revision of tests.

ACHIEVEMENT TEST BATTERIES

Name	Author	Publisher	Cost	Time	Val.	Rel.	Evaluation
California Achievement Tests Forms WXYZ	E. W. Tiegs W. W. Clark 1957	California Test Bureau	$5.60-35 IBM-.04	90-180	Content; Construct.	High	Two scores available in basic skills of reading, arith., lang. Standardized on stratified sample of 341 school systems in 48 states. Administration simple; format clear. Scoring service available.
Iowa Basic Skills Gr. 3-9	E. F. Lindquist A. Hieronymus 1955-56	Houghton-Mifflin	.66 ea. .10 Ans Sht IBM-.03	67-80	Curricular	.70-.96	Tests vocab, reading comp. lang. skills, work-study skills and arith. Grade equiv. and grade percentile norms extensive standardization. Scoring available.
Metropolitan Achievement Forms A, B, C	H. H. Bixler W. N. Durost G. H. Hildreth K. W. Lund J. Wrightstone	World Book Co.	.30 each IBM Ans. .03	165-240	Curricular Course Content	High	Tests reading, arith., lang., soc. studies, science. Extensive standardization. Norms: standard scores, stanine, grade equiv., percentile rank. Scoring available.
SRA Achievement Series Gr. 2-9	L. P. Thorpe D. W. Lefever R. A. Naslond 1954-57	Science Research Associates	.30 each IBM Ans Sht	360	Analysis Instructional Materials	.80-.90	Tests reading, arith., lang., work-study skills and lang. perception. Adequate standardization. Scoring service.

ACHIEVEMENT TEST BATTERIES

Name	Author	Publisher	Cost	Time	Val.	Rel.	Evaluation
Scholastic Achievement Tests	O. F. Anderhalter R. S. Gawkoski J. O'Brien 1953-55	Scholastic Testing Service	.20 each IBM-.15	90-145	Content	Adequate	Intended for Catholic schools. English, spelling, airth., religion. National norms from 304 communities.
Sequential Tests of Educ. Progress Gr. 4-6	Cooperative Test Division 1956-58	Educational Testing Service		70 for each 490 ???	Content	.84-.92	Tests reading, writing, math, science, soc. studies, listening, essay. Separate tests. Random grade samples in 50 schools for normative population.
Stanford Achievement Primary-Tutored	T. L. Kelley R. Madden E. F. Gardner L. M. Terman G. M. Ruch 1953-56	World Book Co.	$6.00-35 IBM Ans. .03	215	Content Analysis of Texts, Courses of Study		Tests reading, soc. studies, science, lang., arith., spelling. Large standardization population in 363 communities. Standard scores, age equivalents, grade equivalent, percentile ranks.

dren. The operation of an effective guidance program requires information that is kept up-to-date regarding the pupil population of the school system, including their educational objectives and community influences seen as a whole. This should be available by individual schools and for the system as a whole. In communities changing as a result of migration into or out of the town, the complexion of the pupil population can change considerably, both in numbers and compositions, in a comparatively short time.

Information which should be available on the pupil population as a whole includes enrollment by grade, size of pre-school population, sex, race, general mental ability, socio-economic background, mode of transportation to school, permanence of residence, numbers of pupils who leave school by age, sex, and socio-economic level, number who graduate and continue on to higher education, number who enter employment, including types of employment.

In the community, information regarding the occupational, educational, and socio-economic status of the adults is needed.

The same form used for the social-status survey of the class can be used in conjunction with a similar survey of the community if time and personnel are available. Lacking this, an excellent summary of such information is available from the U.S. Bureau of the Census which tabulates the data from the U.S. census every ten years by census tract. These summaries list the age distribution, the income distribution, the proportion of the homes built in given periods, the portion of homes owned and rented, and other similar information. Although not as detailed as might be desirable, a valuable survey of the population of a community can be obtained.

Further information about the community which should be available concerns the large businesses, industrial, and government establishments; the churches, parks, libraries, museums, and recreational facilities available; commercialized recreational centers such as theatres, motion pictures, amusement centers, etc.; health centers and clinics, and social service and group work agencies available.

The last named category—social service and group work agencies —are especially valuable to the teacher and the school as resources in their work with children and families who are having difficulties, whether health, financial, or personal adjustment. Two main distinctions can be made in the types of agencies available. The first is between public and private agencies. In this distinction, the difference lies in the source of the funds used by the agency, the public agencies deriving their funds from tax funds—local, state or national—and the private agencies obtaining their funds by private subscription or contribution. Many of the latter derive their major support from the community chest or united community fund drives.

A second distinction that can be made is between financial assistance, casework, and group work agencies, although the variety in social agencies is so great that this distinction becomes blurred in operation. Generally, the public agencies tend to offer financial assistance through the departments of public welfare to the needy, to dependent children under age 18 whose fathers are dead or institutionalized, and to the aged. Exceptions to this generalization exist; for instance, child guidance clinics operated by state departments of mental health, or the foster-child guidance clinics operated by the state for children made wards of the state for any reason.

The private agencies offer casework assistance by trained social workers to individuals or families faced with various problems—health, financial, psychiatric, desertion, alcoholism, etc.—and group work through such agencies as settlement house and recreational organizations. Service organizations such as Kiwanis, Lions, Rotarians, religious organizations, and veterans' organizations add their varied assistance to the complex of agencies offering service to individuals with various special needs. The variety is greater in urban areas than in rural. In the latter, the church, club, and service organizations often offer the only assistance available beyond that which individual members of the community may volunteer. Yet this latter can be quite consequential as a contribution to the physical and mental health of the community, particularly its youth.

With modest effort, a group of teachers could easily make a complete survey of the community resources available to them in their work with children, and, by completing such a survey, discover invaluable resources to which they could turn for assistance in working out solutions to adjustment problems of children. In a city or area large enough to have a classified telephone directory, a listing of agencies available will be found under the heading of Social Services. In smaller communities, town or county offices and churches will have to be consulted. Frequently, services of state agencies may be available if requested.

The following guide (using the heads along the left margin of the page) can be used for obtaining the information regarding community resources. Once obtained, a folder can be prepared containing this information and made available to the faculty, or, where the number of teachers is great, mimeographed and distributed. A form listing the information regarding the Family Service Organization in a community of 50,000 is shown to illustrate, and the meanings of the headings are included:

Name of Agency	*Family Service Organization*
Address:	5 Clemens St.

Classification and description of service
  Medical
  Financial
  Psychiatric
  Vocational
  Recreational
  Social Casework
  Educational
  Other
	A casework agency serving city and surrounding communities with services directed toward helping the individual make satisfactory adjustments in his social relationships and family living. Services include family counseling, psychological consultation, marriage and vocational counseling, child care and guidance.
	Also offers educational and lecture program to community groups.

Eligibility—who is served by the agency.	Non-sectarian. Anyone eligible irrespective of economic status. Focuses mainly on family problems. Anyone may refer, but client must desire appointment.
Personnel—training and experience.	Eight professionally trained workers with M.A. in social work or child psychology. Consultant psychiatrist available.
Costs—to those receiving service.	Fee scale according to ability to pay. Average is $1 per week. Two-thirds do not pay.
Support—source of financial support.	Primarily United Community Fund supplemented by private endowment.
Availability.	No waiting list at present.
Facilities.	9 interviewing offices, 3 clerical.
Coordination with schools and agencies	Referrals come from schools, ministers, doctors, district nurses, and hospitals.

Chapter 18

THE SCHOOL PROGRAM AND ADJUSTMENT PROBLEMS

Certain difficulties of adjustment experienced by children occur as they attempt to master the developmental tasks which occur at successive age levels and find themselves temporarily out of step with the norm. Other adjustment problems are more deep-seated, resulting from unfavorable events and conflicts resulting in difficulties which steadily increase or, in other instances, basic disturbances which emerge unexpectedly under sudden pressures. Many of these can be resolved with sensitive and sympathetic assistance by teachers. Some cannot be without specialized assistance. Yet another kind of difficulty occurs in a different category which can be termed situational, an adjective that is more descriptive than diagnostic. It implies that the source of the difficulties lies within the situation rather than within the individual. It is especially applicable to the school, for it suggests that elements may exist within the school, its organization, and program which create difficulties for otherwise well-adjusted children.

Individual and group self-evaluation is always difficult. We grow accustomed to accepting the way in which we operate as being not only the perfectly natural way of operating but the right and desirable way. In a different sphere, we accept the fact that 35,000 or 40,000 persons will be killed in automobile accidents. In a recent televised debate of bombs, an attitude was expressed that an increase in the number of deaths from leukemia due to radiation hazard of up to 1,500 (in the world) would not be terrible in view of the fact that we accepted the number of motor vehicle fatalities that we do each year; one justifies the other.

In a similar scene, school personnel can be quite complacent about a 40% drop-out rate in high school and never stop to ask if it may not be the school, its program and practices, which are inadequate or inappropriate. We assume the causes of the failure to rest with the individual, without asking if the curriculum is too difficult, too easy, or unsuited to the pupil population; if unwholesome teacher-pupil relationships lie at the root of the problem; if incentive conditions are unsuitable or deleterious; if the pace of instruction is a lock-step program for all regardless of ability.

The analysis of causes of school failure and difficulties of adjustment necessitates a review of conditions within the school and its program which may be contributing to or creating the problem. Two instances come to mind concerning two boys in the tenth grade of school, both referred to by their respective teachers as problems, the first because he was a "clown," "wouldn't work," and the second because he "couldn't do high school work as he had not learned to read."

In the first instance, the responsibility lay squarely on the unwillingness of the faculty to adapt their program. The boy's I.Q. of 88 was seen as a mental handicap by the teachers; they wished the Superintendent would expel him. Inquiry to determine if the boy's total adjustment was similar to that portrayed in school showed that he had worked for several years as a newspaper delivery boy, had always been accurate and responsible with his accounts, had been given the responsibility of supervising a number of route-boys, kept the records of their charges and payments, was accurate and scrupulously honest with his accounts. Tradesmen in the town and neighbors saw the boy as a person who could be trusted with various tasks, including care of children, and be expected to do a creditable job. He participated in group activities outside of school and contributed a major portion of his income to his family who were in marginal economic circumstances. In short, a brief examination showed him to be well-adjusted in all spheres but the school.

In the other case, a so-called illiterate boy was allowed to drop out of school as a failure because of his inability to learn to read. Yet, in fact, he was regularly withdrawing books from the public library on art and electronics, technical books on subjects which appealed to him and which he read and understood. He understood the electronics books sufficiently to be admitted to the navy. Perhaps these instances, however unusual they may be, suggest that in the analysis of adjustment difficulties, the question should always be posed as to what circumstances in the school situation could be causative or contributing factors.

The circumstances may not be as obvious as illustrated above, but the wisdom of being perceptive to the difficulties children are experiencing is shown in the situation of Lisa, an eight-year-old in the third grade. In the teacher's words:

> Lisa is an average and not the least bit unusual third-grader, quiet and unassuming, one of those children it is easy to overlook in a large class because she is attentive and responds conscientiously at all times.
>
> In March her work took a sudden "about face." Her work slipped and her attitude changed. I talked with Lisa and explained what was happening without accomplishing anything. Her reading slipped so badly that I thought it advisable to change her from the fastest to the average reading group. I tried to avoid this by explaining it to her (her I.Q. was 127) without avail.
>
> I knew the mother had been in the hospital in January for two weeks for a serious operation. Looking through the cumulative record I noted that Lisa had been absent 37 days during the second grade (she missed only 4 and 8 days respectively in first and third grades) and what appeared significant was the notation that she had had a mastoid operation when she was three. I wondered if the answer lay in the series of events.
>
> I invited her mother to visit the school for a conference. We had a routine conference in November and I'd found her most interested and cooperative. As our conference progressed I was amazed to discover that Lisa was afraid of the school.
>
> The mother told me that when the time came for Lisa to enter our school, she wanted to go to another one that was made of pink bricks and not the deep red ones which our school and the hospital have. When she was forced to attend our school those red bricks were tremendously frightening to her, and the mother

had to take her to school every day for some time, but she always disliked the school.

A second conference found an occurrence that frightens her —it apparently reminds her of her stay in the hospital—is when the teacher lowers the huge green shades which cover the long windows reaching up to the high, old-fashioned ceiling.

I had no inkling that she disliked school. I could readily understand her feelings and sympathize with her because I could remember spending ten days in the hospital for a similar operation when I was ten.

Next day I asked Lisa if she would like to make up her work that she had missed and stay with the fastest group. She said she would. She has friends in the group and adjusts easily there.

Lisa is most anxious to help keep the room looking nice, so when she requested one afternoon that I let her stay to help, I took advantage of the situation to converse with her. She finds it difficult to express her feelings. She expresses her dislike for school but doesn't seem to know why. We talked about our operations and compared notes but to this point she doesn't consciously associate the school with the hospital. I'm hesitant to suggest the association, but at least I can take steps to develop pleasant associations with school and the people in it.

Several aspects of educational practice which create difficulty for some children can be identified:

Organization of school—age-grade, subject matter division, time schedules

Curriculum—lack of organization and integration, unsuitable tasks, inadequate materials

Teaching Practices—routine drill, unsatisfactory incentive conditions, inadequate evaluation, inadequate provision of fundamental individual difference

Promotional and grading policy

The list will call to mind difficulties which can arise because of the manner in which we organize to educate. The admission of children to school by a fixed age requirement and annual promotion through a series of stepped grades is convenient from the administrative viewpoint, and functional because of the correlation between maturation of abilities and interests with age. The fact that children follow a common sequence of development, and for most this procedes at a common pace, makes an age-grade basis of organization administratively possible. Nevertheless, some children are ready for entrance prior to age 6, others might profit by waiting a year if a fixed rate of progress is expected in learning. Of those admitted, several can learn the "year's work" in a half a year, others will take longer. Yet, too often a child is required to learn at the pace determined by the teacher, not by his own performance and ability. Disinterest and discouragement result.

The tendency to divide learning by subject matter into fairly constant time units standardizes the time and material which one can study irrespective of individual interest and volition. Few people ever read a novel or attend a play in twenty-minute or half-hour units, yet our study schedule in school follows fairly constant units of time. One is supposed to arouse his interest, perform a task, and disengage as if riding a commuter train. The ennui in the classroom is like that on the train—it is an in-between period of little consequence.

The fractionated curriculum often completely lacks the needed inter-locks which tie the parts together, show the relationships of the parts to the whole, and provide some sense of integration of knowledge and skill. Materials fail to keep pace with changing environment. If we teachers kept our materials as up-to-date as toy manufacturers who quickly produce implements modeled on the application of educational and scientific knowledge, the pupils would be much more stimulated to learn.

We speak of providing for individual differences, yet our educational successes have resulted from mass education rather than from effective provision for individual differences. This latter development in education is still ahead of us, especially in the secondary school. The elementary school has seen some gains in this direction. A few teachers are notably skilled, but generally the amount of learning proceeds at a set pace. A fixed number of spelling words are to be learned by a fixed procedure in a fixed length of time. Allow the students to move at their own pace, using self-checking quizzes and examinations, or pairs or trios of children working together and checking each other. Some children will complete the year's work in two months. If they can accomplish this, why should they not be permitted to use the time saved in pursuing other subjects of interest? We still teach too much by rote learning and recitation. Consider the variations in experience and grouping possible in reading in providing for individual differences.[1]

1. *Lockstep*—same text, same rate of progress for all. Workbook used as a filler.
2. *Primitive Grouping*—two to three permanent groups using the same text covered at different rates of progress.

---

[1]Modified from E. A. Betts, "Approaches to Differentiated Guidance in Reading." *Education*, 1950, 70, 9.

3. *Progress Grouping*—Two to four permanent groups based on differences in achievement utilizing different texts in a reading series.

4. *Flexible Grouping*—Three to five groups using different texts in same series. Regrouped as progress indicates. Identification of specific skill needs and provisions for same.

5. *Unified Language Arts*—Three to five groups (flexible) in terms of general language achievement and specific needs. Inter-relation of reading, spelling, writing via instructional units.

6. *Extended Flexible Group*—Flexible grouping in terms of general language arts, specific needs and interests, expanded to include all major subjects. Incorporation of direct reading experiences in other than basal texts. Greater attention to individual analysis of reading difficulty and provision for individual instruction.

7. *Language-Experience Approach*—Flexible grouping on general language achievement, individual needs and interests, and interpersonal relations, an integrated program for developing differentiated language art skills using supplementary materials and experiences.

Most elementary school classes have room for considerable improvement in the degree of differentiation of instruction provided. Yet, failure to do so poses impossible tasks for the less able and insufficient challenge for the capable. In this lies foundation for adjustment difficulties.

Periodic grading on fixed standards of achievement and annual promotion are educational procedures creating additional difficulties. Children who are unable to attain the level of achievement to which they aspire (this level of aspiration being the result of a combination of factors—parental attitudes, group standards, self-esteem, etc.) protect themselves by rejecting the assigned task. The rejection can take the form of daydreaming, disinterest, boredom, or other means of expression.

If the goal happens to be A and B grades on report cards, and they cannot attain them because of limitations in ability (grades are so arranged that only a portion of the group can get top grades putting the less able pupils at a permanent disadvantage) they cease to strive for the goal—the A—on the tasks required to get to the goal, subject matter achievement. Grades, especially in the elementary school are self-defeating. As an evaluation tool in the elementary school, such devises are unreliable; as a communication system with parents, they are confusing. It would be more preferable and more informative to establish the specific skills to be acquired, the tasks to be performed, and note the particular ones which had been completed. Progress in accomplishment of given skills has intrinsic satisfaction which stimulates one to attempt new and more difficult tasks.

The attendance at school required by law produces an interesting concept, that of truancy. Business firms designate non-attendance at work as absenteeism, and in instances of excessive absenteeism, look for environmental, social, and individual factors contributing to the problem with the hope that modification will eliminate or reduce the problem. Absenteeism from school is designated as truancy, with some connotation of moral turpitude to be punished out of existence. Detjen and Detjen[2] list several possible causes and a number of actions which could be taken to alleviate unjustifiable absence and tardiness.

Possible Causes

Undesirable home conditions

Retarded child feeling inferior because he cannot keep up with the class

Dislike of school or teacher (e.g., case of Lisa reported above)

Emotional problem of child.

Suggested Actions

Have special features for days on which most absences occur.

Interest class in forthcoming events.

Find ways of incorporating ideas concerning good attendance and punctuality.

Dramatize causes of recent absences and discuss how they could have been prevented.

Ask children to describe what they do when they're absent, and to tell about times when they were absent when they might have come to school.

Dramatize situations which may lead to absences and what to do about them, e.g., a relative arrives for a visit just before child is to go to school.

Discuss effects of frequent absences.

Send notes and drawings to children who are absent for any length of time so he will feel missed.

Talk privately to a shy child who is frequently absent to determine cause.

Organize campaign for promptness. Urge children to plan ahead and get ready early.

---

[2]E. W. Detjen and Mary Detjen, *Elementary School Guidance.* New York: McGraw-Hill, 1952, pp. 190-194.

Take a vote on the most enjoyable activity in school. Schedule
this activity at the beginning of the day.

Look for particular causes in individual causes needing action.

It should be evident that inflexible organization and practices in
the school can be contributing factors to difficulties of adjustment.
With children who are functioning adequately in areas other than
the classroom, the teacher should look to the unsuitability of the
program for the child, seek and analyze the nature of any learning
problems, and investigate the ways in which the program can be
adapted to provide more appropriate experiences.

A comparison of the causes of school failure offered by pupils,
teachers, and mental hygienists, provides certain interesting contrasts.

Pupils	Teachers	Mental Hygienists
Disliked subject	Absenteeism	Inadequate evaluation
Insufficient studying	Failure in tests	Overemphasis on subject
Discouraged	Insufficient	matter or instructional
Lack of effort	preparation	procedures
Dislike of teacher	Mentally slow	Hostility between teacher
Timid in class	Poor background	and pupils
Slow answering	Lazy	Confusing directions and
No interest in school	Poor study habits	assignments
	Failure to complete	Neglect of individual
	work	differences
		Neglect of exceptional
		children
		Unhealthy incentive
		conditions
		Undesirable home
		conditions

Each person sees the problem from a particular perspective; the
pupil sees conditions which kill his motivation; the teacher sees
inadequacies in academic performance; the mental hygienist sees
inadequacies in the program, environment, or interpersonal relationships. One or the other may be correct, but only through analysis
of individual difficulties will an answer be obtained.

THE RELATIONSHIP OF ACHIEVEMENT
TO ADJUSTMENT

A reciprocal relationship exists between achievement and adjustment. Successful experience in school amplifies a sense of self-esteem,
builds a concept of oneself willing to explore, to create, to risk new

adventures. Failure can be tolerated because it is seen as a temporary event in a sequence of events leading to ultimate success. Repeated failure is destructive. It creates doubts in one's ability, a fear of new experiences which seem likely to present more failure, and a sense of pervasive anxiety in an environment perceived as hostile and threatening. Success in one area compensates and makes tolerable failure in another. Total failure is catastrophic to personality development. Only by adoption of one of a number of possible defenses can any degree of personal integrity be maintained, however obnoxious such defenses may be to one's associates.

Failure and maladjustment feed each other, forming an interlocked, circular reaction, which soon makes cause and effect indistinguishable. Failure produces greater alarm which in turn reduces effectiveness increasing the probability of failure. Except for children suffering from serious personality disturbances, both a diagnostic educational approach and a therapeutic approach can prove successful, because these can break the circular chain of events. Children experiencing reading failure and exhibiting symptoms of maladjustment can demonstrate marked improvement when a remedial program is undertaken which provides a diagnosis of the learning difficulty and appropriate action to develop needed skills. The same children can make progress if a therapeutic approach gives them the help in dealing with their feelings and the emotional support needed as they make further attempts. When closely analyzed, both approaches have much in common. The remedial teacher not only plans for the development of needed skills, but she maintains effective and supporting personal relationships with the pupil and utilizes conditions of maximum incentive to encourage further effort. In some instances, this may suffice, inasmuch as observed progress is self-stimulating, but in others, special instruction to overcome learning disabilities will be needed. Whichever one is started with, the other cannot be ignored. Without progress and some sense of achievement from some source, school becomes intolerable. A curriculum which restricts the range of human ability that can find expression through verbal skills, narrows the opportunities for success available to many children. It is interesting to note that when intermediate grade pupils were given systematic opportunity to develop and pursue their special interests in class, it was their adjustment and group acceptance which showed significant gains.[3]

---

[3]D. D. Durrell and L. J. Savignano, "Classroom Enrichment through Pupil Specialties," *J. Educ.*, February, 1956.

THE TEACHER AS A GROUP LEADER

The word "group" has different meanings for different people. To some, a class of thirty pupils is a group; to others, the seven or eight children seated in their circle of chairs reading aloud to the teacher constitutes a group. For our purposes, these are collections of individuals, not groups. The group evolves with interaction leading to an awareness of a we-feeling, a mutually shared purpose towards which the members act in unity.

Each child who enters the classroom brings with him memberships in many outside groups which affect his thinking and acting. The group memberships have to be recognized because children learn their attitudes and value systems as a function of such memberships. The teacher's effectiveness in being a creative influence in such areas depends upon her capacity to weld her class into a group.

Each of the groups to which a child belongs has its own norms and group standards, whether it be family, religious group, neighborhood clique, club, athletic group, or social-economic class. His family membership defines his status, for his place of residence, his family occupation, or his religious group determines the status he will be accorded. Unless the teacher creates a group with other standards, the existing groups will prevail.

It is simple enough to say that teachers must engage groups efficiently. But we have all seen the first day when a number of individuals find themselves together for the first time. They look around, silently appraising one another, cautious or boisterous, timid or aloof, waiting half expectantly for something to occur. How is the teacher to fuse these elements into a group and get them to work together toward a common purpose?

The teacher has the authority to determine who will interact, for how long, and on what tasks. She regulates the freedom of movement and determines the limits of action, both motor and verbal. She pits individuals against one another in competition, splits them into favored and unfavored groups, determines the atmosphere of the classroom. She does not have complete control of matters, for each individual has his motives and desires to be expressed in one form or another. Some will challenge barriers to determine if the teacher will yield or insist, and on what occasions or for which persons. Others will seek associations which appeal to them, risking punishment if need be. Gradually, a series of interpersonal relationships will evolve between members which can be described by the roles played: friend, leader, clown, isolate, scapegoat, aggressor, blocker, tease, teacher's pet, tattler, etc.

All roles will not occur in all groups, but the ones that exist will be a function of the particular group. The teacher can take an active part as a group leader, or she can let the group relationships evolve by default, restricting herself to being the fountainhead of knowledge.

The first step in fusing the group reduces the strangeness between children by helping them to discover common ground which permits them to lower their guard. This is why many teachers spend time at the beginning of the year in helping children get acquainted. Sharing experiences, feelings, and ideas is one procedure. The narration of "what I did on my vacation" is an attempt, but in groups of diverse economic backgrounds, this is likely to create more differences. For the typical elementary child, a vacation trip across the U. S. is confusing enough to him. His narration of it is meaningless to a group who haven't had similar experiences. But to find how many went to the beach, like to swim, had a chance to go to camp, provides common elements. Asking each other to narrate the most interesting day or exciting event provides shared experiences, for it is the sense of common experience which provides the psychological ground upon which children can approach each other. This is a beginning. More significant is the opportunity to be productive toward a common goal. The morale of a group, or individual for that matter, can be measured by its productivity. Common goals, shared values, and mutual effort are the basis through which the classroom experiences contribute to group development. Perhaps these can be made more specific by a description of a series of events occurring with a group of boys in a special class.

No contention exists that this is a typical group in the elementary school, unless one conceives of the eighth grade as an occasional part. If anything, the opposite is true. The group is atypical and chosen for that reason, for it illustrates effective group leadership in difficult circumstances.

The group consisted of twenty-one boys of 14-15 years old, all but two having intelligence test rating ranging from borderline to normal. All were from lower social-economic status, several from homes broken by death or divorce. The two Negro boys in the group were the only two without moderate to serious adjustment problems. Five were adjudicated delinquents with court records. Most had a marked aversion to school, expressed in a passive disinterest by some, in belligerence by others.

The class schedule called for the group to have shop and physical education during separate periods, the rest of their classes—English, social studies, mathematics, and science with their homeroom teacher. The room to which the class was assigned was a drab, old-fashioned classroom with dark walls. The first day, after taking time to acquaint the boys with one another, the teacher divided the class into two groups, each with a group leader, or foreman, as she termed him. The division and the appointment of the foreman was carried out with class participation in the selection of groups and leaders. Several of the boys proved effective leaders, accepted by the groups, but in one particular case the leader continually tried to have members of his group taken to task by the teacher, necessitating many intercessions on her part. The first job to which they turned was painting the room a light green. The boys were given the responsibility for buying paint, supervising, and carrying out the project. They were completely satisfied and proud of the results. While this project was in operation the teacher discovered one boy making book (taking bets) on a prizefight. The teacher asked the boy if he held his federal license, required of a bookmaker. Lacking it, he was out of business. In the course of the discussion, she discovered that the boy had a keen interest in sports, subscribed to many sport magazines. A sports' corner was established, the boy as manager. A committee was appointed to make a collection of sports pictures, one to represent each sport known. One of the boys, capable at printing, made the signs for the illustrations. The corner was a popular center for spare-time browsing and reading.

The second day, two of the boys skipped two classes, apparently testing the teacher. On their return, one of the boys offered a long, involved explanation of their absence. The teacher listened patiently during the entire explanation while the class waited expectantly. When the excuse came to an end, the teacher shook her head sadly saying, "That one is for the birds." She went on to tell them that the usual referral to the principal or a note to their parents was a procedure used with children. They were young men, and she would treat them as such. She asked them if they would stay with her a few minutes after school to see if they couldn't conjure up more imaginative explanations. Her disposition of the incident was satisfactory for she had no subsequent problems of that nature.

Eighth grade academic work was nearly impossible to teach. Most of the boys had reading difficulty and were adverse to learning. The teacher outlined the courses of study in geography and history and taught only essential facts in question and answer form. She had the boys procure Civil Service Examination Application forms and, by having the boys complete this and write letters in applying for interesting jobs that appeared in want ads, she managed some kind of English instruction. Special credits and demerits were given for home assignments, with the explanation that this was the Classical High School method. Homework was carefully tailored to personal interest and level of ability.

During the second week a cigarette lighter was stolen from the teacher's desk. The next day the teacher asked the boys what kind of penny candy they liked. She brought in some and put it out on her desk along with a container for money. Anybody could take a piece of candy, but he was on his honor to put a penny in the container. The boys didn't know it but only fifteen pieces were out at a time, limiting the risk of teacher's money. The idea worked so successfully that five cent bars were soon purchased, and the money would sit in the jar all day in front of the class. The rule was that if candy and money didn't balance, the privilege would be abolished. The boys felt they were trusted and lived up to the trust. There were no more incidents of stolen goods.

Another critical event occurred when certain parents complained that several boys in the class had ganged up on their son in a fight. The boys concerned were called into the principal's office. The teacher accompanied them and insisted that all the boys be questioned together. During the interrogation, the teacher discovered from the complaining boy (whom she had had in a previous grade) that he had not been alone but had had two companions. The three of them had started the fight and received the worst end of it. On returning to her classroom, the boys who had been called to the office began to express their appreciation. She took advantage of the situation to explain that they could always expect fair play and her assistance if they told the truth.

Trouble and misbehavior broke out between lessons as well as during recess period on stormy days when the group had to remain indoors. The teacher obtained chess, sports magazines, puzzles, checkers, and a table tennis set which was placed in a small adjoining room which they called the game room. Individual boys or groups were given responsibility for care of the equipment. Unsupervised use of the game room was permitted on the condition that there be no unnecessary noise. A choral music group was started, using patriotic songs and songs from the Hit Parade. The group singing seemed to appeal, and soon a few began singing solos.

Many more events could be narrated—the handling of fighting and smoking in the yard, the wearing of neckties, the institution of a sports program, and several excursions—but enough has been described to show the leadership provided by the teacher. She found tasks they could manage and take pride in the result. By "skipping around" in her work, she dissipated the impression that they were always far behind other classes. They could take some pride in studying. She worked with different group combinations. She gave individuals status and responsibility. She supported members of the group when they were under fire, trusted them with money, yet insisted on maintenance of specific standards.

The interaction between the boys developed rather haphazardly at first. They began to enjoy intergroup competition, and worked hard and put in extra time to complete group projects which would be exhibited in the library. However, it wasn't until the games were installed and the teacher and shop foreman rearranged the class groups which went to shop together, that substantial ties began to emerge. The games seemed to serve as a bridge between pairs, the group as a whole was building a group morale, and the two influences coalesced in at least harmonious working relations and more effective learnings. In several cases, there was no noticeable change, but most of the boys accepted criticism and advice more freely as the year progressed; they were willing at least to give ideas a trial instead of rejecting them immediately. They themselves showed evidence of group standards for they ceased to tolerate certain actions. By the close of the sessions they found themselves more responsible members of a maturing group.

A teacher can play a few more roles with a group of children, varying somewhat with the age and background of the children. The roles she plays will be the product of convergence of four sets of conditions—the community demand, the professional role and expectations adopted by the teacher, her own personal intent based on her conscious and unconscious needs, and the images projected by the child and the class. Many of the roles in which teachers saw themselves were identified earlier, but among the more significant are:

representative of society	substitute parent
source of knowledge	target for hostility
helper in learning	friend and confidante
object of identification	object of affection
ego supporter	tyrannical adult
anxiety reducer	faultfinder and critic
group leader and director	

The most important for healthy child development are helper in learning, object of identification, ego supporter, and group leader. Each of these has been discussed in relation to different phases of development. Given the basic knowledge and skill, of knowing something of child behavior, providing for individual differences, recognizing symptoms of maladjustment, utilizing a diagnostic approach to learning and behavior problems, and working with specialists where needed, the successful application of these techniques will depend primarily upon the teacher's capacity to play the roles listed.

REFERENCES FOR PART SIX

Anastasi, Anne. *Psychological Testing.* New York: The Macmillan Company, 1954.

Anderson, H. H. and Anderson, Gladys (Eds.). *Introduction to Projective Techniques.* Englewood Cliffs, N. J.: Prentice-Hall, Inc., 1951.

Baruch, Dorothy. *New Ways in Discipline.* New York: Whittlesy House, 1949.

Buhler, Charlotte, *et al. Childhood Problems and the Teacher.* New York: Holt, Rinehart & Winston, Inc., 1952.

Buros, O. K. (Ed). *Mental Measurement Yearbooks.* Highland Park, N. J.: The Gryphen Press, 1953.

Cruickshank, William M. and Johnson, G. Orville (Eds.). *Education of Exceptional Children and Youth.* Englewood Cliffs, N. J.: Prentice-Hall, Inc., 1958.

Frank, Mary and Frank, L. K. *How to Help Your Child in School.* New York: The Viking Press, Inc., 1950.

Green, H. A., Jorgensen, A. N., and Gerberich, J. R. *Measurement and Evaluation in the Elementary School.* New York: Longmans, Green & Co., Inc., 1950.

Havighurst, Robert J. "Education for the Gifted," *National Society for the Study of Education,* 57th Yearbook, Part 2, Chicago: 1958.

Kirk, Samuel A., Karnes, Merle B., and Kirk, Winifred D. *You and Your Retarded Child.* New York: The Macmillan Company, 1955.

Kough, J. and DeHaan, R. F. *Teachers Guidance Handbook, Vol. I, Identifying Children with Special Needs.* Chicago: Science Research Associates, 1955.

Peters, Herman *et al. Counseling: Selected Readings.* Columbus, Ohio: Charles E. Merrill Books, Inc., 1962.

Prescott, D. *Helping Teachers Understand Children.* Washington, D. C.: American Council on Education, 1948.

Strang, Ruth. *Introduction to Child Study.* New York: The Macmillan Company, 1952.

U. S. Govt. Printing Office, Division of Public Documents. *Handbook of Cumulative Records,* Bulletin #5. Washington, D. C.: 1944.

Ward, Virgil S. *Educating the Gifted: An Axiomatic Approach,* Columbus, Ohio: Charles E. Merrill Books, Inc., 1961.

Warner, W. L. *Social Class in America.* Chicago: Science Research Associates, 1949.

Wood, Dorothy Adkins. *Test Construction.* Columbus, Ohio: Charles E. Merrill Books, Inc., 1960.

BIBLIOGRAPHY

BIBLIOGRAPHY

Ackerman, N. M. *The Psychodynamics of Family Life*. New York: Basic Books, Inc., 1958.

Adler, A. *Individual Psychology*. Paterson, N. J.: Littlefield, Adams & Company, 1959.

—————. *Understanding Human Nature*. New York: Greenberg, 1927.

Alexander, F. and Ross, Helen. *The Impact of Freudian Psychology*. Chicago: University of Chicago Press, 1961.

Allport, G. *Becoming*. New Haven: Yale University Press, 1955.

—————. *Pattern and Growth in Personality*. New York: Holt, Rinehart & Winston, Inc., 1961.

Anastasi, Anne. *Psychological Testing*. New York: The Macmillan Company, 1954.

Anderson, H. H. and Anderson, Gladys (Eds.). *Introduction to Projective Techniques*. Englewood Cliffs, N. J.: Prentice-Hall, Inc., 1951.

Arnold, Magela and Gasson, J. A. *Human Personality*. New York: The Ronald Press Company, 1954.

Averill, A. *The Psychology of the Elementary School Child.* New York: Longmans, Green & Co., Inc., 1949.

Baldwin, L. *Behavior and Development in Childhood.* New York: Holt, Rinehart & Winston, Inc., 1955.

Balint, M. *Problems of Human Pleasure and Behavior.* New York: Liveright Publishing Corp., 1957.

Barr, J. A. *The Elementary Teacher and Guidance.* New York: Holt, Rinehart & Winston, Inc., 1958.

Baruch, Dorothy. *New Ways in Discipline.* New York: Whittlesy House, 1949.

Bennett, Ivy. *Delinquent and Neurotic Children.* New York: Basic Books, Inc., 1960.

Bernard, W. *Toward a Better Personality Adjustment.* New York: McGraw-Hill Book Co., Inc., 1957.

Blatz, W. E. *Understanding the Young Child.* New York: William Morrow & Co., Inc., 1944.

Bloch, H. A. and Flynn, F. T. *Delinquency, the Juvenile Offender in America Today.* New York: Random House, Inc., 1956.

Breckenridge, Marian and Vincent, E. L. *Child Development.* Philadelphia: W. B. Saunders Co., 1960.

_____ and Murphy, Margaret. *Growth and Development of the Young Child.* Philadelphia: W. B. Saunders Co., 1958.

Brill, A. A. (Ed.) *The Basic Writings of Sigmund Freud.* New York: Random House, Inc., 1948.

Brooks, D. *Child Psychology,* Boston: Houghton Mifflin Company, 1937.

Buhler, C. *Childhood Problems and the Teacher.* New York: Holt, Rinehart & Winston, Inc., 1952.

Bullis, H. E. *Human Relations in the Classroom.* I & II, Wilmington, Delaware: Delaware State Society for Mental Hygiene, 1947.

Buros, O. K. (Ed.). *Mental Measurement Yearbooks.* Highland Park, N. J.: The Gryphen Press, 1953.

Carmichael, L. *Manual of Child Psychology.* New York: John Wiley & Sons, Inc., 1954.

Carroll, H. A. *Mental Hygiene: The Dynamics of Adjustment.* Englewood Cliffs, N. J.: Prentice-Hall, Inc., 1951 (rev. 1956).

Chess, Stella. *An Introduction to Child Psychiatry.* New York: Grune & Stratton, Inc., 1959.

Clifford, R. *Brothers in Crime.* Chicago: University of Chicago Press, 1938.

Cronbach, L. J. *Educational Psychology*. New York: Harcourt, Brace & World, Inc., 1954.

Cruickshank, W. M. and Johnson, G. (Eds.). *Education of Exceptional Children and Youth*. Englewood Cliffs, N. J.: Prentice-Hall, Inc., 1958.

Cunningham, Ruth. *Understanding Group Behavior of Boys and Girls*. New York: Columbia University Press, 1951.

Davis, A. and Havighurst, R. J. *Father of the Man: How Your Child Gets His Personality*. Boston: Houghton Mifflin Company, 1947.

Davis, F. G. and Norris, Pearle S. *Guidance Handbook for Teachers*. New York: McGraw-Hill Book Co., Inc., 1949.

Detjen, E. W. and Detjen, Mary. *Elementary School Guidance*. New York: McGraw-Hill Book Co., Inc., 1952.

Dreikurs, R. *Psychology in the Classroom: A Manual for Teachers*. New York: Harper & Row, Publishers, 1957.

English, H. *Child Psychology*. New York: Holt, Rinehart & Winston, Inc., 1951.

Erikson, E. *Childhood and Society*. New York: Norton, 1950.

Forest, Ilse. *Child Development*. New York, McGraw-Hill Book Co., Inc., 1954.

Frank, Mary and Frank, L. K. *How to Help Your Child In School*. New York: The Viking Press, Inc., 1950.

Fried, E. *The Ego in Love and Sexuality*. New York: Grune & Stratton, Inc., 1960.

Fosdick, H. *On Being a Real Person*. New York: Harper & Row, Publishers, 1943.

Garrison, K. C. *Growth and Development*. New York: Longmans, Green & Co., Inc., 1952.

_____. *Psychology of Adolescence*. Englewood Cliffs, N. J.: Prentice-Hall, Inc., 1956.

Germane, C. E. and Germane, E. G. *Character Education*. New York: The Macmillan Company, 1929.

Gesell, A. L. *Developmental Diagnosis*. New York: Hoeber, 1947.

_____. and Ilg, Frances. *The Child From Five to Ten*. New York: Harper & Row, Publishers, 1946.

_____, Ilg, Frances, and Ames, Louise. *Youth—The Years from Ten to Sixteen*. New York: Harper & Row, Publishers, 1956.

Glueck, S. and Glueck, Eleanor. *Juvenile Delinquents Grown Up*. New York: The Commonwealth Fund, 1940.

_____. *Unraveling Juvenile Delinquency*. New York: The Commonwealth Fund, 1950.

_____. *Delinquents in the Making*. New York: Harper & Row, Publishers, 1952.

Goldberg, Harriet L. *Child Offenders*. New York: Grune & Stratton, Inc., 1949.

Goodenough, Florence and Tyler, Leona. *Developmental Psychology*. New York: Appleton-Century-Crofts, 1959.

Green, H. A., Jorgensen, A. N., and Gerberich, J. R. *Measurement and Evaluation in the Elementary School*. New York: Longmans, Green & Co., Inc., 1950.

Gruenberg, Sidonie. *The Encyclopedia of Child Care and Guidance*. New York: Doubleday & Company, Inc., 1954.

Haimowitz, M. and Haimowitz, N. R. *Human Development*. New York: Thomas Y. Crowell Company, 1960.

Harms, E. *Handbook of Child Guidance*. New York: Child Care, 1947.

Hartshorne, Hugh and May, Mark A. *Studies in Deceit*. New York: The Macmillan Company, 1928.

Havighurst, R. J. and Taba, Hilda. *Adolescent, Character and Personality*. New York: John Wiley & Sons, Inc., 1949.

Heffernan, Helen. *Guiding the Young Child*. Boston: D. C. Heath & Company, 1951.

Heyna, P. W. *The Psychology of Personal Adjustment*. New York: Holt, Rinehart & Winston, Inc., 1958.

Hilgard, Ernest R. *Introduction to Psychology*. New York: Harcourt, Brace & World, Inc., 1953.

Hill, A. S., Miller, L. M., and Gablard, Hazel. "Schools Face the Delinquency Problem," *The Bulletin*, 40. (Dec. 1953).

Horney, Karen. *Our Inner Conflicts*. New York: Norton, 1945.

Hountras, Peter T. *Mental Hygiene: A Text of Readings*. Columbus, Ohio: Charles E. Merrill Books, Inc., 1961.

Hurlock, E. B. *Child Development*. New York: McGraw-Hill Book Co., Inc., 1950.

Ilg, Frances and Ames, Louise. *Child Behavior*. New York: Harper & Row, Publishers, 1951 (rev. 1955).

Isaacs, Susan. *Social Development in Young Children*. New York: Harcourt, Brace & World, Inc., 1939.

Jenkins, Gladys, *et al. These Are Your Children*. Chicago: Scott, Foresman & Company, 1953.

Jennings, Helen Hall. *Leadership and Isolation.* New York: Longmans, Green & Co., Inc., 1950.

Jersild, A. T. *Child Psychology.* Englewood Cliffs, N. J.: Prentice-Hall, Inc., 1950 (rev. 1960).

_____. *The Psychology of Adolescence.* New York: The Macmillan Company, 1957.

Johnston, E. G., Peters, Mildred and Evraiff, William. *The Role of the Teacher in Guidance.* Englewood Cliffs, N. J.: Prentice-Hall, Inc., 1959.

Jordan, Thomas E. *The Exceptional Child.* Columbus, Ohio: Charles E. Merrill Books, Inc., 1962.

Joseph, H. *The Emotional Problems of Children.* New York: Crown Publishers, Inc., 1954.

Krech, D. and Crutchfield, R. *Elements of Psychology.* New York: Alfred A. Knopf, Inc., 1958.

Kuhlen, R. G. and Thompson, G. C. *Psychological Studies of Human Development.* New York: Appleton-Century-Crofts, 1952.

Kurtz, V. J. and Swenson, E. J. "Factors Relating to Over-Achievement and Under-Achievement in School," *School Reviews,* 1951, 59; 472-80.

Kvaraceus, W. C. *The Community and the Delinquent.* New York: Harcourt, Brace & World, Inc., 1954.

_____. *What Research Says to the Teacher.* Washington, D. C.: Educational Research Ass'n., 32, 1958.

_____ and Miller, W. B. *Delinquent Behavior.* National Education Ass'n: 1959.

Laird, D. G. and Laird, Eleanor C. *The Strategy of Handling Children.* New York: Funk & Wagnalls Co., Inc., 1949.

Lambert, Clara. *Understanding Your Child from 6-12.* New York: Public Affairs Pamphlets, #144, 1957.

Lee, Grace. *Helping the Troubled School Child.* National Assoc. for Social Workers, N. Y.

Lee, J. and Lee, D. M. *The Child and His Development.* New York: Appleton-Century-Crofts, 1958.

Leeper, R. W. and Madison, P. *Toward Understanding Human Personality.* New York: Appleton-Century-Crofts, 1959.

Leuba, Clarence. *Personality: Interpersonal Relations and Self-Understanding.* Columbus, Ohio: Charles E. Merrill Books, Inc., 1962.

Lindgren, H. C. *Educational Psychology in the Classroom.* New York: John Wiley & Sons, Inc., 1962.

_____. *Psychology of Personal and Social Adjustment.* New York: American Book Company, 1951.

Lund, Helen M. *On Shame and the Search for Identity.* New York: Harcourt, Brace & World, Inc., 1958.

Martin, W. E. and Stendler, Celia. *Child Development.* New York: Harcourt, Brace & World, Inc., 1953.

Maslow, A. H. *Motivation and Personality.* New York: Harper & Row, Publishers, 1954.

Massen, P. H. and Conger, J. J. *Child Development and Personality.* New York: Harper & Row, Publishers, 1956.

Maves, B. *Understanding Ourselves as Adults.* Nashville, Tenn.: Abingdon Press, 1959.

McClelland, D. C. *et al. The Achievement Motive.* New York: Appleton-Century-Crofts, 1953.

_____. *Mental Hygiene in the Classroom: "How Would You Help a Child Like This?"* Chicago, Illinois: American Medical Ass'n., 1956.

Mead, Margaret. *Sex and Temperment in Three Primitive Societies.* New York: The New American Library of World Literature, 1950.

Merry, Frieda and Merry, R. V. *The First Two Decades of Life.* New York: Harper & Row, Publishers, 1958.

Millard, C. V. *Child Growth and Development.* Boston: D. C. Heath & Company, 1951.

Miller, Frank. *Guidance Principles and Services.* Columbus, Ohio: Charles E. Merrill Books, Inc., 1961.

Morgan, J. J. B. *Child Psychology.* New York: Holt, Rinehart & Winston, Inc., 1931. (rev. 1942)

_____. *The Psychology of the Unadjusted School Child.* New York: The Macmillan Company, 1936.

Neisser, Edith. *Brothers and Sisters.* New York: Harper & Row, Publishers, 1951.

Neumeyer, M. H. *Juvenile Delinquency in Modern Society.* New York: D. Van Nostrand Co., Inc., 1949.

Overstreet, H. A. *The Mature Mind.* New York: Norton, 1959.

Parkhurst, Helen. *Exploring the Child's World.* New York: Appleton-Century-Crofts, 1951.

Patty, L. and Johnson, Louise. *Personality and Adjustment.* New York: McGraw-Hill Book Co., Inc., 1953.

Pearson, H. *Psychoanalysis and the Education of the Child.* New York: Norton, 1954.

Peters, Herman and Shertzer, Bruce. *Guidance: Program Development and Management.* Columbus, Ohio: Charles E. Merrill Books, Inc., 1963.

Peters *et al. Counseling: Selected Readings.* Columbus, Ohio: Charles E. Merrill Books, Inc., 1962.

Phillips, B. N., Duke, R. L., and DeVault, M. V. *Psychology At Work In The Elementary School Classroom.* New York: Harper & Row, Publishers, 1960.

Powers, E. and Helen Witmer. *An Experiment in the Prevention of Delinquency.* New York: Columbia University Press, 1951.

Prescott, D. A. *Emotion and the Educative Process.* Washington, D. C.: American Council on Education, 1938.

_____. *The Child in the Educative Process.* New York: McGraw-Hill Book Co., Inc., 1957.

Pressey, S. L. *Psychology and the New Education.* New York: Harper & Row, Publishers, 1933.

Redl, F., and Wattenberg, W. W. *Mental Hygiene in Teaching.* New York: Harcourt, Brace & World, Inc., 1951.

_____ and Wineman, D. *The Aggressive Child.* Glencoe, Illinois: The Free Press, 1957.

Rickman, John (Ed.). *On The Bringing Up of Children by Five Psychoanalysts.* London: Kegan, Trulener, Co., 1936.

Roberts, W. H. *Psychology You Can Use.* New York: Harcourt, Brace & World, Inc., 1943.

Russell, D. H. *Children's Thinking.* Boston: Ginn & Company, 1956.

Sappenfield, B. R. *Personality Dynamics, An Integrative Psychology of Adjustment.* New York: Alfred A. Knopf, Inc., 1956.

Shaffer, L. F. and Shoben, E. J. *Psychology of Adjustment.* Boston: Houghton-Mifflin Company, 1957.

Sherif, M. and Cantril, H. *The Psychology of Ego-Involvement.* New York: John Wiley & Sons, Inc., 1947.

Silverberg, W. V. *Childhood Experience and Personal Destiny.* New York: Springs Publishing Co., 1952.

Slavson, S. R. *Introduction to Group-Psychotherapy.* New York: International Universities Press, 1943.

Snygg, D. and Coombs, A. W. *Individual Behavior.* New York: Appleton-Century-Crofts, 1946.

Spock, B. *Baby and Child Care.* New York: Pocket Books, Inc., 1957.

Stephens, J. M. *Educational Psychology.* New York: Holt, Rinehart & Winston, Inc., 1960.

Strang, Ruth. *An Introduction to Child Study.* New York: The Macmillan Company, 1951 (rev. 1959).

Sullivan, H. S. *The Interpersonal Theory of Psychiatry.* New York: Norton, 1953.

Symonds, P. M. *Dynamics of Parent-Child Relationships.* New York: Bureau of Public Teachers Colleges, Columbia University Press, 1949.

_____. *The Psychology of Parent-Child Relationships.* New York: Appleton-Century-Crofts, 1939.

Taba, Hilda. *Elementary Curriculum in Intergroup Relations.* Washington, D. C.: American Council on Education, 1950.

_____ and Elkins, Deborah. *With Focus on Human Relations.* Washington, D. C.: American Council on Education, 1946.

Teicher, Y. D. *Your Child & His Problems: A Basic Guide for Parents.* Boston: Little, Brown & Co., 1953.

Thompson, G. C. *Child Psychology.* Boston: Houghton Mifflin Company, 1952.

Thorpe, L. *Child Psychology & Development.* New York: The Ronald Press Company, 1955.

Travis, E. L. and Baruch, Dorothy. *Personal Problems of Everyday Life.* New York: Appleton-Century-Crofts, 1941.

Traxler, A. E. *Techniques of Guidance.* New York: Harper & Row, Publishers, 1957.

Tyler, Leona E. *The Psychology of Human Differences.* New York: Appleton-Century-Crofts, 1956.

Wallin, J. E. *The Education of Mentally Handicapped Children.* New York: Harper & Row, Publishers, 1955.

Warters, J. *Achieving Maturity.* New York: McGraw-Hill Book Co., Inc., 1949.

Watson, E. H. and Lowrey, G. H. *Growth and Development of Children.* Chicago: The Yearbook Publishers, 1954.

Watson, R. I. *Psychology of the Child.* New York: John Wiley & Sons, Inc., 1960.

Weaver, A. *They Steal For Love.* New York: International Universities Press, Inc., 1959.

Wheelis, A. *The Quest for Identity.* New York: Norton, 1958.

White, A. L. *The Abnormal Personality.* New York: The Ronald Press Company, 1948.

White, W. *Psychology in Living*. New York: The Macmillan Company, 1955.

Willey, R. D. *Guidance in the Elementary School*. New York: Harper & Row Publishers, 1960.

Winters, J. *Crime and Kids*. Springfield, Ill.: Charles C. Thomas, Publisher, 1959.

Wittenberg, R. *Adolescence and Discipline*. New York: Association Press, 1960.

Wood, Dorothy A. *Test Construction*. Columbus, Ohio: Charles E. Merrill Books, Inc., 1960.

Wylie Ruth. *The Self Concept*. Lincoln, Nebraska: University of Nebraska, 1961.

Index

Index

About The Author

Ralph Garry, Professor of Educational Psychology at Boston University, received his A.B., A.M., and Ph.D. degrees from Stanford University.

In preparing this text, Dr. Garry has drawn upon his years of experience as Project Director for the Foundation for Character Education, consultant to many school systems in New England, and Special Consultant to the Senate Subcommittee on Juvenile Delinquency inquiring into the effects of television on children. His areas of specialization include learning theory, test construction, and group processes.

Dr. Garry has completed two research projects under grants from the Cooperative Research Project of the United States Office of Education with handicapped children and has worked on five projects on instructional television in the elementary school under Title VII of the National Defense Education Act.

Dr. Garry has published extensively in the professional journals. In addition, he is the author of several books, including *The Nature and Conditions of Learning*, written with Howard L. Kingsley. The United States Office of Education selected one of Dr. Garry's research articles on foreign language instruction by television to be included with the fifty most significant pieces of educational research for European publication.

This book is set in Caledonia, one of the most popular and versatile faces in use today. While Caledonia displays touches of both Scotch Roman and Bulmer, it is a distinctly original face. Harmoniously constructed, the face shows little contrast between thick and thin lines. Its bottom serifs are bracketless and meet the upright stems at sharp angles. To complete the book's design, Standard, a simply designed, medium-heavy, sans serif face, is used for the display headings in the text and the front and end matter. Futura Demi-Bold is used for the part and chapter titles in the table of contents.